The Letters of Komitas Vardapet

The Letters of Komitas Vardapet

Translated by Nazareth Seferian

Library and Archives Canada Cataloguing in Publication

Title: The letters of Komitas / translated by Nazareth Seferian.

Names: Komitas, Vardapet, 1869-1935, author. | Seferian, Nazareth, translator.

Identifiers: Canadiana (print) 20210382929
Canadiana (ebook) 20210382937

ISBN 9781771613583 (softcover) ISBN 9781771613590 (EPUB)
ISBN 9781771613606 (PDF) ISBN 9781771613613 (Kindle)

Subjects: LCSH: Komitas, Vardapet, 1869-1935—Correspondence. | LCGFT: Personal correspondence.

Classification: LCC ML410.K73536 A3 2021
DDC 780.92—dc23

Published by MosaicPress, Oakville, Ontario, Canada, 2021.

MOSAIC PRESS, Publishers
www.Mosaic-Press.com

Previously published as Komitas Vardapet - Letters | ԿոմիտասՎարդապետ. Նամականի in 2009 by Sargis Khachents and Printinfo, Yerevan, Armenia

Funded by the Government of Canada
Financé par le gouvernement du Canada

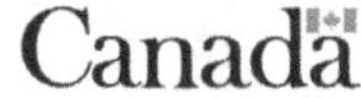

MOSAIC PRESS
1252 Speers Road, Units 1 & 2, Oakville, Ontario, L6L 5N9
(905) 825-2130 • info@mosaic-press.com • www.mosaic-press.com

Հրատարակվել է Հայաստանի Հանրապետության կրթության, գիտության, մշակույթի և սպորտի նախարարության աջակցությամբ՝ «Հայ գրականությունը թարգմանություններում» ծրագրի շրջանակում։

The book is published with the support of the Ministry of Education, Science, Culture and Sport of the Republic of Armenia in the frames of 'Armenian Literature in Translation' program.

Mosaic Press acknowledges the support of the Calouste Gulbenkian Foundation for the publication of this book.

TABLE OF CONTENTS

SECTION 1

The Correspondence Legacy of Komitas Vardapet 3
The Letters Written by Komitas Vardapet 13
The Letters Received by Komitas Vardapet 213
Undated Letters 254

Photo Section

SECTION 2

List of Abbreviations and Contractions 262
The Letters Written by Komitas Vardapet 263
The Letters Received by Komitas Vardapet 446
Undated Letters 471

TRANSLATOR'S BIOGRAPHY

Nazareth Seferian was born in Canada, grew up in India and moved to his homeland of Armenia in 1998, where he has been living ever since. His university education has not been specific to translation studies, but his love for languages led him to this work in 2001. He began literary translations in 2011 and his published works include the English version of Yenok's Eye by Gurgen Khanjyan, The Clouds of Mount Maruta by Mushegh Galshoyan, Ravens Before Noah by Susanna Harutyunyan, Jesus' Cat by Grig, The Door Was Open by Karine Khodikyan as well as Robinson and P/F by Aram Pachyan. He has also translated several short stories by other Armenian authors such as Artavazd Yeghiazaryan, Levon Shahnur, Armen of Armenia (Ohanyan), Areg Azatyan, Avetik Mejlumyan, Anna Davtyan and more. Nazareth's typical work week includes activities in a completely different sector combined with several pages of translation, which is driven by his desire to promote greater availability and recognition of Armenian culture for English speakers worldwide.

SECTION - 1

THE CORRESPONDENCE LEGACY OF KOMITAS VARDAPET[1]

During his highly productive work, Komitas Vardapet would occasionally write open letters and publish the letters he received. The numbers of these publications are not very large – just 6 of his letters or replies were published in the contemporary press.[2] Later, perhaps in the days when the composer was still alive, those studying Komitas began to show an interest on the correspondence heritage of Komitas, publishing a series of letters and writings.

In 1931, in a monograph dedicated to the life and works of Komitas, Toros Azatyan published the letters to which he had access, including those which had already been published in the press (6 letters).[3] Among those published by Toros Azatyan, the letter written by Komitas to Stepan Akayan is particularly valuable, the handwritten original of which has not been found, but a copy was published by this Komitas scholar in his book.

In 1933, a letter addressed by Komitas to Vahram Mankuni was published by the journal *Anahit*.[4]

Starting from 1935, there were a few more publications in the Diaspora and Soviet Armenian press, the largest and most valuable ones of which were those published by Margarit Babayan (12 letters).[5]

---

1 [The Armenian word "Vardapet" is used to refer to a clergyman who has taken an oath of celibacy, and it denotes a certain level in the Church hierarchy, roughly equivalent to the English "archimandrite." It has not been translated into English throughout this book, among other reasons, in order to preserve the name by which the Armenian composer is now known globally – Komitas Vardapet] – Translator's notes.

2 See pages 172, 183, 190, 202, 239, 241 of this publication.

3 **Toros Azatyan** Komitas Vardapet: His Life and Works, Constantinople, 1931, pages 28-29, 98, 107, 112-113.

4 "Anahit," 1933, issues 3-6, pages 228-229.

5 **Margarit Babayan.** Komitas Vardapet Through his Letters, *Mshakuyt*, 1935, pages 153-165. M. Babayan fully or partially published 11 letters written by Komitas Vardapet, and in her article *The Ten Commandments of the Singer* she published another letter ("Contemporaries

In 1935, two of Komitas' letters addressed to Yervand Hakobian were published in the *Annals of Bulgarian Armenians*.[6]

In 1936, Ghevond Tatyan, a congregant of the Mekhitarist Congregation in Venice published two of Komitas' letters with a detailed commentary,[7] while *Grakan Tert* published letters written by Komitas to Siranush and Hovhannes Tumanyan (3 letters).[8]

In 1940, the Soviet Armenian press published two more letters written by Komitas.[9]

Only after the Komitas archives were moved to Armenia did it become possible to study and publish them systematically.

The first serious step in that direction was A. Adamyan's article "New Documents about Komitas," which was published in 1956 in the *Teghekagir hasarakakan gitutyunneri* periodical.[10] The author published 6 letters by Komitas addressed to the congregants of Etchmiadzin (Archbishop Mesrop Smbatyan (2 letters), Kyuregh Srapyan, Father Tirayr (2 letters), Archbishop Gevorg Surenyants) with useful commentaries.

In 1956, the journal *Sovetakan Arvest* published a letter by Komitas to Alexander Miasnikyan.[11]

After Arshak Chopanyan's archives were moved to Armenia in 1958, M. Muradyan published some (20 letters) of Komitas' letters to Chopanyan with brief notes and comments.[12]

---

on Komitas," Yerevan, 1960, pages 133-134). [Mshakuyt, the name of the publication, translates to "culture" – Translator's note].

6 Vol. 1, pages 302-303, later also in the newspaper *Azat Khosk* (1947, 17 November). [The name of this publication translates to "Free Speech" – Translator's note].

7 **Ghevond Tatyan**, Komitas Vardapet, *Bazmavep*, 1936, pages 8-11.

8 *Grakan Tert*, 1936, issue 9, 13. [The name of this publication translates to "Literary Newspaper" – Translator's note].

9 The first was written to Hovhannes Tumanyan, the second to the Catholicos of All Armenians Mattheos II (*Sovetakan Hayastan*, 1940, issue 247). [The name of this publication translates to "Soviet Armenia – Translator's note].

10 Issue 9, pages 101-114. [The name of this publication translates to "Social Sciences Bulletin" – Translator's note].

11 Issue 2, page 9. [The name of this publication translates to "Soviet Art" – Translator's note].

12 **M. Muradyan**, Komitas' Unpublished Letters, *Patmabanasirakan handes*, 1958, issue 1, pages 245-267. [The name of this publication translates to "Journal of History and Philology" – Translator's note].

In 1959, a copy of the handwritten original of one of Komitas' letters was published in the journal *Kulis*.[13]

In 1962, Gohar Aznavuryan published 22 letters addressed to Komitas from different intellectuals (Karapet Kostanyan (7 letters), Arshak Chopanyan (6 letters), Hovhannes Tumanyan (2 letters), Mariam Tumanyan (93 letters), Sargis Kamalyan (2 letters), Vahan Malezyan(1 letter) with brief notes in the journal *Sovetakan Arvest*.[14]

In 1964, the volume called "Spiridon Melikyan – Articles, Memoirs, Letters, Documents" compiled by Satenik Melikyan and Alexander Tadevosyan included three letters by Komitas to S. Melikyan.[15]

In 1966, in the periodical *Banber Hayastani Arkhivneri*, G. Harutyunyan published another 5 letters kept at the Catholicosate, with detailed commentaries.[16]

In 1968, the weekly *Hayreni Dzayn* published a letter from Komitas to Hovhannes Mutafyan.[17]

In 1969, Robert Atayan published a letter from Komitas to Armine Melikyan in the journal *Garun*.[18]

In 1970, two letters from Komitas to Maghakia Ormanyan were published in the *Shoghakat* annals.[19]

In 1969-1974, K. Samvelyan regularly published a piece in *Sovetakan Arvest* called "The Brief Annals of Komitas' Life and Work," which presented the life and work of the composer up to August 1913. Along with numerous useful

---

13 *Kulis*, 1959, issue 302, page 8. [The name of this publication translates to "Backstage" – Translator's note].

14 **Gohar Aznavuryan**, From Komitas' Letters, *Sovetakan Arvest*, 1962, issue 9, pages 50-53, issue 10, pages 53-56. [The name of this publication translates to "Soviet Art" – Translator's note].

15 See the mentioned book, pages 155-156.

16 **G. Harutyunyan**, The Life and Activities of Komitas Seen Through Newly Discovered Documents, *Banber Hayastani Arkhivneri*, 1966, issue 2, pages 149-171. [The name of this publication translates to "Messenger from the Archives of Armenia" – Translator's note].

17 Issue 40 [The name of this publication translates to "Voice of the Fatherland" – Translator's note].

18 **Robert Atayan**, Games of the Pen, *Garun*, 1969, issue 11, page 19. [The name of this publication translates to "Spring" – Translator's note].

19 *Shoghakat*, 1970, pages 15-16. [The name of this publication translates to "Splendorous Light" – Translator's note].

pieces of information, facts and interpretations, the articles also partially or fully reproduced both previously published letters and those that had not been put in print before. The letters by Komitas which were not published in the "Annals" were mainly the undated ones.[20]

In 1981, in the compilation entitled "Nikoghayos Tigranyan – Articles, Memoirs, Letters," published by the efforts of R. Mazmanyan, two letters by Komitas to Sirakan Tigranyan and Nikoghayos Tigranyan were also included.[21]

Thus, from 1931 to 1981, those studying Komitas published a large part of his legacy of correspondence – 96 letters in total,[22] while the vast majority of the unpublished letters (around 50 of them) had been presented in parts or in whole by K. Samuelyan in this "Annals."

In 2000, the Museum of Literature and Art published Komitas' letters as a separate book (153 letters)[23] and a "second, expanded edition" of the compilation (160 letters) was published in 2007.[24] In both publications, the editor notes that "only a small number of the letters had been published over time in the press or other publications. **The majority were published in 2000 for the first time through the archives of originals preserved by the Museum of Literature and Art"[25]** (*emphasis by the editor of this book – G.G.*), while the same compiler demonstrates that contrary to his references in the commentaries – both collections of letters only published a minority of the correspondence for the first time, a large part had already been published from 1931

20 The continuation to the "Annals" was published in the *Handes Amsorya* (2008, issues 1-12, pages 229-247). [The name of this publication translates to "Monthly Journal" – Translator's note].

21 See the mentioned book, Yerevan, ArmSSR Academy of Sciences publishing, 1981, pages 164-165.

22 Some of which were published on more than one occasion (e.g. the ones to Hovhannes Tumanyan).

23 **Komitas**. Letters, MAL publishing, 2000, 224 pages. Text compilation, foreword and commentaries by T. Bekaryan, later KL, 2000).

24 **Komitas**. Letters, MAL publishing, 2007, 272 pages. Text compilation by T. Bekaryan. As mentioned in the foreword, "The commentaries have been significantly expanded compared to the first edition, and have been complemented by new information from H. Bakhchinyan." Later KL, 2000).

25 Ibid, page 13.

to 1981 through the efforts of Komitas scholars and philologists[26] (96 of the 160 letters had been published in full, in addition to which K. Samuelyan had published some in part).

In these two publications, the letters are arranged "by addressee (with last names in alphabetical order), and then in chronological order internally."[27] This approach (an alphabetical correspondence list) is used in archive processing, in order to locate the processed archive items more easily. But in the case of personal letters, it is decidedly inefficient and goes against the scientific principles involved in compiling volumes of correspondence of this kind. Personal and original correspondence has always been arranged in **chronological** order, because otherwise such volumes lose their significance as resources for research, or availing of them requires efforts that can result in confusion. In case of non-chronological arrangement of letters, there is a disconnect between the biographical episodes about the author and the facts regarding his life and activities, increasing the possibilities of misunderstandings and wrong information, which results in their exclusion from scientific research. Such volumes can only tell one how many letters the given author wrote to whom, the kind of data that one can obtain from a simple list.[28]

Regarding the study of original texts, a simple observation showed that the situation here is not a particularly good one either. Without listing the multiple errors in specific publications, we found around 2700 misrepresentations of the original text in just the 160 letters published in these two

---

26 We would not address this non-philological issue and would have considered it a simple error in calculation if this statement had not repeated itself in the second edition. This suggests that the editor or compiler is of the conviction—increasingly so, but nevertheless non-philological—that he should be recognized for publishing the "majority" of Komitas' correspondence for the first time. But this is a case of simply neglecting the work done by the previous generation of philologists who studied the original correspondence. Even when one considers the volume of originals published, the KL published only about 25 percent of the total number of original letters in 2000 and 2007 which is, naturally, not the "majority" of the ones being published for the first time.

27 Ibid, page 14.

28 Let us also note that records of correspondence usually give lists of addressees not in the alphabetical order of their last names, but of their first names. Lists in the alphabetical order of last names are used in literature collections.

editions,[29] starting with a distortion of the author's punctuation, unnecessary divisions into paragraphs of the original, and going all the way up to erroneous readings of the original text, resulting in mistakes and omissions. For a part of these errors—especially those which distort the language and style used by Komitas, sometimes leading to absurd situations in the semantic field—we have written separate notes, considering that those publications are still in circulation and could be the cause of new misunderstandings. In some cases, in order to offer a picture of the work done with the originals in those editions, we sometimes provide a full list of the wrong understanding and omissions by the compiler[30] (see, for example, the letter to Mattheos Izmirlian dated 12 January 1910 and the notes accompanying it). The compiler justifies a part of those modifications through the "modernization" of punctuation, but in many cases, those interventions simply distort the original meaning and author's intent. Let us provide an example of "modernized punctuation" from this letter. Komitas, presenting his program of ecclesiastical choral reform, writes, **"This should be begun first of all, and fundamentally, from the Mother Choir of the Mother Church of the Mother See."** The KL 2000 and 2007 editions have broken up this sentence using commas, resulting in **"The Mother Choir of the Mother Church, the Mother See"** which is senseless because the Mother See and the Mother Church do not have separate choirs – this is a **series of substantives, not a list.** Komitas has used the technique of continuous repetition to make the meaning of the words more powerful. It is obvious that this is not a case of "modernized punctuation," but rather a misperception of the original meaning, which has led to this erroneous division.

With regard to grammatical usage, we have once again maintained the author's orthography and writing style, particularly the "կը" indicative and "չը" negative prefixes, as well as the modifications of the "վ" passive verb ending (վ, ւ, ու) in the original letters.* The issue is that the usage of these

29 In the 2007 edition, which is "corrected" according to the annotation in the book, all these deviations were joined by numerous typographical errors.

30 If we were to include all the lists, this book would be of considerably larger volume.

* [The reference here is to prefixes that are now often not written separately as shown in the paragraph, but merged with the following word, as well as to a verb ending that was spelled in a number of different ways at the time – Translator's note].

particles was not regulated in the study of Armenian literature and in educational institutions at the beginning of the century. While the Gevorgyan Seminary considered it acceptable to write these prefixes in their merged form, the Armenian periodicals of that time, both abroad and in Russian Armenia and its communities, did not show any consistency, and these issues (especially orthography) were topics of heated debate in the Armenian press. In the letters he wrote up to 1905 (which are mainly addressed to Karapet Kostanyants and the congregants at Etchmiadzin), Komitas writes the prefixes in their merged form. However, after 1905, in his letters to M. Babayan and A. Chopanyan, he writes them separately. One should not forget that, taking the linguistic cognition of the addressee into consideration in his letters, Komitas would use both Eastern Armenian and Western Armenian. If we consider this in the issue of consistency, then these specificities—which include not just issues of spelling—are also the results of certain thoughts and considerations by the author.

A study of the language used by Komitas shows that he had a clear talent for style and would freely use certain oratorical artistic tricks to express various tones of voice. And the important thing, as we noted before, is that he would consider the addressee's personality and linguistic cognition when writing his letters.[31] Therefore, such retrospective editing should be avoided, based on the fundamental principles of classic orthography, manuscript study and the need to faithfully reproduce the original.[32]

The letters of Komitas Vardapet that have made it to our times chronologically cover the period from 1894 to 1914 and reflect almost all the important episodes and events in his life and work. A part of them consist

31 This example is noticeably seen in two letters that he wrote on the same day, where he discusses similar issues within the same topic. See and compare the letters written to Margarit Babayan and Arshak Chopanyan on 7 August 1913.

32 In KL 2007, it says, "We have printed those particles (?) fused with the verbs, as is specific to the grammar (?) and spelling of Eastern Armenian" (page 13). The fusion of those particles with the verbs in writing is not specific to "Eastern Armenian grammar and spelling" as the compiler seems to think – they are a consequence of the modern rules of spelling. 19th century Eastern Armenian literature did not accept the fusion of those particles – this issue was raised at the end of the 19th century and the beginning of the 20th leading to a dichotomy in spelling.

of official correspondence – requests, applications, reports sent to different ecclesiastical figures, and a considerable part of them is made up of letters, congratulatory postcards and telegrams to his friends and supporters.

This collection includes the 184 letters, of which we are aware, written by Komitas and 37 of the ones received by him.

Of course, this does not exhaust the legacy of Komitas' correspondence. There is a lot of evidence to suggest that we have discovered only a small part of the letters written by the composer.

According to Margarit Babayan's testimonial, "Komitas Vardapet, who had now left for the Caucasus, would send news to his honorable teacher every week and God forbid if his letter were delayed! Mr. Schmidt would express his concern by telegram from Berlin!"[33] Until now, none of the letters that he would write his teacher Richard Schmidt "every week," nor the telegrams that R. Schmidt would send, have been found and the scholars studying Komitas have, in general, not yet undertaken a study and publication of Komitas' legacy in the German archives.[34]

The letters written by Komitas to Hrachya Acharyan also remain undiscovered, while in his book "Memories from my Life" the latter wrote, "Once, he travelled to Germany. I asked him to send me a postcard with beautiful pictures from each city for the album I had compiled. I received 7 such postcards from different cities, which would have notes written on them such as 'Dear Hrachya, I have reached Vienna,' followed by the date and 'Komitas Vardapet.' Many years later, Ruben Terlemezyan received those 7 postcards from me, when he was compiling Komitas Vardapet's biography."[35] Only one of those postcards has been preserved in the Hrachya Acharyan album kept at the Museum of Literature and Art, we could not find the remaining six in the Ruben Terlemezyan library either.

According to Panos Terlemezyan's testimonial, "I was still in Constantinople when I received a 38-page letter from Komitas, where he described

33 **M. Babayan**, Recollections about Komitas, Contemporaries on Komitas, Yerevan, 1960, page 144.

34 The Kurdish music that Komitas used during his graduation performance also remains unknown, although it should be preserved in the archives of the German Royal University.

35 **Hrachya Acharyan**, Memories from My Life, Yerevan, 1967, page 211. The only one of those postcards that has been preserved is the one sent to Acharyan from Tbilisi, written in Turkish with Armenian characters.

the topic of his lecture and its impact. It is a pity that that letter remained in Constantinople with my things, perhaps it will be discovered some day."[36] That voluminous letter has also not been found.

The massive body of memoirs about Komitas also refers to a number of other letters, some with partial extracts.

In that sense, the number of testimonials left by Komitas himself in his letters is quite large, each with footnotes to make the task of anyone studying them easier.

As for the letters received by Komitas, the vast majority of them never got to us. The number of units at the Komitas library of the Museum of Literature and Art is not much – just 34, while the rough draft of one letter is kept in Arshak Chopanyan's library. However, taking into consideration the references in the letters written by Komitas, we do not have the letters written by Arshak Chopanyan (around 40), Margarit Babayan, Karapet Kostanyants, Hovhannes Tumanyan, Ghevond Tayan, and others, to Komitas. All these references are also mentioned in the footnotes.

A considerable part of Komitas' correspondence is dateless and, in previous publications, these have been placed after the dated letters. In this publication, the dates as well as locations of writing have been mentioned for around 40 undated letters by Komitas, and corrections have been made to erroneous dating in previous publications.

Of the 221 letters written and received by Komitas that have been published in this compilation, 166 (of which 36 – received) are being kept at the Y. Charents Museum of Literature and Art, while 4 letters are located at the Mashtots Matenadaran and 21 are in the National Archives of the Republic of Armenia. The remaining 27 letters are being kept in other archives or have been printed in the press or in other periodicals and books.

***

While preparing the originals we have been guided by the following principles:

A) The originals have been arranged in chronological order. The letters have

36 **Panos Terlemezyan**, About Komitas, Contemporaries on Komitas, Yerevan, 1960, page 195.

been grouped according to the year of writing.

B) In the originals prepared from handwritten texts, we have preserved the author's spelling and punctuation, correcting only mistakes that have all be mentioned in the notes.

C) In letters written jointly, we have written the texts for all authors as they are in the original.

D) In typed letters of unknown authorship, we have preserved the spelling and punctuation of the original printer.

E) The samples of Armenian notation quoted in the letters have been presented in the notes on the letter with European notation.

F) We have included edits and deletions in rough drafts by the author by mentioning them in the corresponding locations within square brackets [...]

G) The differences between the draft and final versions of the same letter have been presented in the footnotes.

H) Additions by the editor to the text in the originals have been included in sharp brackets <>.

I) The sections of text referred to in the footnotes or the differences in the originals are all mentioned by the page and line number of the corresponding section (Page ..., l ...).

GURGEN GASPARYAN

THE LETTERS WRITTEN BY KOMITAS VARDAPET

1894

1. TO KYUREGH SRAPYAN

<18>94 5/7. Holy Etchmiadzin

To the Most Honorable Father Kyuregh
Vice Prelate of Yerevan

If there is a way to support this request, please issue an order by your Most Honorable self to appoint Karapet Ter Astvatzatryan Askaryants, from the village of Vagharshapat, to one of your Armenian community prelacies, giving him the position of Armenian music teacher. He, Karapet, has received complete training in this area a long time ago and is perfectly knowledgeable in this art. He has already provided me his certificate, which shows his qualifications. You can also see his proficiency in these topics in this certificate.

I remain the h<umble> s<ervant> and son
of your Most Honorable self

Deacon Soghomon <Soghomonyan>

2. TO MESROP SMBATYAN

<18>94 6/10 Holy E<tchmiadzin>

To His Grace, the Most Noble
Archbishop Mesrop
My spiritual father
In Christ
With filial obeisance

I have accepted the order from your High Holiness, received verbally from your Honorable Ghevond Vardapet, with willingness, happiness and joy this morning. I examined the person you mentioned and noticed some deficiencies in his ecclesiastical singing. The teaching of the art of music, and the Armenian Ecclesiastical notation, must be undertaken for longer than the wishes of your Most Holy Nobility, if one desires to master this knowledge of art without confusion, and a long time must be appointed as the necessary duration in order to sing without faltering and straying, and in general to learn this vast art, including church music. Two months is not sufficient at all to correct any mistakes, much less lay a strong new foundation and I fear that this will be a misuse of effort and achievement, as well as your support to study in this way.

The humblest servant and son
of the Spiritual Father
In Christ
Monk Komitas

1895

3. TO MESROP SMBATYAN

<18>95, 6/6. Holy Etchmiadzin

To the Most Honorable Holy Father
Archbishop Mesrop Smbatyan,
Deputy Patriarch of All Armenians

Most Honorable Holy Father,
Most Honorable Lord,

If possible, I humbly request that you allow me to go with the seminary students to see Ani, which would also serve as a summer break for me. The seminary administration has divided the students staying there this summer into two groups, and I must lead one of them. I therefore ask the permission of your High Holiness.

The humblest servant and son
Of your Most Honorable self
Komitas Vardapet

4. TO MKRTICH KHRIMYAN, THE CATHOLICOS OF ALL ARMENIANS

The Year 1895, the 25th of July
Holy Etchmiadzin

To the Holy Father
His Holiness Mkrtich I
The Most Holy Catholicos of All Armenians

Holy Pontiff,

I have passed seven months gathering folk songs and dance songs, and I have not yet managed to put the effort to arrange, compile, and seal them.

Armenian folk music, with its simplicity and greatness, is similar to the hymns[37] that our forefathers would play, which would express the lives and thoughts of the people of Hayk.[38] And it still remains hidden and concealed from memoirs and documentation. There are thus many songs of our forefathers' genius preserved in the villages, fresh and untainted with other musical senses, which little by little face destruction with the entry of foreign music. If you do not raise your hand, without your high order, as the Shepherd of the community, you will be condemning them to oblivion and disappearance.

At the same time, these pieces of Armenian folk music have certain lines in common with our church hymns. Each peasant song may shine down like a ray on the naturally brilliant Armenian nation, but this will need various kinds of study.

Therefore, I dare to ask to kiss the H<oly> Right Hand of the Pontiff, and request that you allow me through Your high order, to publish this invaluable treasure, which has been bequeathed to us from our brilliant forefathers:

The humblest and son
Of the Pontiff
Komitas Vardapet Soghomonian

37 [The Armenian word for "hymn" is *sharakan*, and many Armenian musicologists believe that this should be recognized as a separate *kind* of hymn, perhaps a genre of its own. For this reason, they are not in favor of translating the Armenian word *sharakan* into "hymn" and some Armenian texts on spiritual music that have been translated to English have left the word "*sharakan*" untranslated. For the purposes of simplified reading, the word has been translated into the English "hymn" in the letters of Komitas and the corresponding notes] – Translator's notes

38 [Another name for the land of the Armenians] – Translator's notes

5. TO KARAPET KOSTANYAN

<18>95. 28/8. Holy Etchmiadzin

To the Honorable Administrator
Of the G<evorgyan> Theological Seminary
Karapet Kostanyan

I have endured this for long enough. Even if I no longer speak of this, the rocks will shout it out. Enough of this torment! It is as if everyone has accepted a reinstitution of the middle age inquisition – punish someone for a crime he has not committed, murdering him and then justifying him after he is killed.

I am sorry, very sorry, that so many people have heard that slander, that fault I did not commit, which had remained hidden from me for so long, and then came in the form of these accumulated sins. And it never occurred to any of you to investigate the case, because all of you had the appetite to believe it. The word investigation does not exist for us. It is enough to hear backbiting slander about one person, and you believe straightaway that such a thing really happened... I am now so angry, so upset, that no words can express my anger, my surprise at this fault I have not committed, to express that I am *fair, untainted, and pure*.

Did my friends have to display the behavior of Brutus towards me, did they not know me? If I was or am bad, why have they engaged in friendship with me? And if they did not know me, why did they not try to investigate and then only trust their friends. An honest man is one who corrects the fault of others and openly strikes it in their face, instead of concealing it.

Poor me - I pity my young age and my blossomed enthusiasm. I am losing my mind, I am going mad, but all in vain – who will help me? Everyone has turned their faces away. Everyone frowns at me, everyone thinks or believes that I am or can be impudent and shameless. Everyone is spreading the word about the impudence I have not shown, the impudence I have not demonstrated, the actions I have not committed. And I believe who they are – my teachers, my instructors, those who have nourished me. For so many years, they had not recognized any impudence in me, but now a piece of news, a false piece of slander, and everything that was the truth has melted in their ears

– *If I am me*, then who is that person whose impudence is being attributed to me? It is as if Komitas Vardapet was just a piece of cloth, over which everyone considers it their noble duty to rub their feet. Is this the reward for all my work, is this the compensation for all my efforts? Thank you. If all of you were honest people, why weren't you spitting in my face for this fault I have not committed? It is too bad that I have not been a great person, it is too bad that I have not been ambitious, otherwise there would be a court case immediately. Everyone's efforts are directed, after they believe it themselves, to try to make me believe something *I did not do*. Don't they realize that there are courts, there is a state law, which can take over the case? And I truly wish that those who believed, or want to believe it, would not feel shame, would not be overcome with a guilty conscience.

May God not burden them with this silent impudence. I cannot find words to appropriately describe the person who created this slander. It is better that the people who have believed it decide for themselves from here on.

I still believed that I had friends who would investigate the case first before turning their faces away from someone. But the opposite has occurred.

M<ister> Kostanyan, you are my first judge. I humbly ask you to investigate this case. If I am to blame in the way that they whisper together against me, I will give up this holy vocation of my own accord as someone unworthy of it. But if I am acquitted, then may the insolent slander created by a student and a servant be discovered, which others have not just been believed, but have also taken on the dirty work of spreading it further.

If you do not fulfil my request, I will seek the judgment of His Holiness, from where I hope to receive a reply. If there is no judgment there either, I will go to a corporal court and, after a doctor's examination, I will have the same people punished to the extent of the same criminal offense that they wish to force upon me. Shame and reproach to all those who believe it.

This much is sufficient.

Always praying for you
Your h<umble> s<ervant> Komitas Vardapet

6. <TO KARAPET KOSTANYAN>

<18>95 28/8 Holy Etchmiadzin

To the Honorable Administrator
Of the G<evorgyan> Theological Seminary
At the Mother See of Holy Etchmiadzin
Karapet Kostanyan

Letter of Resignation

I humbly inform you that I am resigning from the seminary, and in this regard I send the Honorable Administrator of the G<evorgyan> Th<eological> Seminary this letter, which I ask you to accept.

Your h<umble> s<ervant> Komitas Vardapet

7. <TO KARAPET KOSTANYAN>

28 August <18>95 <Holy Etchmiadzin>

To the Honorable Administrator
Of the G<evorgyan> Theological Seminary

Here are the keys to the grand piano.

Your h<umble> s<ervant> Komitas Vardapet

8. <TO KARAPET KOSTANYAN>

<18>95. 9/10. Tpghis[39]

Honorable
M<ister> Karapet Kostanyan

Respected Sir,

We made it to Tpghis. I handed the letter you had given to M<ister> Doctor Babayants and reminded him of the doctor. He said that he had written a letter and would write a second one as well. I am grateful, he promised support for my work, I have written about it in detail to F<ather> Hussik, he will probably tell you more; I will write to you about how things turn out.

Please, if it is possible, instruct the G<evorgyan> Seminary's Manuscript Library to send me J. Fétis' history of music in five volumes, to use for a certain period of time—*Histoire générale de la musique, t<ome>s. 1, 2, 3, 4 et 5*—of which I have great need. I would appreciate it if you could send it quickly.

The most honorable Holy Father Archbishop Gevorg ordered his people to prepare a room for me at the bottom of the Prelacy.

M<ister> Makar Yekmalyants is completely advising against gaining admission to the conservatory, and considers starting the music school here to be pointless and useless for me. He was so kind as to say that he would go over musical theory with me in great detail. In general, many people advise studying musical theory with Yekmalyants.

I have nothing more to write at the moment. When a final solution is in place, I will write in more detail.

Please give me regards to the Madame and the young lady; also don't forget to mention me to Petros, whom I did not manage to see when I was leaving.

---

39 ['Tpghis' and 'Tiflis' are the old names used by Armenians to refer to Tbilisi, the capital of Georgia] – Translator's notes

Please send the books quickly.

I remain, always respectfully yours,
In prayer,
Komitas Vardapet

9. <KARAPET KOSTANYAN>

30 October 1895. Tpghis

Honorable M<ister> Karapet Kostanyan

Respected Sir,

I received your letter of October 23.

I have already begun regular lessons. I am staying at the *S<oorb> Sargis*[40] with F<ather> Hamazasp, my living conditions are very good. I am at home the whole day and go into town only to attend lessons. For the time being, I am studying the theory of musical harmony and utilization for free with M<ister> Makar Yekmalyants, and I will complete it by the end of the month of May. Until January, I will be occupied only with the theoretical and practical side of harmony, followed by instrumental music up to the extent that is necessary for harmony and vocals, as well as vocal music, which should not take up that much of my time, especially since I need only the practical side. And, in order to prepare myself, I am frequenting the choral music hours at the Nersisyan School, which they have every day, and I am gaining skills in conducting styles, developing and strengthening voices, and methods of dividing into groups. The group at the school is conducted by Yekmalyants himself. They usually ask for a tuition fee of 3 *manets* each for vocal music or instrumental music lessons.

40 [*Soorb Sargis* is the Armenian name of Saint Sergius; in this context, it is a church or monastery that bears his name] – Translator's notes.

If I take 2 lessons of each per week, it comes to quite a sum each month, in addition to the monthly piano fee of 8 *manets*; I don't know what to do. What arrangements need to be made regarding money for me? My monthly salary is barely enough to pay for carriages, books and paper. Additionally, I don't have any winter clothes yet, nor do I have any money to buy them. I have written to Father. Please let him know that the tuition fee situation must be eased, it must be clear where and when I can receive it, so that I can focus my mind on my studies.

Please, make arrangements to send *Histoire générale de la musique* by Fétis, volumes 1, 2, 3, 4 and 5, I really need it.

My regards to Madame, the young lady and the teachers.

Respectfully yours, in prayer,
Komitas Vardapet

1896

10. <TO THE ADMINISTRATION OF THE GEVORGYAN THEOLOGICAL SEMINARY>

1896 April 25

To the Respected Administration of the Gevorgyan Theological Seminary

Subject

I graduated from the Gevorgyan Theological Seminary in the 1892/93 academic year, but I have still not received my certificate of achievement. I humbly request you to provide it.

Alumnus of the G<evorgyan> T<heological> Seminary
Komitas Vardapet Soghomonian

11. <TO MINAS BERBERYAN>

<18>96. 4/6 Berlin

Dear Minas,

After considerable trouble because of my passport, I finally reached Berlin and settled down at Deacon Garegin's place. Give me regards to everyone. Tell Deacon Cheorekchyan that I will write to him soon about the requests he had made. We were so confused in Kharkov that Benik and I did not even get to say goodbye. At the moment, I am busy with German and the piano.

My address is Berlin, Höchste str. 41, Archidiakonus Garegin Howsepianz. Many greetings to father and the rest of your family.

In prayer,
Komitas

12. <TO KARAPET KOSTANYAN>

<18>96. 2/7. Berlin
Koch Str. 73
Pension Frau Ziche[41]

Honorable
Mr. K<arapet> Kostanyants,

Respected Sir,

I could not reply to your letter all this time because my status was as yet unclear. I was supposed to go to Dresden based on F<ather> Karapet's advice, but that did not work out.

I introduced myself to the director of the conservatory here, Joachim, and he affectionately took charge of quickly admitting me as an actual student. My stay here has an additional advantage. There is another establishment adherent to this conservatory – a conservatory of ecclesiastical music, which does not exist anywhere else. I introduced myself to the director of this school as well, Radecke. He promised to enroll me here but as a visiting auditor because they admit Germans exclusively and only 25 people at that. He promised to make an exception in my case.

So I have to be a student of the conservatory as well as the conservatory of ecclesiastical music from October. I am now working on fixing some errors and making as much progress as possible. There is also another good feature here. A student is allowed to advance not on a yearly basis, but based on the

41 [The address was written in German (as shown here) by Komitas in the original letter] – Translator's notes

progress he shows. Demonstrate progress and you will advance to the next class.

With greetings to honorable Mrs. Tiruhi and you, I remain,
Always in prayer and respect,
Komitas Vardapet

P.S. F<ather> Hussik lives in the house of a pastor in one of the villages nearby and is preparing to move to Halle in October. His address is
Archimandrit Hussik Sohrabian
Caltzow bei/ Treptow an / Tollense Pfarrhaus

13. <TO KARAPET KOSTANYAN>

<18>96. 4/22 12/11. Berlin
Koch st. 73^{IV} 1. Hof.[42]

Honorable M<ister> Karapet Kostanyants,

Respected Sir,

I consider it my debt to give you information about my work here. As a friend, you paved the way for me to start studying in a location of my choosing, and you are the true leader of the institution to which I consider myself forever indebted.

I took advantage of my summer vacation and gained practice in German on one hand, while also taking private lessons from head teacher Richard Schmidt and completing the whole *Harmonielehre* course. At the beginning of the winter semester, I registered as a student at the local university in order to attend lectures on music history.

I did not enter the conservatory.

42 [The address was written in German (as shown here) by Komitas in the original letter] – Translator's notes

My teacher, who is the director of the conservatory, tested me and then recommended completely against enrolling. He said that this would be a step back for me and suggested instead that I take private lessons, which he took charge of organizing. The benefit from these private lessons is great and the pace is quick, just as my time is brief. Why didn't I come here 6 years ago?

Two times a week, on alternating occasions, I have lunch with my teachers, whose families have completely opened their doors to me. My teachers often send me free tickets to attend performances at the Opernhaus, Philharmonie, Symphonie and Concert. Thanks to my teacher, I have a broad circle of musical artists who are quite accomplished and respected; this gives me even more encouragement. We write various musical pieces and arrange performances in people's homes, where we play, discuss and debate our music. My teacher arranged to have the musical fragments I had written published at his expense, without saying anything to me or offering to do so. But I am in no hurry. I will not publish anything until I have studied all the deep secrets there are. If there is anything that is causing me difficulty, it is only in playing instruments. Without a teacher to lead me, the erroneous movements of my fingers are taking too long to fix, especially since I have started late as it is.

I have sent "The Fire of Your Love" to you in my letter. The music is taken from our ecclesiastical melodies, but it has been converted to musical order. I have written it for four voices as well as two. Don't publish it, because I know it will be printed wrong, and that error will destroy the whole basis of the harmonies in it. Let them copy from my version, and please keep the original with you, because I only have a draft, which could get lost. I don't have the time to get it copied again. I am sending it along with a guide to teaching it, so that they don't have a difficult time with it.

Please pass on my greetings of respect to Mrs. Tiruhi. Greetings and wishes of success also to all the teachers and families, as well as to our holy priests. Amen.

In prayer for you,
<H>umble <S>ervant Komitas Vardapet

The Fire of Your Love

The first two Amens are written for a male choir, both in the four-voice and in the two-voice versions. The third and the "fire of your love" are for a mixed choir and for strong voices. The third Amen in the two-voice version is meant once again for four voices, but the Alto and Bass simply sing the same note, so that should not cause difficulties. The first voice in the two-voice version should be sung by the Soprano and the Alto together, while the second voice should be sung by the Tenor and the Bass together. The melody has been written with a D Dur variation or in Re Major, but it sounds good with the voices singing half a note higher according to the piano or a tuner, if the Bass cannot sing that low, or on the contrary, with the voices singing half a note lower—which is much more pleasant—if the Sopranos don't have a high range or the Basses have a low voice, which is more suitable. I have written it with a D Dur variation in order to make the notes easy to read, but it is good even if it is sung as it is written. In brief, one of these three variations needs to be used based on the circumstances.

The "Glory to You" should not be sung by the Soprano or Alto, but by the Tenor, in a way that makes for good listening and smooth singing. Naturally, the voice for the "Glory to You" should be adjusted to suit the previous endings.

In places where there is a rise of half a note, the second must be mild and should smoothly transition to the next note or solution, and the opposite should be done when there is a lowering. This makes the singer's job easier.

In the Armenian – (L = lowering) and (m = <m>ild, mm=milder, mmm=very mild or silent=almost unintelligible singing). When forming the choir, there should be a strict selection of voices, especially for the four-voice version. Singers with ability, a good ear and voice should be selected, not those who have voices that are hoarse, sticky, broken or on the verge of changing. Here is the range of selection for each voice.

Soprano  – (si) do-mi
Alto - - .fis – a (fa-la)
Tenor – Like the Soprano, an octave lower

Bass – - . fa-do

This is how I would do the selection

do, re, mi, fa, sol, la, si

c, d, e, f, g, a, h

And, based on this, the prayer translated into Armenian would be

d, e, fis, g, a, h, cis, d,

In this way, the group can consist of up to around 30 people, with the following proportion – Soprano – 2, Alto – 2, Tenor – 2, Bass – 1. This can help you plan even bigger groups. After forming a choir, one should spend a separate two hours on the practice of going up and down 3 half-notes consecutively. When everyone manages this task well, one can then train each of the voices separately and then gradually bring the separate groups together. One can start with teaching the first voices, the second, then bringing them together. Then the third voices can be taught and joined to the rest and so on. Only after this can they all perform together publicly. While singing, strict attention should be paid to the signs marking the nuances in music, which must be performed mandatorily and perfectly as they are written. If there are problems, the groups must immediately be trained again separately. I have written everything that I could foresee, the teacher is in charge of any remaining random occurrences.

14. <TO THE ADMINISTRATION OF THE GEVORGYAN THEOLOGICAL SEMINARY>

The year 1896, 31 December, from Berlin

To the Administration
Of the Gevorgyan Theological Seminary
Of the Mother See of Holy Etchmiadzin

From Komitas *Vardapet* Gevorgyan
A Report of My Studies

Under the high and obliging directorship as well as the direct order of the Patriarch and Holiest Catholicos of All Armenians Mkrtich I, my path led to Germany where I strengthened my incomplete musical education. On the fifteenth day of June of this year 1896 I reached the capital Berlin and mastered the German language by the thirtieth of July, after which I began to take musical instruction by the master of this art *Königlicher Professor und Musik-Direktor* Richard Schmidt, which I completed on the fifteenth of October.

a. The study of musical harmony (*Harmonielehre*).
b. The study of classical music modulation (*Modulation der klassichen Meister*), to be completed in the winter semester.
c. Strict style (ecclesiastical in my case) of musical composition (*Der strange Satz in der musikalischen Compositionslehre*), which I have begun to audit.
d. Free style (*Contrapunkt und Fuge im freien (modernen) Tonsatz einschliesslich Chorcomposition*).
e. Piano (*Klavier*) on going.

In detail, as a student of the capital, I audit these eight classes.

f. History of music from the 16th century (*Musikgeschichte vom 16. Jahrundert an. Prof. Fleischer*).
g. Musical study exercises (*Musikwissenschaftliche Uebungen im Instrumenten-Museum. Professor Fleischer*).

and h. Elements of musical composition (*Die Elemente der musikalischen Composition*).

These are the completed and ongoing studies that I have the honor of humbly reporting to the Administration.

The humble alumnus of your Seminary,

Komitas *Vardapet* Gevorgyan

15. <TO THE ADMINISTRATION OF THE GEVORGYAN THEOLOGICAL SEMINARY>

The year 1896, 31 December, from Berlin

To the Administration of the Gevorgyan Theological Seminary of the Mother See of Holy Etchmiadzin from Komitas Vardapet Gevorgyan

A Humble Statement

I send you with gratitude a receipt for the sum of a hundred (100) rubles.

Komitas *Vardapet* Gevorgyan

Receipt

On the date of 31 December of this year 1896, I received the sum of a hundred (100) rubles sent by the administration of the Gevorgyan Theological Seminary of the Mother See of Holy Etchmiadzin from the kind and gracious Hussik Vardapet Zohrabyan. Dated the year 1896, 31 December, Berlin.

Komitas Vardapet Gevorgyan

1897

16. <TO KARAPET KOSTANYAN>

<18>97. 27/15. 1. Berlin
Koch str. 73^{IV}[43]

Honorable M<ister> K<arapet> Kostanyants,

Respected Sir,

I received your letter a long time ago, but my illness (I had a high fever for two weeks) and my mandatory classes did not allow me to find even a little time to reply immediately. I had just managed to get out of bed when I received your New Year greeting card. It is indeed a New Year that finds me in an educational institution. My holidays have also been celebrated in the diverse layers of a large musical world. Each hour and minute reveal a future scene to me full of endless and caring work.

Your letter of encouragement, which I constantly need in these days of suppressive wandering, motivated and strengthened me – at least there is someone who is looking out for and appreciating me. The deeper I wade into this comedic sea of music, the stronger my conviction grows that both our folk and ecclesiastical melodies, which have been brother and sister for a long time, should also become the focus of study by foreigners. Because their deep roots take one to very ancient times, up to the origin of the Armenian, where it blooms inseparably from him and brings us to our times.

My teacher always repeats this to me - you have created a noble and unique musical style, which passes like a clear red line through everything that you have written and composed.

I call that style the Armenian style–he says–because it is a novelty, given the musical world known to us. I have also had the idea of arranging

43 [The address was written in German (as shown here) by Komitas in the original letter] – Translator's notes

a national melody for our old national songs and it might become a reality. But this is only after understanding the rules of versification and emphasis for our hymnal melodies, because, because the emphasis in the melodies is almost in disagreement with the rules of emphasis and usage for the modern language. I think that our forefathers used a different kind of emphasis. The versification used by the ancient and unknown composers of hymns is very interesting and has now become quite clear to me, because the musical emphasis seems to be preserved and matches the language used.

Was it possible to perform the "Fire of Your Love" or were there difficulties? I would have really liked to send you a sample from a four-voice hymn this time around to see the emotions that our heavenly hymnal melodies can arouse. But, in this case, I found it better to be careful and not to send anything. I was afraid that it might be performed badly, ruining the whole thing. I thought it would be best to only write this much, so that they could get the students used to singing mild notes – they have a habit of always singing medium notes. All this is well and good, but I am having extreme difficulties when it comes to everyday life. I often feel weak – the food I eat is next to nothing, but my tasks are many. I have grown thin and am like a skeleton. I think it would be a great loss for things to end this way. Thank you, the 100 coins you had sent last time covered most of my debts. This stupid subject really costs a lot to study, like the other branches of art. I often give less for food in order to pay for my tuition, but... Holy Father Karapet had written to the boys recently that Komitas is creating too much fuss from there but he should be writing to Mantashyants, and so on. Does he really not know that he only wanted to give me 400 coins at first and that it was only through sheer brazenness that I managed to raise it to 600? Oh... Ah, for the days of the past, at least then people could comfortably dedicate themselves to their studies... it is better to stay silent.

I am sending you a small article for *Ararat* – let them publish it, if they find it worthwhile.

A long time ago, I asked Karapet Vardapet to get one of his students to carefully copy out Samuel Anetsi's *Handwritten Knowledge about Sounds and Songs* from the manuscript library of Holy Etchmiadzin, issue number 1700. But I have still not received it, please remind him.

The publishing house, or perhaps the Catholicos' office, receives the journal *Arevelk.* I would be very grateful if you could somehow send me issue 5600 of the year 1896, it is very important. That is all.

Please give my regards to all the teachers and <H>oly Fathers.

Please also give my respectful regards separately to H<onorable> Mrs. Tiruhi. I am truly happy that you never forget me. I too wish you courage and success in your days and tasks of difficulty. I remain always,

In prayer,
H<umble servant>
Komitas Vardapet

17. <TO THE ADMINISTRATION OF THE GEVORGYAN THEOLOGICAL SEMINARY>

Dated 16/4 February
Of the year 1897, from Berlin

To the Administration of the Gevorgyan Theological Seminary of the Mother See of Holy Etchmiadzin

Statement

I send with gratitude to your administration a receipt for the sum of a hundred (100) rubles.

H<umble alumnus> Komitas Vardapet

Receipt

The administration of the Gevorgyan Theological Seminary of the Mother See of Holy Etchmiadzin has sent me the sum of a hundred (100) rubles, which I have received. Dated 16/4 of the month of February, the year 1897, in Berlin.

Komitas Vardapet

18. <TO KARAPET KOSTANYAN>

<18>97. 14/26 5. Berlin
Koch str. 73[IV] [44]

Honorable M<ister> K< arapet> Kostanyan,

Respected Sir,

During this summer 6-month semester, I am attending the following lessons at university.

1. *Geschichte der Musik im Mittelalter vom Beginn des Christenthums*
2. *Musikgeschichte Frankreichs und der Niederlande*
3. *Einführung in die Geschichte der Kirchenmusik*
4. *Musikwissenschaftliche Uebungen in der Königl. Musikinstrumenten-Sammlung*

And I am taking private lessons with head teacher Richard Schmidt in the following

1. *Formenlehre*
2. *Klavier (Uebungen)*
3. *Moderner Tonsatz*

Next semester, I might be able to start *Instrumentation, Orchestermusik*. I can already freely compose music for the *Streichquartett*. I have fully completed the theory of ecclesiastical music; I am only studying the practical side. These wretched piano lessons are tormenting and wearing me out, progress is very difficult. My fingers have hardened and joints have tightened, that too in the wrong way, such that I am still unable to arrange them straight, [and] faultlessly and properly, I am also often left in despair; nevertheless, I have to learn this as well, it is necessary. My health is limping along as well. I have prepared

44 [The address was written in German (as shown here) by Komitas in the original letter] – Translator's notes

some of our spiritual hymns for four voices, six voices and eight voices; my teacher proposed to have them sung. I am preparing a few more and then my teacher himself will arrange for them to be sung at one of the churches or at the *Singakademie*, as a spiritual concert. I will write more details when we start this work successfully.

My regards to everyone who asks about me. In particular, please give my regards to the honorable Mrs. Tiruhi Kostanyants; I have not forgotten those wonderful evening hours that we would spend at your house, and the Madame was constantly repeating and insisting that you arrange my travel abroad. I am greatly and sincerely thankful for that big and irreplaceable favor that you provided with a double intention – to raise the status of church singing and to drive me forward in the subject that I enjoy.

I have nothing else to write. I too wish you success in your work and well-being.

Your h<umble servant> in prayer
Komitas Vardapet

19. <TO THE ADMINISTRATION OF THE GEVORGYAN THEOLOGICAL SEMINARY>

1897, 14/26 5.
From Berlin

To the Administration of the Gevorgyan Theological Seminary of the Mother See of Holy Etchmiadzin from Komitas Vardapet Gevorgyan

Statement

I humbly send to your Administration a receipt for the sum of a hundred rubles, received from Hussik Vardapet Zohrabyan.

A humble alumnus of your Seminary
Komitas Vardapet

Receipt

I received my living wages of a hundred (100) rubles sent by the administration of the Gevorgyan Theological Seminary of the Mother See of Holy Etchmiadzin through Hussik Vardapet Zohrabian. The year 1897, 26/14 5, Berlin.

Komitas Vardapet

20. <TO THE ADMINISTRATION OF THE GEVORGYAN THEOLOGICAL SEMINARY>

1897, 21/9 July. From Berlin

To the Administration of the Gevorgyan Theological Seminary of the Mother See of Holy Etchmiadzin

Statement

I humbly send to your Administration a receipt for the sum of a hundred rubles, received from Hussik Vardapet Zohrabian, for the months of August, September, October and November of the year 1897, for my expenses.

A humble alumnus of your Seminary
Komitas Vardapet

Receipt

I received a hundred (100) rubles sent by the Administration for my expenses for the months of August, September, October and November of the year 1897 through Hussik Vardapet Zohrabian.

The year 1897, 21/9 July, in Berlin.

A h<umble alumnus of your Seminary>
Komitas Vardapet

21. <TO KARAPET KOSTANYAN>

1897. 10/29 11/10 Berlin

Honorable M<ister> K<arapet> Kostanyants,

These are the lessons I am attending during the six-month semester this winter:

1. *Aesthetik der Tonkunst. Prof. O. Fleischer.*
2. *Die Musik der alten Griechen. Prof. Bellerman.*
3. *Allgemeine Geschichte der Musik. Friedländer.*
4. *Musikinstrumentenkunde. Prof. O. Fleischer.*
5. *Musikwissenschaftliche Uebungen. Prof. O. Fleischer.*

And I am taking private lessons from Prof. Richard Schmidt in the following subjects

1. *Formenlehre.*
2. *Compositionlehre.*
3. *Klavier*
4. *Stimmeinbildung.*

I am very satisfied with my head teacher, who has really helped me progress in music in general during this one year, more than they cover during 6 years of music school here. If there is one thing that is difficult for me, then it is playing the piano, where I am making very slow progress. My fingers have grown rough and my bones have hardened; I can play a little, but I have not yet reached the level that I would like. My head teacher, Richard Schmidt, has set up lessons for me at the preparatory classes of his music school. Under his supervision, I teach lessons in vocal music and am training in gathering a group, training and conducting it, which is extremely useful to me and my experience.

Honorable M<ister> Kostanyants, I have a request. I ask you to send also the stipend for the next 3 (three) months, which I have not yet received; at least that way I would be able to buy the necessary music books, which I need, and I would be able to repay my old debts. Of course, I ask this only if it is possible.

Please give my regards to Mrs. Tiruhi and all the teachers, and other spiritual friends, if you see them.

With regards to you as well.
I remain always grateful
Your h<umble servant>
Komitas Vardapet

22. <TO SIRAKAN TIGRANYAN>

25/6 10/12. Berlin. <1897>

Honorable M<ister> Sirakan Tigranyants,

I received with joy today some of the musical pieces written by your brother, which you had sent me. In accordance with your wishes, I have kept a copy of each and given the rest to the teachers I know, and it is my duty to pass on to you the thanks and satisfaction that they expressed.

The Armenian musical horizon is so narrow and limited that I am very happy and interested to see Armenian melodies printed in European musical notation, especially the many emotions produced by the hearts of our people, which grab my attention and my soul with their simple, natural and austere style, and their profound musical content, which holds the discovery of our nation's unenviable situation.

I sincerely wish your brother success in the work that he has undertaken, presenting our priceless folk treasures to the attention of foreigners. Please give him my regards, if you write him a letter.

My best regards to M<ister> Yevangulyants, as well as from Madame and young lady Strauss, my landlady.

With sincere regards to you,
Komitas Vardapet

23. <TO THE ADMINISTRATION OF THE GEVORGYAN THEOLOGICAL SEMINARY>

The year 1897, 10/29 10/11. Berlin

To the Administration of the G<evorgyan> Theological Seminary of the Mother See of H<oly> Etchmiadzin

Statement

I humbly send you a receipt for the sum of a hundred rubles sent by your Administration, received from Yeznka Vardapet Gyanjetsyan.

A humble alumnus of your Seminary
Komitas Vardapet

Receipt

I received a hundred rubles sent by the Administration of the G<evorgyan> Theological Seminary of the Mother See of Holy Etchmiadzin for my expenses for the months of November and December of the year 1897, as well as January and February of the year 1898, through Yeznka Vardapet Gyanjetsyan. The year 1897, 10/29 10/11, Berlin.

Komitas Vardapet

1898

24. <TO THE ADMINISTRATION OF THE GEVORGYAN THEOLOGICAL SEMINARY>

The year 1898, 30/11 2/3. Berlin

Statement

To the Administration of the Gevorgyan Theological Seminary of the Mother See of H<oly> Etchmiadzin

I humbly send your Administration a receipt for the sum of a hundred (100) rubles for March, April, May and June of this year 1898.

An alumnus of your Seminary
H<umble servant>
Komitas Vardapet

25. <TO KARAPET KOSTANYAN>

<18>98. 5. 5. Berlin
Kochstr. 73^IV

Respected M<ister> K<arapet> Kostanyan,

These are the lessons I am attending during the six-month semester this summer:

Prof. Bellerman:

1. *Geschichte der Musik des Mittelalters seit dem Anfang des Christenthums bis Franco von Cöln im 13. Jahrhundert.*

Prof. Fleischer:

2. *Deutsche Musikgeschichte (dritter Theil) von Händel und Bach an*
3. *Geschichte der Notenschrift*
4. *Musikwissenschaftliche Uebungen im Instrumentmuseum.*

Prof. Friedländer:

5. *Allgemeine Geschichte der Musik vom Beginn des 17. Jahrhunderts ab*
6. *Musikwissenschaftliche Uebungen (Erklärung ausgewählter musikalischer Kunstwerke).*

I am taking private lessons from Prof. Richard Schmidt in the following subjects

7. *Instrumentation und Orchestersatz mit Vocal-, Chor- und Solo-Satz*

   A. *Instrumentation:*
      a. *Instrumentation für gewöhnliches Orchester*
      b. *Instrumentation für das grosse symphonische Orchester*
      c. *Das gewöhnliche Orchester in Verbindung mit Gesang in den niederen dramatischen Formen des Vaudeville.*
      d. *Verbindung des symphonischen Orchesters mit der Vocalmusik in Oper und Orarotium.*

   B. *Orchestersatz:*
      a. *as Orchester und seine Behandlung*
      b. *Der Sologesang*
      c. *Verbunder Instrumental-und Vocal-Satz.*

The last one, the 7th, is a 2½ semester course. I am also giving one lesson a week at my music teacher's school on "Group Organization for Male High Voices" and "Harmony in Free Art" in the senior classes.

Respectfully yours,
H<umble> s<ervant> Komitas Vardapet

26. <TO KARAPET KOSTANYAN>

1898. 11/29 10/9. Berlin
Kochstr. 73[45]

Honorable M<ister> K<arapet> Kostanyan,

These are the lessons I am attending during the six-month semester this winter:

1. *Musikgeschichte des Mittelalters*. Prof. Fleischer
2. *Mozarts Leben und Werke*. Dr. Friedländer
3. *Musikgeschichte des 19. Jahrhunderts*. Prof. Fleischer.
4. *Das deutsche Lied*. Dr. Friedländer.
5. *Musikwissenschaftliche Uebungen*. Dr. Friedl<änder>.
6. *Musikwissenschaftliche Uebungen*. Prof. Fleischer.
7. *Uebungen im Contrapunkt*. Prof. Bellerman.
8. *Ueber die Musik der alten Griechen*. Prof. Bellerman.

And I am going to continue my private lessons in *Instrumentationslehre und Orchestersatz* with Prof. Richard Schmidt, as well as the weekly trial lesson I am giving at his school.

Because I am going to return next year, I have a few suggestions to make in advance.

First, it is necessary that the Seminary procures a good harmonium after my return, because I intend to organize a concert of ecclesiastical music or folk music and song once a week, and the only instrument that suits the spirit of our melodies is the harmonium, which I will always be using to bring our ecclesiastical music to order. It was for this reason that I began learning to play the harmonium, which I will complete by June; it does not cause me as much trouble as the piano does. In a word, I find the harmonium a more suitable instrument for myself than the piano.

Secondly, next year is the 25th anniversary of the Seminary, and we need to prepare a few things, here is what I think. Please ask, on my behalf,

45 [The address was written in German (as shown here) by Komitas in the original letter] – Translator's notes

M<ister> H<ovhannes> Hovhannisyan to write something for that occasion, and as quickly as possible, so that I can come with it prepared, I will not have much time there to deal with such things, and I will focus my main efforts on gathering a choir. In general, keep the older and younger children with strong voices, or allow them vacation up to August 1, I will be coming to H<oly> Etchmiadzin shortly after that. And if you could, please find out what kinds of instruments they play in the Yerevan Military Band, so that I can arrange my songs accordingly. This way, we can celebrate with a glorious concert.

I have already prepared "Save us, Lord" and "Father, Father, your Fatherland" both for a choir and instruments, and I will prepare other selected folk pieces.

I would very much like to audit some lessons in Theology, but my time is very limited, so I will be unable to do so.

If you have any other instructions, please write them to me.

Since I have explained the importance of the harmonium, what remains is that you take on the duty of buying it and bearing its costs – it is not something you can assign to anyone else, they wouldn't be able to do it. I have laid my hope directly on you for this. A good harmonium, that would last long, would require 1500 *manets*, this also includes the transport costs and customs duty. I await your letter.

Please give my regards and respects to your wife, Mrs. Tiruhi and other who ask about me.

Yours, in prayer,
Komitas Vardapet

P.S. Please send me a copy of the jubilee program. Please make arrangements for my stipend to be sent on time.

<The same author>

27. <TO THE ADMINISTRATION OF THE GEVORGYAN THEOLOGICAL SEMINARY>

<The year 1898, 29 September>

Statement

I have received from the Administration of the Gevorgyan Theological Seminary of the Mother See of Holy Etchmiadzin for July, August, September and October the sum sent of a hundred (100) rubles. The year 1898, 29 September, Berlin.

Komitas Vardapet Gevorgyan

28. <TO THE ADMINISTRATION OF THE GEVORGYAN THEOLOGICAL SEMINARY>

<21/2 Oct<ober>/Novem<er>, the year 1898 >

Statement

I have received from the Administration of the Gevorgyan Theological Seminary of the Mother See of Holy Etchmiadzin for November, December of the year 1898, as well as January and February of the year 1899, the sum sent of a hundred (100) rubles. 21/2 Oct<ober>/Novem<ber>, the year 1898

Komitas Vardapet Gevorgyan

29. <TO MKRTICH KHRIMYAN I, CATHOLICOS OF ALL RMENIANS>

1898, 19 November, Berlin

To His Holiness,

The noblest head of clergy and Catholicos of all Armenians,

Having received the most holy order, I make haste to send two young Armenians. They expect to quench their thirst for learning from you, the Armenian Patriarch, as per the request with holy written approval, referenced under number 1189, which Your Holiness pleased to issue on the 17th of October in this year 1898.

I humbly announce that one of these is a native of Cilicia, the other from Constantinople, both being eighteen years of age, without parents. One is called Adom, the other Mikayel Yeretsian. They have studied in Constantinople, in the Mother and Hasköy schools, and both have graduated. They are both children of the true Holy Armenian Apostolic Church. They were sent here to Germany through the German-Armenian Society (but not Dr. Lepsius in Berlin) after the massacres in Constantinople in 1896. Now both of them are at the German institute in the village of Wilhelmsdorf, Württemberg, Germany.

Presenting this letter of proclamation most humbly to you, my Lord, the Most Holy Armenian Father and the Mother of Light, Holy Etchmiadzin, I approach you to kiss your Most Holy Right Hand with deep respect, and remain your son and servant,

Komitas Vardapet

30. <TO KARAPET KOSTANYAN>

1898, 7/12. Berlin
Kochstr. 73^{IV} b. Strauß[46]

Honorable
M<ister> K<arapet> Kostanyants,

Based on what you wrote in your letter, I am rushing to reply.

46 [The address was written in German (as shown here) by Komitas in the original letter] – Translator's notes

a. What I had written about the money was wrong. It was not 3 – I have not received the money for June, because I have been here since June, not July, which makes it 21 months up to March.
b. I am rushing to return as well, but not without seeing things to their conclusion.

In September 1898, it will be 2¼ years since my arrival, while M<ister> Mantashyants had promised to support my stay for 3 years, and had promised a fourth as well if necessary, but I have no need for the 4th. However, there is a lot of necessity to complete the 3rd.

I am going to start higher music, or the art of music, from the 3rd year, and without this it would be almost impossible to bring the ecclesiastical music to order and reform it. I am going to be free of the claws of cut and dry rules only at the end of this month or at the start of the next month. This is not history that one can learn from a book, it is something that only practical lessons can impart and, without this, I would be quite useless as a musician.

Many regards to Madame and the teachers' group.

Your h<umble servant>

Komitas Vardapet

P.S. My predecessor would not have managed over 5 years even 1/10th of that which I have done in this short period.

The same author

1899

31. <TO KARAPET KOSTANYAN>

<18>99. 31/19. 3. Berlin
Kochstr. 73[47]

Honorable
M<ister> K<arapet> Kostanyan,

I consider it my duty to tell you that I will complete the *Compositionlehre* course towards the end of next month. To take advantage of the time available, I decided to improve another weak side I have – for the past two weeks I have been taking lessons in vocal music and vocal training, which is undoubtedly necessary for choral music and in general to train and adjust the voices in the Seminary choir. My teacher tested my voice and decided that I am a baritone who covers the whole range of high tenors and low baritones, 2¾ octaves, 20 scales, my voice has both the flexibility of a tenor and softness of a baritone. Because it is not difficult for me to sing an unfamiliar piece immediately, without learning it, I am able to make quick progress. I am only going to take two subjects this semester, I will write more about that when the time comes. I have also completed learning to play the harmonium.

Recently, the Berlin branch of the International Music Society was founded in the city, where I was invited to become a member. The initiative is being headed by university prof. Oskar Fleischer, and I was the only one of his students who was invited to become a member. I am obligated to correspond with them regularly and provide articles on eastern music. This is definitely a productive force for my future. I am sending you a copy each of the bylaws, you can read more about it there.

47 [The address was written in German (as shown here) by Komitas in the original letter] – Translator's notes

I request once again that you arrange to have my stipend sent at the start of the month. It is a great inconvenience, I now have some major expenses.

I have not received anything on the arrangements I sent you for the Seminary's celebration.

Please give my regards to the Seminary group.

With special regards to Mrs. Tiruhi and you, I remain,

Yours dedicated
Komitas Vardapet

32. <TO THE ADMINISTRATION OF THE GEVORGYAN THEOLOGICAL SEMINARY>

The year 1899, 19/31 March. Berlin

To the Administration of the G<evorgyan> S<eminary> of the M<other> S<ee> of H<oly> Etchmiadzin

Statement

I humbly send you a receipt for the sum of twenty rubles for the month of March, of the year 1899.

A humble alumnus of your Seminary
Komitas Vardapet

Receipt

I received twenty (20) rubles as my stipend for the month of March of the year 1899 through Yeznka Vardapet Gyanjetsyan. 1899, 19/31, March, Berlin.

Komitas Vardapet

33. <TO THE ADMINISTRATION OF THE GEVORGYAN THEOLOGICAL SEMINARY>

1899, 13/1 5. Berlin

To the Administration of the Gevorgyan Seminary of the Mother See of Holy Etchmiadzin

Statement

I humbly send you a receipt for the sum of eighty (80) rubles received from your Administration for the months of April, May and June, of this year.

Komitas Vardapet

Receipt

I received eighty (80) rubles the Administration of the Gevorgyan Seminary of the Mother See of Holy Etchmiadzin as my stipend for the months of April, May and June. 1899. 13/1. May. Berlin.

Komitas Vardapet

34. <TO KORYUN VARDAPET SAHAKYAN>

31 (19) May, <1899, Berlin>
Koch Str. 73[48]

Dear brother,
Father Koryun,

48 [The address was written in German (as shown here) by Komitas in the original letter] – Translator's notes

The time for my return is already approaching, I hope that we will see each other soon. I am writing this letter to you to ask that you do the following for me.

This last year of studies was very expensive for me, and I ended up buried in debts. There was also the behavior of that swindler Grigor Tokatlyan (you probably know him from Holy Etchmiadzin), who borrowed a lot of money not just from me, but from all the students and even from foreigners and then suddenly vanished one day, ran away, with no hide nor hair of him remaining, besmirching the name of all the Armenian students and the nation in general.

I now request you to kiss the Holy Right Hand of this Holiness the Father and ask him to send me 200 rubles, which I ask as a loan that I will repay bit by bit from my salary upon my return.

If you can fulfil this small request, I would be greatly indebted to you.

Reply quickly.

Give my regards in particular to Khoren *ef<fendi>* and those who ask about me.

I remain, your brother, Komitas Vardapet

35. <TO KARAPET KOSTANYAN>

1899. 28/17 6. Berlin
Kochstr. 73[49]

Honorable
M<ister> K<arapet> Kostanyan,

Although I had mentioned to you in my last letter that I would return to Holy Etchmiadzin in August, but my return has been delayed to mid-September because I have an important task that I am obliged to fulfil while I am here. I recently gave two lectures with great success at the Berlin music school

49 [The address was written in German (as shown here) by Komitas in the original letter] – Translator's notes

about Armenian music in general and with particular information about the eastern one. This lecture once again helped me become well known in music circles, especially when I was elected as a member of the International Music Society, where only recognized musicians are given membership. My instructors at the university forced me to have my lecture published, and the first academic journal of the society, which will be published in August, will feature my article as well. So I am now forced to prepare it for publication and have it ready in time. Secondly, I will finish the program planned in my education around August 20. Because I have so many things left to do, please do not expect me at the Seminary before September.

Please give my warmest regards to your wife.

Regards to those who ask about me.

Yours in gratitude,
Komitas Vardapet

36. <TO BABKEN VARDAPET KYULESERYAN>

<1899, October-November, Holy Etchmiadzin>

Gracious Father Babken Vardapet,
Dear brother in Christ,

I have to inconvenience you slightly, [but] I hope you will not reject [helping me in this task necessary for the general success of the assignment].

A few years ago, the Prelate of Caesarea Honorable Bishop F<ather> Trdat Vardapet Palyan had found among the manuscripts of the St. Daniel Monastery [apparently with very interesting content] an old, Armenian manuscript about music, of which he had had a brief summary [very brief in nature, with mainly a list of the relevant headings] published in the *Handes Amsorya* journal. [Because]

I have asked the Honorable Father a number of times, beseeching him to either send me the manuscript or a copy of it, so that I can use it as a musician, extract the H<oly> spiritual Armenian melodies and compare them to the rules of our national *khaz* notation system,[50] but unfortunately the Holy Father replied that he cannot send the manuscript because he fears that it will get lost along the way. And he had promised that he would bring it with him when he came to be ordained as a bishop, so that I might make a copy. When the Holy Father arrived for his ordination, I was studying in Germany, but I had asked my friends and students to copy and send me the manuscript if the bishop came to Etchmiadzin. The Holy Father came and went, but he had not brought the manuscript with him.

So I was forced to write once again and request him to send the manuscript, or have it copied, or to have the pages photographed and sent in that form. He replied quickly and said that he would sell me the manuscript [but he was asking] for 300 rubles, which is a sum that I naturally could not and cannot afford. [Therefore] I am now left to hope that you, honorable Father, can fulfil this wish of mine. If you cannot, then please humbly kiss the H<oly> Right Hand of His Holiness and ask this of him on my behalf. I am full of hope that I will be able to obtain the manuscript this time at least, so that I can copy it and send it back immediately. I would have been very happy to pay 300 rubles and buy the manuscript but, as you know, I am forced to support both myself on my annual 300 ruble salary and the large family of my poor paternal aunt. [If this task cannot be fulfilled without money, then I will make the payment, but in installments.]

I fraternally ask you [to help], you are my only hope for help and know that, if you succeed [in helping], you would have provided a big service by supporting the development of our ecclesiastical music.

Awaiting your reply
I remain with you in prayer
Komitas Vardapet

---

50 [The English word for notations of this kind is "neumes" but many Armenian musicologists believe that the Armenian *khaz* should be recognized as a particular *kind* of neume, perhaps a genre of its own. For this reason, they are not in favor of translating the Armenian word *khaz* into "neume" and some Armenian texts that have been translated to English have left the word "*khaz*" untranslated. For the purposes of simplified reading, the word has been translated into the English "neume" in the letters of Komitas and the corresponding notes] – Translator's notes

1901

37. <TO NIKOGHAYOS TIGRANYAN>

22/1 Holy Etchmiadzin. <1901>

Dear Nikoghayos Tigranyan,

Sirakan reminded me of my promise to send you my works immediately after returning from Tiflis. Don't think that I had forgotten to do so, I was waiting for them to be published, which is why it took so long. I received one the other day, but not the other. Unable to wait any longer, I am sending you these two torn right out of the collection – a) *Interpunctionssystem der Armenier* and b) *Armeniens Volkstümliche Reigentänze.* The second is a small extract from the big piece that I will publish next year – the printed version didn't come out the way I had wanted it, and there are a few minor errors, which you will probably notice yourself, but I suppose I could expect no more from a German who speaks no Armenian and has no concept of our dances. I had also had pictures published, so that the samples of the songs I had placed at the end would be easier to comprehend for foreigners. Anyway, this is how it turned out. My intention has been to only provide a small hint about our melodies to foreigners, the composition and rhythm of which can teach them a lot. The examples I have selected are partly purely folk, partly composed as bard music and then turned into folk songs. But I don't need to drag the explanation any further, you are quite well aware of it yourself.

The rest of my work has not yet been published, you will receive it over time as well. At the moment, one article that is ready for publication and will be printed in Paris is "Armenian Ecclesiastical Music in Eight Voices, its Locution and Keys." Meanwhile, an article on Armenian Folk Songs, Intonation (the intonation of songs) and Prosody, which highlights the origins of our folk song melodies, will be printed (I have already mentioned this to you) in the compilations of our musical society. I am now developing the history of the Armenian notation of ancient and modern epics as well as ecclesiastical music (that is to say, *Neumengeschichte, die Bedeutung*).

The Seminary lessons are really impeding my studies.

This summer, I intend to travel around the villages and check the melodies of folk songs one last time, then have them published in parts.

What are you doing? Have you written any new Persian music, have you published anything new? I am sure you are doing a lot, knowing you I can imagine that you will not give yourself a quiet moment. Give my regards to my acquaintances and those who ask about me.

I wish you wellbeing and constant enthusiasm.

Yours, Komitas Vardapet

38. <TO HRACHYA ACHARYAN>

<1901, 19 May, Tiflis>

Bu gün çıktım, Çok selam sana ve kızkardaşına.[51]

Komitas

<Translation>

I went out today, regards to you and your sister.

Komitas

39. <TO SARGIS KAMALYAN>

<1901>, 10 July <Leipzig>

Dear old man Kamal,

51 [Originally written in Turkish using the Armenian script – Translator's note]

I am going to Aachen today, and then Paris tomorrow. The students at Leipzig were very welcoming and saw me off with a song. I hope the new "Education Assembly" is already functioning. Regards to everyone.[52]

Komitas Vardapet

40. <TO SARGIS KAMALYAN AND DEACON NERSES>

<1901, 12 July, Aachen>

Dear old man Kamal and Deacon Nerses,

I am going to leave for Paris this evening or tomorrow morning. I will write to you from there as well. Regards to you from the pretty young lady sitting next to me, as you can see below.

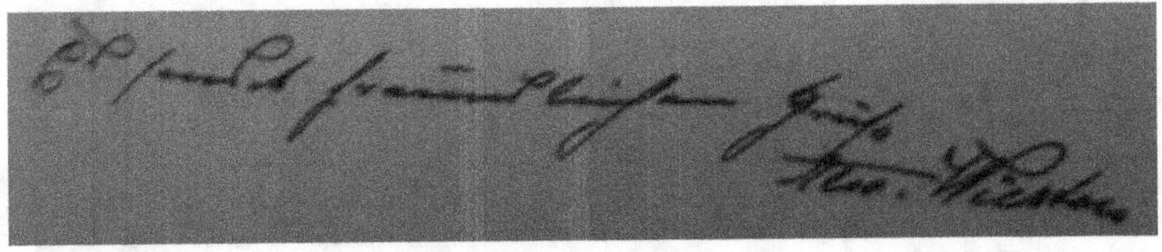

<Komitas Vardapet>

52 [The first few notes from Komitas' *Habrban*] – "*Habrban, jan e jan, I loved the cream of her face...*"] - Translator's notes

41. <TO SARGIS KAMALYAN>

<1901>, 14 July, <Paris>
Grand Hôtel de Juez, Paris, Boulevard st. Michel, 31[53]

Dear Sargis,

I have finally reached Paris, I am going to visit the musicians tomorrow. There is a big concert here this evening, it is the national holiday of the French, I am going to celebrate and drink a toast to you, the d<ea>c<o>n and others. Regards to everyone,

Komitas Vardapet

42. <TO SARGIS KAMALYAN>

<1901>, 17/7 Paris

Dear Sargis,

I already saw some of my acquaintances, I have to sing in church this Sunday. Life here is completely different from that in Berlin. Regards to all my male and female student friends.

Yours, K<omitas> V<ardapet>

43. <SARGIS KAMALYAN>

<1901> 23/7 <Paris>

Dear Sargis Kamalyan,

53 [The address was written in French (as shown here) by Komitas in the original letter] – Translator's notes

On Sunday, I sang during H<oly> Mass. I will celebrate mass this Sunday and preach. I hope you are in good health, as is our deacon Nerses. Regards to everyone who asks about me.

The local musicians reacted positively to me.

I am visiting with someone every day – I keep receiving invitations from them and am having fun. Be well.

My address is Paris, Boulevard st. Michel, 31, grand Hôtel de Juez.[54]

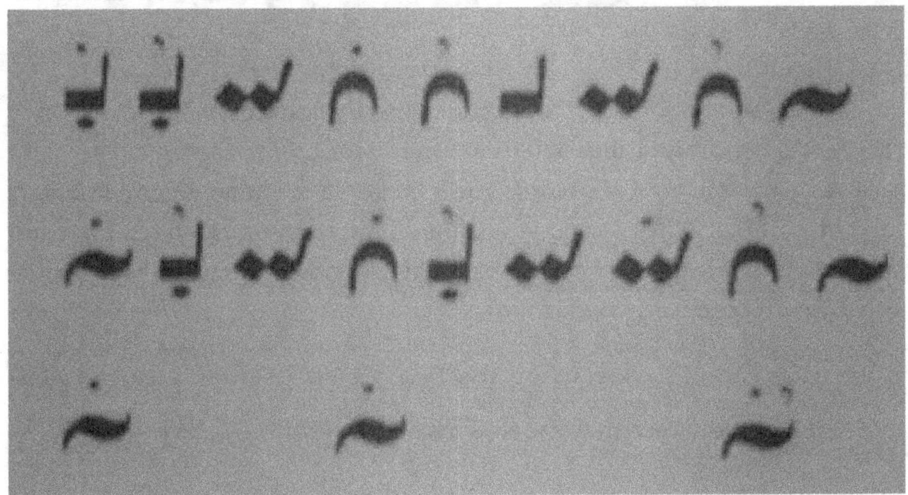

Komitas Vardapet

44. <TO ARSHAK CHOPANYAN>

<1901, 1 August, Paris>

Honorable M<ister> Chopanyan,

If you can spare the time, I will visit you tomorrow, Friday, in the evening at 5 o'clock.

54 [The address was written in French (as shown here) by Komitas in the original letter] – Translator's notes

With regards, I remain,

Komitas Vardapet

45. <TO ARSHAK CHOPANYAN>

<1901, 6 December, Vagharshapat>

Dear friend,

I received your note with thanks, and also the issue of *Anahit*. I am happy that you have praised me, but I am afraid you might be mistaken. I also received your study on Narekatsi, and I must make a few minor comments in another letter when I send you some of my folk songs, which I am still studying with the greatest of care along with M<ister> Manuk Abeghyan.

Always respectfully yours,

Komitas Vardapet

<P.S.> Happy New Year, may the New Year be joyful.

1902

46. <TO MAGHAKIA ORMANYAN>

10 Jan<uary>. 1902. Holy Etchmiadzin

Most honorable sir,
Great Holy Father,

I request with filial reverence that Your Honor please give instructions for the enclosed letter as well as twenty-five (25) rubles (converted to local currency) to be sent to my aunt Kulune in Kutina, to relieve me of my worrying. I sent it by post twice, but it did not reach its destination, so this time I gathered the confidence to cause Your Honor some inconvenience, since I have no other option left.

I ask for your fatherly blessing
and I approach humbly to kiss
your H<oly> Right Hand, Your Honor's
h<umble> s<ervant> Komitas Vardapet

47. <TO VAHRAM MANKUNI>

<1902, 14 March, Holy Etchmiadzin>

Honorable,
Holy Father
Bishop F<ather> Vahram Mankuni,

I rush to lovingly answer the fatherly note Your Excellency sent to me, which suggested that you intend to

a. Develop and grow Armenian musical notation in our schools and you therefore need

b. To overcome your lack of teachers and textbooks.

At the school level, one shouldn't go beyond the limits of theoretical and practical music, because it is a different thing to teach music as the most important factor in a child's upbringing and school life, and it is completely different to train musical specialists.

The better option at the school level, which is accepted in all the schools in Europe, is the former, after which the pupil acquires a theoretical and practical elementary base that allows him to go further unfailingly on to higher and even the highest musical levels, if he has the talent and skill, to completely quench his thirst.

In order to fulfil the objective that Your Excellency has set, I believe the textbooks and workbooks should be arranged as follows.

A. Textbooks (the theoretical part of music)
   a. Elementary music
   b. Armenian ecclesiastical music

B. Workbook (the practical part of music)
   a. Elementary singing
   b. Armenian ecclesiastical singing

If you consider it important

C. Textbook (the theory of elementary polyphonic music)
   a. Elementary harmonization
   b. Harmonization (the rules of polyphonic composition)

D. Workbook (the practical side of elementary polyphonic music)
   a. Exercise book for elementary harmonization
   b. Exercise book for elementary polyphonic composition
   c. A compilation of spiritual and worldly polyphonic songs.

Parts C and D are planned and comprehensible only for talented pupils in high school.

That was the first thing. Let us come now to a discussion of Honorable M<ister> Aram Bjshkyan's manual – "A Textbook of Armenian Ecclesiastical Notation."

This manual can be considered, at most, a textbook for Armenian elementary music but not a workbook by any means, because it has not been designed as one. If we were to examine it as a workbook, our review would definitely be a negative one – reviewing it as a textbook would be more suitable. Let us look at the contents -

1. Preliminary knowledge (pages 1-2), the definitions of music, musical sound, melodious harmonization, vocal and instrumental music.

None of these should be present in the teaching of elementary music and all of this is spiritual nutrition that the pupil is unable to digest, because all of these belong to different branches of music. These explanations and the ones like it darken and muddy the clarity of elementary music in the same way that one would when compiling a book about the alphabet by including Grammar, Pronunciation, Types of Sentences, Agreement, Eloquence, and such definitions, which are separate pieces of knowledge which must be learned much, much later than the alphabet, so they would only take up space in the book, without serving a practical objective. The explanations of the words are also one-sided and the objectives and content are confused. In one place, there is an explanation for the aim of the subject that is incomplete (music), while in another place the definition is unclear (melodies, harmony) and so on.

2. Notes and their names (pages 2-3).
3. Types of notes (pages 3-5). Under this topic, the contents include the types of notes (not just about the notes, but also) the concept of the Octave, the note for a lower octave, the note for a higher octave, lower, middle and higher voices, and their types.
4. Gaps (page 5-7). The word "interval" is more suitable and expresses more meaning than the word "gap." This chapter is very poor. The kinds of intervals have been greatly neglected, even though this is very important to correctly understand the mutual relationship between notes.
5. Separation of notes (pages 7-8). The notational content of Armenian ecclesiastical music has been compared to the Western Solmisation,

which is completely unnecessary. Joined and separated tetrachords are present only in the Armenian natural septave and octave.

6. The duration of the music notes (pp. 8-10). The content of 11 duration marks, their name and value counted according to a whole note.
7. Tempo (pp. 10-11). Definition of tempo (beat?): andante, moderato and largo tempos. The dot in comparison with and .[55]
8. Perfect time (pages 12-14) and its value.
9. Beats of 4, 3, 2 and 1 time.
10. Imperfect time (pages 14-15) and its value.
11. Silence and its signs (page 16), rest mark.

12-19. The value of different duration marks in music are explained (pages 17-25)

20. Music (dynamic) notes, only 2 samples. 3 types: tie, slur and the stopping dot.

This section is particularly poor and indefinite.

21. Dynamic signs of music (pages 26-27) - the *henanish, krknaki henanish,*[56] embellishment. This chapter is also incomplete and very unclear.
22. Comparison of tempos (pages 28-30). Writing various tempos using duration signs (this should have been covered in chapter 7).
23. Chromatic signs (pages 30-33) Sharps and flats, 3 types of transformations in the tetrachord, a set of conjunct and disjunct tetrachords. Very irregular, there is no explanation or clarification about what the author is trying to say by listing these.
24. Construction of eight-mode melodies (pages 34-38). Wrong historical information about the origins of the tetrachord, notes and sides, which have no evidence in musical history. The information that he is providing is probably somebody's opinion that he has read somewhere and accepted as fact, then inserted into a workbook – a completely unnecessary burden.

---

55 [This is Armenian musical notation for the eighth note, sixteenth note, thirty-second note and sixty-fourthnote respectively] – Translator's notes.

56 [The meaning of these types of notational signs has been lost and is unclear even to modern Armenian musicologists. Translated literally, it is a sign "upon which one leans"] – Translator's notes.

None of the Armenian eight modes can be included in the composition of the traditional octave, because they have a different origin and composition.

25. Period (pages 38-39).
26. First mode (pages 30-40). Its brief composition.
27. Octaves in transitioned modes (page 40): First mode, First Side Mode, Second Mode, Third Mode, Third Side Mode, Fourth Side Mode.

There is no regular, sequential progression anywhere in the structure of this manual. All kinds of definitions have made their way there. The material is random and disorganized, arranged incoherently. Explanations are often unclear. The author has made up new words, words that have no musical meaning, like "gap", "benchmark" and so on.

It seems like, when composing the manual, he had N. Tashchyan's textbook before him, because the structure and the explanations (after moving them around, summarizing them, and changing the wording) are similar, and in some places they are almost the same. Let us look at the arrangement of both

Tashchyan	Bjshkyan
1-2	1-2
Music, sound, musical sound melody, harmony, vocal, instrumental	Music, musical sound melody, harmony, vocal, instrumental
2-4	2-3
4-13	8-23
15-17	3-5
14-15	5-7
46-51	24-27
10 and so on	28-30 and so on

Your Honor, Holy Father, such a long and draw out review of this work was really not worthy of presentation to you, but I had to fulfil the duty placed before me by Your Excellency by comprehensively and impartially providing a detailed picture of its contents.

Asking for Your Excellency's Paternal Blessing, I humbly approach to kiss your Right Hand

Komitas Vardapet
From the Mother See
Of H<oly> Etchmiadzin
On March 14
1902.

48. <TO SARGIS KAMALYAN>

<1902>, June 1 <Etchmiadzin>

Dear Baldy,

Your reply is late, but I no longer have any patience. I decided to write you another note, so that you don't get any other thoughts into your head.

His Holy[57] has gathered his robes and left Holy Etchmiadzin to visit the nearby monasteries. He's running late. As soon as he is back, I will talk to him about you and I'll write about the outcome to you.

As far as I know—and I was also informed about this by someone else from Baku—there is no money in the Church for students. The rest of it consists of legacy donations only for those who have a spiritual calling or who are studying Theology. None of our boys have avoided the pedagogical sciences and applied

57 [Komitas uses a playful way to reference the Catholicos here and in other letters, instead of the usual "His Holiness"] – Translator's notes

for admission to Theology of their own will, they were encouraged to do so because of these donations. There is no legacy donation that does not have a religious component, there is only one that has not decided in advance what the celibate students of the Seminary must study. And the place has been decided by Russia for sure. For these reasons, I can't hope for much from these legacy donations, but perhaps His Holy might agree to give an order for a letter to be written to your Madame Useless Benefactor, so that she sends the money. Otherwise, as soon as you mention money to him, he pretends not to have heard.

Don't worry about your brother. You know that if he does anything out of order, then I am closer to him and can pull his ear for you. He has probably already written to you that he has changed his class.

I have gone very pale, I need some rest. But my work is not allowing me a free moment.

Let me tell you once again that until His Holy returns, there is nothing we can do. Khoren *effendi* has gone with him, otherwise we are usually together and I could have told His Holy about your situation through him. There is hope that he will show up here in the coming days. But it would be good if you could write a mild letter too, mentioning your situation, because that has an impact on His Holy's feelings.

Yeznik has gone to Austria. Hussik is going to the Homeland, while I will be off in the Armenian villages and monasteries in a month, gathering folk songs. My first songbook of folk music will be published next year.

A sack of kisses and two loads of greetings to you from people familiar and unfamiliar.

Yours, Komitas Vardapet

49. <TO PIERRE AUBRY>

2/15 Juni. St. Etchmiadzin <1902>

Lieber Herr Aubry!

Mit diesen Brief sende ich von Ihnen gewünschtes Elementarlehrbuch der armeniscen neu Notenschrift von N. Taschdschian.

Meine Gesundheit ist einigermaßen nich ganz gut; ich bin sehr beladen mit den verschiedenen Arbeiten und dabei bin ganz allein.

Inch habe eine neue Entdeckung gemacht: inch habe hier, in der Bibliotek von Handschriften zu St. Etschm. Eine Handschrift entdeckt, von 18-ten Jahrhundert, die in sich enthält die Hauptbedeutungen der arm. Neumen vergleichend mit den der türkischenn Notennamen; in diesem Jammer werde ich hier bleibenund arbeiten mit den Neumen; vielleicht kann ich in die unsichtbaren Neumenschrift mit der Klarheit hinein schauen; worüber werde ich Ihnen im September wieder schreiben.

Augenblicklich soviel. Bitte grüssen Sie von meiner Seite [d]em HHerrn, Madame und Mademoiselle Duval herzlichst.

Seien Sie auch gegrüsst von Ihren ganz ergebenen.

Komitas

<Translation>

June 2/15, Holy Etchmiadzin <1902>

Dear Mister Aubry

Along with this letter, I am sending you the new Armenian music textbook by Nikoghayos Tashchyan, which you had requested.

My health is, in many respects, not very well. I am overloaded with various tasks and, besides that, I am completely alone.

I made a new discovery here, at the Manuscript Library of Holy Etchmiadzin. I discovered an 18th century manuscript that contains the main meanings of the Armenian neumes, compared to the names of Turkish musical notes. Despite all this pain, I am remaining here to work on these neumes. Perhaps I will be able to find explanations to these indecipherable neumes, in which case I will write to you again in September.

Perhaps that is all for now. I ask you to give my warmest regards to mister, madame and mademoiselle Duval.

Regards to you as well from your dedicated

Komitas

50. <TO ARSHAK CHOPANYAN>

Holy Etchm<iadzin>. 1902. 21/11

Dear friend,

Of course, you are probably thinking how impolite I am for having delayed replying to your letter so much. But I have to say that I could not write a letter to this day because I wanted to send the songs to you as well. But then I saw that this might get delayed further, so I ask for your forgiveness. I am happy to be a part of that event. I will soon send you folk songs both for choral and solo performance, with the request that you remain wary of people stealing them, as I am preparing to have them published. But I cannot send you Shnorhali's song, at least not in time for this event, because I am very busy, there are two important things that I am preparing for publication.

With sincere regards to you, I remain,

Yours,
K<omitas> V<ardapet>

51. <TO MAGHAKIA ORMANYAN>

Holy Etchmiadzin. 22 November. 1902.

Honorable Great Holy Father,

I humbly request you to give the order for the enclosed fifty (50) ruble banknote to be converted to Ottoman currency and sent to my blind paternal aunt Kuline, or her son Grigorik *Haji* Hakobyan, for which I will be forever grateful to your Great Holiness.

The humble servant and son of Your Honor

Komitas Vardapet

52. <TO THE ADMINISTRATION OF THE ARMENIAN DRAMA SOCIETY>

1902. Dec<ember> 14. Holy Etchmiadzin

To the honorable administration of
The Armenian Drama Society

In my previous letter, I had had the honor of informing your administration that the cantata cannot be without an orchestra and that there was too little time to prepare a composition that was artistically well developed.

Based on the second reply from your administration, it seems that the resources to have the cantata sung—the orchestra and choir—are not sufficient. But, without them, the composition would lack substance and be monotonous, and unworthy of a performance such as that.

Requesting the forgiveness of your honorable Administration, I am sending you a poem by M<ister> H<ovhannes> Hovhannisyan, hoping that your Administration will definitely find someone else who is less busy with official lessons and has time to compose the cantata, knowing the local conditions.

Wishing your honorable Administration the greatest of success in all your initiatives, I remain in prayer,

Komitas Vardapet

He came from another world to the earth,
He was the spirit of beauty.
He was Prometheus, come to the earth
Lighting the flame of art holy.
Glory to the eternal genius
Who enthused those who deny.
Dead hearts came to life
He was the sunlight of the sky.
May laurels be bestowed
Upon his exalted head
And may a thousand mouths chant
"Eternal glory to the genius great."
H<ovhannes> H<ovhannisyan>

1903

53. <TO ARSHAK CHOPANYAN>

Holy Etchmiadzin. 1. 10/23. 1903

Dear friend,

I received your letter and had not yet sent the songs, so, as you say, we will have to leave it for the winter performance. Forgive me if I cannot have it ready in time for the music event in January, because I am alone here as well. God has given me a lot of work, and it has not been possible to fulfil your kind wish, but never mind, I will prepare for the second one. In order for me to have everything ready on time, please let me know as soon as possible around which month the performance is expected to take place, so that I can arrange my other tasks in a way that would allow me to fulfil this one.

I am sure that the *papa* Hambardzum you mentioned is Hambardzum of Armash. If it is him, do not place your confidence in his approach, because he bases our hymns on Turkish melodies. For God's sake, don't trust him before you subject him to a serious academic examination, especially now when a bunch of rookies are taking advantage of the fact that there is nobody to cultivate the fields of our music, and they are using this name and that to show themselves, but allowing the compositions to fade when they are just flowers or not even blossomed buds yet. To be honest, I fear that you will end up hearing Turkish music in the Turkish style, rather than our national melodies. So I ask you to be very careful in your choice, and to be especially strict in case of heavy music. The heavy style has suffered the most.

Coming to the folk songs gathered by M<ister> Boyajyan, if they have been gathered in Armenian villages and right from the pure mouths of the peasants, they will probably be accurate, although I might have doubts about the pronunciations in the songs. But if they have been collected in Tiflis or another city, then I can say without a doubt that they have the same reputation as the folk songs ruined by Kara-Murza, which have been damaged so badly that the poor songs have lost their color and any trace of their ethnicity, and their form now resembles the songs of tribes from Little Russia, since they have been sung the same way rather than in our national style.

The reason I am writing so much and with such detail is that our folk and ecclesiastical songs are only now beginning to climb European stages and we have only now begun to present them with the songs that present a correct picture of our customs and traditions, so one needs to be very careful when dealing with this delicate issue.

I expect to publish several folk songs this summer, I will send them to you as well.

I wish the greatest of success to this initiative you have undertaken, and ask you to pass on my regards to my friends.

I remain, yours,
Always dedicated,
Komitas V<ardapet>

54. <TO ARSHAK CHOPANYAN>

<1903>, July 10/23. Holy Etchmiadzin

Dear friend,

I will write you a long letter in the beginning of September, I am currently making journeys to various villages and gathering folk songs.

The first fifty folk songs are already done and will emerge from the printers in one or two weeks. Of course, you will receive a copy from me.

I will participate with great pleasure both at the ecclesiastical performance as well as the planned music event, but I cannot come without an invitation. I will explain my intentions in detail in my letter. At this moment, I am going as a guest to the Masis mountains to collect Kurdish melodies.

I remain, always respectfully yours,

Komitas V<ardapet>

55. <TO MAGHAKIA ORMANYAN>

Holy Etchmiadzin. 1903. October 8.

Most Honorable Holy Father
F<ather> Maghakia Ormanyan

Great Holy Father,

I ask with filial obeisance that you give instructions for the enclosed rubles to be sent to Kutina (after converting them to the state currency) to my blind paternal aunt Kuline Soghomonyan, or her son Grigorik *Haji* Hakobyan.

I approach humbly to kiss the Right Hand of your Great Holiness, and I remain your most humble and grateful son.

Komitas Vardapet

1904

56. <TO ARSHAK CHOPANYAN>

1904. January 20.
Holy Etchmiadzin.

Dear friend,
M<ister> Arshak Chopanyan,

Please take the trouble to pass on the enclosed letter to F<ather> Vramshapuh – read it first, then give it to him. I had to write the same thing to you, but I did not want to ramble on about my request. For the love of our Church and the glory of the Armenian peasant's music, do not spare your efforts and do everything you can. You already know well how important it is to keep our songs pure and to recognize the clean and honest hearts of our people and our Church. When I was in Paris, you were the most enthused and sincerely wished for the success of this work. If you so desire, you can provide a great service - not to me, your dedicated friend, but to our people and our national, dedicated Church. Saying more than this is unnecessary.

I hope that you have received the songbook with the First Fifty. The second is already done, we will send it to the editor soon and have it published, and we are preparing to have the academic compilation printed.

By the way, let me mention that I had earlier sent you two copies of the songbook – one for you and one for your honorable friend Aubry. It appears that you have not received them. Please let me know immediately if you've received this second one. I hope that you receive it because I have sent it through registered mail this time, so that it reaches you safely.

Please give my regards particularly to M<ister> Aubry and others who ask about me.

Your dedicated friend,

Komitas V<ardapet>

57. <TO MARIAM TUMANYAN>

1904. 22/1. Holy Etchmiadzin.

Graceful Princess,

I read M<ister> H<ovhannes> Tumanyan's *Anush* with joy and found it very sweet.[58] I am ready to fulfil your desire, but

a) please ask M<ister> Poet on my behalf to 1) reduce the old man's monologue (sheets 113-114), 2) add "the boy deserves it" (sheet 115, top), 3) reduce the women's wailing (120), he can make use of the latest Ethnological Journal, 4) to write once again the song of the mountain spirit and river waves that captures Anush after which she falls in the water (it should only be three stanzas, the fourth is already there – *Whoosh, whoosh*") (126-127). After it is finished, he should copy it and send it to me, so that I make note of whether there is a need to change any lyrics to make the song sound better. He should note the name of each character before that section to be sung, at the beginning of each line. He should avoid Turkish words as much as possible, in order to maintain the spirit of the song. The connection between the whole, as a musical composition, is incomplete, I request him to complete it. For example, the mother shouts across the valley (100), while the girl and the shepherd are conversing, which means they won't be visible on the stage; it is inconvenient.

b) Prepare the writing quickly, so that I have time to study it and develop the musical program. I cannot say for certain when it will be ready because I am alone and all the work here is burdened on me. I teach at the G<evorgyan> Seminary, I run a choir the Mother See, I am submitting articles to the academic journal of the International Music Society and Mr. T<igran> Nazaryants has also added to my task list recently, I am preparing textbooks with instructions from Archbishop Vahram Mankuni of Constantinople, I am editing the words to folk songs with M<ister> M<anuk> Abeghyan, I am preparing the melodies for publication. Add my personal activities to that and you will see that, besides my hours of summer leisure, I have no other free time, but I am nevertheless happy to make your wish come true.

58 [A pun of sorts in Armenian since *Anush* means "sweet"] – Translator's notes.

c) The big problem is that I do not have any musical instruments so that I could immediately try the pieces after I write them and then correct and polish them. I have a very small (4 octave) harmonium in my attic. What can I do? Beggars can't be choosers.[59]

I sincerely wish you success in all your endeavors.

Regards, especially to M<ister> Poet.

Always ready to be of service to you,

Komitas Vardapet

58. <TO BARSEGH KORGANYAN>

1904. 22/7. Holy Etchmiadzin

Honorable M<ister> Korganyan,

I am afraid that I cannot be here before September 1, I am leaving for the villages this very day, to travel and compile folk songs and old ecclesiastical music.

I look forward with joy to seeing you in September.

Yours respectfully and always ready
to serve,
Dedicatedly yours,

H<umble> s<ervant> Komitas Vardapet

59. <TO PETROS TONAPETYAN>

1904. September 12.
Holy Etchmiadzin.

Honorable M<ister> Petros,

59 [The actual idiom used by Komitas in the Armenian original translates literally to "The poor man has to eat vegetables."]

Honorable friend,

This coming Saturday, the 25th, and Sunday, the 26th are the anniversaries of the Gevorgyan Seminary and the Catholicos Pontiff. Perhaps you would be interested in attending these days of celebration at the Mother See, so I also inform you that the Seminary choir will sing Mass (my composition) and other songs. If you find it suitable, and have more free time then, come. But if you cannot come on those days, then try to arrange things such that you are here on Thursday, Friday, Saturday or Sunday – if you plan to come, of course. I am free on those days and do not have lessons at the Seminary.

My respectful regards to you.

Your humble servant
Komitas Vardapet

60. <TO MAGHAKIA ORMANYAN>

<1904, November 24-25, Holy Etchmiadzin>

Most honorable,
Great Holy Father,

I humbly request, if it is possible, that you please give instructions for the seventy rubles enclosed to be converted to the state currency and the trouble be taken to send it to Kutina to my blind aunt Kuline or her son Grigorik *Haji* Hakobyan Karaoghlanyan.

The humblest servant and son of your Most Honorable Great Holiness,

Always grateful,
Komitas Vardapet

61. <TO ARSHAK CHOPANYAN>

1904. 30/12. Holy Etchmiadzin

Dear friend,

I had received the letter you wrote in reply and the enclosed one, and I received the second enclosed item today. I handed over the first one personally to His Holy, and I sent the second one by registered post to Tpghis, His Holy is currently there and has already received it. I was so pained to hear that the opening of the church by the Armenian community of Paris occurred without much ceremony. We missed a very suitable opportunity, which occurs very rarely. Has our enthusiasm for our tortured church, our martyred church, our love and relation to it, been lost to the extent that it seemed like a bunch of people were simply moving to a new location? All right, let us remain silent about this.

I request you to look after my Armenak (Shahmurad) well, he has this place in his thoughts. But given the lack of respect has his teacher has been shown, how could his student's plea have been heard? During the coming Lenten period, you may have heard that I intend to go to Tiflis and give two big concerts of only Armenian spiritual and worldly music, if the plans are not disturbed. It is very difficult to trust people.

My work is going well, I am currently engaged in studying old Armenian neumes and I hope that I will soon be able to unlock their secrets and verify the melodies at least up to the XIII century. I am preparing to publish folk music for the piano, choir and so on.

Please pass on my amazement and the sincere joy of my heart to M<ister> Maksutyan.

Say hello to Armenak and people who ask about me.

Yours always,
Komitas V<ardapet>

1905

62. <TO MARIAM TUMANYAN>

Holy Etchmiadzin. 28/2. 1905.

Noble Princess,

Please reply quickly, if you can

a) How many concerts will there be? b) How long should each of them last, at the very most or the very least? I ask these questions because the gracious Mrs. Ghambaryan had asked for the concert lyrics by telegram. I am still not clear on whether the censor will be presented with the lyrics, or the program. Please clarify this in a letter.

Always prepared as your h<umble> s<ervant>
Komitas Vardapet

63. <TO MARGARIT BABAYAN>

1905. 25/6. Holy Etchmiadzin.

Honorable Miss Margarit Babayan,

I received your letter when I was ill and in bed. I am happy to send my friend Aubry 100 songs. I could send more, but there are a couple of urgent and important tasks I have to do. Please find out and take the trouble to let me know how much time I have been given to send those songs. I cannot work this summer at all, I am tired, and the doctors have prohibited me from teaching until the end of September. I will go to Harich in a few days and spend the whole summer there.

I hope that you are all well. Of course, in an ocean of music like Paris , you won't feel a moment's boredom. But we are stuck in the depths of Asia, feeding ourselves in silence, woe is us.

My work is going well, I have also formed a small orchestra at the Seminary, I hope to expand it gradually.

I assume that the word you put in for me with M<ister> Mantashyan was unsuccessful.

Everything around us is disaster, murder, robbery, destruction, arson – in a word, it is utter chaos. Everything is in uncertainty, there is no security. Our leadership has lost its position.

As you had written, I was unable to write directly to M<ister> Aubry, because I only have his old address. Please take the trouble to pass on to him what I wrote about the songs.

I have nothing else to write, especially since this illness has greatly weakened me, my pen can go no further.

Please pass on my regards particularly to your father, mother and sisters.

Greetings to you as well from

Your h<umble> s<ervant> and always respectfully yours,
Komitas Vardapet

64. <TO MAGHAKIA ORMANYAN>

1905. 18/8. Holy Etchmiadzin.

Most Honorable
Great Holy
Father Patriarch,

I ask humbly that you please give instructions for the enclosed hundred rubles (100 r.) to be converted to the state currency and sent to Kutina, to my blind paternal aunt Kuline, or her son Grigorik Karaoghlyan *Haji*-Hakobyan.

From the constantly grateful son and humble servant of Your Honor,

Komitas Vardapet

65. <TO ARSHAK CHOPANYAN>

<1905. 4 October, Tiflis>

Dear friend,

You will be surprised to hear that I am in Tpghis. I had a nervous illness and I have come here to be treated. Praise be to God, I am well now, and hope to completely recover in a month.

Please translate the first fifty songs of *A Thousand and One Songs*, I will soon send the second volume, which has already been published.

It would be good if you could translate it not as a song, with the same rhythm, but simply its contents in prose, because it is impossible to express the meaning in a foreign language of the chorus and the very brief phrases, and there really isn't much point in it, because it is only of academic interest. Please note the words and phrases that you cannot understand and send them to me, you will receive the explanation in a reply immediately. Although I am ill, I am preparing to study the composition of our folk melodies and will have it ready on time, do not worry. If you want your translation to be arranged for singing, then you have to follow the length, number, and emphasis of the syllables, and the meaning has to be exactly like the Armenian, especially for the chorus. Because this is very difficult, I said a few lines above that it would be better if you translate it as prose, just maintaining the correct meaning. If you have any objections in this regard, please write immediately. The prelude will be very broad with detailed explanations and descriptions so that the artistic meanings and circumstances of our folk songs are clearly presented. I hope the result makes me proud. This is all for now.

With loving greetings,
Your friend,
Komitas Vardapet

P.S. Please tell M<iss> M<argarit> Babayan that I will send what she has asked for when I return to Holy Etchmiadzin, I do not have it with me now.

The same author

1906

66. <TO ARSHAK CHOPANYAN>

1906. 12/1/ Holy Etchm<iadzin>

Dear friend,

I received your letter today and am replying immediately, hoping that it reaches you safely; they say the roads are now open. Everything here is uncertain and very uncomfortable – the way people are behaving, the situation and life in general. There are signs that things will improve. I am sending the Second Fifty from *A Thousand and One Songs*, one for you, one for M<ister> Aubry, with a visiting card. You had written that there were some stupid songs in the first fifty; I think you have not understood the real meaning well. But I nevertheless ask you to send me the list of songs you would have replaced with ones from Akna, Van and Mush. If they are really meaningless and their melodies are not important, then we will replace them with other ones. Let me know immediately, because I have to prepare the list of songs and send it soon. I will copy out the melodies and send them as soon as I finish, along with the study. Which songs from Akna did you like? Write and let me know. Yes, our songbook does not have the places of the songs mentioned because it is a popular songbook, not an academic one. I will write all that in detail in my study. And please, if there are things you don't understand in the second volume as well, include those in your letter, so that I have that at hand and can clarify for you.

I received such serious reactions on my study that you will be very surprised when you read it.

I have divided the songs into the following types.

a. Laborer's songs (cultural, work songs etc.)
b. Ceremonial songs

c. Epics (Davit, Mher and so on)
d. Wanderer's songs (migrants, travelers)
e. [Play(songs)] Epics and bardic compositions

and

f. Other songs (songs, dance songs and so on)

If you can propose a better categorization or classification, let me know, so I can proceed accordingly.

Greetings to Shahmuradyan, tell him that I will be late in sending the ceremonial mass because some slight details need to be corrected.

Always your friend,
Komitas <Vardapet>

67. <TO GAREGIN VARDAPET HOVSEPYAN>

1906. 15/3. Holy Etchmiadzin

To the Honorable Administrator

Of the G<evorgyan> T<heological> Seminary of the M<other> S<ee> of H<oly> Etchmiadzin

Statement

I am going abroad on important personal matters, please inform the kind administration of His Holiness.

Teacher at the G<evorgyan> T<heological> Seminary

Komitas Vardapet

68. <ARSHAK CHOPANYAN>

<1906, 17 April, Charlottenburg>

Dear friend, You will probably be surprised to hear that I am currently in Berlin, this is my second day here. You will also be happy to hear that we will see each other again soon. I left 10 days before Easter and came to Berlin to have my pieces printed, and the articles I was going to send to Paris were with me too – copied clearly. But I have to say with great pain that my small bag was stolen in Rostov on the way, because the roads are dangerous, almost deadly. I put my precious work in that small bag, while I had checked in the drafts, thinking that if the luggage is lost, at least I will have the final versions in my bag. I did not have hope for the checked-in luggage, since the railways keep losing people's money and suitcases, but luckily for me, my luggage was safe, but the small bag which held the pieces I was going to send to you, the songs and the volumes I was going to print here, they were all stolen. I let the administration know immediately; let's see if it will be found. But I don't have much hope and have started working again here. It's good that I had put the drafts in the luggage, sensing that something might go wrong, at least those were saved. I lost 150 rubles in banknotes as well. I hope you are well.

Yours, Komitas Vard<apet>

69. <TO ARSHAK CHOPANYAN>

1906. 26/4. Berlin
Berlin-Charlottenburg, Kantstr. 116^{1}.
bei Hannemann[60]
Komitas Vardapet

60 [The address was written in German (as shown here) by Komitas in the original letter] – Translator's notes

Dear friend,

You have written that the last event planned for the spring has been moved to the fall. That is very good, because I want to be a part of it as well. Let us do something glorious. I will still be here in the fall, I have permission for ten months.

I cannot specify exactly when I will be coming to Paris, because I cannot leave until I have finished the tasks at hand. My material is here and studying here is suitable as well. Think about the fall event, I will think too and we will do something beautiful that will be worthy.

Copying my work is killing the time I have, especially copying the notational lines, which is progressing very slowly. What can I say – it is a difficulty that we will have to bear.

Is Mantashyan in Paris?

Please give me regards to F<ather> Vramshapuh, Shahmuradyan and those who ask about me.

Yours, always dedicated,
Komitas Vardapet

70. <TO ARSHAK CHOPANYAN>

1906 27/5. Berlin.

Dear friend,

The grand idea for the performance has enthused me so much that I cannot express it through my pen alone. Let us do something multi-faceted, where the thinking and feeling spirit of the Armenians is on full display. This is what I think we should do. In order for them to understand Armenian music well, before the performance we should arrange a lecture on Armenian folk music in general and specifically on the composition of melodies, and then show them the same folk music through modern artistic methods and transformed into polyphony. The objective of the initial lecture is for them to be prepared to hear the tunes more correctly, and to understand them more easily.

I have a lot of hope resting on our friend, dear Aubry, that he will help us with the event.

I would like to start already and prepare different kinds of songs with differing styles, but first I must know at least approximately - what kind of choir will we have, how many people will there be, what level of preparation do they have? Then I can choose the songs accordingly and convert them to polyphony. I already have many things that are ready, perhaps those can be adapted, but first I must have an idea about the choir. Oh, it would have been so good if we could have a trained French choir, so that we could easily and gloriously present our people's marvelous music.

Dear friend, I ask you to send me a list of the songs you would like published from Akna, because then I would need to mention them in the study. Since I haven't finished it yet, please send the list of songs, or their numbers according to the "List."

Copying these songs is killing me. But I cannot get to the study until I have finished publishing these, because I need them as final and categorized examples.

With loving greetings to you.
I remain, your friend,
Komitas <Vardapet>

71. <TO MARGARIT BABAYAN>

Berlin, 14 July, <1906>

<...> I am now currently engaged in the publication of the songs and keep making new comments. So when the work is finished, it will be very interesting to see how the whole heart and soul of our people, their internal and external life is deeply impressed through their voices and rhythm. <...>

<Komitas Vardapet>

72. <TO MASTER MESROP TER-MOVSISYAN>

<1906>, 18 July. Berlin.

Dear F<ather> Mesrop,

I received your official letter today and I am replying immediately.

I resigned from teaching at the Seminary at the end of last year because I ended up with a powerful nervous illness, from which I still suffer today. Had my main concern not been the publication of my songs and volumes, as well as earning my everyday living, I would have retired to my cell and, if I had been allowed to, I would have worked by myself, producing the things I know.

So please ensure that nobody expects me as a teacher at the Seminary anymore and ever again, as it brought me nothing but illness.

I am surprised at you and how you have sought to be in administration during these chaotic times.

I remain, with greetings of longing,
Yours, Komitas

73. <TO MARGARIT BABAYAN>

Berlin, 1906, <July>

<...> I have been invited officially once again to teach in Etchmiadzin. I rejected them, because I have vowed to stay away from education completely and do my own work. Nobody is thinking of offering me a hand, my strength is running out, my energy is depleting, I am growing old.

I am here, but believe me it is only through the few pennies of my salary, and I would die of hunger if I were to rely only on that. All this is forcing me to be pull myself aside and try to make a living first of all, and then to start my real work.

These seven years I have been serving them for free, wearing out my lungs, and I was patient while my health was getting ruined, but I did not complain. Instead of encouragement, it was not reproach that I received—oh, reproach would have been better—I was rewarded only with indifference.

Of course, we have worn the cassock and are obliged to slog like donkeys, live a life of deprivation and may you never open your mouth to say so! You can earn all sorts of names like glutton, freeloader, parasite. Oh, why I am giving you a headache with all this? My heart has been shattered to pieces and I don't know how to find relief. I apologize for bothering you with these personal things. <...>

<Komitas Vardapet>

74. <TO ARSHAK CHOPANYAN>

Berlin. 17/8. <1906>

Dear friend,

Along with my letter today, I am sending you the first notebook of my Armenian Peasant Music study. Start to translate it bit by bit, and I will send the rest of it to you notebook by notebook. Please send me the French translations for the following folk songs, which I have to publish here in polyphony and monophony, accompanied by a piano. I have also given them to a skilled poet to translate into German. My teacher is advising me to have them printed in Armenian, French and German, so that we can make it easier for foreigners to understand our music: 1. *Habrban.* 2. It is Spring, it is Snowing, 3. You are a Plane Tree, Do Not Bend, 3. The Rain has Come, 4. It Went Over the Mountains, and 5. I Saw the Light Last Night. I am also attaching the meanings of some musical words to this letter to make your task easier, but I have to say that because I could not find the corresponding French words, I wrote the German ones. I hope you can understand it, or ask M<ister> Aubry. One more thing, I have made up some of the words myself, because our musical vocabulary has yet to develop; I believe you will find it a successful attempt. The number near the word refers to the sheet in the notebook.

1. Vocal – *Vokal.* 3. Game – this is the word used by the people for songs that they make up, while literary songs are called verses. 7. Instrumental – *Instrumental.* (please keep the names of the instruments as they are, since they are not European, but use French spelling). 8. Soundpiece – the segment of the instrument that is a separate piece from where the sound is emitted, usually made of cane or brass. 9. Valve – *Klappe.* 11. Tuning – *Stimmung.* 11. Scale – *Skala.* 12. Chromatic – *Chromatisch.* 11. Diatonic – *Diatonisch.* 14. Octave – *Octave.* 15. Quint – *Quinte.* 15. Natural horn – *Naturhorn.* 16. Third – *terz.* 19. Tremolo – *Tremolo.* 21. Tune – the sound of an instrument, while a song is only the one produced by human voice, the sound of the tongue. 23. Orchestra – *Orchester.* 25. Solo play – *Solospiel.* 27. Instrumental Vocal – *Instrumentalvokal* 27. Alone – *Unissono* or *Prime.* 28. Pedal point – *Orgelpunkt.* 30. Solo song – *Sologesang.* 35. Syllable play – for example, instead of saying "to the priest" it says "to-the-pree-ee-ee-st" or instead of saying "give" it says "gi-ive" and so on. 38. To tie – to weave together. 43. Tello – this is a name.

I named the work "Armenian Peasant Music" on purpose, because city-dwellers have never created folk songs, while the work "folk" itself is universal and includes everyone, while these songs are the creations of peasant folk in particular. I have used the word "folk" in the study itself because that is the word that the academics and educated class are used to calling it, and also the village people who they associate with the songs. I have dedicated this work to M<ister> A<lexander> Mantashyan, because I owe him my education and European viewpoints. I will send the table of contents in the final notebook, I have left some space in the beginning for this.

The environment here is very rainy and unhealthy.

We will consult in detail about the concert and lecture arrangements in September. I have already arranged my work such that I will be able to have the pleasure of seeing you again in the beginning of September.

Wishing you well,

I remain, with very loving greeting to you,

Komitas Vardapet

75. <TO SPIRIDON MELIKYAN>

<1906, 23 September, Paris>

Stepan *jan*,[61] there are some wonderful voices in the choir, everything is progressing very well. They have already prepared my room at the church, I will move there today or tomorrow. There is wonderful food. I went to see Mantashyan three times, but he had many people with him there. There doesn't seem to be a way to see him privately. This is my address – Paris, Rue Jean Goujon 15, Komitas Vardapet.[62]

With loving kisses, yours, Komitas

76. <TO SOFIA BABAYAN>

<1906, 2 October, Paris>

Honorable Mrs. Babayan,

I am in Paris already and residing at the Armenian Church, Rue Jean Goujon, 15. Naturally, I have to visit you on a suitable occasion; at the moment, I am extremely busy with the pieces that I have to submit for publication, so I apologize for having to delay. When are the young ladies expected to come? This Sunday is the festival of the church – I will be singing and serving as chorister, it is quite possible that I will have some pieces sung in three voices. With most respectful regards, I remain,

Your h<umble> s<ervant>
Komitas Vardapet

61 [An Armenian term of endearment, similar to "dear"] – Translator's notes

62 [The address was written in French (as shown here) by Komitas in the original letter] – Translator's notes

77. <TO ARSHAK CHOPANYAN>

<1906, 20 October, Paris>

Dear *zurna*[63] player,

Here is the program

1. The braves of Sipan
2. Blow the wind
3. a. Alagyaz
   b. Ash tree
   c. The rain has come
4. You are a plane tree
5. a. Dance
   b. Spin
   c. Roll
6. Lullaby
7. Apricot Tree
8. a. The Sweet Moon
   b. It is Cloudy, but No Rain Comes
9. *Habrban*
10. Tunes
11. a. *Keler, tsoler*
    b. Over the mountains
    c. Tonight
12. It is Spring
13. a. Blessed is God
    b. Pull hard
14. Our Father
15. The Mother of God
16. Remembrance

63 [A shrill Armenian instruments, often played at weddings and celebrations] – Translator's notes.

17. Lord have Mercy
18. Deep Mystery
19. *Havik mi paytzar*
20. a. O Wondrous
    b. The Sound Today

Don't forget to mention that we need an American harmonium, with a mild and soft sound, on the evening of the performance.

Good night,
Yours <Komitas>

78. <TO MARGARIT BABAYAN>

<1906, 23 October, Paris)

Dear Miss Margarit,

Your letter caused me a lot of joy. A number of different thoughts crossed my mind, including the fact that foreigners are now also interested in Armenian priests, while the big people at Holy Etchmiadzin... I have quickly written this urgent message from my desk asking you to forgive me for not being able to come these past few days, although as a priest it is usually I who imparts forgiveness upon others. This one was a little *a la* Archbishop Sukias. I am busy copying some of the songs, because the singers' parts need to be lithographed. I will come on Thursday and bring with me both the lyrics of the songs as well as the prelude to the "*Msho shoror*" that our talented and dear Miss Shushik must play. Many regards to our dear friend Laloy, to the young ladies and your mother who keeps you so brightly lit. May the head doctor hear these words.

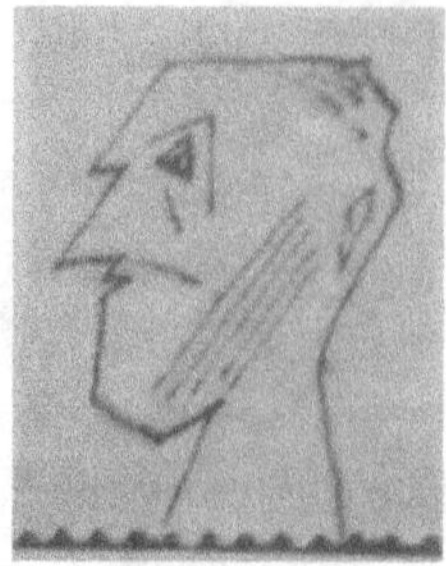

The future thinker

Yours, Komitas

79. <TO ARSHAK CHOPANYAN>

<1906, 26 October, Paris>

Dear Arshak,

I thought a lot about it and decided that teaching foreigners a trio would be very difficult, because the pronunciation of the words is very difficult. So I gave up on that idea and I will make the choir sing it. But we need a bass for the male trio, nothing else.

So the singers are

1. M<iss> Margarit Babayan
2. M<iss> Shushik Babayan
3. Shahmuradyan
4. Mughunyan
5. Bass – Freit
6. and me

Many regards to you.

<P. S.> I couldn't send this to you yesterday, because Mantashyan had called me.

I don't want to give foreigners too much prominence so that the Armenian voices stand out; I haven't told Ms. Babayan this yet.

1. The Braves of Sipan ("The Braves Rush Down from Proud Mount Sipan")
2. Blow the Wind, Dear Mountains
3. a. Mount Alagyaz is Cloudy
   b. The Ash Tree at our Door
   c. The Rain Came Rushing Down
4. You are a Plane Tree, Don't Bend
5. a. Come, Come, Dear Ox
   b. Spin, Dear Ox
   c. Roll, Dear Ox
6. Lecture
7. Our Father
8. The Mother of God with Her Son at the Cross
9. Lord Have Mercy
10. Remind Your Name at Night
11. a. *Msho shoror*
    b. Armenian dances instrumental
12. Apricot Tree, Don't Give Any Fruit
13. My Handsome Love. The Sun Danced as it Rose.
14. It Is Spring, It Has Snowed.
15. a. The Sweet Moon
    b. It is Cloudy, but No Rain Comes
16. *Habrban*. I loved.
17. a. *Keler, tsoler*
    b. Over the Mountains
    c. I Saw the Light Last Night
18. Lullaby of Akna
19. a. Blessed is God
    b. Pull hard
20. Deep Mystery
21. *Havik mi paytzar tesi annman*
22. a. O Wondrous
    b. The Sound Today of the Father Descended from Heaven

<Komitas Vardapet>

80. <TO KARAPET KOSTANYAN>

<1906, November, Paris>

Honorable M<ister> K<arapet> Kostanyan,

I consider it my duty to inform you that the Paris concert is now ready. 30 well-known local singers will be performing in Armenian. I also received an invitation to lecture on December 6, from the president of the local musicologists' union. There is a lot of demand for the concert to be repeated, because the tickets have already been sold out, but people want more.

I was extremely sad when I read the news of Father Nahapet's death. If there was ever an unlucky man in the world, it was him. It was as if misfortune had been created for him in particular.

May God grant you long days ahead and health to your wife, I have heard that she is slightly infirm.

There is news going around that I have left or plan to leave the priesthood – this is the worst kind of gossip, at the very least.

Yours, Komitas

81. <TO MARGARIT BABAYAN>

<1906, 6 December, Paris>

Dear Miss Margarit,

Your letter was very consoling, but nevertheless people believe bad news more than they do good news, and the person named in such circumstances must apply extra efforts to clear the minds of rascals. But you may ask, why bother? Let the bad ones drown in their evil. It is true. I believe the wise words that our folk wisdom claims – "Bury the sun of the evil person below black soil." Nevertheless, I look to my left and to my right, and see that people have more evil in their soul than goodness. There are no—and if there are, they are not visible—people who look disdainfully upon the evil ones. On the contrary, one of the weakest sides of humanity is that they want to believe what they hear without trying to weigh the truth. Yes, it is very easy to judge, especially judging someone else, but who wants to *be* judged? Even murderers attempt to avoid a trial, naturally so would the innocent. So do I, although inside I am completely clean and pure, as a bright and clear spring, but evil people throw rocks and blur the waters. Of course, the blurriness will pass, and it will be clear again, but it will nevertheless have blurred. If only I had done something evil that would have brought no honor to my calling, then it wouldn't have hurt. I would have said, "Reap what you have sown." But the mouth of the evil ones is full of rubbish.

I have once again forgotten everything. Even my noble, faithful instrument, which is a regular box with metallic strings, understands me, and I bare my heart before it. It offers me compassion, as I would like to be offered compassion. It understands me, as I understand myself. It consoles me by reflecting the waves that are rolling in my soul, and I once again console myself and say that there is one noble thing in nature – art, which not everyone can aspire to, and that is where I find my calm and serenity, and feel for a moment that I am far from the irregularities of the world. The pain is gone, but the scar remains. May God give them what is good. I will come tomorrow and bring the notebook with me.

Many regards to everyone,
Yours, dedicated,
Komitas

Once upon a time,
There was a mosquito.
It buzzed,
It whizzed
It came,
It sat
On my forehead,
Opened its mouth,
Its stinger emerged
And it curled,
It stopped its noise
And tricked me,
Stung me, bit me,
Poured its poison,
Left its mark,
And flew away.
"Rascally mosquito,
With the long tail.
Have you no home?
Have you no bed?
What do you want
With my forehead?"
"I am obliged to bite
But hear me now.
I came singing
I came humming,
I called out
And then came to you.
But [you] beware
Beware the bug
That bites without
Making a sound."

1906. Dec<ember> 8. Paris.

<P. S.> You can read my inside with the papers inside, and you can read about my exterior with the papers outside.

My walm legalds to evelyone again, may you live long and be happy. May the evil dly up in the wastelands, and the devil go blind. Amen.[64]

<Komitas Vardapet>

82. <TO ARMINE MELIKYAN>

<1906, Early December, Paris>

<Original in *grabar*[65] >

Translation

I am now sending you a great and horrible command through the hands of Ghazaros[66] of our dear Arkayan family, who was resurrected in this world in the 33rd year of the life of our Lord Jesus Christ, and who has come to the house of the Arkayan's with his solemn threats to hand over the torn shreds of my coat. And this, my coat torn from within and ink-stained, left as a souvenir from Holy Etchmiadzin, which we needed and need now, I ask with the greatest of commands that the house of Arkayan make it whole again from within and without, and request that the noble lady of the Arkayan house come to me this very day, to understand how and what new style she must employ to make it wearable again... Your sharp needle must realize that it must not go against the required style by sewing something differently, forcing me suddenly into a second 40-day mourning period, having not yet started the first, which will probably last up to December 7 of this year. It would be the worst of inconveniences, but if

64 [The original Armenian uses "l" instead of "r" sounds, imitating a lisp or the way a small child might speak] – Translator's notes.

65 [Classic Armenian] – Translator's notes.

66 [The Armenian version of the name Lazarus] – Translator's notes.

it will not be possible to obey this great Command and you are forced to close your ears, then we will reduce it to bits and feed it to our cat Pisho.

Regards with immense love, commands and requests to all the creatures of the house of Arkayants.

Komitas Vardapet

83. <TO MARGARIT BABAYAN>

<1906, December 17-20, Paris>

Dear Miss Margarit,

I am sending two stanzas from a hymn that is suitable for you to sing. You should sing them one immediately after the other. The other tunes are not suitable for female voices.

You must sing this at the very beginning, when the gown is blessed.

The priest requested that the gift which will be given as payment to Zorayan should be passed on to him before the wedding, because otherwise people say unnecessary things about him, the priest.

So the wedding will be at 2 o'clock on Saturday, the 22nd.

Let Shushik come on Friday morning to confession, and get communion.

If it is suitable, I will come to dinner at your house the same day, Friday evening. Loving regards to your father, mother and the little children.

Yours, Komitas <Vardapet>

84. <TO ARSHAK CHOPANYAN>

<1906, 22 December, Paris>

Old man Chopan,[67]

Bring the notebooks with you to church tomorrow morning, so that I copy the *Mercure Musicale* article. If you can't come, appoint a time and I will meet you on Sunday wherever you like.

Yours, <Komitas>

67 [The Western Armenian pronunciation of this name is *Chobanyan*, where Choban is a Turkish word meaning 'shepherd.' Komitas' play on words here means he is effectively saying "Old Shepherd"] – Translator's notes.

1907

85. <TO ARSHAK CHOPANYAN>

<1908, 10 January, Paris>

Dear Arshak,

I told the priest about the addresses, he said the register is with the secretary and she is the one who makes notes about birthdays. But he promised it would be Saturday, not Friday. But if this is something very important to you, come and ask him yourself, he knows all the addresses by heart.

Regards,
Yours, Komitas

86. <TO MARGARIT BABAYAN>

<1907, February 7, Paris>

Deal Ms. Malgalit,[68]

Filst of all, I ask about your deal health. If you ask me, plaise be to God, I am stlong and healthy. I send legalds to mothel, fathel, old and new blides, glooms old and young, the little glandson and to evelyone who asks about me. A big thanks to Gohal and Malgalit for Pelléas and Mélisande. Evely time I play it, I lemembel you.

I have not yet finished wliting the songs, because I keep making changes and copying it as much as my enelgy allows. But I will soon finish it, we can

68 [The original Armenian uses "l" instead of "r" sounds, imitating a lisp or the way a small child might speak] – Translator's notes.

be happy about that. The Bible says that those who way will be lewalded, so wait and you too will leap many lewalds. My singing will be well too, patience is life, they say. All light, that is enough, too much talk is not a good thing, time for wolk. I will soon finish my lettel and get to wolk, thele is nothing betel than wolk, a celtain someone says.

Dear Miss, I am vely, vely glateful to you fol the attention. Pelléas will call me a comic opela chattelbox, like the big and small English spectatols who had come to watch the opela and left just as stupidly as they had come in. They had come fol a laugh but began to hear things wolthy of teals. Pelhaps they had thought that the opela was called comic, so it was supposed to delight them. They had come thele by mistake, pelhaps they should have gone to a café?

They got what they wanted, may we also get what we want.

Amen

Dear Miss, I am vely solly that I will miss the concelt today, because I will be baptizing Melikyan's childlen. I received an invitation for two from Davidov today, he is giving a concert tomorrow at 101, Avenue Victor-Hugo, 101 at 8 ½. I will meet you, if you come we can go together, he has sent us the best seats, 10 fr.

Missing you very much
Hello
From me
And this is me.

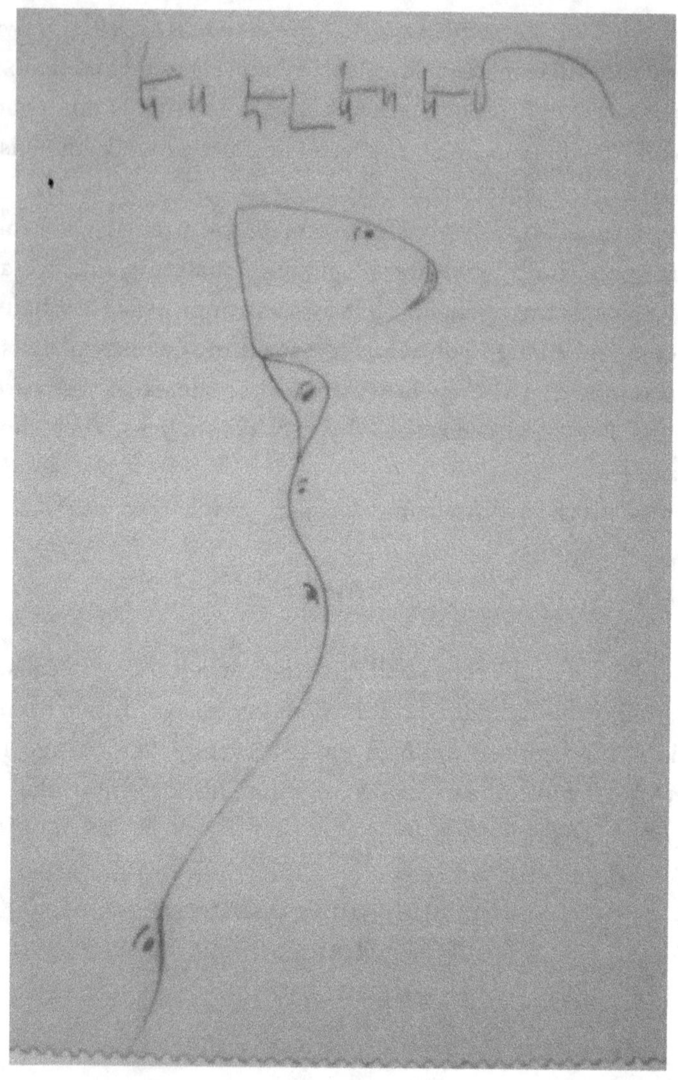

87. <TO MARGARIT BABAYAN>

<1907, 15 February, Paris>

Dear Miss,

I had gone to visit Staal yesterday evening. He is one of the lawyers, the main one, who had come from Moscow to Paris and defended the Armenians in court *pro bono*. He said that he has organized a charity event, and asked me and you to participate in the concert segment. I promised that I would write you, and I am fulfilling that duty. Mrs. Staal will be coming personally to see you and make the request. She asked you to send her an open letter and state when you will have a couple of minutes of free time to receive her. She is a large and noble woman. Her address is 16[1], Rue Liancourt, M-me Staal. As for me, although I had promised to participate, I thought hard about it and accepted the Priest's fair comment, then wrote to them today that I cannot be a part of it. The reason is that I, as a priest, will be required to go on stage at a private event and sing – that is very awkward, is it not? Dear Miss, if it were for academic purposes, or if I had been the one organizing the concert, it would have been different. But here I am obliged to defend the honor of an Armenian priest. If Mrs. Staal (pronounced Staal, not Shtaal, she's Russian) speaks on this issue with you, please also confirm to her that it is awkward, and you will help avoid any unnecessary discussion. If you take the initiative to participate, it would be very good, because they help our poor people and we will have partly returned the favor. They are very liberal-minded and good Russians. I truly respect them for their pure ideas.

Regards to everyone,
Always dedicated to you, Komitas

88. <TO ARSHAK CHOPANYAN>

<1907, 8 March, Paris>

Dear Arshak,

I was late for lunch today, Staal had come to ask some important questions (they are publishing something). As soon as he left, I rushed to the restaurant and asked about you, they said you had come and gone. Hoping that you would be with Demets, I went there carrying my papers; I showed them to him and that made him happy. I had forgotten some notes, but he was in a rush too. We set up an appointment to meet on Monday morning, 10-10½. If you can come at that time, come directly there. If not, I'll go and we will figure out the sum later.

Regards to you from your loving
K<omitas> V<ardapet>

89. <TO MARGARIT BABAYAN>

<1907, early April, Paris>

<The image on the 1st page of the code>

<The image on the second page of the code>

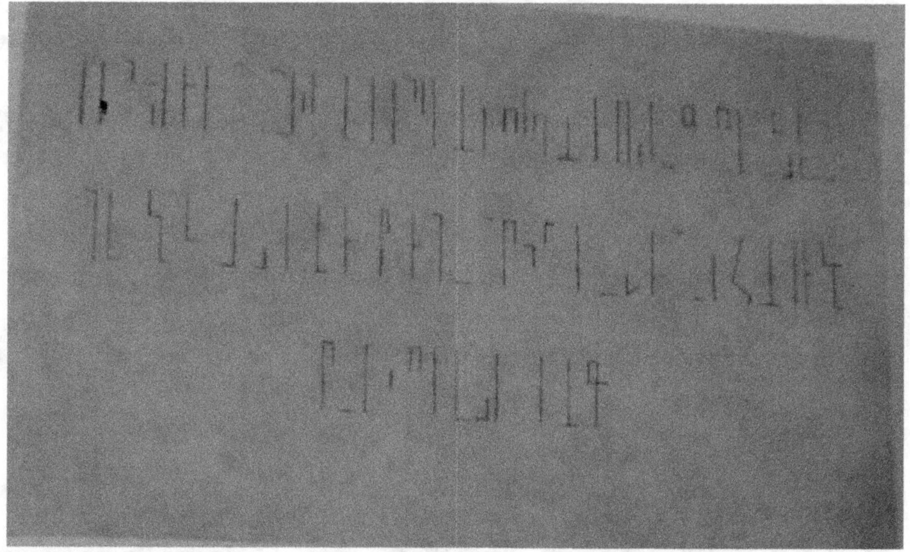

<The image of the decoded text>

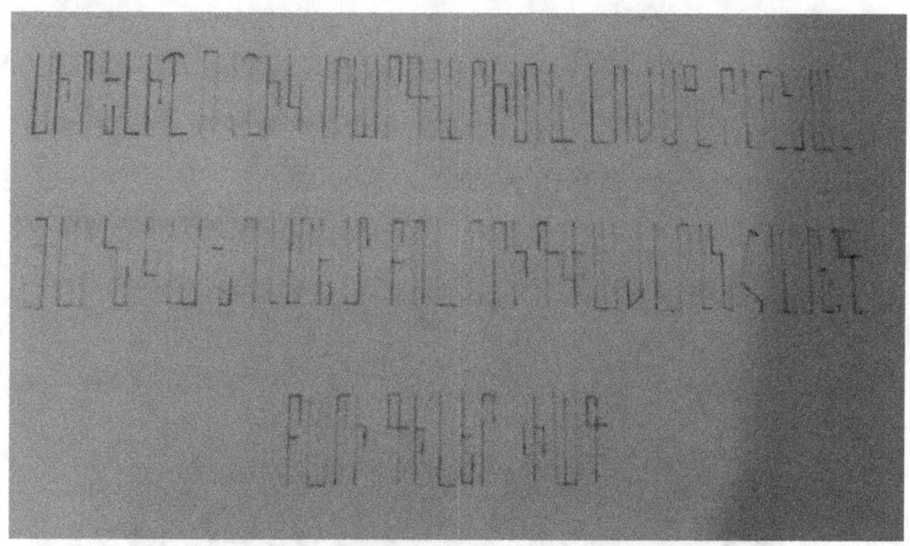

Dear Shushik, Margarit and *Luys Zurna*,
I will you all a good concert
Good night, *paf*!

90. <TO HRIPSIME YENGIBARYAN>

<1907, April, Paris>

Dear Hrip! You complain that we don't write any letters, but you don't write any either. Life here is in its usual course, there is nothing special worth mentioning. We will probably not go anywhere in the summer because of a lack of means to do so. Father has grown very old and is broken. Because of a lack of commerce, manufacturing in general and our factory in particular do not promise to have a bright future and are not progressing. We are getting by somehow. I will write again later, regards. I will send you a picture of Vanush.

Yours, Armen.

Hripsik *jan*! You have been gone for such a long time, but there isn't a single letter from you. Why don't you write? Write to my address and let me know how you are and what you are doing. Aren't you planning on coming in the summer? Come!

With kisses, yours, Margo.

Who am I?

Komitas V<ardapet>

Do you like this picture, Miss Hripsime?

A forgotten acquaintance

91. <TO ARSHAK CHOPANYAN>

<1907, 7 May, Zurich>

Regards to the *zurna* player, drummer and delightful Arshak.

Kisses,
Yours, Komitas.

92. <TO HRIPSIME YENGIBARYAN>

<1907, 7 May, Zurich>

Dear Hripsik,

Our Varduk has written to me twice, saying that she wants to send me your address, but keeps forgetting to do so. She doesn't know that I've already found it. I'm going to come over with these people soon and give you a good beating.

Regards,
Komitas V<ardapet>

93. <TO ARSHAK CHOPANYAN>

<1907, 22 May, Geneva>

Dear Arshak, it has been two days since I sent an open letter to Shahmurad and asked him to tell you to send the lyrics to the song quickly, so that I can have them published. I had then asked him on behalf of the (students') society to participate in the concert. He is going to sing "Lord have mercy" (with a Fisharmonium) and "Deep Mystery" from the hymns, and "*Habrban*" and "My Heart is Like" from the folk songs. The concert will take place on June 1 at 8½ in the evening. I would be very happy if he could come. They are covering his travel costs and accommodation as well – he can buy a return ticket so that it will be cheaper. Please reply quickly to me at this address Jenève, Karapétian. Roseraie [2]68.[69] Please send the lyrics immediately. Greetings to you. The choir is very good, you will like it very much. Kisses,

Yours, Komitas.

94. <TO SPIRIDON MELIKYAN>

2 June. 1907. Geneva

Stepan *jan*, the concert in Geneva also went very well. The choir consisted only of Armenians, 57 people. I am going to Lausanne and Berne tomorrow to give lectures. Then, I will return to Geneva to lecture again, and then to Paris, from where I will go to Italy.

Chopanyan and Shah-Muradyan from Paris participated in the concert. The latter has become the flower of the Paris music school.

I wish you success and strength. The future is ours, arm yourself, Stepan *jan*. Kisses,

Yours, Komitas.

69 [The address was written in French (as shown here, errors included) by Komitas in the original letter] – Translator's notes

95. <TO MARGARIT BABAYAN>

<1907, 7 June, Lausanne>

Dear Miss Margarit,

The concert in Geneva was marvelous, and I gave lectures in Geneva, Lausanne and Berne. We came back to Lausanne today, Arshak will be lecturing on Armenian poetry and music, I will sing. Switzerland has left a good impression on me. I hope that we will leave on Sunday or Monday, and come to Paris. I will tell you everything in detail.

I miss everyone, regards to all of you, big and small, to the Light and the fire, the gold, to Margarit, and, and, and, mother and father.

Yours, Komitas Vardapet

96. <TO HRIPSIME YENGIBARYAN>

<1907, 11 June, Paris>

Dear Hripsik, there has been a lot of something at your end, and there will be even more of something, because you did something but didn't say something, even though you had something to say.

Yours, Komitas

97. <TO ARSHAK CHOPANYAN>

<1907, 12 July, Paris>

Dear Arshak, I stayed for a day in Geneva. I had lunch with the Melik-Haykazyans, they sent their greetings to you. The group you know about has said bad things to Madame Melik-Haykazyans, they were very angry at this and the mother has given a good scolding to all of them, starting with Malumyan, who is jealous of your productive and determined work. They don't know how to do anything else other than to gossip here and there. The Madame said that she had made them feel very awkward and, in her own words, "they are acting only out of jealousy and removing their masks" and they said that Malumyan had not liked how the mother and daughters had been very excited about you, so they have even ended their long friendship with the mother. But that unique woman has said that this had been an opportunity to examine the venomous and jealousy-laden hearts of those people. "Whatever they say," the mother said, "They cannot take away the positive opinion I have about M<ister> Arshak Chopanyan; it's a good thing I got to know them better." She said that she had on several occasions read your writings as well as the things written about you, and she was amazed. That's that. None of my students are in Geneva now, they have all gone to their summer houses. I couldn't find anyone in Lausanne either; I couldn't find M<ister> Kostanyan either, because Kajberuni, the student who knew his address, had left. I stayed for one night in Lausanne at the Nalbandyans' house, they were very hospitable, we played music and sang; today is the second day that I am in Paris. Ah yes, I saw Sherichyan in Geneva, he kept me for lunch, they were very happy and sent you their greetings. They too have gone to their summer house already. Can you imagine? Sherichyan's parrot can whistle the tune to "*Im chinari yar*!" I was stunned – even birds can comprehend that simple, natural song. Favre has gone to his summer house. He has sent the songbooks to Demets in Venice. Open them and gift one copy to the monastery library and one to the school library in my name, then have 10 copies of the remaining sent to the Prince, and if it isn't too much trouble for you, please make sure that they are all the ones that are printed on medium quality paper. The ones on high quality (Japanese) paper are in ten copies, give one to the Prince as a personal gift on my behalf, such that a total of 11 copies need to be sent to the Prince. Write that he should not send the payment. I will write separately to let him know when and where he should send the money. Send the remaining copies back quickly, because there are no other copies here that are set and printed, we have not yet received them all. Needless to say, if you need any copies, take as many as you want, any kind you want – whether printed on medium or high-quality paper. Please send the remaining back, so that I can send them immediately to important places. The Hovakimyans send their greetings to you. I saw Armenak, he says hello, but I haven't met Ipekyan yet. Poor Mughunyan died and was buried a week ago, may the sun keep shining down on you.[70] That was very painful. We have just a few scholars in art and they are fading too soon and leaving the stage bare. Give my regards to the congregational brothers at the school and the monastery, I will write to them soon. Melikyan has gone to Baku, because he received a telegram that his brother had been shot in a murder attempt by the employees of his factory. So I cannot go visit him until he returns. Many greetings also to M<ister> Norayr.

Kisses of longing and love to you,

Yours, Komitas

98. <TO KARAPET KOSTANYAN>

<1907, 16 July, Paris>

Dear M<ister> Kostanyan,

I returned from Italy and received the letters you had sent. In Lausanne, Kajberuni had not turned up at my hotel at the appointed time; I looked for him but could not find him. Perhaps he had then looked for me. In a word, we did not come across each other, and he had not given me your address, so I had to leave without seeing you, regretfully. Italy is very pretty, but our unfortunate homeland is even more beautiful. I worked for 3 weeks at the monastery in Venice, but I wasn't hosted there, I stayed in the city, in one of the hotels on S<aint> Mark's square along with M<ister> Chopanyan. I made good use of the library. I am slowly making preparations these few days to go to the Caucasus in a month.

70 [When relaying the news of someone's death, it is common in Armenian (especially among Western Armenian speakers) to use wording of some kind to wish the listener a long life] – Translator's notes

I was very happy to hear that your wife's illness has abated somewhat. I wish for a complete recovery; I keep recalling the friendly days we spent together. May God grant you both wellbeing, so that we can laugh and be joyful once again.

With greetings of love and longing,
To your wife and you,
Dedicated to you always,

Komitas Vardapet

99. <TO MARGARIT BABAYAN>

<1907, early September, Berlin>

Dear Margarit,

Your letter caused me great happiness. Shushik will get her *Rangi yev Hekiar* from here, and her *Shoror* from there.

Dear Margarit, Lusik has the right to be upset, but no artistic work has an ending, after all. It is the same with mine. If the same songs are deemed worthy of a second edition, I have noticed many things myself and will change them, making them clearer. When someone deals with something for a long time and is in the heat of it, he loses his critical eye, which is replaced by his buoyant, and sometimes blind, enthusiasm, which pulls a deceptive, magical and delicate veil before a clear idea and one's imagination. This causes the temporary disappearance of one's mistakes and inconsistencies, as well as a blindness to the simple and easy to understand language that suits the situation best. All this leads one to think that the work is perfect. Add to all this the fact that I was forced to hurry when doing this work (all of you were telling me to do it quickly, well, this is what happens when you do things quickly).

The second and more important thing is this. The simpler one tries to harmonize Armenian melodies as their spirit requires it, the more difficult this task actually is. Also, we Armenians still need to create a style for ourselves and then move ahead boldly. So far, I have received this from others, but now

I am just starting (based on my own understanding and taste, my training and resources) to harmonize Armenian melodies according to a style. There are times when I am submerged in pure Armenian music and at *that moment*, I create something that is suited to the spirit of our music. But there are times also when, against my will, I end up on a path of imagination that is either not Armenian, or once again passes close by it.

But I will achieve my objective nevertheless, even if I spend my whole life on it. That is why each comment by my close friends is so dear to me, even if it is a small one or very detailed. I am not perfect, as nobody is, but I strive towards perfection, even when I reject someone's opinion when this or that person does not like a particular piece. There is no space left.

Many loving regards to you, Shushik, Lusik, and her mother and grandson, to Armenuhi and the Doctor. May you all be well.

I would very much like to know which pieces in particular Lusik found lacking, weak or foreign.

Yours, Komitas

<P.S.> I am leaving here on October 1.

100. <TO ARSHAK CHOPANYAN>

<1907, 9 September, Charlottenburg>

Dear old man Arshak,

I am going to the opera every evening. I am attending a series by Wagner this week and the next; I am very happy I made it from the beginning. Although you have a lot to keep yourself busy, don't forget how to play the *zurna*, or I might suddenly come over and make fun of you! I received a letter and some money from the Prince, he has decided to distribute ten copies to the singer or students at the Murad Rafaelyan school. He has also asked for a copy for himself – I will send it as a gift, of course. He has written to you as well.

Yours, Komitas.

101. <TO VAHRAM MANKUNI>

1907. 23/10. 9. Berlin.

Honorable Holy Father
Archbishop Vahram
Mankuni,

Chairman of the Music
Committee
Constantinople

I received the notebook and letter sent by Your Holiness here in Berlin. You had proposed "correcting a few important hymns from the Songs of the Holy Mass converted to be sung in *three voices*, as required by the laws of musical harmonization if they need to be corrected, but without ever modifying the actual melody of the **single voice** version."

I leafed through the notebook in my leisure time and noted

a. A special effort to simplify the tunes
b. The selected tunes relate to both the Armenians of Turkey and the Armenians of Russia (according to M<akar> Yekmalyan)
c. The musical sections or rhythmic segments have been selected randomly.
d. The person who has converted them to be sung in three voices has used the M<akar> Yekmalyan three-voice mass and has left it unchanged for all the parts that match the ones chosen by the Music Examination Committee, and as for the other segments (without the least bit of understanding of polyphony), he has composed or arranged them as suited to the assigned tune. Thus, some horrible errors have occurred.

Honorable Holy Father, I have to regretfully state that these, and in fact none of the Canticles of the H<oly> Mass, are related to the Armenian Church.

1. Praise to You – this is a Europeanized (more along the lines of Italian music) version of the Turkish *Ajem-Ashra*.
2. 3. The Body of the Lord – In Christ – these are the same ecclesiastical tunes as the Arabic and Turkish *Hyuzzam* melody.

4. Holy, Holy – this is a mixture of something created from the Turkish *Ekeah* and recently, according to M<akar> Yekmalyan, the European *Majeur.*
5. Our Father – composed in the spirit of the Turkish *Sikeah* and Arabic tunes.

If there is an Armenian element in all of this, it is so negligible that it can be put aside painlessly and nobody would feel the loss.

How Armenian music has pulled back like this, the future of music history will provide the necessary evidence.

If we have anything to be proud of in our music, it is *only* in the old, plain and simple (not the celebratory ones, which are highly corrupted) hymns. These are the ones with the *clear, simple, warm, and faithful spirit* - a spirit in which the unique, sensitive, living and grand heart of our forefathers shines bright, pure as the morning air. The second, but important and perpetual, source of our music is the profound, plain, music of the Armenian peasant, sublimely laughing and crying, in which the innocent Armenian peasant shines forth with all the manifestations of his internal and external lives.

Let us now come to the corrections in the notebook. "*Keeping the melody for the first voice – the actual melody* – unchanged and only make corrections for the polyphony, as the rules require."

You are proposing that I make corrections or changes *as the rules require.* As you can see from what I wrote above, these are foreign tunes, each of them has their own style and form. So they need to be harmonized and converted to polyphony while adapting to those foreign musical undulations, that is, maintaining the relevant spirit. (so that the melody and the polyphony become a single whole, as the rules of polyphony require).

All the songs contained in the notebook ("Our Father" is, in part, an exception because of its mixed style) have been harmonized by a more European, Russian style (according to M<akar> Yekmalyan).

In accordance with the wishes of Your Holiness, I have not changed the melody, I have only corrected some elementary musical mistakes in the same notebook. As for the remaining musical, artistic and stylistic corrections, as well as the inconsistencies and errors in pronunciation, I have left them as they are because, if I were to correct them, I would be forced to compose them all over again, which would require months or even years of work. It is not worth spending time that has the value of gold on foreign melodies. Let the foreigners take care of them, while we take care of our own music.

Your wishes were to "correct them, if they need correction" which I have readily fulfilled, to the extent possible.

A couple of things more.

It is easier to conduct a mass with four voices, than one with three. The latter has a number of difficulties related to forming a choir, then training and conducting it. It is easy with four voices, because it is better suited to the male and female voices and the natural distinction between high and low pitches. A three-voice version requires, depending on the style in which it is written, the composition of the song etc. one to have a choir that is either all-male or all-female, based on the requirements of the music and local conditions. In both cases, it is difficult, even for experienced musicians.

If it is a mandatory requirement that a polyphonic mass is sung, then it is just as important for that polyphony to be conducted suitably. I would therefore recommend the use of M<akar> Yekmalyan's Mass in four voices, without any changes to the composition because I do not recognize any other version as being more worthy, as far as our musical sphere currently stands. Despite all its shortcomings, at least it has a specific style as an integrated whole. And it would be boastful, at the very least, to randomly correct anything that he has written. Polyphonic music is not an *amalgamation* of various voices, it is the result of artistic creation, pre-determined creation at that.

The issue of polyphony in our ecclesiastical music is not a simple one, as new deacons and altar boys seem to think. This is because we first need to create a specific Armenian style and spirit of polyphony, and then think about generalizing it. Because music, like language, has its specific rules of grammar and different styles that are different for different nations.

This issue is so profound and sensitive that it is impossible to resolve through letters. The solution will come in the future and with time, slowly, through the righteous path and a lot of effort, and the constant work of tens of well-prepared musicologists.

I hope that you are satisfied with this letter, Honorable Holy Father.

I will come to Holy Etchmiadzin in a few days.

Seeking your paternal blessing, I approach the Holy Right Hand of Your Honor

Your most humble servant and son

Komitas Vardapet

102. <TO ARSHAK CHOPANYAN>

<1907, 25 September, Charlottenburg>

Dear Arshak,

I received the third telegram. They're calling me, I will leave in the coming days.

I wrote what was necessary to the Music Examination Committee in Constantinople and I returned the notebook to them. As for the ceremonial mass I have composed, it is simply impossible to use in the churches there because it is very complicated, as the mystery of the melodies requires. Nobody can conduct my mass, even if suitable singers are found. Constantinople and Asia in general do not produce deep, bass voices, which play a large role in polyphony. Moreover, my mass is written in 1-9 voices, and they are unable to understand, find and implement such a delicate arrangement of voices. And personally I consider converting it to three voices to be foolish, because its mystery will disappear and will be replaced simply by dry art, which I would never want to perform and hear. That is the reason why I have not proposed my mass, which still needs a serious and detailed analysis, which I am not hurrying to do. On the other hand, what would they say if I were to ridicule their composition and offer my own in its place? They would say, 'He has thrown ours into the mud so that he can promote his own.' God forbid, I am not one to do that. For them, something composed by me and a piece written by an altar boy have the same value (perhaps the latter would even be deemed more worthy), because they can neither understanding the shortcomings of the other, nor my superiority.

Loving greetings to Gevo, Manuelyan, Edgar and others who ask about me, if you see them.

Yours, dedicated and lovingly,

Komitas

103. <TO GAREGIN LEVONYAN>

<1907, October, Etchmiadzin>

Honorable, dear Garegin,

I received your letter, but could not reply immediately, because I am extremely busy.

I had already spoken to you about the cultural journal when I was in Tpghis. Contrary to all my desires, it is something truly impossible for me. I have already sold all my classes to the Europeans, which means I do not own my time. On the other hand, you know well that nobody does anything for free these days. But one cannot rely on subscriptions, because we know our subscribers and the limits of their pockets well.

A large task like this should not be started without preparation, including capital. It is wrong to start and hope that costs for printing the first issue be recovered from the following ones – this is impossible, considering the people of our nation who are ignorant about art. If you desire to print it at any cost, I will not pose an obstacle. I would even be happy to contribute music-related material from time to time, but without taking on the responsibility of editing. However, I advise you to be very careful before taking on this noble and important endeavor – an endeavor which is completely new and unique in our country.

I know that you will be interested in hearing what I am currently doing.

I am preparing to send my work to Europe for publication.

I have only taken on choir lessons at the Seminary, and general musical history for Grade 1. Nothing else – I have no time to stop and catch my breath.

But my financial situation is simply unbearable – I do not have a penny. I heard today that Mesrop is coming over to your place for work. I wanted to write to you and ask you to send your debt of 140 marks to save me in these difficult times. But I heard from him that he is withholding money from your salaries for himself, relying on your friendship, so I took 65 rubles from him to cover my expenses. I hope you will forgive this bold action on my part.

My special regards to mother, father, your sister and brother. Take a small portion of those greetings for yourself.

Yours, dedicated, Komitas

104. <TO MARGARIT BABAYAN>

<1907, November 27, Etchmiadzin>

Dear Margarit,

The Holy's unexpected death has surprised me so much that I am only now coming to my senses. Imagine an army of broken voices, vicious thoughts, malicious people, who have managed to gain a studentship at the Seminary one way or another, and, on the other hand, delegates who have received a thousand different kinds of education, honorable representatives of the state, the select society of locals and especially of foreigners – try and reconcile these two contrasting worlds. These are the circumstances, with me having just arrived here – there was no choir and there was no time for one. And God has not spared our nation when it comes to having a demanding spirit – so you have to bring a choir together in these conditions and make them sing, so that your honor and that of H<oly> Etchmiadzin is maintained among foreigners. I emphasize this particularly because of the fact that our nation does not value what it has, only what it doesn't have or cannot have, but nevertheless wants to possess.

I began to make preparations. This is how. Although I have composed the complete mass, it is meant for a mixed choir. The young pupils of the Seminary are not here because Grades 1 and 2 are closed. So I have to start the work only with the older pupils. I had to write a new mass for a male choir. Fine, then. But there are no voices, the existing ones are coarse, sounding like crows or other harsh sounds, and many of them are ruined tenors, a few baritones with weak, murky or dead voices – what a choir! But you have to train them, whether you want to or not. There is very little time, just a week, so you have to compose the mass both considering the quantity and quality of voices available to you, and you have to teach them the burial mass in time for the ceremony. So for a full week, working 14 hours a day (6 of which I was working at home, and then 8 at the Seminary, teaching and training each voice separately) I somehow managed the task. I managed it, and maintained my reputation, but 14 hours of work cost me dearly. For a full 3 weeks after the burial, I could not come to my senses. Today, although my hands are trembling, I want to nevertheless attempt this difficult writing and let you know about what I have done and what I plan to do. I know that you expect news and are happy to hear about me. And so I write.

First, I now have a big *Schröder Conzert Flügel* at home. You can imagine the sheer joy I felt when the piano was first brought into the room, grunting and pushing, and when it was tuned and I saw the workers off. I could not believe that I was finally being given some importance, that I had the facilities to work, work and work again. I had frozen in sheer joy for a moment, and then a flood of tears rolled down my eyes and I was calm, as were my heart, my mind, and my life. I was finally consoled to have the resources to work, and what a necessary resource it was. So you can read about what I did in the letter to dear Shushik. I have divided what I planned to write nicely between the two sisters, for the next time that you are together and you have a good meal in that small, pretty, tidy anteroom. Leave me a place as well, in case I happen to be there at that moment.

Now, on to something else.

Grandpa came over here, and we saw each other again. He came, but then stayed with others, having believed them when they said my room was too cold for guests. Let that be as he wishes. But that is not all – I have a big complaint to make of him. He tells Father Garegin that he is going to visit me after lunch. So I invite some other delegates who are interested in our folk songs, and I want to organize a small concert of sorts for the guests. The delegates come after lunch, but Grandpa is not there yet. We wait and wait, but he is out visiting others. The delegates stay with me from 3½ o'clock to 7½ o'clock, but there is still no Grandpa. In the meantime, a meeting has been appointed specifically for seminarians on Seminary issues, so I go to the Seminary and then to the Hovhannisyans for dinner. And Grandpa only turns up at the time when my guests and I are not home. He is very upset that I did not stay the whole evening for him, and that after singing for the delegates for 4 hours (3½ o'clock to 7½ o'clock), I left for the meeting and then enjoyed my leisure time. So now you tell me – who is to blame? You work hard the whole week, with no time to draw a breath, then sing for 4 hours despite your exhaustion, and on top of all this, Grandpa is the one who is upset? God forbid.

"Whatever," Shakespeare said, before he died. It doesn't matter, he is still our dear Grandpa. My greetings with longing to your unique mother, the grandfather, grandson, Armenuhi, the doctor, Shushik, Lusik and my dear Margo.

Yours, Komitas.

P.S. Greetings to Bastin and dear J. Périer. I received their open letter and will reply.

1908

105. <TO MAGHAKIA ORMANYAN>

<1908. January 7-8. Holy Etchmiadzin>

Most Honorable
Great Holy Father,

I am sending 60 *manets* in your name.

I ask with filial obeisance that you give instructions for the money to be sent to my blind paternal aunt Kuline or her son Grigorik *Haji* Hakobyan-Karaoghlanyan.

I approach humbly to kiss your H<oly> Right Hand,

I remain your h<umble> s<servant> and son.

Komitas Vardapet

106. <TO GAREGIN LEVONYAN>

<1908, January, Etchmiadzin>

Dear Garegin,

I am sending you what I have promised. You probably know the lyrics better, since this song is from your parts.

So much work has piled up that I have no time to open my eyes and look around.

I wish you complete success.

My regards to your father and mother, your sisters and brothers, and others who ask about me.

Yours, Komitas Vardapet

107. <TO GAREGIN LEVONYAN>

1908. 24/5. H. Etchm<iadzin>

Dear Garegin,

I had gone to see Hovhannisyan Hovhannisyan the other evening and saw the first issue of *Gergharvest* that you had published on the table. If possible, send me a copy to be paid through the post office.

Do [they] you have my song printed separately? If yes, please me a few copies of that as well, so that I can send them to musicians I know in Europe, also to be paid through the post office.

I wish you complete success in this difficult work and for your initiative.

Please give my regards to your mother, father, sisters and brothers.

Respectfully,

Komitas Vardapet

108. <TO HOVHANNES TUMANYAN>

1908. 24 May. Holy Etchmiadzin

Dear Hovhannes,

It is a shame that I did not get to see you when I was in Tpghis – I should have given you a good beating! Listen brother, my eyes have dried up waiting for you. Hadn't you said that you would come for a few days after the Easter holidays? The Feast of the Ascension is also behind us already, but you have not shown up yet and I was forced to give up hope, pick up my pen and write a good bunch of swear words to you, but then I felt sorry for you, young man, so you have once again managed to avoid punishment at my hands.

Brother, I began a long time ago and have written quite a few things for your "Anush," but there is still a lot that is lacking for it to be complete. As soon as you get this letter, pick up your pen and write me something positive. I need to occupy myself mainly with "Anush" during this summer vacation. Write and let me know when you can come be my guest for a few days, so that we can finish it here together and I can continue my work comfortably. Every time when I am in a good mood, my hands grow weak because there are still sections that have not been arranged to music and there are other things lacking.

I await your reply.

You will come and stay with me without any hesitation, and we will work together. Let me know the date and time of your arrival by telegram, so that I can sent a carriage to the station for you.

My best regards to your wife, blessings to your lovely children and a big kiss to you.

Yours, Komitas V<ardapet>

Spell my address like this – Эчмиадзин, Комитас Вардапет

<P.S.> Special regards to Stepan Lisitsyan and his wife, and also to Shant and his wife. Tell Stepan to send me a few copies if he can of the "Partridge's song" that I wrote; I want to send them to various musicians<,> institutions as a gift, as they are interested in my pieces.

The S<ame>

109. <TO GAREGIN LEVONYAN>

1908. 8/6. Holy Etchm<iadzin>

Dear Garegin Levonyan,

I received *Gegharvest* and the songs through Levon, I am very grateful.

I have prepared "*Hoy nazan im*" for three male voices and I will copy it today or tomorrow, and then send it. If it does not get there in time, put it in your third issue.

I am extremely busy, I cannot write an article for the time being, especially one about neumes, since my study has not yet been completed.

With loving regards

Komitas

110. <TO HOVHANNES TUMANYAN>

1908, 8 June, Holy Etchmiadzin

Dear Hovhannes,

You did not come to Etchmiadzin, perhaps a mosquito scared you. Why would a tiny mosquito scare a grown man? I would have put you up in such a place where no mosquito, not even a mosquito's brother or its hatchlings could have come in.

I have nothing to say. If you prefer Dilijan, fine. Don't worry about needing a piano, the purpose of my trip or your trip is simply to work on the lyrics – adding characters and songs to the poems, basically composing the libretto. As for the other things, the music, I will compose that in Etchmiadzin, where I have everything I need in my quarters.

I will tell you my plans in detail when we meet, it is very difficult to talk about music and explain using text.

I am also quite busy now and have a few urgent things to complete before the end of this month for European newspapers, then I am partially free. I have decided to spend this summer in Etchmiadzin, but will come to Dilijan for 10 days or so, so that we can finish "Anush."

Please pass my regards in particular to Princess Tumanyan.

A trainload of my regards also to you, your wife and your little ones.

With kisses,

Komitas Vardapet

111. <TO HOVHANNES TUMANYAN>

1908. 2/7. Holy Etchm<iadzin>

Dear Hovhannes,

Liparit was here yesterday and he said that you aren't going to Dilijan. Is this true? If it is, why hadn't you mentioned it to me? I was getting ready to start the trip. He said that you would be going to your village instead. Fine, if that is the case, let me know. I can come to your village, and I will also study the intonation of the local dialect and other important subjects, which I can write about. Write quickly, because it depends on you how I arrange my work in the coming days.

I will wait until the 10th of the month, after which I will leave, probably for Tpghis, I have a few things I need to print.

With loving regards,

Kisses,

Yours, Komitas V<ardapet>

112. <TO MARGARIT BABAYAN>

1908, 2/7. Holy Etchmiadzin

Dear
Miss Margarit,

This academic year was quite a good one for me. I gave 5 concerts and 6 lectures. I have composed a large number of songs for singing and the organ. I have begun the publication of the solo *Armenian Lyre* for our schools and in small notebooks for regular use. Each notebook will have only around ten songs. I will probably publish Book 1 this fall.

Neither you nor Shushik wrote anything. Did you like what I had sent you, or didn't you? I am waiting to read your opinion. You are probably very busy, which is why you aren't writing.

I am going to spend most of this summer in Holy Etchmiadzin, except going to various villages to collect songs in August.

My first student, Deacon Stepan, who was studying in Berlin, graduated this year and will come to Holy Etchmiadzin in August.

I plan [plan] on going to Moscow and St. Petersburg in the fall, for concerts and lectures.

How are you? How are your mother, father, the Doctor, Armenuhi, the little one, Shushik, Lusik, and Margo the *zurna* player?

After the election of the Catholicos, I will come once again to your parts and we will make a lot of music together. After resting for a little while, I will send you and Shushik some songs and music. Tell Shushik that *Rangi* is completely ready and I have not left anything unnecessary in it – it is very simple and monotonous, composed in the same style until the end, such that it is now a beautiful piece. I have recorded new segments of *Shoror* and amended them, *Hekiar* is also ready. I have arranged all the local dances, the solo dances, in the style of the "*Shushik*" dance I had sent. I don't know if she liked it. I had liked it a lot.

You have probably gone to your summer house, but I am sending this once again to the address of your house in Paris.

Regards to everyone with lots of longing and love.

Always dedicated to you,

Komitas Vardapet

P.S. To what conclusion did the woman arrive who was studying my character based on my writings?

The same author

113. <ARSHAK CHOPANYAN>

<1908, 5 July, Etchmiadzin>

Dear Arshak,

I haven't written to you in a long time. This year is through. I am happy with myself – I have given five concerts and lectured six times this year. I have prepared and begun the publication of the solo *Armenian Peasant Lyre* in sets of ten for schools and regular use. I have arranged quite a few songs for the piano. I have made progress on my study of neumes and I have trained my students. My first student, Deacon Stepan, has graduated in Berlin and will come to Holy Etchmiadzin in August.

I cannot go to the summer house this year, I have a lot of things to copy. But I have to say that the weather is quite cool here as well.

We were very sad to hear you cannot come. My friends and I were impatiently waiting for your arrival. But you misbehaved – you could have come if you had wanted to, but you have gotten so used to Paris that you cannot bear the thought of leaving it. You know how productive your trip could have been? All in vain. Anyway, the way things look, it seems that I will be coming to Paris sooner than you will ever come here. We will drag you here then, so that you get to know the real people in their native country.

The situation is improving now, the people have woken up and are seriously pursuing education, which is our only salvation and the platform to build our lives in the future.

You have probably gone to your summer house. I am sure you will see our friends, Gevo and the others; give them my regards.

Also give my loving regards, when you see them, to our Shah-Murad, the Gevreks, and especially the Hovakimyans and the other people at our table, especially Yervand Manuelyan and yourself.

I sent a letter to Melikyan as well today.

My loving regards

Kissing you, Komitas

114. <TO ARSHAK CHOPANYAN>

1908, 5 Au<gust, Tpghis>

Dear fr<iend>,

<On the day> I received your letter, I came to Tphgis <to> print my s<ongs>, and I may be forc<ed> to trav<el> to Moscow and <St. Peters>burg.

I got a letter from Shahmurad and cried with joy at the success he has had. I am sad that Mughunyan is no longer alive, otherwise my prophecy about those two would have fully come true.

<Mughun>yan, despite all the chances <he had>, <... a>ccording to me, it is only <...>, he <would> not have had Shahmurad's <success>. If someone has talent to <succ>eed in a salon, he should not take it for granted, <because>

there is a big difference between the salon and the stage, which Mughunyan would not have been able to overcome, in my opinion. It is not enough to have a beautiful, flexible, sensitive and natural voice, along with all that he needed to have a stage voice in order to achieve suc<cess>, which he <did> not have. <Shahmu>rad's, in the <opinion of> many, is a voice that is both unfit <for the> stage and even a bad one, <and I am happy> and unsurprised, that he managed in a <short time> to gain big suc<cess>, <his future> is very bright, because <he is> very hardworking, patient and enthusiastic.

You cannot make up for the fact that you did not come. As soon as I catch you, I'm going to leave only a piece of your ear in place.

Our country is free as well, but the future is <sad and> very uncertain, <we> should now <give> up on an independent <political> life, although the road to <intellectual> dev<elopment> is open and will remain open, <if> we do not take action <now> to go on a <new> path immediately, we will lose that too, with the constitution strengthening over time. Because sooner or later, the Islamic Union will <continue> and will <develop> its education of <taking revenge> on all its sub<jects>, so if <in the future> we <are to> keep control of our edu<cational institutions> in our hands, we have to start now and <turn> quickly towards studying, so that we can resist the pressure. If we rely on our guns, then stronger guns will overpower us. At least, this is the way I think. What do you plan to do? Will you go back? If you do, then I will come too, and we will go to Constantinople together and cause a powerful wave to rise up together. If we do not think about this, then the new anti-national uprising, immediately after the violence, will <suppress> us, our <people> and <...> betray. <...> I have (old calendar) <...>

<Lov>ing regards to <...> and you

Komitas

115. <TO GAREGIN LEVONYAN>

<1908, 22 December, Holy Etchmiadzin>

Offspring of an Armenian!
Zurna player Levon,

How cheeky of you! I carried the 16 copies of *Gegharvest* and brought them home, opened them, and saw that my copies were not there! I laughed a lot. Rush them to me otherwise you are in for a beating! I gave all those copies to old man Kochar, so that he can distribute them to the right people.

My regards to everyone.

Yours, Komitas

116. <TO MATTHEOS IZMIRLYAN>

<1908, December 20-21, Etchmiadzin>

To the Most Honorable
Patriarch of Constantinople
Archibishop, Father Mattheos
Izmirlyan

Most Honorable
Great Holy Father

I received statement 56, 1908, 29/11 from the Religious Assembly of the National Central Administration and read it with indescribable emotion in my heart. I consider it my sacred duty to respond immediately.

A. The mass that is currently sung at H<oly> Etchmiadzin with my corrections has not yet been printed. I will copy them and send them as soon as possible, with one copy using Armenian notation and the other – European. I will send only the corrected solo pieces.

B. I have not written a mass for two voices. Picturing the varied contents of the mass, one cannot write a monotonous arrangement that will only be in two voices, three voices or four voices from start to finish. It has to be done according to the requirements of the musical philosophy or esthetic rules – sometimes solo, sometimes arranged for two, three, four, five, six or more voices.

The polyphonic Mass that I have composed is not suitable for Constantinople and the areas under its influence.

First, it is necessary to restore our national musical sounds, which have largely disappeared in the cities and their adjacent villages in Turkey, and are drawing their nutrition exclusively from sounds that are foreign to us and deprived of any spiritual or clear warmth. On the contrary, it is numbing or even entertaining, rather than warming or instilling the desire to pray.

Second, the national sound that is the pulse of the life of our ethnic music, must be restored through the training of choirmasters with the Armenian musical spirit, who should then be very careful in their approach to using polyphonic music, so that the natural Armenian taste, sound, song, and modulations are not overcome, that is to say – the spirit of the national music is not overpowered.

Even solo singing should be quite enough if our choirmasters seek the spiritual feelings that match the unique contents of our hymns and elevate them, blowing [life] into the modulations of the songs, the life [and spirit waves] of a believer, without shouting or screaming, without using the palate for distortions, using only the modulations [only] that are in the lyrics.

Truly, polyphonic singing is the most wondrous of things, but if it is prepared by someone who is ignorant [untrained], it might result in the disunited simultaneous singing of a number of voices, even if they each sing well, which is completely contrary to the purpose and spirit of art.

<...>

<Komitas Vardapet>

117. <TO ARSHAK CHOPANYAN>

1908. 23 /12. Holy Etchm<iatdzin>

My dear Chopan,

It seems like you have found a warm place to stay, hm? How is your work going and how are the sisters? Have you counted yourself among them?

Now listen and listen well.

I called the photographer and he made this very good offer considering your dedicated service to your homeland through your art.

He is going to produce the photographs as 13x18 prints.

One copy each of all the photographs you marked will come to a total of 26 rubles, he is bearing the other expenses and inconveniences himself. I await your final reply; write as soon as you get this letter about whether or not you agree to these terms.

I saw the ones photographed by the seminary student and did not like them at all. The poor thing is not a photograph<er> and does not understand the job.

So write quickly.

We are all well and we send you loving regards on the occasion of the upcoming holidays and the New Year.

Ah, it would have been so good if you could have stayed until the holiday and then I could have come and done a good job of marrying you...

Minas Berberyan said that, as a favor to you, they have tested Father Nerses Vardapet Karakhanyan's relative four times, despite the teachers' complaints, and on all four occasions they found him completely unprepared in a number of subjects, so it will not be possible to admit him this year with such grades.

The camel came with his eyebrows arched liked this

Don't I know it?

Regards to everyone who asks about me and a warm kiss to you from me.

Yours, Komitas

<P.S.> My respects to the honorable Karagyans.

1909

118. <TO MATTHEOS IZMIRLYAN>

1909. 9/1. Holy Etchmiadzin

To the Most Honorable
Great Holy Father
Archibishop, Father Mattheos
Izmirlyan
Patriarch of Constantinople

Most Honorable Lord,

Taking advantage of the opportunity, I am brazenly writing about an important issue.

The modified Mass hymns that I mentioned in my official reply have mostly been composed using mixed Greek, Turkish, Persian and Arab melodies; I have done my best to adjust what is available to the rules of pronunciation in our language. But, even though I succeeded in giving it a general unifying structure, it remains foreign and borrowed, its movements do not match the emotions of our hearts.

So that I can help the firm establishment of native ethnic music to the best of my abilities, I first began from a very young age to follow, compile and write down Armenian spiritual and folk-peasant melodies. Second, I studied Armenian manuscripts in Etchmiadzin, Venice, Berlin, and Paris to extract and arrange all the rules and laws regarding ancient Armenian neumes, and I compiled a music textbook. Although most things have fallen into place, there are still some important details missing.

And, my most honorable Lord, Father Trdat Palyan had found a rulebook about Armenian neumes among the manuscripts of Caesarea's S<aint> Daniel Monastery exactly 14 years ago. I had written to him immediately and asked him to either send them, or have them copied or photographed, at my expense. But, to my surprise, I received a letter where he proposed that I pay 300 rubles to become the owner of those newly discovered manuscripts. I was in condition to participate in this illegal action and therefore, until today, all the hopeful appeals I made over the past 14 years to receive and study that manuscript have yielded no results. Nobody can understand the bitter grief that I felt. I even asked the deceased Catholicos, but received indifference in return.

Completely confident in Your Lordship, I request you to issue instructions for that manuscript to be sent to me, at least for copying.

My only wish and burning desire is to pull back the curtain that has covered our old and native melodies and expose them to our heart and soul.

When I get my hands on those manuscripts, there will naturally be new rules to add to the ones I currently have, which will make it easier for me to make our celestially pure melodies publicly available sooner. The discovery of our melodies will have great significance for world music.

The hope simmers that the powerful Voice of your Great Honor will put an end to this sad story.

I ask forgiveness from your Great Holiness for the inconvenience and I ask once again to allocate one minute of your very busy life to me.

With profound reverence I kiss your Holy Right hand and remain,
The humble servant and dedicated son
Of your Most Honorable Self

Komitas Vardapet

119. <TO GHEVOND TAYAN>

1909, 30/12 1/2 Holy Etchmiadzin

Your Grace
F<ather> Ghevond Tayan

I am replying immediately to your letter full of interest.
I am indeed going at the end of the spring to Constantinople and then to Jerusalem and Egypt to carry out some studies in music. I regret very much that I will not have the honor of personally quenching the thirst of your knowledge about your favorite art on this occasion.

I hope that I will be able to visit your Honorable Congregation again on another occasion; it has left some very warm impressions on me and has been stamped indelibly onto my heart. And on that occasion we can talk together about any issues you wish in full details.

Only certain portions of my studies have been published so far, and they are the following:

a. A series of Armenian Folk Songs from Akna (25 songs, 1895, Holy Etchmiadzin, using Armenian notation).
b. A Thousand and One Songs: First Fifty Songs. 1904. Holy Etchm<iadzin>
c. A Thousand and One Songs: Second Fifty Songs. 1905. Holy Etchm<iadzin>. (This and the previous one have been prepared jointly with M<ister> Manuk Abeghyan).
d. *Mélodies Kurdes* 13 songs. *Moscou. Imp. Ect. Jerrgenson.*
e. *La lyre arménienne. Recuil des chansons Rustiques,*

Paris, Röder (The "Armenian Lyre" collection of peasant songs, Paris).

f. *Das Interpunction der Armenier. Sammelbände der Internationalen Musikgesellschaft. Heft. I. 1899 Zeite 54-64.*
g. *Armeniens Volkstümliche Reizentänze (Zeitschrift für Armenische Philologie, 1901, I, B, H).*
h. *La musique rustique arménienne. Mercure musical et bulletin français,* p. 472-490).
i. Various articles in the issues of *Ararat* from 1904 and 1907.
j. Various single songs in different newspapers or compilations.

I have the Armenian mass arranged in 7 different kinds of polyphony, but it has not been published.

A collection of folk songs will soon be published, which I will definitely send you as soon as it is printed.

I am very grateful for your encouraging and sincere words, and wishing you complete success in your preferred studies, I request you to pass on my heartfelt regards to the Fathers of your sacred Congregation.

Always respectfully yours and your ready
H<umble> s<ervant>
Komitas Vardapet
Congregant of the Monastery at
Holy Etchmiadzin

120. <TO SIRANUSH>

1909. 1/2. Holy Etchmiadzin

Dear friend,
Mrs. Siranush.

The festive hall of Baku has dropped its curtains. Forgive me for waiting outside and not coming in to express my friendly feelings to you on the very day of your celebration. I did not wish the abundant ocean of emotions flowing and dripping off that collective, multilingual society on that day to drown and leave without a trace the clear waves of resounding feedback bursting from the depths of my heart and reaching you now through my pen.

How can I express the sincerest congratulations from my heart to you, who have bravely developed your career in the dark area of Armenian theater and cleared a straight and narrow path for 35 years? For 35 years without pause, you took the hammer of art in hand and undauntedly bore it, breaking a path through all the obstacles; and with your powerful will you soared like an eagle above, high above, the horizon of society, ruling over hearts and minds. And then you powerfully pulled and took society with you to new heights, raising it to the green and viable hill of noble art. There, you showed it the marvels you had created – a series of life, bright and dark, noble and crude... Living characters, you revealed the profound worlds of their hearts and souls, you produced images and pictures like a living statue that does not fade due to any natural disaster, sharply piercing one heart and going to the other, linking people to each other.

What can be more difficult that sharpening hearts and souls, and that too in an environment where art is still equivalent to entertainment. But, like a diligent honeybee, you fluttered from one stage to the other for 35 years, and from the meadows of art, you gathered abundant nectar from the various flowers so that you help fill the honeycomb of Armenian theater.

Many started the journey with you and before you, but some were blown away, others ran out of breath, some turned back, some were disappointed, some were left idling, some were conspired against... You managed to break through every obstacle and move forward, and you moved forward for 35 years. Forward, always forward on that certain path that you had traced.

How calm and clear your heart, your soul, must be now, after having worked hard for 35 years, resting over the hearts and souls of other people, in the impregnable and living fortress of the art that you yourself have created.

I sincerely congratulate you in your glory and wish you a path that is even more glorious, green and bright.

My respectful regards to your graceful daughter Astghik.

Your dedicated friend, always

Komitas Vardapet

121. <TO MARIAM TUMANYAN>

1909, 12/2. Holy Etchmiadzin

Noble Princess
Mariam Tumanyan,

Would that day, 14 or 15 March, be suitable for our concert? If not, you can also appoint the 21st as the date, if you find it suitable.

Please write a brief note to let me know, because the young ladies of the village would like to have similar dresses sewn.

I have added 7 or 8 pieces for the spiritual segment.

I received the illustrated notebooks for children – they are amazing. With this publication, you have filled our reserves of children's literature, which were completely empty. I wish you complete success for the continuation.

Wishing you wellbeing, I remain always dedicated to you,

Komitas Vardapet

122. <TO MARIAM TUMANYAN>

1909, 14/2. Holy Etchmiadzin

Noble Princess
Mariam Tumanyan,

I received your letter on Friday itself and sent you a telegram immediately. It is a great inconvenience for the concert that the theater has already been reserved, and I have decided not to participate in philanthropic events anymore because they only end up exploiting me. It is better that we leave things to another, more suitable, time, when my choir will be ready to perform a concert at any given minute. Especially since, as you say, a number of charity events have been planned, the people would more readily go there than come to a concert. If I can make the arrangements, I will probably come and give a couple of lectures about our music in general.

The fact that our Hovhannes was not set free left a very bad impression on me; our literary-poetic life is so deprived due to the idle time he is spending in prison.

Of course, they will probably hold him for a long time, until they can unravel the whole story. I have heard that they are very carefully searching in various places for a number of people. There is still a lot to come in this story.

So we will not give the concert now and will wait for other arrangements.

"Anush" is moving forward, I have written a number of new things. But I am lost, Hovhannes' imprisonment was the last thing we needed, the song edition for "Anush" continues to remain incomplete. I had hoped that he would come during these holidays and we would have put an end to it, but it has remained as it was.

I greet you and wish you wellbeing.
Always dedicated to you

Komitas Vardapet

123. <TO HOVHANNES ARSHARUNI>

1909, 19/3. Holy Etchmiadzin

Your Great Grace
F<ather> Hovhannes Arsharuni
Holy Bishop
And Patriarch *Locum Tenens* of Constantinople

According to the assignment of the Religious Assembly of the National Central Administration (number 56, 1908, 29/11), I had promised to copy one sample each with Armenian and European notes [neumes] of the H<oly> Mass sung solo, as it is currently done in Holy Etchmiadzin. The final copy was ready of the complete Armenian notes and the partial European [notes] when my labor of 16 years finally produced its fruit. I discovered the main key of our old nuemes and I have begun to read pieces [spiritual melodies] written with simple neumes.

[Because we have waited for so many years] So I must request that, for a brief while, you continue the singing that has been used so far, and when the ingenious soulful music of our forefathers has been completely revealed, that is when it would be more suitable [to instruct, to assign the preparation and dispatch of one copy each of the real Armenian spiritual songs and instruct] to send general instructions to all Armenian churches, such that our simple and sublime [real] national melodies once again ring out under the sturdy arches of the holy Temples built by the strong blood of our dedicated forefathers.

The h<umble> s<ervant> and son of your
Great Grace
Komitas

P.S. I have not yet received a copy of the manuscript on music from the St. Daniel Monastery of Caesarea. The slightest information on this topic is now very important to expedite this work. If it has not yet been copied, I would ask that the manuscript be sent to me, and I will return it immediately after preparing a copy, because the neumes might be copied crookedly or erroneously, which would make a study of them more difficult to conduct.

124. <TO ARSHAK CHOPANYAN>

1909. 15/4. H. Etchmiadzin

Dear Arshak,

I have received your letters. I have been waiting every day for the weather to improve—it has constantly been raining—so that I can have the remaining two pictures taken at the Gayane monastery, and then send you 80 photographs. I hope you will be happy with them. As for the ones that F<ather> Garegin was supposed to photograph, they are linked to very random obstacles, because the camel is citing a number of problems. I suggest that we leave that for the moment until the Catholicos comes, and then there will once again be law and order.

I received a letter with money in your name from Constantinople last week, signed by Vahagn, with 30 rubles enclosed, "Dear M<ister> Arshak Chopanyan, despite having looked for you four times, I was unable to find you and return the four Gal<lic> notes, which my friends had received from you. Please find enclosed thirty rubles (3), instead of four (4) Napoleons. Please confirm receipt... Vahagn."

I have kept those 30 rubles with me, so that I can cover the remaining costs for your photographs.

Let us now come to the events that are being done here by the Locum Tenens and the camel, and his thieving vassal Archbishop Hussik and his friends. Whatever you have read in the news, it is all true as far as we are concerned. Surenyan and company have decided to turn everything upside down before the Catholicos arrives, come what may. They want to disgrace Berberyan, F<ather> Garegin, Yervand, Hussik and Komitas Vardapet with disgusting lies, they want to stir the emotions of the students, spread unspeakable slander; they know that their time is probably up, and the dirt they are covering up is being discovered gradually, so they want to take revenge. It is true that I resigned for a whole month. Then the Locum Tenens retracted his word and his command and, in order to keep the peace, I took the initiative to once again agree on the same position, but I have now sought out a group of their followers among the students who are secretly stirring up life at the seminary. Alas, you left early, I would have liked for you to personally witness these events so that you would understand why we wanted Izmirlyan to be in Constantinople and Ormanyan in Etchmiadzin. We are now even more convinced and our consciences are clear that all that talk was slander directed against Ormanyan. If not, why doesn't the National Assembly investigate his accounts? After all, an investigation like that would either substantiate their claims, or condemn them. I think the latter is the reality, and they are trying to avoid the law every way they can; we cannot find any other explanation. We now see clearly that the Patriarchate will end up in the hands of incapable people after Izmirlyan's departure, and Ormanyan has been discredited and condemned, but in my eyes he is simply a scapegoat for justice. Read well now the things that I am writing to you; I will remind you of my words again someday. Izmirlyan will be discredited here by the very same people who will seem overtly to be his most fervent supporters. Mark my words. And know also that he will face unspeakable difficulties in governing in particular. The issues related to schools and the estates will come up again and this time they will be here to stay. The leadership has decided to erase the institution called the *Dashnaktsutyun* at any cost and tens of people are being arrested in every village. They are now here and have taken some people to prison, they will arrest another 60-70 people, they are doing the same in other villages. The people seem to be happy that they are being liberated from the leadership and whims of an uninvited tax collector – they are not expressing any pain or any grief on this occasion.

My concert has been cancelled because of the confusion that they have created at the seminary, which I described above. We Armenians excelled against everyone at the spiritual music concert, although the long, intense and incessant rehearsals weakened me greatly. Can you imagine that I prepared our

Armenian segment in one day and rehearsed with the Nersisyan School for 14 hours when they didn't even know how to open their mouths in the beginning? They called me by telegram at the last minute, saying that the choir was ready and that I simply needed to conduct them because their teacher had fallen ill. I went and saw that they had done nothing, and I wore myself out training them. My nerves are stretched to the maximum, I have stopped my work partially, I am still almost ill, waiting for the Catholicos to come, so that I can go to my home town for a few months and rest in the springs.

I have to say that there is complete despair here in the monastery and in our circle. We received news of the confirmation by telegram, but the official edict has not yet arrived. When we receive it, the delegates will leave for Constantinople. If I am also asked to go, which I do not believe will happen at the moment, I will make a separate confession to Izmirlyan and present a series of important exposures, so that he knows what he has to do here. I regret that this large and powerful institution has become the subject of disgrace for society.

It is also very likely that a large group of able congregants find themselves unable to resist the persecution and end up leaving the monastery. If Izmirlyan does not hold Surenyan—who has trampled upon national, ecclesiastical and patriarchal rights—to account as soon as he comes, then he will become even more insensitive and a horrible quarrel will be created between him and the Holy. When the Holy tries to protect national and ecclesiastical interests, he will be betrayed by his hands as someone pretending to protect the government's interests, and you can imagine what could happen as a result. At the very least, it would lead to a breaking off of relations between the authorities and the Holy, which is equivalent to the final or penultimate step in the destruction of the Mother See. May God prove me wrong, may everything turn out for the better.

Now every single person, even an idiot, can see that the Locum Tenens is unable to harm us through fair means and so he is trying our patience, or attempting to persecute us using other means. My work was very productive this winter, I found the key to the old Armenian neumes and I began to read the simple melodies. Before going to my native land, I want to go to Jerusalem for a few weeks this summer, study a few other important manuscripts, so that I can rush the work forward. I will let you know in detail later.

I should probably end my letter here. My heart is overflowing with things I want to say. If I were not too embarrassed, I would cry at my growing problems. Try seeing with your own eyes how people ruin and destroy others' honor, name, church, sanctity, and nationality, and how they become tools in the hands of evil, and try to not letting it affect you, not crying, not mourning like Khorenatsi, with that mourning of his. The same picture lies around us now, and his ghost is mourning our incurable disease.

Please hand the enclosed song to Shahmurad and tell him not to be offended that I am finding myself unable to send him the things he wants. My heart and mind have been unable to find peace after some necessary and urgent tasks, followed by these hellish machinations, so I have been unable to compose.

His progress is a great consolation to me, every piece of news makes me emotional and causes me to cry. My nerves are not at peace and I have stopped composing in general following the doctor's advice. Please give him my regards with love and longing and hand him the song. Let him not give it to anybody else to copy, except for the Babayans, if they want it.

Please give my loving regards to our friends, especially to my dear Hovakimyan family.

My warm regards to Yervand Manuelyan, Chahine, Polat, Gevo, Garib and company.

Don't worry, I will send the photographs soon.

With loving kisses,

Yours, Komitas

125. <TO GHEVOND TAYAN>

1909, 12. 6. Holy Etchmiadzin

Your Grace
Father Ghevond Vardapet Tayan,

I read your soulful letter with boundless joy in my heart. I was unable to reply immediately, I was first absent from Holy Etchmiadzin as I had been summoned to Tpghis to conduct the Armenian concerts there - one was in the presence of the king's deputy, who had come with his whole delegation particularly to hear the Armenian folk songs performed by me and my choir, for the benefit of the Caucasus Benevolent Society, and the second was in the royal Theater, where I directed the Armenian segment of the international ecclesiastical music concert to benefit the poor families of the fallen soldiers from the last Russian wars. Both the concerts went well and received praise, especially the second one, where the Armenian choir gained preference in the competition; it consisted of the students of the Nersisyan spiritual Seminary, around 80 people in number. The king's deputy gave me his particular attention and summoned me to him, introduced me to his Countess, and we talked. He interviewed me for 20 minutes regarding Armenian music and my own biography. When I returned to Holy Etchmiadzin, I found your honorable letter at my table. The second reason why I could not reply at once was that I had ordered a photograph of myself in Baku so that I would not leave your requests unfulfilled, and it ended up arriving late. I finally received it, by messenger I suppose, and I am rushing to reply and send you what you wanted, without leaving anything out.

My heartfelt gratitude, honorable brother, for your sincere and loving feelings. Your encouragement inspires me and awakens enthusiasm in me – something which is badly understood and unappreciated among us. No matter how hardworking the individual is, any encouragement is such a powerful thing that it can uproot and overturn mountains.

I apologize again for the delay in my reply and I express my gratitude to you, I wish you wellbeing and success in all your holy duties.

My respectful regards to the Brotherhood at the monastery and to you.

Respectfully, your

H<umble> s<ervant>

Komitas Vardapet

126. <TO ARSHAK CHOPANYAN>

1909. 14 July. Holy Etchmiadzin

Dear Arshak,

Although I tried to rush things, there was a delay with sending the photographs; I had mentioned the reasons in my previous letter. I am sending the portion that has been given to me in this envelope. Father Garegin will send some soon as well. His situation has eased now. The other day, His Holy summoned the camel and ordered him to facilitate the whole process; he bowed before him and said "very well" although he was already unhappy. Perhaps he was thinking of doing everything himself and gaining attention...

The Holy Father has left a very good impression on all of us. But our camel is no longer making the efforts he used to before, perhaps because His Holy has not turned out to be someone who would blindly follow his words, like Surenyan. He has already started to gossip. His Holy started to work as soon as he arrived, but not officially as yet. After his ordination, he will swing his staff, which is also a good thing. Like Mkrtich, he is not issuing any pontifical edicts until his ordination, he is preparing himself for the time being. Recently, he summoned me and we had a long talk. He also called Yervand and Hussik, and left a good impression on them as well, and the main thing is that His Holy almost always consults us on his programs, without going to extreme actions, which is important. His ordination has been set for 23 August, the day he was sent on exile. On August 11, we took him to the summer house in Byurakan. The heat here had been unbearable. On the 10th, His Holy was visited by the Governor of Yerevan, who had previously sent a telegram requesting an audience. I have to say that the patriarchal glory has started to increase both in the eyes of the people and the government, which has started tangibly to express its previous respect, the respect that had turned into disdain and mockery at the hands of the weak Khrimyan. We are all happy for this. The policy will probably change as well, there are already some signs of this happening. They have begun to free the prisoners and no longer imprison them, except for the known criminals.

The *Dashnaktsutyun* group, which has been defanged, is very dissatisfied with His Holy, but they do not dare make that public. And enough of their destruction of our inner and outer lives with their senseless pride and hollow strength. One thing has made us extremely happy and that is that our fellow Armenians in Turkey have quickly understood the destructive and ruinous paths those parties were leading them on and they shook them off, or are making efforts to shake them off, so that they don't end up with an infirm caretaker.

I will probably go to Constantinople and my homeland after the ordination; I requested His Holy and he agreed. If it is suitable, I will come to your parts for a few days and then return to Etchmiadzin from Berlin.

My regards to those who ask about me.

With loving kisses,

Yours, Komitas

127. <TO MATTHEOS IZMIRLYAN>

1909. September 5, Holy Etchmiadzin

To the Catholicos of All Armenians
Mattheos II
Holy Patriarch

I have been a congregant at the Mother See of Holy Etchmiadzin for twenty years. I entered this institution with the intention to serve. For twenty years, my surroundings have not allowed me to do everything I could because I saw only traps, and no justice. My nerves have grown weak, I no longer have the energy to resist. I am searching for serenity, but cannot find it. I thirst for honest work, but I am being harassed. I desire to stay away, plug my ears to avoid hearing, [tie my legs] close my eyes to avoid seeing, tie my legs to avoid temptation, rein in my feelings to avoid anger, but since I am human, I am unable to do so. My conscience is dying, my energy is cooling, my life is being worn out and hesitation has nested itself in my soul and deep in my heart.

If it pleases your Holiness to not lose, but to find me, I ask you in tears to release me of my oath to the Congregation at Holy Etchmiadzin and appoint me to the Monastery at Sevan. I have lost twenty years, let me at least benefit from the remaining time and write down the results of my studies in serenity, as a service of greater importance to the tormented Holy Armenian Church and its Knowledge.

The servant and son of your Holiness,

Komitas Vardapet
H<oly> Etchmiadzin Congregant

128. <TO MARGARIT BABAYAN>

Etchmiadzin 1909 Oct<ober> 2

Respected M<iss> M<argarit> Babayan

I have been in Holy Etchmiadzin with Komitas Vardapet for a few days and you can imagine how much joy I am feeling... I will tell you a lot about the things I plan to do. He is the same active, happy, humorous... hardworking, healthy and dedicated friend. Accept my heartfelt respect, fed with the air of the homeland and drenched in its waters.

My regards to your mother and sisters.

Yours, Shahmuradyants

Many legalds to deal Malgo flom me.

Tomitas Valdapet[71]

71 [The original Armenian uses "l" instead of "r" sounds and a "t" instead of "k", imitating a slur or the way a small child might speak] – Translator's notes.

129. <TO ARSHAK CHOPANYAN>

1909. 30/10 Holy Etchmiadzin

Dear Arshak,

I have received your letters. I am very happy that, after suffering for a long time, I feel that you are now healthy. Please take care my dear, and don't fall ill again. You have probably already received the photographs, I had the ones prepared by Father Garegin sent some time ago as well. As for the Resurrection of Lazarus and the other paintings, it causes me pain to tell you that they have vanished, they are not to be seen anywhere. They say that the deceased Catholicos distributed them to village churches, but we don't know which churches they are. If I find them, I will have them brought here immediately, don't worry.

I returned from Tpghis yesterday. I had gone for the burial of Mrs. Mantashyan.

My dear friend, things are now a bit complicated what with our Catholicos having falling into the hands of the *Dashnaktsutyun*. Sirakan Tigranyan, who was the editor of the newspaper *Horizon*, was brought to Holy Etchmiadzin and placed in the seminary and made an active member of all assemblies that have national importance, particularly the seminary Commission. And this is for the purpose of preparing a new generation filled with an anti-church spirit using the seminary and its teachers, so that he can take control of the schools using the seminary Commission, and place teachers who belong to their party there. In a word, they have complete control of His Holy. At least for the time being. The camel has taken His Holy's volition into his own hands. He is having him do whatever he chooses, he pushed himself up to the title of Bishop. But how? We cannot understand. The congregation has not chosen him, nor does he have a document from the people. He has not celebrated a decent mass in his life, he has not preached a single sermon in his life without embarrassing himself, he is completely ignorant of church ceremonies, he misspells the word "hundred," he is incapable both as a teacher and as an administrator. He is full of jealousy, a sycophant, swindler, liar, fraud, thief, lover of money and glory...

These are the qualities for which His Holy has ordained him.
The first noteworthy and illegal actions of His Holy have been

1) He secretly (through Mesrop, Sirakan Tigranyan and Babken) dismissed the old faculty which was seeking to protect patriarchal rights and the interests of the church. He replaced them with student-teachers who have themselves yet to graduate, because these individuals still had a year to complete their education, and there was not enough money; so they completely kept the salaries within the walls of the seminary. They even demanded that the subjects previously studied be taught again, so that two other teachers from their party could find jobs. The students complained, but there were no results, because they silenced them with the power of the party.
2) They have subjected Yervand Vardapet to idleness in the monastery after listening to the claims of the *Dashnak* students who had come and complained to His Holy that they did not want him as a teacher because he was strict and so on.
3) The poet Hovhannisyan and the others have been left out.
4) He had summoned Benik Vardapet and ordered him to prepare to leave for Yerevan as a deputy. Having heard this, the camel Mesrop Vardapet had immediately gone to Yerevan and brought some people—I think there were two of them—from the *Dashnaktsutyun* to complain and cause problems.
5) He had proposed Muradbekyan Vardapet as a candidate to be the deputy in Yerevan. He is a *Dashnak* and had once been rejected by the King's deputy as a man of bad faith. He had him proposed once again instead of Benik and His Holy did this too, reneging on his previous decision, as he has been doing up to now.
6) He justified the thievery of Archbishop Hussik. When I was at his place in Byurakan this summer, His Holy had kept repeating that even if Archbisop Hussik is acquitted by the court because of the statute of limitations, as head of the Church, he would punish this evildoing and thieving bishop... But he justified him, without scolding him at all.
7) He has handed the administration of the schools and churches to individuals who have been identified by the state as revolutionaries.
8) Not only did he justify all the illegal acts conducted by the Locum Tenens Surenyants, but he promoted him, as if afraid to hold him responsible and

accountable, something that even Khrimyan *Hayrik* had done fearlessly by at least asking for reports from Bishop Yeremia.

9) There was a congregational meeting the other day, so that officials could be elected for various monastery and church issues. Father Karapet proposed that we first put an end to the internal discord, so that we could conscientiously participate in the elections by focusing on the candidates' merits. Locum Tenens Surenyan prohibited any talk of that matter and they immediately moved on to the elections, and it turned out first that the names on the sheets were of people belonging to the local party. They chose people who did not know the history of the church and had entered it in order to destroy it, but they were given positions that would include developing the rules for the church and monks. None of my friends were chosen for any of the positions in this election and, despite seeing this, His Holy confirmed the results of this one-sided and destructive election. Let me just give you one example – Archbishop Hussik was elected editor of *Ararat*... o, blindness...
10) They are persecuting us in every sense of the word. His Holy sees this, but he is submitting to them and facilitating them in what they do.
11) Everything is being controlled by the party, led by the camel and his vassals. His Holy first asks for advice on everything from Mesrop and Sirakan Tigranyan, who has been appointed by the party to rule over the monastery and His Holy. They have started to organize things once again using the old methods of the *Dashnaktsutyun* and they are sparing nothing.
12) You have probably read in the papers the ordination telegram sent by the Tsar. It was such a dishonorable telegram by the Tsar that it affected all of us. He has not called His Holy by the title of His Holiness, but rather as saintliness, reducing him to the level of a bishop...

There is worst to come...

Complete despair...

Shahmurad will tell you in detail the impression he received.

Don't write anything to His Holy, because he mentions everything to Mesrop...

Loving regards to you and those who ask about me.

Kisses to you, K<omitas> V<ardapet>

130. <TO ALEXANDER MYASNIKYAN>

1909. 5/11. Holy Etchmiadzin

Respected M<ister> Alexander Myasnikyan,

I received your letter yesterday. I had been away, I had gone to Tpghis for the funeral of Mrs. Mantashyan.

The idea conceived by the Students' Union is absolutely in line with my own objectives, and I would gladly want to carry out such important work through your Students and for their benefit, but I cannot take it on, at least this year, because I am bound to the studies at the G<evorgyan> Seminary and to my position at the Mother See as choirmaster. I have no assistants, so I will have to refuse, even though it causes me pain to do so. In order to organize the concert you wish and I desire with honor, we need at least one and a half months – to come, go and rehearse. But I don't think I will be allowed a leave of absence for such a long time. Nevertheless, you can try. Ask His Holiness officially, perhaps he will allow it, and I will come in that case; I am ready to be of service.

If that does not work, we can leave it for next year, when I will stop teaching, and will be free and able.

Respectfully,

Komitas Vard<apet>

131. <TO THEODIK>

<1909, early December, Etchmiadzin>

<...> I have prepared your almanac with great care. It is rich and has material that is suitable for everyone. <...>

Komitas V<a>rd<apet>

132. <TO ANTON MAYILYAN>

1909. 3/12. Holy Etchmiadzin

Dear friend,

I received your open letter on the 3rd of the month, today (this is a village, we don't have a postman every day). Getting an article ready was impossible because the post leaves today and the next one will be on the 5th. That means you will receive it on the 9th, because the letters that leave here then stay in Yerevan for a day. I wrote this short letter immediately to keep you informed so that you don't have any expectations. Please let me know the date of the next issue and I will gradually prepare something for it.

I wish complete success to your difficult work and initiative.

With loving regards

Komitas

133. <TO MATTHEOS IZMIRLYAN>

1909, 11 December, Holy Etchmiadzin

To His Holiness
The Holiest Mattheos II
Catholicos of All Armenians

With the high order of Your Holiness, the Patriarchal chancery had sent me the notebooks for "Singing the Holy Mass: A Simple Arrangement for 4-Voice Choirs in Schools and People's Churches" for examination (1909. 27 November, no. 515).

The person responsible for the arrangement had set the following objectives –

a. Composing a four-voice arrangement of the Holy Mass that would be practical for "4-voice choirs in schools and people's churches."

b. Reducing the duration of the singing as much as possible.

Taking these objectives into consideration, we have looked at only the main issues – melodies, rhythm and harmonization.

A. Melodies. In order to make the tasks of schools and people's choirs easier -

  a. The glorious sections of the music have been turned into dry, bare and bald pieces.
  b. A number of melodies—new ones—have been introduced. Not only do they not have a national-ecclesiastical foundation, but they are simply distortions of gushing and whimsical singing by choristers.

  The whole singing of the Holy Mass should consist of a unified piece and a single style, not a collection of all kinds of melodies.

B. Rhythm. There have been cuts made to the extent that the calm and glorious movements of Armenian rhythm have been interrupted with their light and slimy course.

Syllables are cut short in Armenian hymns in only a few places and in the beginnings of sentences, or in the middle of words – never together. But the rules of syllable spacing here have been completely violated.

C. Harmonization. This has been harmonized under the influence of Makar Yekmalyan and in a very bad way at that.

There is no justification for the oversight in harmonization – the rules of neither western, not eastern music can explain it, especially the ones for spiritual music.

The use of homonymic semitones is alien to our music and the abuses of harmonization are not suitable. The harmonization choices have been made carelessly – they do not represent a thoughtful connection, but rather an artificial attachment of harmonies.

The fact that it is eastern does not make it something that is devoid of rules and laws, nor is it true that abusing these is characteristic of eastern melodies. And let us not even mention the fact that our melodies are neither absolutely eastern, nor absolutely western. No. Our melodies are also very regular, just like eastern music. One should seek and find the rules specific to them instead of slapping together

> some borrowed regulations. You can't sew a red patch on a black piece of cloth, no matter how valuable the former is.

In general, one should not allow a musical arrangement without subjecting it in advance to the detailed scrutiny of a specialized assembly. Otherwise, we will end up with a mess of hymns (and even without this our spiritual music is currently in disarray), which will be impossible to regulate.

All the compositions pass through the test of historic and national value, and cannot be seen independent of them, if of course our objective is to keep our values pure. Our past hymnologists and musicians, without exception, have composed a unique, national musical style, which they have consistently followed, developed and then given to us, their descendants, a complete entirety, which is ours. We should also follow their example.

The music of each nation springs from the four indivisible elements of that nation's language – measure, modulation, pronunciation and spirit. These are the things that form the worlds of our thoughts and emotions. Until we study in detail the four characteristics mentioned above, until we understand their rules and use them, we cannot have a perfect harmonization of any spiritual or worldly song.

Presenting all this to Your Holiness, I approach to kiss your Patriarchal Right Hand,

Your h<umble> s<ervant> and son

Komitas Vardapet

134. <TO RUBEN GHORGHANYAN>

<1909, end of December, Holy Etchmiadzin>

<...>

a) The melodies are foreign and do not match the style and spirit of Armenian spiritual music.

b) The rhythm has been disrupted. There are foreign accelerations and excesses, which do not originate in the basic spacing rules of our language.
c) The harmonization does not have a common style, a common unity, and does not match the style of music.

Language is the pulse of music. Armenian language and music have rules that are characteristic of them. The German Mozart and Weber, the German Beethoven and Wagner, and others are all separate interpreters of their mother tongue. The borders of the musical sea created by any musician are unstable – the closer you get to the border, the further away and more expansive it becomes. We have not yet understood and probed Beethoven and Wagner. Composers should not accommodate public desire, they should not sacrifice something beautiful for the sake of the miserable situation in everyday life. Polyphonic singing is weak in our tradition because of our elementary musical ignorance, because our polyphonic hearing has not developed well <...>

<Komitas Vardapet>

135. <TO MARGARIT BABAYAN>

<Holy Etchmiadzin, 1909>

<...> I was so happy to receive your letter. Indeed, I had not written anything in a long time to you or my friends, who are very close to my heart even though they are very far. I have turned into a nervous wreck – my brain and mind are not working well. I am running out of patience. Imagine that I am surrounded by a thick fog, I want to see a light, a bright light, go up, very high up, and live with the burning sun. But I can't find the way, and I am suffocating in this unjust air. There is nobody to whom I can open up, nobody who can say something I need to hear. I sit from morning till night at my desk like a hoopoe, writing and writing more... The time comes to relax and I look for someone to whom I can sing and play what I have composed, and hear an

opinion, but I find nobody. I go out and roam about here and there like a tiger, on my own, in my garden and on my roof.

It surprises me – how is it that I have not lost my mind in the unfair conditions of this deceitful environment? I sometimes want to fly away, far away and alone, and other times I want to lock myself in, alone and live like an ascetic. But am I not living like an ascetic already? Yes, but not that kind. I want to live alone with my muse, so that my heart does not blur over, my mind does not get corrupted, my soul does not get angry and my conscience does not die... But I have not despaired. I keep working, I have composed many things, I have done a lot. I haven't forgotten you and I have prepared your parts too, which I am sending you with this letter, as a sample of the remaining lot. I have completed Shushik's *Shoror* and the other pieces she likes, but I cannot find the time to copy them. I have some very interesting tasks at hand that I don't want to delay <...>

<Komitas Vardapet>

1910

136. <TO ARSHAK CHOPANYAN>

1910. 5/1. Holy Etchm<iadzin>

Dear Arshak,

I received your letters. It has only been possible to send you a positive reply today – the photographer was not here, his child had fallen ill and had been taken to Tpghis for treatment, with the news always being that he would come 'today or tomorrow.' He finally arrived yesterday, but he did not have large pieces of glass. I had them ordered immediately and we will receive them in the coming days, and we will send everything that you wanted. Rest assured, my dear, and write to His Holy, he called me and asked me to expedite things, and I told him the situation.

My heart is very sad to hear that you have still not regained your health. Let me put it simply – only marriage can cure you. I hope to see you in Paris this year. I will be coming for a month to your supremely honorable parts.

There are no signs of anything new in our internal or external lives. It looks like things are getting more complicated; we are living in very dangerous times, my dear.

I cordially wish you health, and success to your work. All of our priests send you their regards with longing.

Loving kisses to you,

Yours, Komitas

137. <TO MATTHEOS IZMIRLYAN>

1910, 12 January, Holy Etchmiadzin

Following the verbal high command of Your Holiness, I report the following for your kind consideration.

A. Over the past 20-30 years [up to now] one can see the gradual decline of our spiritual music in Armenian churches in general. The real pieces of Armenian spiritual music, our hymns, are falling and disappearing, being replaced by the singing of the mass.

The songs of the mass are almost all foreign in origin and consist of tasteless melodies. In Turkey, they are Turkish-Arab-Greek, in Persia they are Persian-Arab in origin [and in our motherland, [ara] you can add others]. In Russia, they are European, mainly Russian, while in our motherland it is the sum of all of this, and in our migrant communities—with the exception of Old Jugha—it is an unimaginable distortion, including all kind of graceless music [but] with no common origin or style in the songs.

Our national taste has grown foreign and alien—even more, I would say it has become the subject of mockery—thanks to ignorant [musicians] and selfish choirmasters, who do not know that which belongs to them and they do not even want to search for it and learn. They ignore it all and can present theirs as something beautiful and select, while it is really destructive music. The barrenness that is now prevalent in our spiritual music should therefore come as no surprise.

If we were to watch carefully how our mass is sung, we would immediately notice that there is no common mother tongue, no style that matches our cordial spirit, but that it is just a pile of tasteless, ugly, graceless melodies, lacking any spiritual feeling, selfish without any community spirit, ignorant and borrowed as a crude chain where there is nothing healthy, like God have mercy, Amen and unto your soul, Holy Holy, Almighty – in a word, everything is as varied as the number of singers and choirmasters we have ever had. There is no healthy, probing singing of the mass, one that matches our soul, our language, our thinking, one that could be the interpreter of our feelings and thoughts. The whole singing of the mass does not have any Armenian rhythm, any Armenian emphasis, while these two are the vital national-musical arteries, which are the only ones capable of consecrating the national heart. Enough said about that.

The real national melodies—the spirited, simple and sublime music of our hymns, which are the images and mirrors of our ancestors' enviable souls, which were always humming—have now been condemned to disdain, loss and reproach; what is more, they are taking our hearts and souls to foreign paths that are choking us. If we extinguish the last bit of the old that is left, then we will see with our own eyes how our hearts are being buried, and it will be like extinguishing the furnaces of our own lives.

One of the big contributors to the decline of hymn singing consists of long and extended, unnecessary elongations (early notes that are out of place, the resting composition, composition extracts, pieces that are unsuitably fancy) which, instead of causing enthusiasm, have choked the pure and simple melodies. Society is now tired of seeing things stretched out, which has happened only because of the tasteless innovations that have developed over the last few years. Honey is a sweet thing, but one cannot eat too much of it. Each person, no matter how devoted, no matter how good a Christian they are, cannot digest such a conglomerate of food at once. If music—the role of which is to educate and purify, by instilling a feeling of spiritual music in the heart and soul of the believer—is offered in an unsuitable manner, it will naturally lead to a decline and will drown out the soft strings of the heart and will then cut them. It will turn off the heart and soul, which are inseparable brothers working together through music in our lives.

Because it is still not too late, we must raise our hands and cure the wound, no matter how much it costs us, otherwise an irreversible loss is inevitable.

A. [Immediately] Look for means to write down what we had and what remains, as material to be studied and the basis for the restoration of our spiritual music.
B. Gather at once the people who know the old melodies and verify the current situation for pronunciation, emphasis, rhythm, musical formation, style and so on.
C. Examine the state of spiritual music locally in the center and in a few isolated places.
D. Prohibit willful changes, not allowing choirmasters and musical conductors to govern as they wish.
E. Examine the level of national legitimacy of all spiritual music pieces, without exception.

F. Regulate and improve the acolytes' choirs.
    a. Allow people who are trained and experienced, harmonious, those who understand the hymns, to come closer to serving in the choir.
    b. Reduce to the extent possible the participation of children in singing, especially during songs that are difficult for them to understand and harmful for them to sing.
    c. Improve the standing of the acolytes' choir in the eyes of the public, both materially and morally.

G. This should be begun first of all, and fundamentally, from the Mother Choir of the Mother Church of the Mother See. [where one should train]

H. At the Mother See, one should train choirmasters and send them to each [sister] daughter church, appointing them based on their skills and the availability of suitable places.

I. All of this can be achieved quite easily if no resources are spared.

J. I am personally ready to put in as much effort as possible and train as many people as I can, if I am given the facilities.

After all this, I have the boldness and confidence to say that it is already the 11th year that I have spent educating myself and serving the Mother See for the glory of its music. But I have dropped here like an unnecessary bud, left to the winds of chance, and as [time] this golden time passes by, the flame in my heart, the enthusiasm in my soul, is starting to die out, and despair and desperation are near, sieging me like a two-headed monster, after which there will be only one way out – looking for another place, different circumstances, so that I do not remain here like an unwanted fruit.

Demand [might be] the almighty call to action, but having to sit like a hen plucked of its feathers is like being a man for whom a beautiful set of clothes has been sewn, but which remain hanging on the wall, while the man is naked and unclothed.

Having said all this to Your Holiness, I beg you to enthusiastically [undertake][search] make efforts to raise the reputation and preparation of our powerful spiritual music. [If] Your Holiness [so desires] can find all the resources necessary to cure this fundamental disease.

I submit these neighborly comments with admiration and approach to kiss the Holy Right Hand of Your Holiness,

Your h<umble> s<ervant> and Holy Etchmiadzin congregant

[K<omitas> V<ardapet>]
[Komit<as>]

138. <TO THE EDITORIAL BOARD OF *TACHAR*>

1910 March 15, Holy Etchmiadzin

Honorable Editor,

Please be kind enough to provide a small corner of space to this letter in your fortnightly journal *Tachar*.

In the second half of the past century, the 18th, the Armenian press of Constantinople was publishing pieces on Armenian ecclesiastical music – a series of analytical, critical and especially argumentative articles. In the current issue of *Tachar* dated 1910, 31 January, issue 6, F<ather> Abraham Epeyan is proposing that I publicize my theories about the hymnal neumes.

It is true that I have found the key to the Armenian neumes and I can even read simple compositions, but I have not yet reached the end. In order to comprehend the mysterious meaning of each neume, looking through tens of manuscripts, it is a task that sometimes takes months. And the neumes that I have with me at the moment, the ones whose titles are known, are currently only 198 in number, while the ones with unknown names are much more.

Thus, it is impossible to write about such specialized topics in the pages of our press for the following reasons – first, the number of pages in these publications is very limited; second, there is no point in engaging the public in a study that is purely academic and has been ongoing for years; third, it is huge and very costly; and fourth, I have not yet completed my examination.

Let me summarize in a few words, for the time being, the elements that make up Armenian neumes –

A. Neumes for pitches
B. Neumes for musical nuances
C. Neumes for embellishment
D. Neumes of dynamics
E. Neumes of duration
F. Neumes for keys
G. Neumes of prosody
H. Punctuation neumes
I. Stylistic neumes
J.Connecting and disconnecting neumes
K. Chromatic neumes, and so on

In order to complete a study like this, one should perfectly master these basic concepts and sciences – rhythm, syllable spacing, word spacing, line spacing, prosody, emphasis, punctuation, neume spacing, neumic understanding, language (the real and true origins of the words), philosophy (geometry, arithmetic, astronomy and music in the classic sense), the origins of neumes, their development and decline, their modern history, comparative neume studies – and only then will that which is secret begin to come to the fore. May Armenian society be forgiving and—particularly—patient, until I finish my excruciating sixteen-year study. I hope that, in the near future, it will become the property of the public, in several volumes.

IN PRAYER
KOMITAS VARDAPET

139. <ANTON MAYILYAN>

1910. 22/3. Holy Etchm<iadzin>

Honorable M<ister> Anton Mayilyan,

I am sending you my small study on "Armenian Peasant Dances" which has already been published in German (*Zeitschrift für Armenische Philologie*, 1901,

I, B. H.) in a journal, but has not yet been published in Armenian. I offer you this study unconditionally. I only ask that, if it not an inconvenience to you, you take the initiative and have as many copies as you can printed; my intention is not to sell them, but to give them to my friends here and there as a gift.

I received with thanks your first issue of the journal *Tatron yev Yerajshutyun*[72] and its supplements.

The promotion of the Adamyan sisters is good news, I was following closely the progress they were making in their concerts and reading about their glorious achievement filled me with admiration.

Who is that G. Verdyan who is attacking so mercilessly the mild song of the sorrowful Armenian villager? I am surprised at our society, which is pushing out true art from its hearts through people like this.

Wishing success and wellbeing
To your work and yourself.
Regards,

Komitas Vardapet

140. <TO ANTON MAYILYAN>

<1910, April-May, Holy Etchmiadzin>

Honorable M<Ister> Anton Mayilyan,

I apologize for the uncomfortable situation in which my proposal had placed you. I did not wish for you go into debt because of me. Therefore, if you have not yet had them typographed for printing, please do as would suit you best–print as many copies as suitable, send me as many as you like. I understand the difficulty of the job very well and would like to support you as much as possible in order for you to progress on this agreeable initiative. Please do not cause yourself any discomfort on my account.

I send you my regards, wishing you wellbeing and success,

Komitas Vardapet

72 ["Theater and Music"] – Translator's notes

141. <TO MATTHEOS IZMIRLYAN>

1910. May 10. Holy Etchmiadzin

To His Holiness
The Holiest Patriarch of All Armenians
Mattheos II

Holy Patriarch,

Armenian ecclesiastical music has been going through a decline in the past centuries – the 18th and especially the 19th. Among other powerful reasons, it is in decline because our churches only pay attention to the Holy Mass and its distorted singing, which has completely lost the melodies sprinkled with simple and sublime, uncomplicated and childlike naiveté as well as seeped with sincerity and faith. It has been replaced by a conglomerate of unsuitable, inadequate, borrowed and pitiful singing. The hymns—warm as the sun, pure as air, lively as water—of our ancestors have been relegated to positions of secondary importance and even fully to the background, they have been condemned to oblivion, thus cutting the arteries of our music. Therefore, hymnologists are reducing in number every day, and the hymns are growing more obscure because of this disrespect, and in their place, undereducated, ignorant, inexperienced and tasteless choir singers and choirmasters are coming up, who are musicians without any theoretical training, and whose unimpeded and energetic willfulness has been charged with the art of spiritually and responsibly educating the Armenian people. I am not talking about the majestic and educational role of spiritual music, but in the simplest of outlines, I am emphasizing below how one can reignite—through the revitalization of our national spiritual music—the frozen heart of the Armenian Christian, and once again rekindle the hidden flame of enthusiasm.

A. Open an Armenian spiritual music school to arm the teachers, singers, choir singers, choirmasters, musicians and all clergymen in general, to save the splinters of the music of our ancestors from oblivion, to develop national culture and to introduce our rich musical literature to foreigners by doing research and giving concerts.

B. Open a musical publication department at the Mother See printing house and print, with the oversight of the supervision body, all kinds of books and notebooks on Armenian spiritual singing.
C. Make a common version of spiritual singing mandatory for all Armenian churches.
D. Establish a daily choir in Armenian churches.
E. Select choir singers using strict criteria. For choir masters, the requirements should include perfect mastery over ecclesiastical concepts and music. Choir masters should be confirmed in their appointments by the closest high official in the church, and they should work under the supervision and care of that official.
F. Establish regular singing classes and basic music as part of the academic program in Armenian schools, taught by certified instructors.

The Mother See should be the one providing the first example, and it is obligated to establish the foundation for a permanent and exemplary choir through the following steps.

a. For polyphonic singing that is of a quality worthy of the name and position of the Mother See, the choir will have at least 40 excellent singers.
b. For solo singing, twenty-four singers.
c. The choir must be independent of the students at the Seminary, whose vocally talented members may join in on feast days, in order to have singing of a more celebratory nature.

I am ready, from this very day, to dedicate all my efforts and energy to a sacred duty of this kind. A sacred duty that has attracted and bound me to the Mother See. A sacred work that has inspired hope in me for exactly twenty years, but also a sacred duty that has embraced me with silver hope, seeped into me and raised me, without becoming a reality. And thus, I have been left to burn in that same hope, to grow old and to leave this transient life like a desiccated plant, which bends and dries with the blows of the wind and thirst.

Holy Patriarch,

I have put my foot into the second threshold of my life, but once again with that same undying hope. Although that energetic young man has now become serious, and that youthful pace has grown milder, my courageous energy and perpetual hope are only just coming to a boil.

Having delivered this letter to Your Holiness, I remain with undying hope,
The h<umble> s<ervant> of Your Holiness and congregant
of the Mother See of Holy Etchmiadzin

Komitas Vardapet

142. <TO ANDREAS BABAMYAN>

1910. 10 June, Constantinople

Dear Andrush, I have safely reached Constantinople and I will go to my birthplace in a couple of days. My regards to your wife and those who ask about me.

Yours, Komitas

143. <TO VARIKO VRATSYAN>

1910, 18 August <Bursa>

Honorable Miss Variko,

I asked Levon Yeramyan to take a picture of you from a distance. Take a look – do you believe me? Do you look like this picture? I am leaving my birthplace on the 20th of this month.

Many regards to everyone

Komitas

My regards to you

Yeramyan Levon

144. <TO THE EDITORIAL BOARD OF THE NEWSPAPER *JAMANAK*>

Bursa, 1910, Sept<ember> 22

An Explanatory Letter from
Musicologist F<ather> Komitas V<a>rd<apet>

L<evon> *ef<fendi>* Ch<errahyan> had published an article in your newspaper where he has not expressed my words correctly, and he has confused the general questions and answers with our separate interview. The viewpoint that I have presented in the article was not in reply to a question during our interview, it was something I said to the whole audience when answering questions from various people. During our separate interview, the main issues which we covered were A. where I am from, B. where I had studied, C. what songs I have composed and D. where I have given concerts and lectured.

I did not say that "Armenian musicians in Constantinople are far from being valuable" but rather, when asked about the "three-voice and four-voice singing" prevalent in Constaninople, I had said, among other things, that they cannot be valuable (the three-voice and four-voice singing) because there are no music schools in the whole of Turkey and the "Armenian musicians of Constantinople are people who have grown and studied within the confines of Turkey."

I did not say that "they do not even have the drive towards self-development and, despite not being worth much, they are very confident of their abilities," but rather that "I even know some Armenian musicians in Constantinople who are not worth anything, but are critical of other's work in the papers and sign their names with the title 'specialist musician.'" I had also given an example of how (I think it was in the *Manzume-i-Efkâr*), someone who did not even have elementary knowledge of polyphonic music has, without any reservations, criticized Chilingaryan's mass for three voices, which, with all its shortcomings, was definitely worth something more than the revised version submitted by the person who considered himself a 'specialist musician.' It is these kinds of people who "do not even have the drive towards self-development and, despite not being worth much, they are very confident of their abilities."

I don't want to burden your readership's minds with other minute details and issues. One's actions are more powerful than words or the pen. However, I will say that I have not "been dazzled by my own abilities." I have not said or written that the Armenian musicians of Constantinople would have been better or worse musicians and musicologists if they had enjoyed the patronage of people like my renowned benefactor M<ister> Alexander Mantashyan and travelled to Europe. The heaven-blessed talent of music has not come down upon Komitas Vardapet alone. Therefore, although I am conscious of the fact that I do know something in this area, I have never pretended to be or declared myself the "ONLY MUSICOLOGIST" or the "GOD OF ARMENIAN MUSIC." On the contrary, on many occasions, I have had the opportunity to confess before a large audience that if fortune had not smiled upon me and if I had not gone first to Holy Etchmiadzin and then to Germany with the support of my invaluable benefactor M<ister> Alexander Mantashyan, I would be in my birthplace of Kutina, a cobbler at most, because my uncle Harutyun who brought me up as orphaned child was also a cobbler, and it is obvious that I too, in all probability, would have become his apprentice.

I don't like dealing in such issues and making others deal in them, but I was forced to write this letter to prevent any misunderstandings. If you find it suitable, please be so kind as to publish it.

Komitas Vardapet

145. <TO MARGARIT BABAYAN>

1910. 17/12. Smyrna

Dear Miss Margo,

I received your letter, I am very happy that all of you are well, and that you remember me from time to time.

My dear, I organized 5 concerts this summer in these parts, starting with my birthplace. I am writing this letter from Smyrna, where I am working on the 6th one. Then, I will go back to Constantinople and give a 7th one to benefit the national hospital, and then I will go to Atabazar to give the 8th one. If I don't receive any invitations from elsewhere, I will come to Paris directly via Vienna. But I don't know when this will be, I will write again. You can't imagine what I have been through, the tricks that the stupid choristers tried to pull here, but I won and made our Armenian music ring out once again. I will come and tell you in detail so that you can see how corrupted people's morals and life are here...

I miss all of you very much; it makes me so happy to think that we will see each other again.

Many, many regards to all of you and those who ask about me.

Always dedicated to you

Komitas Vardapet

<P.S.> Happy New Year, have a good year and a Merry Christmas.

146. <TO STEPAN AKAYAN>

1910. 22/12. Smyrna

Noble Stepan *ef<fendi>* Akayan,

I received your letter yesterday and am replying today.

I have begun immediately to write up the fundamental statute of the union and its program because it is not an easy task, so I cannot do it quickly, please be patient for a few days. And in order to save time, it is best that you spread the news about the need for this organization and seek the means for fundraising.

- - -

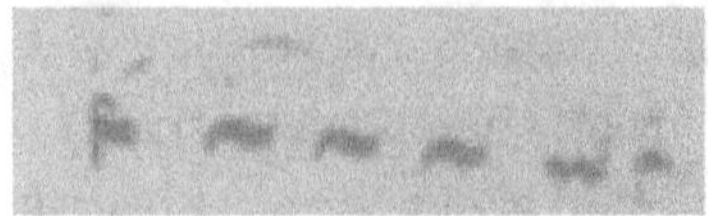

I congratulate you on the occasion of the feast bearing your name – eat, drink and be merry.

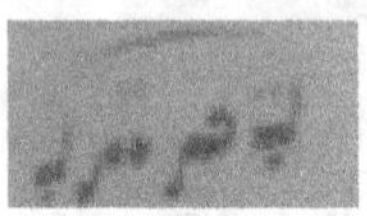

Give my regards to our boys, and grab whichever of them you come across by the collar, stop them and say hello to them from the *kertenkele*.

I am well, but I am not very happy with my work. There is a serious scarcity of Baryton[73] and Bass singers, if a choir of 50-60 people comes together, then that is quite an achievement.

There are other things to say, but let us be silent for now.

My regards to Harents and Ashchyan *effendis.* I have things to write to the latter, but I will do so after I complete the statute for the organization – the one who endures to the end will be a spinach eater.

Regards, Komitas

73 ["Baryton" and "Bass" were written using Latin letters in the original letter by Komitas. This translation has not corrected the misspelling] – Translator's notes.

1911

147. <TO HOVHANNES MUTAFYANTS>

1911. 29/1. Smyrna

Honorable
M<ister> Mutafyants,

I would happily take the initiative to come to Alexandria and give a concert of Armenian ecclesiastical and peasant music, as well as to give two lectures on the origins, development and current state of a. Armenian peasant and b. Armenian ecclesiastical music. Regarding the training of a church choir and regulating their spiritual singing, this is unfortunately impossible. Firstly, I only have one and a half months, or two months at the most, of time that I can dedicate to Alexandria, because I must go to Europe for important personal reasons. Second, it is more important to train a choirmaster than to prepare a permanent church choir – a choirmaster who is knowledgeable and skilled, at least regarding the spirit, style and especially the pronunciation of Armenian music. And third, it is not possible to prepare both a choir and a choirmaster in this brief time. Additionally, there is no point in expending efforts to train one choirmaster because the choirmaster must be almost a musician, and must first learn what he has to teach and then teach it.

You had asked about my conditions.

a. Please make 60-80 people of both sexes, young and old, available for the choir. The more people you can arrange in excess of this number, the more content I will be. We need at least 40-50 female voices or those of young boys, and 20-30 adults. How many Tenors, Basses or Barytons[1] can you find? Please write and let me know.
b. I will take 2/3rds of the proceeds from the concert for the publication of my works. If I could afford it, I would have settled for a fifty-fifty split.

1 ["Tenor," "Bass" and "Baryton" were written using Latin letters in the original letter by Komitas. This translation has not corrected the misspelling] – Translator's notes.

c. The full proceeds from my lectures will be mine.

If you do not have any specific suggestions on your part, I will arrange the concert, pending your agreement, for 1 May, Sunday. I will leave Constantinople immediately after the concert benefitting the National Hospital on 6 or 13 March, and I will begin preparations immediately after arriving in your city.

The Smyrna concert is on the 30th of the month, and I will leave for Constantinople on 2 February. If you write me a letter, please send it to Constantinople, to the *Soorb Lusavorich* church in Galatia, and I will receive it there.

With my warm gratitude to your enviable art-loving Armenian community, I give you my regards and remain, respectfully yours

Komitas Vardapet

148. <TO HAKOB>

<1911, February-March, Constantinople>

Hakob *jan*,

I regret that we are invited to Martin Hakobyan's this evening. You silly thing, you *kertenkele*, why hadn't you said anything the other day, so that I would have been at home?

Regards to every<one>.

Komitas Vardapet

149. <TO MARGARIT BABAYAN>

1911 25/12/4
Alexandrie, Eglise arm.[2]

2 ["Alexandrie, Eglise arm." was written this way in French by Komitas in the original letter] – Translator's notes

Dear M<iss> Margarit,

You are probably surprised to see that I have ended up here. This trip of mine was like one taken by a wandering Jew. We will see each other soon, in about another 2 months. I am going to give one concert here, then move on to Cairo and Jerusalem to see some manuscripts, and then I'll be coming to Paris via Marseille. I have many, many things to tell you that will make you happy. My work has already reached the level of princes, and that is a good thing. I will come and tell you, it is impossible to describe one by one in a letter all the things that have been thrown at me, but I ended up victorious nevertheless. The main reason I am writing this letter is the following.

A young lady from Constantinople, from a very good family, whose house had been plundered during the recent destruction, has very good potential to become a pianist. She already has a lot of training, a great ear, wonderful taste, but lacks in musical development and resources, something which she has been unable to get in Constantinople. I advised her to come to Paris. She really wants it, but her parents are afraid to send her abroad, because they have never let her out of their sight in the past. I promised to facilitate things through you. So, how much money would be needed annually for a young lady to live in a guest house and to study with a private tutor or at a music school? She can afford 60 rubles every month. Can she live and study on this amount? Is there a family, Armenians or French, who has lodging available? If not, then of course there are a number of guest houses where she can safely stay. She is very elegant and a straight talker; she is 20 years old and has a wonderful personality.

I ask you to reply to my questions immediately, so that I can put her at rest and make her happy. Her parents would agree if they are convinced that their daughter is in a reliable place.

She would be a good force for us.

That is all for now; many, many loving regards to all of you.

Yours, Komitas

150. <TO MARGARIT BABAYAN>

1911 12/6 Cairo

Dear Miss Margarit,

I received your letter, my heartfelt gratitude for the exhaustive and direct explanations you gave.

The concert in Alexandria was also very successful and I am now in Cairo. The Armenians here wanted to transport the choir and repeat the concert. I will go to Jerusalem from here and, after seeing the manuscript library, I will come directly to Paris. If you are not there, I hope to be able to come and find you, even if only for a few hours.

Many things have happened, but I shouldn't tell you about them with a pen, I should use God's gift of the spoken word. I hope to open a music school in Constantinople, but the plan is so far just at the level of talk. When the *hos-hos*[3] start taking action, that is when things will be successful. I have given 17 concerts this year and lectured 12 times.

Give my loving regards to everyone and everybody.

I remain, always dedicated to you,

Komitas Vardapet

151. <TO MR. AND MRS. LALOY>

<1911, August 2, Shanklin[4]>

My dear friends,

I congratulate you on the birth of Nicolette, may she babble like a bright star above your home. My regards.

Komitas Vardapet

3 [A word used to mock the Armenians of Constantinople, possibly originating from the Western Armenian word for "here" (pronounced *hos*) which is very different from the Eastern Armenian word ("*aystegh*")] – Translator's notes.

4 ["Shanklin" was written this way in English by Komitas in the original letter] – Translator's notes

Susutchki, we are having a wonderful time with our little Holy Father; it is like both of us are in heaven. Too bad none of you are here. Many regards with longing and kisses, congratulations on the occasion of Nic<olette>'s feast.

Margo

152. <TO VARIKO VRATSYAN>

1911, 3/8 <Shanklin>

Honorable young lady Variko Vratsyan,

Many regards to you, to the Madam, Nikol and little Anahit (I want my nose back) and all the members of our group, from the Isle of Wight in England, the city of Shanklin. Soon, I will go to Paris, Berlin, Vienna and Constantinople.

Respectfully, Komitas

153. <TO TIRAYR VARDAPET>

21 August 1911
St. Malo. Villa Franc-Val.[5]

Dear Tirayr,

Father Komitas is with me for a few days and we are having a very good time together. We constantly recall you and talk about the situation of our poor Eghpaneu. Please accept the regards of my whole family, and loving regards from me too.

Yours, Hambardzum Melikyan

---

5 ["St. Malo. Villa Franc-Val" was written this way using Latin letters by Komitas in the original letter] – Translator's notes

Old man *Zmbltoros,*

You are something else. You left Paris and ended up in the doghouses of Kishinev. Ha! Good, you deserved it! I am with Hambardzum as you can see, as his guest, and will go tomorrow to Paris, Berlin, Vienna and then Constantinople.

Many regards to you and your baldness.

Yours, Komitas
Mara Melikoff

154. <MARGARIT BABAYAN>

1911, 18 September
Charlottenburg, Kantstr. 150A
Komitas Vardapet[6]

Margo *jan*,

I think the young man who visited you is one of the singers from the concert at Constantinople. I think he will be a bit of a mess in music – he has no money, no training and, if I remember correctly, he was one of the regular voices in the choir, with a slight oriental tinge in his skin. I don't know, be careful that you don't cause yourself any problems. Nothing good can come of people of that type. He had written to me from London and I had replied that he wouldn't be able to get into a music school. I am busy with copying now, when my work is in order, I will write a long letter. Regards to everyone. Please ask Shushik for the final copy of the dances, I will get them printed and want to look them over again.

I have no time to write anything new, I'm barely able to copy out the songs to be printed. You must probably be stuffed... I was very happy that your voice

6 ["Charlottenburg, Kantstr. 150A, Komitas Vardapet" was written this way using Latin letters by Komitas in the original letter] – Translator's notes

is ringing out and is blowing hard as hard can be. Regards to everyone once again.

Komitas

155. <TO ARCHBISHOP GEVORG SURENYANTS>

1911. 26/12. Constantinople

Honorable Locum Tenens
Of the Patriarch
Of All Armenians Archbishop Gevorg

Great Holy Father,

Since I am to stay in Constantinople, I ask you to kindly instruct [for] my congregational salary at Etchmiadzin to be cancelled.

I would like to come and personally say goodbye, but the representatives of the Russian government—the Embassy and Consulate—did not approve my visa, saying that the law recognized me as a priest resident in Turkey (exactly 4 weeks have passed since they wrote to Petersburg and I have still not received a reply from the superior authorities), and I have already started to work in order to avoid wasting time.

I approach to kiss the Holy Right Hand of your Great Holiness, and remain the

H<umble> s<ervant> and son
Of your Honorable Self

Komitas Vardapet

156. <MARGARIT BABAYAN>

Constantinople, 1911, <December>

<...> I have a lot to write, but my soul is not at ease; as you can see, I am now in Constantinople. Let me write briefly this time. My songs are being published

by *Breikopt und Hartel* and will be available in one or two months, in parts, in small notebooks, which are convenient for both the seller and the buyer.

The people are very positive about my work, which is good news and gives me strength. Oh, you don't know how much I want you to be here with me now, so that I could tell you everything – very interesting things. I subjected the songs to quite a few changes and they now have a better shape, air, space, and picture. <...>

<Komitas Vardapet>

1912

157. <TO THE EDITORS OF *HOVIT*>

Constantinople, Feb<ruary> 19, <1912>

I regret that your honorable publication has echoed false news. I have simply asked the Most Honorable Locum Tenens to cancel my salary, that is all, because I have moved to Constantinople, so it is not right for me to receive a congregational salary. I have never given up my spiritual vocation and the thought of leaving the clergy has never crossed my mind.

I remain, always, an official of the h<oly> church,

Komitas Vardapet

158. <TO VAHAN MALEZYAN>

1912. 24/2 Constantinople
Pangalti N 83 (47)[7]

Dear friend,
M<ister> Vahan Malezyan

I barely managed to find time, although I had already begun the work a month ago, but please forgive me if the fulfillment of my promise was slightly delayed.

The Committee for the Armenian Music School has been organized, with Astvatzatur Harents being elected as Chairman, Eduard Karageozyan as Treasurer, and Sisak Ashchyan as Secretary.

7 ["Pangalti N 83 (47)" was written this way using Latin letters by Komitas in the original letter] – Translator's notes

So, I know have a place to stay and an income. I am working with my group, private lessons, and on my own compositions. I work for myself until noon, and for my students in the afternoon. I have a group of young people consisting of 12 individuals who are studying harmonization and choir conducting, so that they can organize and conduct choirs. This group is studying for free. I have a choir consisting of excellent voices and mature individuals – 160 people. I selected them strictly and carefully because this is a permanent choir, studying regularly and for free. I am sending you enclosed a copy of the contract on becoming a member of the choir, for your information. I am already training them, and the first performance will take place on New Sunday[8] to benefit the music school, and the second a few weeks later to benefit the National Hospital. Some excellent voices and talents have come to the fore; I grow happier every day seeing their progress. The concerts this time are peppered with national music, peasant songs and foreign pieces, so that we can make ours more familiar to others while growing familiar to the foreign ones. Yesterday, the chief of protocol for the Sultan, Ismayil Cenan *bey* came to visit me. He has very good taste and a good understanding of both European and foreign-oriental music. He was very satisfied. Sing him a couple of things.

The excellent singer Shahmuradyan is now the honored guest of the Egyptian Armenians. The unprecedented success he has had has made me very happy and I am truly pleased when foreigners learn about us through science and art, and are left with a good impression; such work is of undeniable and progressive value. Shah-Murad, who is the seed of the Armenian soil, having drunk Armenian water and basked in Armenian sunlight, has an excellent, bright and energetic voice. How many more occasions will he provide for us Armenians to be proud, he is still in the spring of his career. The foreigners were jealous and conspired against him, but we are obligated to nurture and nourish him.

I had promised to compose a song for the Union and you promised to send some songs written by various people. Now you know my address, and I have the facilities to work. So, I ask you to please send me a few suitable things, so

8 [The literal translation of the Armenian term for the Sunday after Easter, called 'Low Sunday' in some western church denominations] – Translator's notes.

that I can select from among them. But it would be good for it to be brief and direct, using language and a style that is easy for common people, so that it could spread through the schools. I plan on composing it for two, three, four and more voices, so that, depending on the place and the requirements, it can be possible to sing in a number of ways. It would be good if it consisted of two or three stanzas. If words with the same rhythm were to repeat in the stanzas, then the melody itself could only be for one stanza, and that would set the tone for the rest. But if the stanzas differ in the content or if the other ones grow more serious, then in that case the melody will probably change as well. In a word, the simpler, the better, and the more prevalence and popularity it will have. But I beg of you, do not let it sound like just a series of good wishes.

My regards with longing to all my friends, each of whom I cannot mention separately.

I remain, always dedicated,

Komitas Vardapet

159. <TO MARGARIT BABAYAN>

1912. 15/28. March, Constantinople
Constantinople, Pangalti
N 83 (47)[9]

Dear Margo *jan*,

You can't imagine how many times I have picked up a pen to write you a letter, but something has interrupted me every time – either my lessons, or visits. I decided today that no matter who comes, I will make them wait and write you a letter. Let them wait till they can't take it anymore. Let me worry about that. They are hosting me; they are covering all my expenses – accommodation, a servant, food and so on. I have formed a choir and given two

9 ["Constantinople, Pangalti N 83 (47)" was written this way using Latin letters by Komitas in the original letter] – Translator's notes

concerts – one on New Sunday, the other the following Sunday. I will probably repeat the same in the other districts. I have a permanent choir consisting of 200 individuals, people of both sexes and with excellent voices. I have conducted their selection and admission in a strict manner, so that this work starts off on a strong foundation. I have now redoubled all my efforts to start the task of the music school. I was to begin by finding a building, so that it can be a permanent location. This is delaying things a little bit, but that's all right, my hope remains strong, I will definitely be able to solve this and drag you out here as well. An Armenian girl came the other day, I tested her voice – *akh*, Margo *jan*. If only you had been here and heard it. I nearly went mad with joy. Nature has given her everything perfectly – her voice, her height, her beauty, brains, poise, feeling, grace... in a word, I went mad. But... but... that was the end of it all. Her mother will have her married right after this Easter, on New Sunday. Her mother had come to me as well. I got very angry and said that she was a murderer for extinguishing talent of this kind. The girl started crying and confessed that she had begged her mother to send her abroad to study. She had felt that there was something within her, it had burned inside. She had heard last year that I was heading to Europe and had finally convinced her mother to send her with me to Europe but, bad luck, I had already left the previous day. They had come asking for me and I had already been on the way to Egypt. Things went dark for her and she was disappointed. I tried hard to convince them for her to go with her fiancé and develop her talent, but that is not possible. Her fiancé cannot leave his work here. So you see what losses we are facing and how, what talents and geniuses are vanishing, burning due to ignorance. Coming to Miss Gavanozyan, whom you hosted so hospitably, she is a very nice girl, they said that she was extremely proud of herself because she had not seen another singer here, and she may have been falsely accused, but I knew that after entering your room she would finally understand who she was and how much she still had to learn. I'm glad to hear that is what happened. Imagine that, if you compare her to the girl I mentioned, her talent is actually nothing!

You had sent the program, I was very happy that our folk singers and glory are spreading in the music world. And I have no reason to be upset at your initiative to have the song published – you have done the right thing.

The printing of my songs has come across a problem. My manuscripts, which I had handed to Breitkopt-Hartel, had been sent to my address in Etchmiadzin, and none of my friends are there now. I can't trust the others. They have been in Petersburg for a few months, as witnesses for the Dashnaktsutyun case. So the printing has been delayed. Until I get the manuscripts, I cannot send them for publication. I have the drafts, but I have no time to copy them, so things have remained as they are.

Akh, how I wish that our music school would open and you would come here so that we could push our music forward together in society. You can't imagine how much talent there is here and how they love art. Although they aren't well prepared and don't understand much, when the school opens, we can do a lot. As soon as the process is in a more stable situation, I will write to you and you can come. I give private lessons too, but not many. I don't want to waste too much of my time on lessons.

I work until noon for myself every day and then engage in my lessons. So, I have managed to write quite a few new pieces; I know you will like them a lot. I have also written two Turkish songs—one dedicated to the Sultan, the other to the constitution—so that my work is successful and I can gain quite a broad circle of acquaintances in the palace. The Sultan's chief of protocol had visited me yesterday. You can't imagine how ignorant they are of music, although this one in particular understands quite a bit of it – he has a good education and lots of power. That is all for today. Many regards from me to everyone at home and all the boys.

Loving regards with longing, with blessings to you and anointments

Komitas Vardapet

<P.S.> I just received the last program you had sent, thank you. I was very happy to see that you are sparing no efforts in putting Armenian songs and music on the right path. Bravo!

Dear and respected
M<iss> M<argarit> Babayan

I am following your success from a distance and it makes me proud.

I beg you to accept my sincere congratulations and regards. Many regards from me to your dear sisters, your honorable mother, and your brothers-in-law, as well as to Mathveev and the Gyurjyans. Father Komitas and I are staying at the same house together, so the address is the same. Please also do the favor of giving my regards to other people who know me.

With loving regards,
P<anos> Terlemezyan
20 March 1912
Constantinople

160. <TO TIRAYR VARDAPET>

1912. 22/3 Constantinople
Pangalti, N 83 (47)[10]
Komitas Vardapet

Dear Tirayr,

Father Mattheos Hekimyan, our seminarian friend from Bilecik, had come from Bursa;

I'm sure you remember him. He was pleading in sorrow to be transferred to the Bessarabia Diocese, if a vacancy for a priest could be found there. The local priests are envious and are not letting him feel at ease. He has a family of 3 people – he, his wife and their child Stepan, who is studying at a state school. He is already 19 years old and is a very nice boy – smart and a quick learner. So I told him that it was not likely to happen, because there is the issue of getting Russian residence. But I am writing to you in any case, for his sake. If it is possible and you have a vacancy, he is a very good priest and he can be very helpful to the people. The income here is so low that people are barely making enough to eat. Please let me know immediately somehow, so that I can inform the poor man.

10 ["Pangalti, N 83 (47), Komitas Vardapet" was written this way using Latin letters by Komitas in the original letter] – Translator's notes

I kiss the H<oly> Right Hand of the Holy Father and
Send you kisses

Yours, Komitas

161. <TO ARSHAK CHOPANYAN>

1912. 10/5. Constantinople
Pangalti N 83 (47)[11]

Dear Arshak,

I was very happy to hear that you are feeling completely recovered.

Your anniversary should definitely be postponed because the situation is tense and it is a season of anniversaries. So we should wait a while until the circumstances change, so that we can arrange a glorious event and present the real literary figure and literary art. This is how I would like it.

Coming to my work, I was forced to postpone the publication until I could also arrange my new discoveries, which have great value. So I will not rush things. I am therefore very busy. But my work has been well organized, so I am not depriving myself of anything.

With warmest kisses

Yours, dedicated, Komitas Vardapet

162. <MARGARIT BABAYAN>

1912. 12/5. Constantinople. Pangalti N 83 (47)[12]

---

11 ["Pangalti N 83 (47)" was written this way using Latin letters by Komitas in the original letter] – Translator's notes

12 ["Pangalti N 83 (47), Komitas Vardapet" was written this way using Latin letters by Komitas in the original letter] – Translator's notes

Dear Margo,

My 4th and final concert is this Sunday. I went to Izmit, Atabazar, Armash and Partizak last week to lecture and sing. I am well, for the time being. I have arranged my work in such a way that I engage in my own tasks until noon and then work with my students. I will go to Leipzig[13] in two weeks. If I can afford it, I will stop by in Paris as well, particularly to see you.[14] My choir, which I have named "Gusan" (in honor of the old Armenian bards and singers of Goghtan, who were called *gusans* by the people), has seen a lot of progress. It will be even better next year, and I will be able to do a lot. I am popular among the people, but they are still not ready to move. Slavery has suppressed them so much, that they do not have the energy left for independent and confident work.

You had written about going to America, but I am forced to push this thought back for the time being, until I can get some things done.

Akh, I have a lot to write, but my time is arranged such that I cannot compose lengthy letters.

I am sending you the photograph of me that you had requested, and the program of one of my concerts.

I am happy that you too are happy with your students and are doing a lot of work. You have already been appreciated in Paris, that is a big and powerful factor for the success of your work. What is important is that your future has brightened and you have occupied a big spot in the history of Armenian music with your relentless and energetic work in a foreign setting, where they perceive you better than in your own homeland. But our people are not the ones to blame, art is only just beginning to enter our lives and I hope that we will move forward soon because there is a lot of timber to work with, but the levels of skill vary.

---

13 ["Leipzig" was written this way using Latin letters by Komitas in the original letter] – Translator's notes

14 [Komitas uses the Armenian ձեզ which is the respectful or plural form, in contrast to the other instances of 'you' in the letter, which were in the singular. He is probably referring to the whole Babayan family on this occasion] – Translator's notes.

Money has become an issue here because of the war, and this has affected my work a little. But an end to the war will have an immediate effect and the door will once again open, and I will work and work.

My loving regards with longing to your father, mother, the Laloys, the Carbonels, and our honorable, learned boys, whom I know you have already gathered around yourself.

Loving regards to you as well,

Yours, Komitas

163. <TO MARINOS STAMPOLYAN>

1912, 15/28 10 Constantinople

Dear student
To [Miss] Marinos Stampolyan

Greetings to your new life.

Move forward undaunted, humbly, like a lily of the valley; sincerely, like a rose in the orchards and like lightning, the choicest gold.

Greetings to your new life.

Your hope is abundant, like the spring,

Your efforts are bright, like the summer,

Your work is replete, like the fall, and then you rest, like the winter, so that the door to a new spring may open.

Greetings to your new life.

K<omitas>

164. <TO MARGARIT BABAYAN>

1912. 15/12. Constantinople
Pangaldi, N 83 (47)[15]

Dear Margo,

I am truly guilty; I have not written anything to you in all this time. What can I do? I am not very fond of letters.

I am very, very happy that you are finding success under a foreign sky and in an environment where it is difficult to please. That is proof that you have the means, grace and energy to work, may you always stay that energetic and bright.

I only saw Mannik twice. Her voice is good, her tongue has emotion, but she seems uncontrolled, unstable and, in particular, lazy. She had done nothing the whole summer and, importantly, when she had come to me and I had offered her my help, she only took one lesson and did not reappear. I wanted to teach her the sounds of the Armenian peasant songs and then study those songs with her. I noticed the last time she came that she had a cold. I prohibited her from singing until she got better. And then she did not return. It seems like she has a good voice and talent, as well as the faculties to learn, but there one small thing she does not have – the *will* to learn. She seems very distracted, absent and bored. I told her to go back to Paris immediately and finish her studies with you – after all, she loves you so much and admires you, she is happy with you.

I would have been happy to have had her sing solo in my choir, but things did not work out well and we left it at that. I wouldn't advise her to go to Tpghis because I don't think she would be happy there – they are well trained there and demanding, she would be miserable. And I am not sure about giving private concerts here and making a living – she is not yet known. But that is still something if the alternative is to do nothing. You had not written anything about Tigran Nalbandyan. It looks like this is a common problem

15 ["Pangaldi, N 83 (47)" was written this way using Latin letters by Komitas in the original letter] – Translator's notes

we Armenians have – we cannot see things through to the end. We let them develop superficially or not at all, we train people who end up lacking. I don't want to discuss the reasons, they are justifiable for the moment. In my opinion, Tigran is also a person without any form or character. He is worldlier than in the higher realms of the abstract and artistic. But his voice is soft and velvety, unrestrained, but not boundless. And he has managed to survive simply because of his charm, but he does not have the foundation to go further, to serve on the most prestigious stages, as far as I know. Life, too, is behaving very unpredictably. This is my personal opinion. He can prepare perfectly and perform in a way that would smooth his whole career ahead of him – naturally, only if he works with all seriousness.

Coming to Iskuhi Ghavanozyan, she also has energy, talent and is hardworking, but the bad thing is that she tends to try and do a broader range of things, rather than go deep into her singing, which can be a serious obstacle for her future. She will not progress if she keeps pushing herself to things that lie on the exterior, things that are visible, rather than to dive in and breathe in the spirit of the song.

Both of them have good sides and bad sides, but the negative tends to dominate in them both, so I don't think that they will be able to serve high art or to find a place for themselves the way that Shahmuradyan has done.

I am working on a number of academic and artistic things, which I will tell you about at the right time, when I finish. My life is good. My apartment is comfortable, my students are attentive; I am training people in the villages to teach and form choirs. And you know that I am not wasting my time. My time is my own till noon, I work on my personal tasks. My afternoons are sometimes mine and sometimes my students'. I suspended half my groups because of the wars, I will restart them as soon as peace is declared. This year, I am mainly teaching wedding songs and a few choral songs from Wagner and Verdi, and also my large and expanded mass, which I hope to have sung during this feast. I have already reached "Holy, Holy" and it is going very well.

The current uncertainty has not yet passed, and I have therefore not received my songbooks from Leipzig[16] although they are published and ready.

16 ["Leipzig" was written this way using Latin letters by Komitas in the original letter] – Translator's notes

I am waiting for the outcome of the war. I will send you one as soon as I receive them. I am sending you a photograph of me with a small memento for you.

I wish you success and wellbeing. My loving regards to your father, mother, Charles, Luys, Armenuhi and Shushik, and one loving kiss to each of the little ones.

Regards to you, I remain with yearning,

Praying for you,

Komitas Vardapet

Very dear and respected M<iss> Margarit

Happy New Year! I wish you perfect health and success. I shake the hands of your dear sisters, your mother and M<ister> Laloy, and wish them good things.

Is Mrs. Armenuhi (Carbonel) working?

My regards to everyone, with longing

P<anos> Terlemezyan

Bravo, Panos *jaaaan*...

What about me? Bravo to me too, right?

<Komitas>

165. <ARSHAK CHOPANYAN>

1912. 25/12. Constantinople
Pangaldi, N 83 (47)[17]

Dear Arshak,

I have been planning to write to you for a long time, but I keep putting it off and that is why it has taken me a while.

17 ["Pangaldi, N 83 (47)" was written this way using Latin letters by Komitas in the original letter] – Translator's notes

I have been receiving some information and now know that you are working on something sacred and noble, something you love and cherish, something you have weighed and thought through – the future of the Armenians is the subject of your attention, so you have rightly directed all your strength towards that supreme objective. The Armenian nation already owes you a lot; you were the first person to fully understand that, I order to smooth a path for our own future, we needed to make ourselves more familiar to foreigners, to show them that we are viable, that we are the bearers of light and pioneers in the darkness, that we are builders... If we have lacked in foresight and unity, the reason was that we had not been allowed to breathe freely, even during the days of our supposed independence we were persecuted by darkness and ignorance, by ruins and destruction, by the sword and fire... But we have something invincible within us, an undying hope; we stare towards the lantern of the future, towards the lantern that the Armenian nation had hung—after losing its kingdom and power—on the celestial summit of Mount Aragats, from the invisible ceiling of the sky using an indiscernible string, so that nobody could touch it with a dark or destructive hand, and so that the trace of its light could shimmer on our faces as we imagined our future lives. You were the first who described the creative souls of our forefathers using paper and books and displayed them for the foreign world to our brothers in civilization. You showed them that we, too, are on this path, we have also walked on this road, we have also held a light in our hand. Even though the demons tried to blow and extinguish our lives, it was they who drowned, while we sparked anew from the ashes, relying on the science and education that had originally been ours, as children of the east, though it had escaped us to enlighten Europe. So, because the archetype of our minds and our ability is not unfamiliar to us, why should we not hold our own lantern of light in our hands, rather than rely on the one that is in Europe? You were the first one who invited Armenian art, introducing it to the civilized world... So, enjoy what you have done and be happy, take strength from it and give more back, stand firm, so that the centuries-old billows and waves that rise up as they seek independence do not crash against the cliff and shatter once more, a course of events that might result in loss for our nation.

Let us now put emotions aside and judge our reality.

I think that, unless we take a positive first step at the very least, we will never be able to think of the second one, or have big ambitions. From the very beginning, our country has been a tasty morsel for advancing empires and the powers that surround us, and even now we are in the same situation. We are now truly an object of interest for the Russians. It has been decided that our country will, today or tomorrow, become a part of the Russian state. So we can strive for independence in two ways - although the end point for both is the same, the paths are different. The first is to stick out maximally as a bulwark in front of Russian diplomacy by being self-sufficient and independent, and the second is to rely minimally on Uncle Russia and forge a united Armenia. They both the same thing, but the second can be made a reality by relying on common interests, while the first is not possible. The Russian government suffered in the Far East, so their path towards expansion will be on this side. Persia has already truly been divided between England and Russia. Thus, the Armenians will be freed from the Persian yoke and will join the Armenians of Russia, mutually strengthening each other. Then the turn is ours – the Armenians of Turkey. I cannot imagine that the Russian government would sacrifice its interests for us, since it cannot allow this part to be better off than its own Armenians. So they will always strive to make us feel a need for them (if we do not join their country), so that we become a suitable territory for future occupation – our large massacres are already proof of what I say. And the Russian papers are continuously emphasizing this very point – that we will hammer and forge our independence at the gates of Petersburg. This was what Loris Melikoff had once said, when warning Catholicos Gevorg IV (during the Russo-Turkish war, when the Catholicos hoped for and saw our salvation at the hands of the Turks, and was almost sitting in Etchmiadzin and waiting or the Turks to come). You already know well that this was the main purpose for the union of England, France and Russia. So there is no salvation without Russia. Moreover, all Armenians need to be united under one power, under one law, to grow and develop morally and materially, and time itself will bring us this great independence. If we rush and jump into the second step without completing the first, we will lose everything. Do not have any expectations of the Turks, don't hope for anything. Their brains are like rock cliffs, they are unable to develop, they are only good for destroying and crushing beneath their feet.

We should not be divided. We should not be fooled by various promising illusions from Europe. We have to unite and go down the practical path. In my opinion, the first step is to unite all the Armenians under Russian rule, and the second step is to develop economically and morally on a purely national basis, without paying heed to ideas that are foreign to us and untried. The third step is the Russian revolution that will occur—not one that we will undertake—while we benefit from that process by preparing to go down a nationalistic road, like the Poles did. The European ideas of humanity are excellent and very desirable, but we do not need them. The plants of a cold country would burn up beneath our warm sun.

I have no fear that we would melt under the Russian government. No matter how much we do melt, our self-consciousness has awoken and if we act wisely, we will benefit. This is what I believe.

My heartfelt wish for you is energy, strength and courage, so that the New Year's gift you bring us be something humble and tasty.

With kisses and longing,

Yours, Komitas Vardapet

Dear, respected friend
M<ister> Arshak Chopanyan

Happy New Year!
I wish you perfect health and success to your initiatives...

I shake your hands
P<anos> Terlemezyan
27 Dec<ember>

1913

166. <TO MARGARIT BABAYAN>

1913. 9/2. Constantinople

Dear Margo *jan*,

I have a problem to relate to you in this letter. I want to buy a *flügel,* the small kind, for my personal use. Could I, as an artist, get a good *flügel* through you at a discount, from Paris?[18] I leave the choice to you as to which factory you get it from which one you select. But I like the ones that produce a soft, melodious, calm and smooth sound. So please find a good one immediately at a suitable price and have it sent in my name. I hope you will be able to put all your skills to use to send me something excellent. I can send you the money immediately, buy it and send me a letter telling me how much you want for it, or how much you spent on it.

Our situation is uncertain, it is very bad. Life has come to a halt, there is no work. I have suspended my group for the time being, because of a lack of security.

I have limited myself to private lessons and my personal work.

I have not yet been able to get my songbooks from Leipzig[19] - they have written to say that it is unsafe to deliver at this time.

Shah-Murad came and left for the Caucasus. He visited me twice. He sang – he is the same as he was before...

18 ["Paris" was written using Latin letter by Komitas in the original letter] – Translator's notes

19 ["Leipzig" was written this way using Latin letters by Komitas in the original letter] – Translator's notes

So, Margo *jan*, I ask you to hasten and complete the task regarding the instrument. Lalois[20] can help you too, please ask him on my behalf.

My regards with longing and love to your mother, father, Shushik, Armenuhi, Carbonel, Luys, the little ones and yourself.

I wish you success and wellbeing,

Yours, Komitas Vardapet

<P.S.> Panos sends his regards to you and everyone.

167. <TO HOVHANNES HOVHANNISYAN>

<1913, 27 April, Constantinople>

[Text in French]

[Translation of text in Russian. English below translated from Russian]

We express our admiration to the great poet and noble gentleman Hovhannes Hovhannisyan.

Komitas Vardapet
Panos Terlemezyan

168. <TO HOVHANNES HOVHANNISYAN>

<1913, 20 May, Constantinople, Bera>

My most heartfelt congratulations.

Komitas Vardapet
Father Mesrop Maksudyan
Terlemezyan

20 ["Lalois" was written this way using Latin letters by Komitas in the original letter, the misspelling has not been corrected] – Translator's notes

169. <TO SPIRIDON MELIKYAN>

1913, 9/6. Constantinople

Dear Spiridon *jan*,

This Saturday, I am leaving for the Caucasus and Tiflis. I will write or wire you the date of my arrival from Batum and we will sit and talk to our heart's content with each other.

I am very happy that you have finally married and even brought the heir of your royal throne into this world. And here I was asking myself, what is this soprano[21] I hear through the distant clouds and the Tiflis horizon? Why it was our Tsteban, perhaps a little sneeze.

You just see how badly I am going to beat you up when I get there, I am going to make mincemeat out of you, so that you don't fall ill again. Found time for that, hm?

I read in the news about the music union founded there and guessed immediately that it was you who had moved the musical swamp of your city. And I was even happier to read that you resigned its chairmanship in order to give it a secure future, because otherwise the frogs would have croaked against you. Bravo! My kisses to you, Tsteban *jan*.

We will speak with each other face to face, I am waiting for the permission of the minister in Petersburg, without which clergymen cannot enter the Caucasus. They won't cause any problems, the ambassador was a friend of mine.

Many, many regards and blessings to your Satik (not Arazyan's), who has become a good and dedicated companion to you, and lots of kisses to you and your child. I will come and marry you two again - I don't accept the previous one, that's no way to get married.

Yours, Komitas

<P.S.> I sent the songbooks today.

---

21 ["Soprano" was written this way using Latin letters by Komitas in the original letter] – Translator's notes

170. <TO MARGARIT BABAYAN>

1913, 9/6. Constantinople

Dear Margo *jan*,

Your open letters caused great joy, and even more came from the success that you have had and will have in your capital. My heart gets profoundly emotional at every single word that I read about your activities, and I am happy to hear about the appreciation of Armenian art.

I was able to give only two concerts this year, because the war and insecurity were obstacles to doing more. But I am happy to say that all the diplomatic representatives here, without exception, have come to my concerts and I have been invited by them and praised on several occasions. They are all in awe of our art, and the church where I go to sing is always the focus of attention of many foreigners.

Margo *jan*, I am going to the Caucasus this Saturday to collect songs. I will stay till September, when I will return to Constantinople. If we can work it out, I can come to Paris for a couple of weeks at that time and we can organize a grand concert. It is the perfect time to show that Armenians are a people important to humanity, to show their creative abilities – this is the only path to our future and salvation that I can see.

An Armenian girl from Egypt will be coming over to your parts; her name is Hranush Polad and she wants to improve her voice, so I have directed her to you and your school, she will come to study from you personally. She is a good girl, well-educated and has a lot of love for singing. Her voice is good if the useless teachers in Egypt haven't ruined it; they tend to prefer throaty ones.

So stay well and hopefully we will see each other soon. My loving regards to everyone and to Gavanoz and the [illegible]s.

Loving greetings from your *kertenkele*.

Yours, Komitas Vardapet

171. <TO HOVHANNES TUMANYAN>

1913. 19/7. Holy Etchmiadzin

Dear Hovhannes,

Despite my desire to do so, I was unable to see you in Tpghis.

I have only come here for a short time, my dear. I am examining some manuscripts and collected peasant songs. I have to be in Constantinople in September, where I have now settled and work. I have a school of my own, where I train choirmasters and singers. I have a choir called "Gusan" consisting of 300 people of both sexes. I am organizing concerts and giving lessons. That is my life in brief - my new life.

I deeply regret that I will not be able to participate in the literary event organized by the Armenian Writers' Society because, as I said, my work forces me to stay in Constantinople.

I wish your Society success.

My regards to your family and the people who ask about me.

With loving regards,

Yours, Komitas Varapet

172. <TO MARGARIT BABAYAN>

1913. 7/8. Holy Etchmiadzin

Dear Margo *jan*,

As you can see, I am in Etchmiadzin, but I have not come here to stay. There is nobody who is asking me to stay, either. I am working in the manuscript library and collecting peasant songs. I finished the first task and I will start the second one tomorrow, and then return to Constantinople in the beginning of September to get back to my work.

I just received a letter from Chopanyan too. He wrote that he had gone to the springs. He also wrote that the concerts and gatherings this winter had been very successful and that you and the others participating with you had sung very well. I am so happy and proud when I hear about the appreciation of Armenian art. We should have held this weapon of hearts and minds a long time ago, instead of going for the wooden and metallic ones, which were destroyed at once by the most powerful blows of the most powerful enemies. But the weapon of hearts and minds is so transparent and viable that foreign hearts and minds have no choice but to submit to it. This is a living weapon, whose soldiers are both you and I, as well as all the others who present the noble hearts and minds of their nation, thus moving the frozen heart of the cold politician to look a little upon our viable and useful people and nation, to think about us.

The monastery left a very pitiful impression on me. Its head is headless, its passion has awoken... They didn't even ask me once why I wasn't going to stay, why I don't remain, why I am leaving the monastery... Even if they had poured gold on me, I would not have stayed, but at least they could have made me feel like I had been there once, I had worked and expended my efforts there selflessly. The singing at the monastery has become worse than in a village – noise, clamoring, cacophonous screaming, that's singing for you...

Don't write me any more letters until I write from Constantinople about my arrival there, because I will be in the villages and will constantly be travelling around.

I miss you greatly and send my loving regards to your whole family.

Yours, Komitas Vardapet

173. <TO ARSHAK CHOPANYAN>

1913. 7/8. Holy Etchmiadzin

Dear Arshak,

As you guessed I received your letter here. I have not come to stay, just to work with the manuscript library and collect peasant songs. I finished that first task yesterday and will start the second one tomorrow. I will be back in Constantinople by mid-September. Tomorrow, I will head for the villages. A number of new things have come up.

You have done well by going to the sea baths. They will have a very good effect on you and you will recover. Stay there as long as you can.

I am following your activities with pride and joy, especially in the circumstances when we do not have a stronger weapon than the display of the scientific and cultural abilities of our old and new churches, and our worldly side. Let them see that we are not asking them for a handout, we are coming to the public as a strong nation that is a part of humanity. If only we had picked up that weapon from the very beginning. Instead, we picked up a weapon that those stronger than us shattered. But what we have is invincible and unsinkable – it is the heart and soul of the Armenians that is ringing out as a weapon. Better [never] late than never. Especially when it is the Armenian genius that is on display – Armenian individuals, organizers, singers, musicians, and speakers, forcing all prejudices to lay down their arms immediately.

Coming to the work here, there is nothing of consolation. You know the saying about the one who works his field. And you know His Holy personally – glory-seeking, money-loving, miserly, incapable, weak and a fancier of flattery, easily taken in, not knowledgeable about his work - he does whatever they tell him to do. There is nothing of consolation. The situation is hopeless. He is a toy in the hands of a few people who have taken the top positions from 1 to 7, while my friends have been left without any standing both within the monastery and outside it. One is a teacher at the Russian gymnasium, the other has other problems. Holy Father Karapet doesn't even have a room at the monastery; he has been stuffed into Hussik Vardapet's room and works in the manuscript library along with Garegin Vardapet... The buildings are new here and there, built in stone, while the inner buildings and the monastery are in ruins.

I have barely escaped this swamp, why would I come back? Nobody even asked me once - why aren't you coming back, why aren't you staying? The singing at the monastery is worse than in a village.

My work in Constantinople is going very well. I am training students in order to lighten my own burden.

All my friends send you their regards.

I will you perfect wellbeing and success to your work.
With kisses,

Yours, Komitas Vardapet

174. <TO MARGARIT BABAYAN>

1913. 7/20. November. Constantinople.
Pancaldi, N 83 (47) Péra[22]

Dear Margo,

I received your letter a long time ago, but my work was in such a mess that I did not have the time to take my pen in hand. My work kept getting interrupted by a number of events. Finally, I am writing my first letter today, to you. The series of articles you had written in the pages of *Azatamart* left a very good impression on the people and was the subject of discussion for quite some time. They got to know you, I am very happy about that. Those choristers have been defanged, they no longer have any power or reputation. The things they had written were the cause of a decline. Armenak Shah-Murad was here, with me at my house. His concert went very well, he is preparing for the second one, after which he will go to Izmir, Moscow and Petersburg. I will come to Paris at the end of spring for a music conference, I have already been invited to participate with a lecture. I have taken it on and will speak about "Armenian Neumes and Peasant Music." I had already written that I would participate and requested them to send me the *Réglements*[23] but I have not heard from them so far. I wonder if my letter reached them or not. Please ask our Lalois[24] whether or not they received my letter. If they haven't, tell them that I have committed to [speaking] lecturing on these two topics.

22 ["Pancaldi, N 83 (47) Péra" was written this way using Latin letters by Komitas in the original letter] – Translator's notes

23 ["*Réglement*" was written in French by Komitas in the original letter] – Translator's notes

24 ["Lalois" was written in French this way by Komitas in the original letter] – Translator's notes

A. The Armenian Neumes – our Ecclesiastical Notes
B. Armenian Peasant Music

One more thing to tell them is that they could perhaps grace us with the opportunity to sing a few samples—organizing a small concert—before the delegates at the conference, which would leave a very good impression about our music. If you agree, those of us that are there—you, me, Shah-Murad has already promised me he would join us, Mannik, Iskuk and the others—can sing, and our dear Shushik can play the piano. No? Is this a good idea that I have had? So let us prepare a program about what we will do and get to work accordingly. My first group of students have graduated and are teaching in schools, and everyone is happy with them. This was the reason for the grumbling of some people in Constantinople. Jealousy, jealousy, jealousy, jealousy...

I am working, I have written new compositions. You will see them when I come over.

Many regards with longing to all of you and to Iskuk, Mannik and all those who ask about me.

Yours, Komitas Vardapet

175. <TO THE CURACY OF THE ARMENIAN PATRIARCHATE IN CONSTANTINOPLE>

1913. 27 November. Constantinople

To the Curacy
of the Armenian Patriarchate
Constantinople

I have "replied" with "immediate" effect to letter number 1512 from your honorable Curacy.

If I had any official circumstances, the Respected Religious Assembly of the National Central Administration would have been aware of it.

Komitas Vardapet

1914

176. <TO MARGARIT BABAYAN>

1914. 17. 2. Constantinople
Pancaldi 83 (47)[25]

Dear Margo jan,

I received your letter only when it was too late and the doctor had submitted the paper to the attention of the National Assembly, where it had already been read and even published in the newspapers. But the will is nothing financial, it consists simply of advice and recommendations on the life of our nation, coming from your father's patriotic and practical spirit. The good thing is that everything went by without much noise or chatter. You have no reason to be concerned. I regret that your letter arrived very late, otherwise I would not have allowed even that to happen and I would have asked them to open it beforehand, in my presence, before reporting on it, had there been anything to report, to the National Assembly. Anyway, it seems this was for the best.

We will see each other in a few months and tell each other of our sorrows and joys.

Regards with longing to everyone. I have a concert this Sunday, on the 22nd. I am sending you the program.

Yours, Komitas Vardapet

25 ["Pancaldi 83 (47)" was written this way using Latin letters by Komitas in the original letter] – Translator's notes

177. <TO ARSHAK CHOPANYAN>

<1914, 4 June, Paris>

My dear friend,

I too was taken by surprise, and so I had no time to write to you. I will be reading the last lecture, on Armenian peasant music, tomorrow, Friday, morning around 11, rue Blanche 19.[26]

The first one got a wonderful reaction.

With loving regards,

Yours, Komitas

P.S. Please send Shah-Murad a *pneumatique*[27] immediately for him to come tomorrow to the church for rehearsal at 3 in the afternoon.

I have lost his address

<The same>

178. <TO HIS STUDENTS>

1914. 14/6. Paris.

My dear students,

You don't how uncomfortable I am at not being able to write a single positive thing to you. I have seen a number of people, starting from managers, to teachers to advisers – a thousand mouths and a thousand ideas, not one of them fitting the other. Only one thing is for certain, that the Scola Cantorum,[28] whose manager is d'Endy, is full of talentless and horrible teachers,

26 [The address was written by Komitas in French] – Translator's notes

27 [The word "pneumatique" was written by Komitas in French] – Translator's notes

28 [The words "Scola Cantorum" were written by Komitas using Latin letters] – Translator's notes

while the *Conservatoire*[29] is so narrowed by some of its rules that it is accessible to very few people. But there is one thing that might be possible, and my friends will be working on it. That is that it might be possible to enter the *Conservatoire* as an independent auditor and to benefit from its lessons. I should be able to get permission for that. But at the same time, if you can locate a reputed choirmaster and organize yourself to get group lessons from him, that would be much more suitable. The conference just ended today, but I have been chosen a member of the executive committee, so my work will continue as before.

I have spoken also about forming a choir at the church and giving you a monthly stipend, but the locals are peddlers, let's see what they will decide, they have not given me an answer yet, although they are not lacking in staff.

There is no point in you coming before the right time, because the people will be leaving in a few days and the weather here is unbearable.

I cannot write the introduction to the children's songbook until I get to Constantinople, because the work of the conference committee is unending and I am very tired, I'm not myself.

Don't hasten here until all the arrangements have been made. If any of you face the danger of military conscription, then that person has to find a way to hide for a while, or only he should come. The cost of living has gone up sharply, so one needs 120-150 franks a month. If the church gives each of you 30 franks, then it might come to something. But it is difficult to get them to understand something, they are so thick-headed. There are many students suffering here.

They have come and called me to a meeting. Goodbye and my loving regards with longing and kisses to all of you.

Yours, Komitas

29 [The words "d'Endy" and "Conservatoire" were written by Komitas in French] – Translator's notes

179. <TO HIS STUDENTS>

1914. 22/6. Paris

My dear students,

There have been various promises of free lessons at the music school, but without the ability to participate in the final competition, because that is linked to a number of pre-conditions that are unfortunately not in our favor. The other schools are useless and nobody recommends them. There is also another way – taking private lessons with someone. I have asked a couple of people and I hope to be able to have some success on this front as well. So either that or this, or both together, will work for us. Coming to the financial part, I have not yet been able to do anything. The locals have their pockets closed and are untouchable; the people I would like to speak to are not here. I spoke to a few other people; let's see if we will be able to soften their hearts, or not.

Coming to the church, the choir singers get 30 franks a month for full time singing, which is not suitable.

It is the foreigners who are robbed by us, but when it comes to dealing with our own... May God save us all...

If something comes up, I will write immediately. For the time being, I have received invitations from private institutions to lecture on our music – the Armenians of Manchester and the French of Marseille. I am waiting from an official invitation from the former, so that I can go to England.

The weather here is unbearable and the streets of the city are crumbling, swallowing people up. A miracle saved me from ending up in one of these collapses. I had passed before a spot 2-3 minutes before it crumbled and took a number of pedestrians and their carriages with it. The flood came and all of them ended up 8-10 meters beneath the mud. Thanks be to God for saving me from that calamity.

Be safe, my dears, and with the hope of God's help, your problems will also be solved.

Kisses and regards to all of you and the greetings of a *kertenkele* to everyone who asks about me.

Yours, Komitas

P.S. Our ecclesiastical music is also causing admiration.

180. <TO MARGARIT BABAYAN>

<1914, 23 June, Paris>

Dear Margo *jan*,

I have been invited for dinner at Garibyan's today. I deeply regret that I will not be able to stay with you. But I will definitely stop by; I have some important things to tell you.

I will probably go to England tomorrow. I have received an invitation to lecture on Armenian music.

With lots of regards and longing,

Yours, Komitas

181. <TO ARSHAK CHOPANYAN>

<1914, 2 July, Paris>

Dear old man Arshak,

I will come at 7 in the evening to your place. Today is the birthday of Shah's ragamuffin, I think you are supposed to be present and give your blessings too, so that he does not end up like his father... As I said, I am not going to be there and I am happy that I supposedly cannot be present.

With love,

Yours, Komitas

182. <TO ARSHAK CHOPANYAN>

1914. 22 July. Constantinople
Pangaldi N 83 (47)[30]
Komitas Vardapet

My dear friend,

I finally arrived in Constantinople.

I did quite a lot of work in Vienna and Philippe. I spoke, sang and strengthened their school and education. Now I will rest for a couple of weeks. My mind is tired.

Unfortunately, Bishop Yeghishe Duryan has also played a bad role regarding my case during one of the Religious Assemblies. So this jealousy is pervasive, and even seems to be guided by the leaders of the older generation.

What is important is that the Turkish music school will be opened and also has a music department. Cemel Pasha has asked about me in my absence and requested that I keep him informed about my arrival. Perhaps they are planning to give me a position of some kind there, I don't know. I will write to you as soon as something comes up.

The government keeps hatching something and is once again not kindly disposed towards us Armenians.

I was met warmly in Vienna and especially in Phillipe. The whole city was on its feet, without exception, to honor me.

Many regards to "I won't, I won't" and our dear friends.

With kisses,

Yours, Komitas

30 ["Pangaldi N 83 (47), Komitas Vardapet" was written this way using Latin letters by Komitas in the original letter] – Translator's notes

183. <TO YERVAND HAKOBYAN>

1914. 13/26. <October> Constantinople.
Pangaldi N 83 (47)[31]
Komitas Vardapet

My dear friend,
M<ister> Yervand Hakobyan,

You are probably thinking that I left and forgot about you. Indeed, my circle of friends has been broadened with the entrance of new ones. I have forgotten nobody, and it has not been the circumstances as much as my work that has made me lazy in picking up my pen and writing to my noble friends. Very often, I sit to write a letter and each time I ask myself, "What should I write?" and I grow lazy, and then use my correspondence time to further my work.

I am trying to stay far from the savagery of the times and keep my emotions busy with my important studies. I have not been able to start my group classes and concerts yet due to the military conscription of my students, but I have begun the preparation work for organizing a new choir in Çabtus. I am hoping to have the Liturgy of the Holy Mass with our most ancient of melodies ready by the Easter holidays, and I will teach it to my new choir.

The city authorities are about to lay the foundation for a music school where I too have been appointed among the faculty. I did not refuse them, but I only took on the harmonization lessons, so that I can spare and care for my voice. I will send two copies of my photograph – one for you, the other for Father Vaghinak. They have been delayed because I have ordered them from Egypt.

My respectful regards to everyone in Philippe.

With loving regards to you and your graceful wife,

I remain, in prayer

Komitas Vardapet

---

31 ["Pangaldi N 83 (47), Komitas Vardapet" was written this way using Latin letters by Komitas in the original letter] – Translator's notes

184. <TO YERVAND HAKOBYAN>

<1914, Constantinople>

My dear friend,
M<ister> Yervand Hakobyan,

My tasks around Easter prevented me from replying to your letter immediately. I was very happy that you had organized those cultural events and concerts.

You have decided to print out copies of my photograph and sell them for philanthropic purposes – I have no objection. Do so, if you think it will be useful.

My regards to all my friends, to father Vaghinak, who does not use grass incense but rather spreads his own soul over my garden and their families.

Regards to your noble wife and yourself

Yours, Komitas Vardapet

THE LETTERS RECEIVED BY KOMITAS VARDAPET

1. <FROM OSKAR FLEISCHER>

[Original letter in German, translated version is based on Armenian translation]

Translation

Berlin, 16 July, 1899

Honorable Priest

I consider it my duty to express gratitude to you on behalf of the International Music Society for the willingness with which you provided your lectures on Armenian music for the purposes of our society. Your skilled and profound lectures helped us penetrate deep into the music that was almost completely closed to us until now, and it can teach us westerners a lot. The work you have undertaken is not easy at all, and I speak on behalf of everyone who has heard your lectures (including very special people who have reached a level of global renown in academic circles) when I claim that your determined work and efforts have not been in vain. You would have provided an invaluable service to modern science if you publish your works, and I would be exceedingly happy if I were able to support you in that task.

With the greatest of respect,
Yours dedicated
Oskar Fleischer

2. <FROM MAX SEIFFERT>

[Original letter in German, translated version is based on Armenian translation]

Translation

Berlin, 19 July, 1899

Honorable Priest,

It is a great pleasure and honor for me to express the sincere and warm gratitude of the Berlin branch of the International Music Society for the extraordinary willingness you displayed to lecture three times, thus informing us about the history and characteristics of Armenian music. The penetrating view you provided us of the magnificent abilities of a great and developed civilization distant from us, the surprisingly skilled presentation of everything that is truly important to understand the oldest western civilization, your perfected art of lecturing and singing – these are things that caused amazement and will remain embedded in the memory of your audience. With this, you have achieved not just the gratitude of our branch but, most certainly, also the appreciation of the role of your homeland in civilization.

Adding my own expression of great reverence to everything mentioned above, I have the privilege, honorable Priest, of signing this letter as

Dedicated to you
Doctor Max Seiffert
Secretary of the Berlin Branch
Of the International Music Society

1905

3. <FROM MARIAM TUMANYAN>

19[/]3/III <19>05

Dear Holy Father,

M<rs.> Ghambaryan has taken on the costs for the concert and I immediately made her aware of the contents of your letter, she has promised to reply immediately. I hope that she will fulfil her promise. I am very happy that I will have the opportunity to make your acquaintance and talk to you about the opera "Anush." If you can, please bring the notated pieces with you, I've heard that they've turned out very well.

Respectfully yours, M<ariam> Tumanyan

4. <FROM N. GHAMBARYAN>

[Original letter in Russian]

Translation

Telegram from Tiflis to Etchmiadzin
To Father Komitas
25.II.1905
Reply Paid

Can you give a concert on 27 March? We have to rent a hall for the concert. Please send the text immediately.

Ghambarova

5. <FROM N. GHAMBARYAN>

2 March 1905, Tiflis
Laboratornaya 13[32]

Honorable Holy Father,

I have already replied to your letter by telegram. I repeat that, without the text,[33] that is the lyrics of the songs, I cannot begin anything. I have to get them translated, so that I can present the whole program[34] to the governor, we need at least 16 N (the more the better for repetition). One question now, since your choir will consist of students. In order to avoid a lot of transport expenses, I can request a whole wagon from Ivanovsk as if for a field trip.[35] I can say that I received the request from there. But I need the consent of Mr. Kostanyan. In that case, the 600 r<ubles> will remain ours. Please speak to the administrator and telegram me as follows – "request it"[36] – nothing more, I will understand. One more thing. Please tell me which is more suitable – a theater hall or a concert hall, and what instrument you will need.[37]

I repeat my request for you to send the program[38] quickly.

Respectfully yours, N. Ghambaryan

---

32 ["Laboratornaya 13" was written in Russian] – Translator's notes

33 ["text" was written in Russian] – Translator's notes

34 ["program" was written in English letters with British spelling – programme] - Translator's notes

35 ["field trip" was written in Russian] – Translator's notes

36 ["request it" was written in Russian] – Translator's notes

37 ["a theater hall or a concert hall, and what instrument you will need" was written in Russian] – Translator's notes

38 ["program" was written in English letters with British spelling – programme] - Translator's notes

6. <FROM N. GHAMBARYAN>

M<arch> 25 1905 Tiflis
Laboratornaya 13[39]

Honorable Holy Father,

I sent the administrator 300 r<ubles> today to cover transport costs, but if you cannot get permission in Ivanovsk to get the group a separate wagon or "student tickets"[40] I will send a telegram immediately, so that you don't end up buying tickets unnecessarily. The money will remain for the group. You will decide what to do with it.

They say that there is a lot of disorderliness going on in the train system; I am worried that you might be late. It would be better if you left on the 29th, not the 30th.

Please do not forget that the students must bring their pillows, blankets and bedsheets with them - pillows, blankets and bedsheets.[41] I still don't have your program.[42] Everything is ready, tickets are being sold. We await you with impatience.

Respectfully yours, N. Ghambaryan

39 ["Laboratornaya 13" was written in Russian] – Translator's notes

40 ["student tickets" was written in Russian] – Translator's notes

41 ["pillows, blankets and bedsheets" was written in Armenian the first time and in Russian on the second] - Translator's notes

42 ["program" was written in English letters with British spelling – programme] - Translator's notes

1906

7. <FROM KHACHATUR HATSAGORTSYAN>

1906, May 22

Dear Holy Father,

Naturally, you, more than anyone else, would be interested in my progress in art. I am working on it as much as I can and am always careful to paint as attentively as possible. I have graduated to 6th grade from the 5th, they say that they might send me to the summer house. Levon went to tour around the Sukhumi region, mainly to paint, but we have no news from him to this moment. He has not written us a letter, nor do we know his address, so we cannot write and find out what has happened. The conflict is growing more acute here as time goes by, all kinds of tragic news is coming in from everywhere. A conflict broke out in Yerevan yesterday but luckily it was brief. The outcome is not clear but, according to some news, 30 Armenians and 5 Turks were killed. One of the slain Armenians was our *Hajji*[43] from the Museum, who had left on other business and had had quite a large sum with him. As he was passing next to the meat shops, a butcher killed him. M<ister> Abeghyan, M<ister> Altunyan, and M<ister> Mesrop were also all in Yerevan at that time, and they were spared by a miracle and made it to Etchmiadzin. Ending my letter, I would ask that you give my regards to Father Stepanos.

With regards to you, your student,

Khachatur Hatsagortsyan

---

43 [A term used to denote someone who has completed the Holy Pilgrimage. In the case of Muslims, this is the *Hajj* to Mecca, while Armenians in the Middle East often used it to refer to fellow Armenians who had been to Jerusalem. In this letter, it was written with a capital H and there is therefore also the possibility that this was the person's name] – Translator's notes.

8. <FROM ARSHAK CHOPANYAN>

<1906, December, Paris>

Honorable F<ather>
Komitas Vardapet Gevorgyan,

Honorable compatriot,

The <central> council of the Arm<enian> Union of Paris considers itself obliged to express its profound gratitude to you for the valuable support you personally provided during our Armenian concert.

In order to express it gratitude to you [and to make the appreciation of your musical works known to every Armenian in society], the council has decided to allocate 1000 francs [for the printing of] for the purpose of publishing your unpublished works.

We ask you to please accept the assurances of our highest esteem.

<Arshak Chopanyan>

1907

9. <FROM MAURICE BASTIN AND JEAN PÉRIER>

<1907, early November, Paris>

[Letter in French]

Translation

Maurice Bastin has fond memories of the meeting with honorable Father Komitas and is already looking forward to the pleasure of meeting him again.

Maurice Bastin

Honorable Father Komitas, may this postcard deliver the most sincere greetings of your young friend to the most distant landmarks.

Jean Périer

10. <FROM KARAPET PARTIZPANYANTS>

<Constantinople, 12 December, 1907>

<...> Yekmalyan's harmonized pieces, so will probably hear yours too. Naturally, I will let your Honor know about the outcome, although you will probably hear about it from the press as well.

Finally, I will wait with impatience for your reply, in which I ask you to note if you have any particular instructions for singing, or about any melodic nuances.

I have enclosed two folk songs for your collection *Lele*, which you had mentioned in your last reply, so that I may be useful to you to the best of my abilities. For a philologist like you, I find it unnecessary to add explanations for any of the difficult words.

[FOLK SONGS ARE IN TURKISH AND
ARMENIAN DIALECTS, NO TRANSLATION]

ԿԻԿՕՆ Ի ՔԱՍԸՄ-ՓԱՇԱ

Լէ՛, լէ՛, լէ՛, լէ՛, խըրպան է,
Խասըմ-փաշա մէյտանէ.
Օխտը դուրուշ կունտելիք,
Քիրէճ-խանէն կու պանէ:

Մըր խօր պապկէ գերեզման
Թողի, էստեղ կի գեամ ման.
Խոգիս կ'ելնի եուքի տակ,
Խաստա, դիժար ա վաստակ:

Ա՜խ, իմ աղբերք, Իստամբօլ
Կ'ասէք ջո՞չ է, փարէն բօ՞լ.
Խասրէթ մ'անէք, մեզ ճալալ
Մըր խօր մուլքն է ու մալալ:

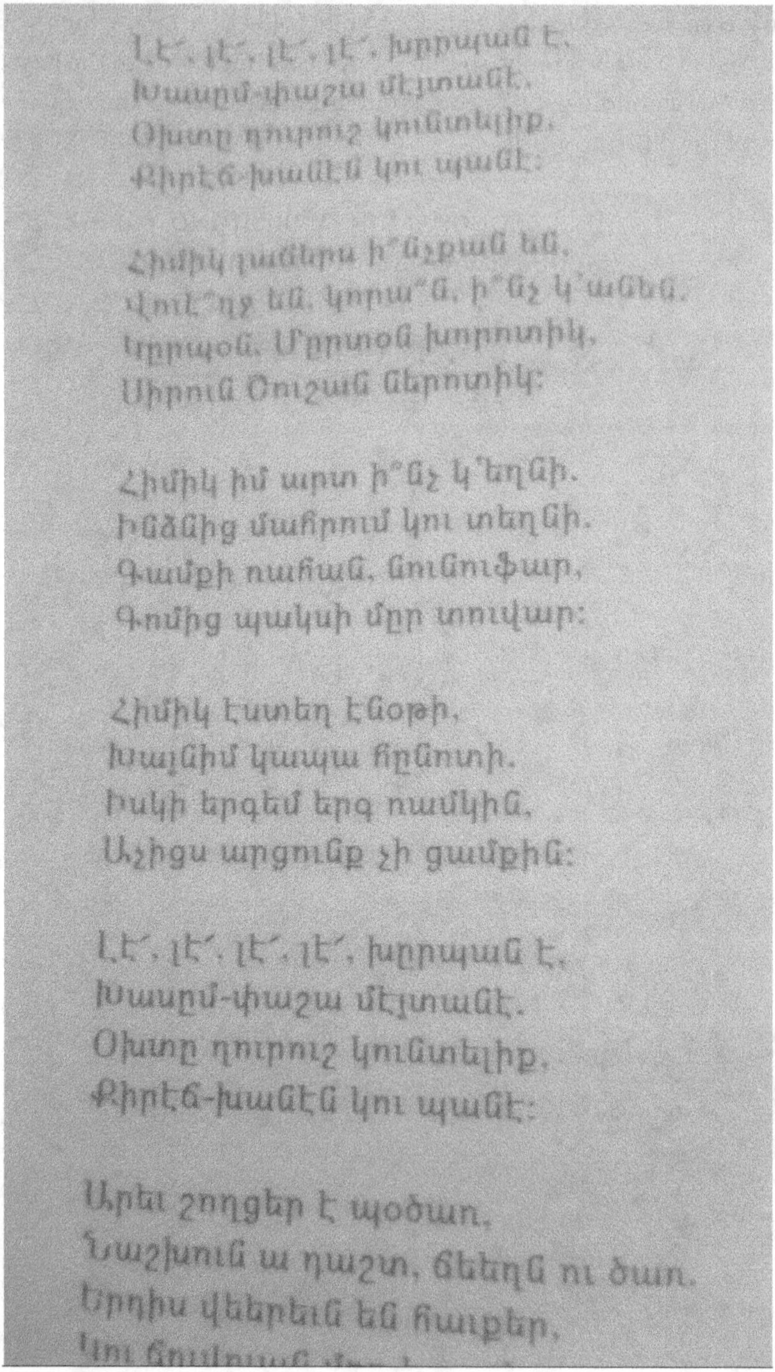

Լէ՜, լէ՜, լէ՜, լէ՜, խըրպան է,
Խասըմ-փաշա մէյտանէ.
Օխտը դուրուշ կունտելիք,
Քիրէճ-խանէն կու պանէ:

Հիմիկ լանկրս ի՞նչքան են,
Վուէ՞ղջ են, կորա՞ն, ի՞նչ կ՚անեն.
Երբալօն. Մըրտօն խորոտիկ,
Սիրուն Շուշան ներոտիկ:

Հիմիկ իմ արտ ի՞նչ կ՚եղնի.
Ինձնից մահրում կու տեղնի.
Գամքի ռահան, նունուֆար,
Գոմից պակսի մըր տուվար:

Հիմիկ էստեղ էնօթի,
Խայնիմ կապա հընոտի.
Իսկի երգեմ երգ ռամկին,
Աչիցս արցունք չի ցամքին:

Լէ՜, լէ՜, լէ՜, լէ՜, խըրպան է,
Խասըմ-փաշա մէյտանէ.
Օխտը դուրուշ կունտելիք,
Քիրէճ-խանէն կու պանէ:

Արեւ շողցեր է պօծառ,
Նաշխուն ա դաշտ, ճեեղն ու ծառ.
Երդիս վեերեւն են հաւքեր,

Ա՜խ, բաշխո՞ւմ եմ, ի՞նչ էրի,
Ղարիպ եղէ, սիրտս կիլէրի.
Լո՜ւռ կաց, աշուղ, ի՞նչ պէտք երգ,
Կը գեամ, կը գեամ, իմ տիղերը:

ՍԻՐԱՀԱՐ ՆԻԿՕՆ

Բլբուլ թառա բանձըր քարին,
Կիւլայ դարդեր իր ճիկէրին,
Էս լէ դուրբան կ՝եղնիմ եարին,
Ծի մօտ տարէք Սիփնա սարին:

Սիփնա սարը դուման մըժ է,
Էս ա՛խ կէնեմ, էն լէ փօշ է,
Կ՚ասեն արախ դարդին խօշ է,
Էլպէթ Նիկօն ճիպ սէրխօշ է:

Էս սէրխօշ եմ սիրով էնջախ,
Քօռ ու ջահնամ էղնի արախ,
Եա՛ր, դիւ մարիս իմ տան օջախ,
Քեզնից մահրում կէնեմ ախվախ:

Մըտիկ դըրէք, բըլբուլ դուշեր,
Քընց զըմէն եար իմն անուշ էր,
Թուշն էլ խնձոր, աչք լէ նուշ էր,
Վըր իւր ծոցի խով մըշմըշէր:

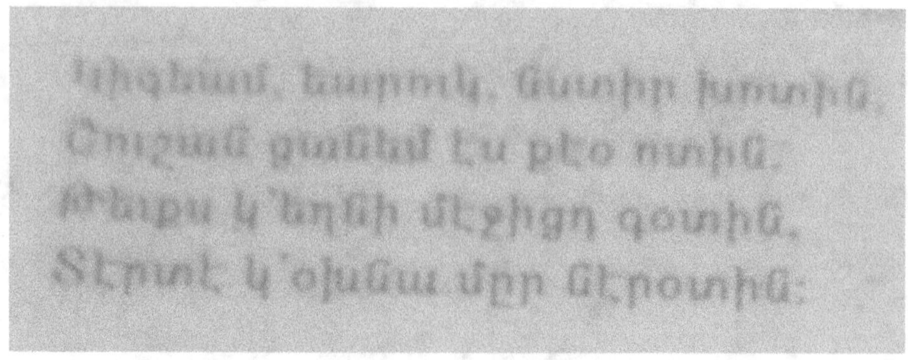

- - -

I hope you accept the assurances of my most profound esteem.

I remain, kissing your Holy Right Hand
Karapet Partizpanyan
Constantinople, 12 Dec. <1>907

My address is the following – Garabed Bardizbanian
Imprimerie de la Dette Publique Ottomane
Constantinople[44]

P.S. – I have now been admitted to the French section of the Public Debt Office, which is the best printer in our capital. I served for more than twenty years in Armenian publishing houses and it pains me to say that I had not seen elsewhere the appreciation for my education and abilities that I enjoy here on the part of the European staff members. Thus, besides a decent salary, my family and son will also be cared for during my old age, or after my death. Please also provide information about your current life, the Seminary and the monastery. The 5 years I spent there being the best of my life, I am always interested in hearing more. I kiss the Holy Right Hand of my notation teacher, Holy Father Ghevond, and give my regards to anyone else who asks about me.

The Same

44 [The name and address were written in Latin letters here] – Translator's notes.

1908

11. <FROM SAMSON HARUTYUNOV>

(from lawyer Samson Stepanovich Harutyunov)

<Tiflis, 1908>

Dear Holy Father,

I am sending you our program, where you can see that your choral performance has been arranged in two parts; it was complicated to do it any other way, first, because you were saying that it is difficult to sing them one after the other and, second, that [illegible] and his wife are going to come for the second part, and they want to hear you and your choir. So please prepare your choir with this program in mind. Because the program is big, you should not give your students the chance to sing solos; we should only have choral performances.

With profound respect, Samson Harutyunov

1909

12. <FROM MEHMED EMIN>

[Letter in Ottoman Turkish]

Translation

Istanbul Chamber of Commerce and Industry,
351

Sir,

A group of responsible experts has been appointed for the examination of the concert hall at the Gulkhane Military Band Institution, and the corresponding payment has been made; we have therefore prepared a letter of invitation to be personally present on this 18th of January, Wednesday, at 10 o'clock European time, at the mentioned institution, to the Mehmed Ali Pasha hall in Galata, at the Istanbul Chamber of Commerce and Industry.

1327 [1909] January 16
Chairman, Istanbul Chamber of Commerce and Industry,
Mehmed Emin

1910

13. <FROM MARGARIT BABAYAN>

<1910, May 15-20, London>

Dear little Holy Father!

What is going on? We haven't heard from you.[45] I am writing to you from London, where I am spreading F<ather> Komitas' songs everywhere. We should have done that together, dear little Holy Father... When are you coming to our parts, we miss you a lot, after all, and your valuable right paw.

I have a lot to write to you, I will write in more detail from Paris.

Yours, in prayer, M<argarit> B<abayan>

14. <FROM GHEVOND DURYAN>

Constantinople, 20 November, <1>910

Your Grace
F<ather> Komitas S<upreme>
Vard<apet> Soghomonyan
From Constantinople

We regret to inform Your Grace that the Sacred Law and Order of the Armenian Church are completely opposed to the performance of hymns from the

45 [Armenian has two forms for the word 'you' (the singular/informal and the plural/formal), like French, Russian and some other languages do. Margarit Babayan uses the formal 'you' when addressing Komitas in her letters, even though the general tone of her letter is quite informal] – Translator's notes.

H<oly> Mass on worldly stages, such as the one in "Petit Champ." We therefore prohibit you from carrying out the first part of your program in order to appease those of the faithful who are angry and we permit the second part, in order to satisfy those interested in your unmatched talented singing.

I remain, dedicated to you,
Deputy Patr<iarch>
Ghevond S<upreme> Vard<apet> Duryan

1911

15. <FROM HOVHANNES MUTAFYANTS>

16/1 March 1911 <Alexandria>

Honorable Father
Komitas Vardapet
Constantinople

I had the honor recently of receiving your privileged letter dated the 29th, in reply to which I first extend my thanks to you for the warm willingness you have shown in response to our invitation, as a result of which you are ready to stay in Alexandria for up to two months, to organize concerts and give lectures on Armenian music.

For the concerts, there are a sufficient number of boys who can form a choir. Regarding your other conditions, we are in complete agreement.

So in expectation of your arrival,

I remain with profound respect

H<ovhannes> Mutafyants

16. <FROM TIGRAN KAMSARAKAN>

To Father Komitas

VARDAPET,

I regret that I will not have the good fortune of attending your concert, but I will be with you in spirit on the evening of June 5.

I heard both your lectures, through which you acquainted us primitive Christians and pagans with the heartrending vocal art of Armenian sacred and peasant music. I heard your melancholic singing as you kneeled in the church, before the extensive altar, and also your lightning sharp speech, which is like another song in itself...

My soul has never before enjoyed that noble and supreme delicacy of art, that profound and sweet Armenian feeling, that you have given us, "may your voice ring out forever," Vardapet.

You are such a wonderful reminder of our former and current Armenian beauty. With a faithful heart and fully dedicated efforts, you have studied, searched and brought to life our sweet spiritual hymns and blessings, through which you have allowed the spirits of our sacred ancestors to kiss us. But this alone was not enough for your burning musicological and patriotic curiosity. You have allowed us, Vardapet, to know and love the fluttering, cooing and charming corners of our homeland, from where you have brought our Armenian peasant poetry out of dusty burrows, rediscovering it and breathing new life into its heartfelt stammer and its virgin beauty.

I said you were a reminder, but you are more like a Cicero in a monk's robe. By singing and speaking in dialect at the *Université Populaire* hall the other day, sometimes amusing us and always engaging us, you took us on a pilgrimage to Armenia, or perhaps it is better to say that you brought a piece of Armenia to the Armenians of Egypt. We would think that an Armenian clergyman coming from Etchmiadzin can bring only chrism with him. You brought the Masis and Aragats to us for a moment. Who said that mountains cannot walk?

We walked up with you to the very summits of our homeland's mountains that have been "watching over" Armenians for four thousand years, and then we came down together to these flowery meadows and heard the sound there of our Armenian springs, with their loud voice, singing, laughing, rejoicing... Well, Vardapet, is this all true? The Armenians of Armenia also have shouts of joy, calls and cheers of happiness; our poor brethren do, we did not know that, the surprise moved us...

And who will ever be able to forget these happy scenes of the homeland that you offered before our charmed eyes through your song and words. For your song, Vardapet, is a perfect painting, with color and variety, depth and atmosphere—the atmosphere of our country—light and shadow, our Armenia... we saw it all.

When you came to us to remind us and reproduce for us this wonderful and familiar Armenian beauty, of which we were ignorant since birth, we were confused. Having now heard the beautiful fluttering sound of our estranged homeland, had we, the Armenians around the world, been bad countrymen? If so, why then did our hearts quiver in their very depths when we heard your "Crane," "Prince of the Magi" and "The Braves of Sipan"...

Oh master Vardapet, what should I admire more in you – your artful voice (**flowing abundantly**, as Koryun would say) or your delicate art, your saturating knowledge or your fiery oration, the charming speaker or the... You are a magician, Holy Father.

I was present at the rehearsals for your concert, so that I could at least partially sample your performance. It was a perfect parade of vocal art. The Armenian spirit is present in that concert; it loves and prays in turn, it whispers and thunders alternatively, it talks about itself. What a united melody and pervasive harmony! What majestic singing, and what pagan delight as well! What colors, form, fresh emotion and depth! But, particularly, what natural emphasis, what flavor, and what sweet inspiration you have produced and blended with the knowledgeable and difficult to digest music of the west. And if the Armenian lyre has fused with western music in such a natural way thanks to your reconciling art, is this not proof that our Armenian talent lends itself easily and deservingly to the west and strives towards it. Your concert is a credo in itself, Holy Father, of the great talent and endless perfectionism of the Armenian tribe.

You, Vardapet, caused a small miracle to occur among us. One hundred and fifty children, who just yesterday could not sit in front of the piano and produce the first note, are now singing "like a choir of Seraphims." It is the homeland that began to beat in the beautiful depths of their hearts, it is a miracle from the past. Who would have thought that there was such harmony hidden in these young throats? Through your spirit, Holy Father, another miracle also occurred here. Do you see how, during your concert, it is not just the children who sing? Next to them, I saw our "young men" too. Those young men, until yesterday, would differ on "issues of principle" and, instead of finding the LOVE of their nation... they would find hatred. Through the power of your violin bow—I should actually have said through the enchantment of your flute—they have been calmed, "lowered from anger" as you might like to say yourself. And for the first time, they stand together for that "first song," singing with each other in unison and harmony. Bless this musically talented army, Holy Father, this is the first trace of Armenian unity, for which we are in your debt. The old saying goes, "Words do not make action." This is true, but you have even led to song becoming action. Didn't I say you were a magician?

But you are also a harp, in particular, on which the soul of the centuries-old Armenians play their mysterious tunes. You are, therefore, a "chosen" one, more than a clergyman. If you had acted proud because of it, you would have sinned, for the lyre you write is not your own. It is a rustic tradition handed to our tribe by peasant singers, which you have had the good fortune to keep and preserve, in your chosen hands. And your duty is to care for and guard them; they are a national heritage, they are Armenian property.

Go forth with that sacred tradition in your hands, Holy Father, go forth into the entire world, may your lyre ring out to our estranged Armenians, who have only heard of Alishan between the nightingale of Avarayr and today. That nightingale has perched on our date trees now.

See, Vardapet, what a simple patriotic excitement you caused in our sluggish souls. We lived through a few brilliant weeks of the homeland through you. You, Holy Father, gave us Armenia as our "communion."

Fourteen centuries ago, your meritorious and glorious spiritual brothers, Yeghishe and Khorenatsi, Yeznik and Koryun, as well as others, came to Alexandria with "perpetual wisdom" in the words of the historian himself. And you, like them, came in this same direction like a messenger of good news. Should I see a connection here? They serenaded "for the glory of the Armenian lands," they eulogized, they sang. Continue, Vardapet, and go forth with this golden voice and deliver the good news of Armenia's valuable beauty to the dispersed Armenians, whose religion of patriotism you will revive. Any Armenian who hears you will have a reason to be proud of his nation. You are like a town crier for our whole nation.

And if, one day, you decide to seek the restoring sources of the homeland to revive yourself after singing and charming, touching and moving others, I have two things to beseech of you, Vardapet. First, please bow on our behalf before the grave of the blessed musician Yeremia, one of your forerunners who has now been resting next to the Aragats incorruptibly and undamaged for one thousand two hundred years, as you told us with restrained fondness. And then, when you are given the chance to go up the mountain that presided over the origin of the Armenians, especially when you do it "with the first rays of the sun," ascend it and "remember us too," Holy Father, so that you can stand on its flanks and breathe in the scent and spirit of its flowers as your voice echoes from it to the Armenians uprooted from their lands into all parts of the world, becoming for us, a filial message of longing.

Tigran Kamsarakan

17. <FROM MARGARIT BABAYAN>

<1911, 18 October, Paris>

Dear little Holy Father! What happened? We haven't heard from you. How are you? Write about yourself. A young man with the last name of Msergjyan came to see me recently. He said he was your student. He was hungry and wants to learn *composition*[46] here. My impress<ion> was that he has talent, but the poor thing doesn't know anything yet. What is your opinion? I think so much about you. What decisions are you going to take now? Please write about what you are doing. I am being tormented, one of my students is going to participate in the *concours*[47] at the conserv<atory>, I am getting another one of them into the theater group, and so on.

Our whole household sends you its greetings and a thousand good wishes. Périer was very grateful for your card.

Yours, Margo

46 [The word "composition" was written in the original French by Margarit Babayan] – Translator's notes.

47 [The word "concours" was written in the original French by Margarit Babayan] – Translator's notes.

18. <FROM G. RÉÏCIAN>

[Original letter in French]

Translation

Alexandria, 14 June, 1911

Graceful Father,

That wonderful concert, which I attended with great joy, simultaneously revealed the greatness of the work that you have undertaken. By reviving our ecclesiastical and folk songs with this interpretation and harmony, which are faithful in the way they preserve the character and style of our art, you have restored and consolidated within us the adoration towards our glorious past. I am writing to confirm, graceful Father, the appreciation that I have for the material you have tastefully selected and sent to me. I have promised myself to focus my attention on those beautiful songs as often as possible. They are full of uncomplicated simplicity, but at the same time are not devoid of any profundity of emotions, which have breathed life into them and which reflect the spirit of a whole nation, its ability to love, suffer... and hope.

So, graceful Father, along with my gratitude, I send you the assurances of my highest esteem.

To graceful Father Komitas

G. Réïcian

1912

19. <FROM AVETIS AHARONYAN, GASPAR IPEKYAN, Y. HAMAMCHYAN, HAKOB GYURJYAN>

28 February, evening, 12 o'clock, Paris <1912>

My amazement, love and greetings from the distant west to the wonderful and greatly majestic poet Siamanto, and F<ather> Komitas Vardapet, who holds the holy and tear-filled soul of the Armenian people in his hands.

A<vetis> Aharonyan

We have a "brother" in Paris, my dear Siamanto, and a lyre – Father Komitas.

Gaspar Ipekyan

We are waiting for "Care and Love"

Y. Hamamchyan

We recall our dear friends at the small hall of the d'Anquerre in Paris and regret that they are not hear with us.

H<akob> Gyurjyan (sculptor)

20. <FROM MARGARIT BABAYAN>

<1912, 21 July, Paris>

Dear little Holy Father,

How happy I was to receive your card! How I wanted to see you. I am very happy and grateful about the songs.

Lately, I have been very tired and sick, and these days I am going to our naughty little Bay View[48]—do you remember it?—in order to relax completely and regain my strength. I don't think that you will return to Constantinople so soon. Karapet Kostanyan will stay for another week in Villa Bethilden[49] in Viltungen. I wish you a lot of success, dear little Holy Father, you little monkey; and don't forget your Margo.

I would be very happy to receive the notes.

I sent you a card in Berlin, but I suppose it never reached you.

My whole family asks about you often, they send you greetings.

Ipik graduated with flying colors.

Everyone at home is ill with the *grippe*,[50] as am I. We are taking care of each other, as we are all ill.

I mention our address in England here again –

Bay-View

Shanclin, Angleterre[51]

Give me some news about yourself

<Margarit Babayan>

21. <FROM MARGARIT BABAYAN>

<1912, 23 July, Paris>

Dear little Holy Father, you little monkey, "immediate Ipik" is with me, I am going to our White island today, send the notes there, I await them

48 [The words "Bay View" were written in English by Margarit Babayan] – Translator's notes.

49 [The words "Villa Bethilden" were written in English by Margarit Babayan] – Translator's notes.

50 [The word "*grippe*" ("influenza") was written in the original French by Margarit Babayan] – Translator's notes.

51 [The text in italics in these two rows was written using Latin letters and has been reproduced as in the original, although Shanklin is misspelled] – Translator's notes

impatiently. How are you, little Holy Father? Write something about yourself, how I would have liked to be with you now...

Yours in prayer, Margo

Dear Holy Father *jan*. I have graduated and am going to Egypt in 2 days. Perhaps I will come to Constantinople from there, or perhaps I will stay in Alexandria. My heartfelt kisses and wishes of success for your new endeavors. Kisses.

Gaspar Ipekyan

22. <FROM KARAPET KOSTANYAN>

24/VII. <1>912 <Berlin>

Dear Father Komitas,

Greta had mentioned to us that you are in Leipzig. My wife and I were very pleased to receive your postcard. That means you have not forgotten us. My wife joins me in sending you our greetings and says that we will leave here in a few days. Perhaps we will pass through Leipzig and meet; if not, you are welcome to visit us in Berlin.

Yours, K<arapet> Kostanyants

23. <FROM MARGARIT BABAYAN>

<3 November, 1912, Geneva>

Dear little Holy Father,

A heartfelt memento from Geneva. My thoughts are with you, all of you, I am thinking of all of you very much. May God be with you!

I am singing the Mass here in their main cathedral and then returning to Paris the same evening.

I haven't heard from you in months. How are you?

Yours always, Margo

1913

24. <FROM MARGARIT BABAYAN>

<1913, 10 April, Paris>

Dear Holy Father, I am moved and consoled by the lines you wrote in your letter. We are now sitting in a café[52] together listening to non-Armenian music and thinking about Armenian music and you.

Margo

Dear Vardapet

Iskuhi <signature>

Greetings to you and the other one – Terlemez

S. Yervandyan
A. Yervandyan

52 [The word "café" was written in the original French by Margarit Babayan] – Translator's notes.

Let's leave these monkeys to us while you have all the swans and beautiful lakes in the world. We know that you will leave us our "share"...

Have you received my letter, little Holy Father?

My heartfelt greetings to our Mannik, Siamanto, and Terlemezyan, and profound gratitude, sweet memories...

25. <FROM THE PARIS DEPARTMENT OF THE INTERNATIONAL MUSIC SOCIETY>

<1913, 18 August, Paris>

[Original letter in French]

Translation

FROM THE PARIS DEPARTMENT OF THE
INTERNATIONAL MUSIC SOCIETY
19, LA BO□TIE Street, Phone. 598.12

PARIS CONGRESS
1914

Honorary President – Henry ROUJON
President – Louis BARTHOU
Vice-Presidents – H. DEUTSCH DE LA MEURTHE
J. ECORCHEVILLE
PROF. GARIEL
Secretary General – J. CHANTAVOINE
Assistant Secretary – A. GADAVE

Dear Sir and colleague,

We have the honor of inviting you to participate in the Congress organized by our Society, which will take place in Paris from 2 to 8 June 1914. The Congress will include the following sections–

1. Non-religious History	–	Mr. André Pirro (31, Vaneau Street, Paris) Messrs. Brenet and J. Tiersot
2. Religious History	–	Mr. A. Gastoué (52, Vavin Street, Paris) Mr. P. Raugel
3. Esthetics	–	Mr. L. Dauriac (8, Nouvelle Paris Street) Mr. Poirée
4. Ethnology	–	Mr. L. Laloy (17 bis, Capucins, Bellevue (Seine & Oise)
5. Acoustics	–	Mr. Gabriel (6, Edouard Détaille Street, Paris) Mr. Gustave Lyon
6. Instruments	–	Mr. L. Greilsamer (32, Duperré Street, Paris) Mr. Ch. Mutin
7. Bibliography	–	Mr. L. de La Laurencie, (20, Rapp Avenue, Paris) Mr. Henry Expert
8. Theory and Education	–	Mr. Maurice Emmanuel (42, Grenelle Street, Paris) Mr. Paul Vidal

We would like to direct your attention to the specific topics which we would like to present for discussion at the Congress –

1. All the issues that define the borders of music and distinguish it from other areas (science and art).
2. All the issues that relate to the interaction between French and foreign music over the course of the history of music.

We would be happy if we could get confirmation of your participation, and we request you to inform us the sector in whose work you would like to participate with a separate lecture.

The agenda for the Congress will be sent to you later, based on your reply.

Respectfully yours,

President of the Paris department

J. Ecorcheville

26. <FROM ARCHBISHOP ZAVEN>

The Armenian Patriarchate
Constantinople
Constantinople, 14 November, 1913

S<ir>

The Jubilee Organization Committee has invited a special meeting next Monday, 18 November, at 3 o'clock in the afternoon at the Galatia Parliament.

We therefore ask you in your nobility to please definitely be present at the decided time, so that it would be possible to complete the work and present the report and accounts to the National Central Administration.

We remain in prayer,

Patriarch of the Armenians of Turkey
Archbishop Zaven

27. <FROM THE EDUCATION COUNCIL OF THE NATIONAL CENTRAL ADMINISTRATION>

The Armenian Patriarchate
Education Council
National Central Administration

Constantinople,
13 Dec<ember> 1913

Your Grace, Father Komitas Vardapet,

Taking into account the mandatory requirement for the review and improvement of the special education program in our national schools, our council has found it necessary to conduct this important work through the organization of a committee, with relevant people to supervise each subject by preparing the special program over seven years in their area.

Thus, our council found it necessary to hand the care of the special program for music to Your Holiness, knowing well your achievements and skills in that area, and we therefore request you to please conduct this work either on your own, or with the participation or advice of individuals you consider appropriate if you find it necessary, and provide it to us by January 15 at the latest.

Along with this letter, we are sending you a copy each of the old academic program and the new organizational statute, as well as an academic program that had previously been considered for your subject, to facilitate the process.

Confident that you will acquiesce to take on this important work and thus provide your valuable support to the sphere of education for the benefit of all, we thank you in advance and remain respectfully

Representatives of the Educat<ion> Council

Undersecretary H. S. Chelalyan
Chairman M. Nalbandyan

MUSIC PROGRAM

7-9 Years Old
Learning simple ecclesiastical and school songs verbally.

Arm<enian> Notation
9-11 Years Old

Basics of Arm<enian> notation. Notes and pitches. Duratio marks, exercises using whole notes, half notes, quarter notes, dotted eighth notes, eighth notes, and sixteenth notes. Signs for rest. Learning hymns from the H<oly> Mass verbally.

11-13 Years Old

Hymns of medium difficulty, Half-tones and their application. Brief information on the eight-mode system. Notation of regular hymns and singing them. Reading the notes for celebratory hymns.

13-15 Years Old

Advanced hymns.

Largo tempo. Exercises with durations of dotted thirty-second, thirty-two-second and sixty-fourth notes. The eight-mode and its expanded usage. The process used for modulated types of hymns. Writing notes for and singing *taghs*[53] and melodies.

European Notation

9-11 Years Old

Basics of Europ<ean> notation. Notes, G-clef. Recognizing pitches. Durations of the notes and their signs. Double, triple, and quadruple tempo. Rest signs. Reading notes for duration and conducting (without singing).

11-13 Years Old

Hymns from previous course.

53 ["Embellished hymns"] – Translator's notes.

Solfegio exercises. Major scale, minor scale. Half tones. Chromatic signs. Reading and solmization of musical pieces (in one and two voices). 3/8, 6/8 and so on, introduction of compounds tempos.

13-15 Years Old

Hymns from the previous course.

F clef. Writing a musical piece with different notes. Reading and solmization of musical pieces (in three and four voices)

1914

28. <FROM PANOS TERLEMEZYAN>

9 May 1914 Constantinople

Dear Holy Father,

I have received your card; I am well and am preparing to take a trip, probably towards Van. M<ister> Portugalyan is still with us, he sends his regards. My greetings to my friends, and kisses to you.

P<anos> Terlemezyan

Mrs. Jalti's address is 201 Boulevarde Péreire Paris[54]

29. <FROM THE PARIS DEPARTMENT OF THE INTERNATIONAL MUSIC SOCIETY>

[Original letter in French]

Translation

FROM THE PARIS DEPARTMENT OF THE
INTERNATIONAL MUSIC SOCIETY
19, LA BOËTIE Street, Phone. 598.12

PARIS CONGRESS
1914

54 [The address was written in French] – Translator's notes

Honorary President – Henry ROUJON
President – Louis BARTHOU
Vice-Presidents – H. DEUTSCH DE LA MEURTHE
J. ECORCHEVILLE
PROF. GARIEL
Secretary General – J. CHANTAVOINE
Assistant Secretary – A. GADAVE

Paris, 20 May, 1914

Sirs,

As you know, our Society is organizing a large conference in Paris dedicated to the history of musicology and music from June 1 to 11 this year.

The conference will include various performances of spiritual music, the first of which will be of Catholic spiritual music in one of Paris' churches, the second will display Protestant Huguenot music at the Cathedral on Requépine Street. We are very touched, with the grace of your loving benevolence, to invite our attendees to a religious ceremony at the Armenian Church, benefitting from the arrival in Paris of one of our well-known members, Holy Father Komitas. Holy Father Kibaryan and Holy Father Komitas have agreed on the details of the ceremony.

Hoping for a positive response, Sirs, we ask that you accept the assurances of our highest esteem.

<signature>

30. <FROM THE PARIS DEPARTMENT OF THE INTERNATIONAL MUSIC SOCIETY>

[Original letter in French]

Translation

FROM THE PARIS DEPARTMENT OF THE
INTERNATIONAL MUSIC SOCIETY
19, LA BOËTIE Street, Phone. 598.12

PARIS CONGRESS
1914

Honorary President – Henry ROUJON
President – Louis BARTHOU
Vice-Presidents – H. DEUTSCH DE LA MEURTH
J. ECORCHEVILLE
PROF. GARIEL
Secretary General – J. CHANTAVOINE
Assistant Secretary – A. GADAVE

Paris, 8 June, 1914

We have the honor of informing you that we will be gathering to discuss the constitution of the Folklore Commission on Wednesday, 10 June, at 4 o'clock in the main office on LA BOËTIE Street 29.

Professor GARIEL
Maurice EMMANUEL
Louise LALOY
Gabriel LEFEUVE
Julien TIERSOT
Henry EXPERT

31. <FROM TIRUHI KOSTANYANTS>

VII/5 <1>914 Vienna[55]

A special thanks to Father Komitas for the letter. The same to you, my dearest ones, Gret-Ams-Shushik, for remembering us. Many greetings with longing to you along with the Holy Father. May God allow us to meet soon.

Always yours, T<iruhi> K<ostanyants>

55 [In the original letter, the city name is written in Germany as "Wien"] – Translator's notes

Special greetings for beautiful Vienna.

Always respectfully yours and forever remembering you, Tir<uhi> Kostanyants.

Please give this to Father Komitas.

1919

32. <FROM GRIGOR VARDAPET HOVSEPYAN>

Smyrna, 10 Dec<ember> 1919

Your Grace,
F<ather> Komitas Vardapet Gevorgyan Soghomonyan

Your G<race> and my brother in Christ

You will probably not be able to understand who I am from my signature, so I feel that I should first introduce myself. I am a resident of Constantinople's Gürü Çeşme district, the third son, Grigor, of a countryman of yours and very much a relative, Mr. Karapet Hovsepyan. The one you used to refer to by saying "Old man Geogor ran away" and "*Zmbl Toros*."

I had managed to disseminate in Constantinople to the best of my abilities the Armenian spiritual and folk music you had collected and composed, even during the most horrible period of the war. With the intention to work in the regions as well, I was called to fill the position of gen<eral> choirmaster for Smyrna where, by the grace of God, after finding quite a bit of success, it seemed like I was ordered all of a sudden to serve the church in order to work with you, your majestic and immense works, and thus to fulfil my debt as a student.

Therefore, I was full of enthusiasm and got ordained as a priest while retaining my old name, so I am now called Grigor Vardapet. I am now undergoing my forty-day period of renunciation, after the completion of which I plan to organize a peasant music concert, which I hope will end up being successful, through your paternal prayer.

Inspired by the faith from which a bit the size of a mustard seed can move huge mountains, I am sure that, after you read this letter and are informed of the situation, a big revolution will take place in your body which will immediately be followed by a complete recovery, by the grace of Our Lord Jesus Christ.

Armenia has taken shape already. That day which we dreamed about has finally arrived and the time has come for you to make a reality all the wonderful plans that you mentioned on multiple occasions during our walks along the hills of Gürü Çeşme.

So wake up, Holy Father, get yourself together, and send me news immediately, so that I can hasten to you and we can start the work commanded by God.

I place a filial kiss on your H<oly> Right Hand

Grigor Vardapet

UNDATED LETTERS

33. <FROM HAKOB HARUTYUNYANTS>

Respected Holy Father,

When I had told you that I would be able to rent a piano in Sarygamish and practice music, it turned out to be false. I said all that based on a letter that they had written from over there in order to trick me and bring me over. I am in an unenviable situation now, especially from a moral point of view. The people who tricked me did so to further their own interests. It is now very difficult for me therefore, from a moral point of view, to live in their house, but I currently have no possibility of living anywhere else. I plan on going to the homeland soon, if the political situation there is good. What do you advise? If I go, I will have the opportunity to notate many songs and send them to you. I have notated 2-3 dance songs (solo dances) at the moment. The first is called "Pululik", its tempo is *Vivo*, neither very soft, nor very loud, with graceful movements. It's time is 12/8

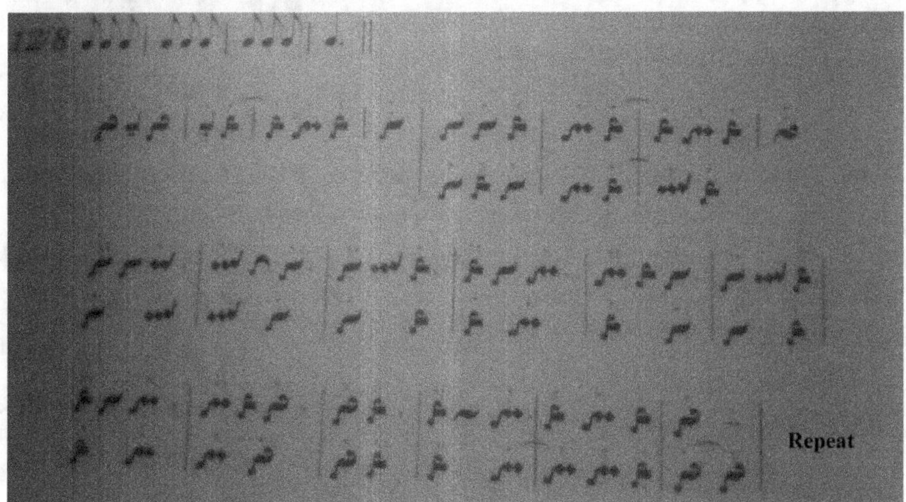

The second dance is called "Galalin" and is also sung with lyrics, but the melody is the same in both cases. It is sung in 3/8 *allegro*, more soft than loud.

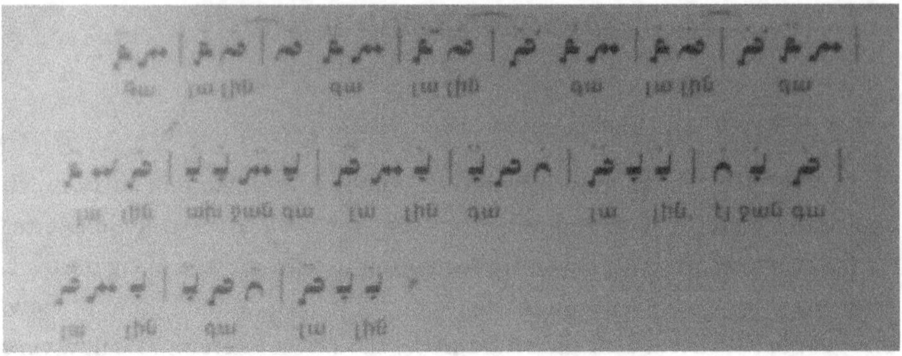

The last piece (from # to #) should be repeated and then the whole should be completed.

The third one is called “Dzor”, 6/8, joyful

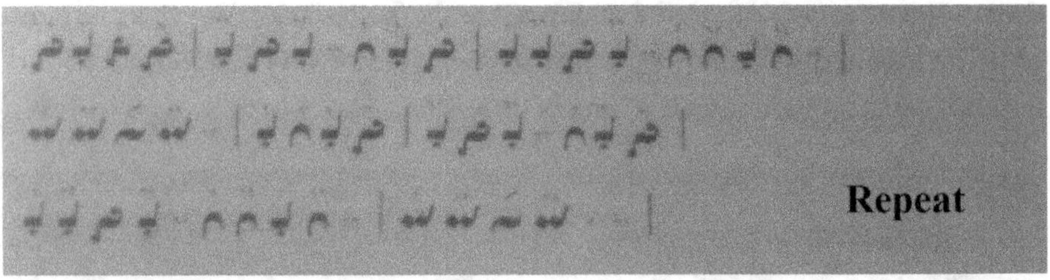

Repeat

What happened to your plans, were they accepted? What do you plan to do and when? Are you leaving, and when? If you leave, please send me your new address. Has Khosrov left? After I receive your letter, I am going to write you a long and serious one. Write to me at the following address – Sarygamish (Karssk. Region), to Mr. Tigran Aykyants,[56] and ask for it to be given to Hakob.

With heartfelt greetings

Hakob Harutyunyan

56 [The address was written in Russian in the original] – Translator’s notes.

34. <FROM HAKOB HARUTYUNYAN>

Respected Holy Father,

You had asked for the lyrics of variants of "Mokats" but I have unfortunately not been able to send more than 2-3 stanzas because the servant tried very hard to recall (at least this is what he claims) but could only remember this much. The meaning of each stanza is the same in general, just the names of the flowers change and, in part II, it is in Kurdish, arranged once again like the Armenian part# (by flower names).

Here it is –

I. I don't like roses at all # *vay, vay*
Your mother was a thorn # *vay, vay*
χ̇ A thousand thorns χ̇ *vay,* alas
The smell was sweet

II. I don't like jasmines much # *vay, vay*
It was a blue flower # *vay, vay*
It may be blue a thousand times over χ̇
But the garden was green

III. I don't like primroses, they were *deshush* (?)[57] on the hills
They were a thousand times *deshush* (?) *vay*, alas
The smell was sweet.

IV. I don't like primroses # *vay, vay*
They grew on old stones # *vay, vay*
Say it a thousand times
But they were like new.

*V. (Kurdish)*58 *Give me a bow* *vay, vay*
Made from a walnut tree *vay, vay*
Give me a lover *vay*, alas
Who has not yet been bitten (kissed).

57 [This word is written in Armenian letters but not translated or explained in the original, and the question mark appears in the same way in the original letter] – Translator's notes.

58 [In the original letter, the Kurdish text appears after the parentheses, using Armenian letters, with an Armenian translation in the footnotes.] – Translator's notes.

I longingly send my greetings to you and F<ather> Stepan. There are two more songs (from the village of Mastara) but I did not write them due to a lack of space and because it is late.

Accept once again my ward regards.

I remain, with p<rofound> r<espect>, Hakob Harutyunyan

35. <FROM AN UNKNOWN SENDER>

Dear Holy Father

It was only recently, when my students and I were on an excursion to Hamberd and Byurakan, that I found out where you were, so I am hastening to write you a letter full of longing.

Before I move on to the main subject of my letter, I want to let you know a piece of news – music news. The other day, I happened to notate the death lamentations of the people of Shirak, and see how amusing it turned out. Manukoghlyan had come to Harich and, among a few other songs, he sang that lamentation as well as if it were a comedy or absurd performance. And indeed, at first because of its amusing words, it left the impression on me too of being a useless street song. Here are the lyrics:

Chsho *jan*, Chsho *jan*, Chsho

If my Karo had died, it would not have been as painful to me #
If my Aram had died, it would not have been as painful to me #
I would die for your soup ladle ears #
I would die for your peddler's face and eyes #
I would die for your *zurna* nose #
I would die for your ox-shed mouth #
I would die for your axe-shaped teeth #
I would die for your shovel tongue #
I would die for your priest staff legs #
I would die for your tail shaped like a girl's hair #

A villager is thus praising his dead donkey and singing this balderdash about his "dear ones" in a tune of lamentation. This one song truly tells us more about the confused emotions of our wild villagers and the extent to which they are unrestrained—it has reached the limits of indecency—than tens of volumes of folk songs. This lamentation <illegible> has been composed by tetrachord and has a complicated, recitative tempo.

I am not sure whether or not I was able to relay the tempo.

<...>

36. <FROM AN UNKNOWN SENDER>

<3 September, Paris>

Dear Father Komitas!

It is with great pleasure that I am fulfilling little Margarit's wish, who had desired to send you her photograph, saying, "Holy Father, say 'ho.'"

All of us always remember with joy the days that we happily passed together and we hope that we will deserve to see such days again.

My profound and heartfelt respect
My kisses

37. <FROM MARGARIT BABAYAN>

Dear little Holy Father, you probably remember this woman who cried a lot when she heard your songs. She asked me to pass on her greetings to you and send you this beautiful photograph. The other three young people were Czech (*Tchèque*) teachers who had been staying here a few days. So this is our first local society. Our young lady sends you her greetings. With loving regards

Yours, Margarit Babayan

1911, յունիս, Կահիրէ
Cairo, June 1911

SECTION - 2

LIST OF ABBREVIATIONS AND CONTRACTIONS

ACF – The Arshak Chopanyan Fund
ANA – The Armenian National Archives
BHA –*Banber Hayastani Arkhivneri*
GLF – The Garegin Levonyan Fund
GKF – The Gevorg Karpisian Fund
HFJ – The History and Philology Journal
HMF – The Hovhannes Malkhasyan Fund
KF – The Komitas Fund
KKF – The Karapet Kostanyan Fund
KL 2000 – Komitas, Letters, Yerevan, MAL, 2000
KL 2007 – Komitas, Letters, Yerevan, MAL, 2007
MAL – The Museum of Literature and Arts named after Yeghishe Charents
MBF – The Margarit Babayan Fund
MM – The Matenadaran Institute for the Study of Ancient Manuscripts named after M. Mashtots
MTF – The Mariam Tumanyan Fund
NTF – The Nikoghayos Tigranyan Fund
RTF – The Ruben Terlemezyan Fund
SA – Soviet Art, a journal
SF – The Siranush Fund
SKF – The Sargis Kamalyan Fund
SMF – The Spiridon Melikyan Fund
TF – The Hovhannes Tumanyan Fund
VMF – The Vahan Malezyan Fund
VSF – The Vardan Sarsgyan Fund
doc. – document
f. – file
fn. – fund
fol. – folder
l. – list
r. – row

THE LETTERS WRITTEN BY KOMITAS VARDAPET

1894

1. <TO KYUREGH SRAPYAN>

The original is located at the MM, Kyuregh Srapyan Fund, fol. 82, doc. 811.

The letter was first published in the *Teghekagir hasarakakan gitutyunneri* journal, 1956, issue 9, pages 104-105, and then in KL 2000, page 167 and KL 2007, page 197.

Most Honorable Father Kyuregh – He is addressing Archbishop Kyuregh Srapyan, a congregant of the Mother See of Holy Etchmiadzin.

Has received complete training – This has been misrepresented in KL 2000 and KL 2007, with the *grabar*[1] ‘ի լիր reproduced as **1/2** լիր**.**

2. <TO MESROP SMBATYAN>

The original is located at the MM, Catholicos' court, fol. 236, XI, doc. 169.

The letter was first published in the *Teghekagir hasarakakan gitutyunneri* journal, 1956, issue 9, pages 104-105, and then in KL 2000, page 165 and KL 2007, page 195.

A. Adamyan had first dated the letter **6 February 1894**, which was reproduced in KL 2000 and KL 2007, but this is an obvious mistake, since Komitas had dated it <18>94/6/10, that is **6 October 1894**. Adamyan had confused the Armenian letter ժ[2] with the number 2 (ժ=10=October). The fact that the letter was written in October 1894 is also supported by the author's signature "**Monk Komitas**" (which was erroneously "corrected" to "**Komitas Vardapet**" in KL 2000 and KL 2007), while Komitas was ordained to the level of *vardapet* on 26 February 1895. Deacon Soghomon was ordained a monk on

1 [Classic Armenian] – Translator's notes

2 [Also used to denote the number 10] – Translator's notes

11 September 1894 (see *Ararat*, 1894, issue 9, page 290).One of the deacons ordained with Komitas, Deacon Stepanos, wrote the following in a letter addressed to Kyuregh Srapyan on 11 September 1894:

"Honorable and dear Holy Father Kyuregh

Before my ordination, I had prepared a telegram to ask for your holy blessing, but Deacon Karapet assured me saying, 'I have heard that Holy Father Kyuregh will be coming today,' so I did not send the message, hoping that you would be present at my ordination.

I know, o father, that you will bless me now and I believe that your prayers were with me when I was asking the Heavenly Priest for strength and the ability before the holy altar to take on lightly and without self-pity the burden which is eased only for those *vardapets* who love the Cross.

Blessed be the angelic Patriarch who consoled us with boundless paternal compassion and love, encouraging us to take this oath under the patronage of the Mother See, over the grave of Catholicos Gevorg whose memory is blessed, before the Father, the people and the just brothers who share our spiritual meals.

The Patriarch blessed us with new names. Karapet remained Karapet, Stepanos became Babken, Soghomon – Komitas, Ghevond – Yeznik, Hussik remained the same, Tigran became Tirayr. A couple of words about work. I received your Honor's letter only after returning from Byurakan. When I read it and informed Deacon Karapet that I will be leaving for Yerevan for a teaching position, he said, "I heard today that this arrangement has changed. I think you will be a prelate administrator." I have not verified this with any other sources and I do not know what I should do now.

Of course, everything will be decided when you come, I can only wait.

I kiss the Holy Right hand of your Honor with yearning, and I remain a dedicated son always,

Monk Babken (Deacon Stepanos)

I forgot to express my pain regarding Vahan. We tried many things for him to be ordained, but His Holiness the Catholicos refused categorically. He said that when you are a Bishop soon, he will send Vahan to Yerevan as well and you will ordain him there.

The Same Author
1894, 11 September
Saint Gayane Monastery
(MM, Kyuregh Srapyan Fund, fol. 82, doc. 826).

Archbishop Mesrop – Archbishop Mesrop Smbatyan (1833-1911), a congregant of the Mother See of Holy Etchmiadzin. For his biography, see *Ararat*, 1911, issue 2, pages 87-90.

Ghevond Vardapet – He is referring to Priest Ghevond Hovakimyan (1852-1915), a congregant of the Mother See of Holy Etchmiadzin. He was appointed on 1 September 1881 as the singing teacher at the Gevorgyan Seminary, and was ordained a bishop during the reign of Catholicos Khrimyan on 13 May 1901, after which he held the position of head sacrist at the Mother Church until his death. Ghevond Vardapet "was skilled in Armenian vocal notation and knew the ecclesiastical rites of the Armenian Church and its ceremonies very well" (*Ararat*, 1915, September-October, pages 728-729).

Your – The Armenian original Ձերոյին is misspelled and is represented as Ձերոյն in KL 2000 and KL 2007.

This morning – The Armenian original ՚ի սերկեան աւուրս is misrepresented as ի զերկեան աւուրս in KL 2000 and KL 2007.

To master – The Armenian original սակս is misrepresented as նախ in KL 2000 and KL 2007.

The Armenian original իցեն is misrepresented as իցէն in KL 2000 and KL 2007.

The Armenian original չքաւեմ is misrepresented as զքաւիմ in KL 2000 and KL 2007.

Monk Komitas – This has been misrepresented in KL 2000 and KL 2007 as **Komitas Vardapet**.

1895

3. <TO MESROP SMBATYAN>

The original is located at the MAL in the collection of letters of Armenian writers, unprocessed.

It was first published in the *Teghekagir Hasarakakan Gitutyunneri* journal, 1956, issue 9, page 105.

To the Most... All Armenians – This section of the letter has been published for the first time.

4. <TO MKRTICH KHRIMYAN, THE CATHOLICOS OF ALL ARMENIANS>

The original is located at the ANA, fn. 56, f. 353, l. 15, fol. 4.

It was first published by G. Harutyunyan (see *Banber Hayastani Arkhivneri*, 1966, issue 2, pages 156-157).

5. <TO KARAPET KOSTANYAN>

The original is located at the MAL, KKF, 1086.

It was first published by Gohar Aznauryan, *Sovetakan Arvest*, 1962, issue 9, pages 50-51, and then in KL 2000, pages 76-78 and KL 2007, pages 93-96.

Fault I did not commit – According to the memoirs of Vardapet Benik Yeghiazaryan, "After the death of the martyred Catholicos Makar and the exile of a number of monks who were encouraging us, the condition of us deacons grew very bitter. Some of the students taught by the new teachers of the Seminary, the 'new regime,' simply persecuted us. We became targets of scorn and mockery to them. We were certain that the behavior of those students was dictated by the advising ‘Ahikars’ who stood behind them. But we bore those insults in silence and disdain, convinced that they would not last long because every evil eventually comes to an end. We understood that the advice that was being given, harming the moral training of the students, was designed to drive us out of the seminary, so that we would not ‘infect’ the wards of the ‘new regime’ with our ideas. And we vowed to stay, waiting for them to expel us.” (MAL, KF, 77, pages 55-56). These persecutions and bad talk continued later as well, and “Komitas could not be exempted or excluded from it although, it is true, he was driven by his own idealistic work and did not participate in any conflicts, but continued to be persecuted by the Tsar’s prosecutor, his satellite monks and their foolish brigade.” (Ibid., pages 58-59). Unable to bear the persecutions, some of the seminarians left the Mother See. “That ugly stone-throwing dismayed our new friends – Deacons Poghos, Kostandin, and Grigor, who were like-minded to us and had followed us when they came to the monastery, but now could not bear the mockery and scorn of the new regime. So they removed their vestments and left the monastery for a new life.” (Ibid., page 61).

In the next two letters, which were written the same day, Komitas presents his resignation, which was not accepted.

Brutus – Marcus Junius Brutus, 85-42 B.C., Roman politician, a friend of Julius Caesar and one of the organizers of the conspiracy against him. Tradition suggests that he was the first to stab Caesar.

Behavior – The Armenian վարմունք is misrepresented as զարմանք (**“surprise”**) in KL 2000 and KL 2007.

Whisper together against me – Ps 41:7 – “All that hate me whisper together against me: against me do they devise my hurt.”

6. <TO KARAPET KOSTANYAN>

The original is located at the MAL, KKF, 1085.

It was first published in *Sovetakan Arvest*, 1962, issue 9, page 51, and then in KL 2000, pages 78-79 and KL 2007, page 96.

Which – the Armenian ընդ յար is misrepresented as ընդ յոր in KL 2000 and KL 2007.

7. <TO KARAPET KOSTANYAN>

The original is located at the MAL, KKF, 1087.

It was first published in *Sovetakan Arvest*, 1962, issue 9, page 51.

8. <TO KARAPET KOSTANYAN>

The original is located at the MAL, KKF, 1089.

It was first published in *Sovetakan Arvest*, 1962, issue 9, page 51, and then in KL 2000, pages 79-80 and KL 2007, page 97-98.

The letter you had given - The letter has not been found.

Doctor Babayants – He is referring to the renowned senior physician Avetik Babayan (1844-1913), Margarit Babayan's father. A. Babayan received his higher education at the St. Petersburg Military Medical Academy, participated in the Russo-Turkish war, and then worked as a military physician in Abastumani and Tiflis. He authored more than 50 scientific articles, of which the following were well known in the beginning of the 20th century – "Issues of Healthcare in Schools" (1881), "Healthcare in Kindergartens or Fröbel Centers" (1882), "Modern Approaches in Healthcare and Medicine" (1886), "Consumptive Lung Disease and How to Battle its Dissemination" (1899), "Influenza" (1904), "Ecclesiastical Healthcare" (Book I, 1909, Book II, 1911). See *Ararat*, 1914, issue 2, pages 135-140, *Hay Anvani Bjishkner*[3], Yerevan, 2002, pages 73-74.

I have written about it in detail to F<ather> Hussik – He is referring to Mother See congregant Hussik Zohrapyan, with whom Komitas was ordained a monk in 1894 in the Saint Gayane monastery (*Ararat*, 1894, issue 9, pages 289-291), and with whom he had afterwards left for Europe for higher education (*Ararat*, 1896, issue 4, pages 189). The letter Komitas wrote to him has not been found.

J. Fétis' history of music in five volumes - François-Joseph Fétis (1784-1871), renowned musicologist, founder of the *Revue Musicale* journal (later,

---

3 [Renowned Armenian Physicians] – Translator's notes

weekly newspaper), published the 5 volumes of his work in Paris between 1869 and 1876. Komitas has used this work by Fetis on multiple occasions in his articles and research.

Archbishop Gevorg ordered his people to prepare a room for me at the bottom of the Prelacy – Archbishop Gevorg Surenyants (1847-1930), later the Catholicos of All Armenians (1911-1930). As Komitas mentions in his 30 October letter addressed to K. Kostanyan, Archbishop Gevorg's order has been carried out. "I am staying at the *S<oorb> Sargis* with F<ather> Hamazasp"

M<ister> Makar Yekmalyants – Komitas studied "the theory and execution of musical harmony" (see the letter dated 30 October 1895 to K. Kostanyan, under the tutelage of M. Yekmalyan for six months. The reason he studied with M. Yekmalyan was his intention to get transferred to St. Petersburg, which Father Tirayr mentions in his 14 October 1895 letter to a friend – "Soghomon – Komitas – had written that I ask on his behalf whether he could come here. It is very difficult to come, because one would not get the necessary salary. There is one way. Next year, Yekmalyan has to bring 6 trained singers and one conductor for the church here. Soghomon could be that conductor, receiving a salary of 50-60 r<ubles> at most, if they allow him to come here; there is no other way. So if he is willing to accept this condition, he has to go to Tpghis this winter or in the spring, so that he can acquaint himself with his work as a conductor with Yekmalyan and his choir, and then come with them in May. Think about it and act accordingly." (MM, Tirayr Fund, fol. 128, doc. 30). The letter addressed by Komitas to Father Tirayr has not been found.

Regards to the Madame – Meaning Mrs. Kostanyan.

Petros – It is not clear to whom Komitas was referring.

9. <KARAPET KOSTANYAN>

The original is located at the MAL, KKF, 1088.

It was first published in *Sovetakan Arvest*, 1969, issue 11, page 56, and then in KL 2000, pages 80-81 and KL 2007, page 98-99.

I received your letter of October 23 – The letter has not been found.

At the *S<oorb> Sargis* with F<ather> Hamazasp – He is referring to Etchmiadzin congregant Vardapet Hamazasp Hamazaspyan, who was appointed a member of the Tiflis statutory Consistory through a decision of the Synod on 13 November 1891, while simultaneously being the manager of the estates belonging to Etchmiadzin and the abbot of *Soorb Sargis* monastery. In 1898, Hamazasp Vardapet was appointed a member of the Monasterial Administration of the Mother See, and in 1906 he was made the treasurer of the Synod (*Ararat*, 1915, September-October, pages 730-731). In the archives of Senekerim Ter Hakobyan, located in the Mashtots Matenadaran, there is a photograph of Komitas gifted to Hamazasp Vardapet. "A friendly gift to Father Hamazasp Vardapet, Deacon Soghomon Soghomonyan. 93. 22/9. Holy Etchmiadzin" (MM, S. Ter Hakobyan's archives, fol. 73, doc. 1).

I am studying... with M<ister> Makar Yekmalyants – See the letter to K. Kostanyants dated 9 October 1895 and the corresponding notes.

I have written to Father – He is referring to Khrimyan *Hayrik.*[4] The letter has not been found.

4 [*Hayrik* is the Armenian word for "Father" and was an affectionate way to refer to Catholicos Mkrtich I Khrimyan] – Translator's notes.

1896

10. <TO THE ADMINISTRATION OF THE GEVORGYAN THEOLOGICAL SEMINARY>

The original is located at the ANA, fn. 312, f. 1352.

Segments of it were first published in *Sovetakan Arvest*, 1969, issue 11, page 56.

My certificate of achievement – Komitas' tri-lingual certificate is located in the fund of the National Archives (ANA, fn. 312, f. 1352).

11. <TO MINAS BERBERYAN>

The original is located at the MAL, MBF, 160, section III.

It was first published in KL 2000, page 45, and then in KL 2007, page 59.

The letter was sent to Nor Nakhijevan. "Нахичевань н/Д (Russland). Высокоблагородному Г-ну Минасу Берберяну."[5]

Dear Minas – After Minas Berberyan (1871-1919) graduated from Moscow University, he taught for one year (1894-1895) at the Gevorgyan Seminary and from 1896 to 1906 he held the position of honorary judge in Rostov. In 1907, through a special patriarchal order, he was appointed administrator of the Gevorgyan Seminary (*Ararat*, issue 9, pages 781-782).

Deacon Garegin – As the address in the letter suggests (Archidiakonus **Garegin Howsepianz**), the Garegin referred to is Deacon Garegin Hovsepyan.

Deacon Cheorekchyan – Gevorg Chorekchyan (1868-1954), later Catholicos of All Armenians (1945-1954). Deacon Gevorg Chorekchyan served for many years at the Holy Illuminator Church of Nor Nakhijevan.

5 [Translated from Russian – Nakhijevan (Russland). To the highly noble Mister Minas Berberian."

Benik – He is referring to Vardapet Benik Ter-Yeghiazaryan, with whom Komitas was ordained a monk in 1894 at the St. Gayane monastery (*Ararat*, 1894, issue 9, pages 289-291). Benik Vardapet later wrote extensive memoirs about Komitas (see MAL, KF, 77).

Many – The Armenian բազմասցի (“**becomes many in number**”) is misrepresented as բարեմաղթէ (“**wishes**”) in KL 2000 and KL 2007. Բազմասցի is the verb բազմանալ (“**to multiply, to become many**”) in the future tense, in the singular third person form, and is common usage when expressing good wishes, for example in the Armenian version of Paul’s First Letter to the Romans “Grace to you and peace.”

12. <TO KARAPET KOSTANYAN>

The original is located at the MAL, KKF, 1091.

It was first published in KL 2000, pages 81-82, and then in KL 2007, pages 99-100.

F<ather> Karapet’s advice – He is referring to Mother See Holy Etchmiadzin congregant, philologist Karapet Ter-Mkrtchyan (1866-1915). In 1899, during the time of Catholicos Makar, Deacons Karapet and Gevorg (Chorekchyan) went to Germany at the expense of the Kamoyents Church – one of them seeking training in theology, the other in music. After their return in 1894, K. Ter-Mkrtchyan was appointed a teacher of theological studies and assistant to the inspector at the Gevorgyan Seminary, and he also ran the theological section of the *Ararat* journal (*Ararat*, 1915, November-December, pages 851-853).

Joachim – Joseph Joachim (1831-1907) was a Hungarian violinist, composer, and educator. He worked in Germany and was the founder of the Joachim String Quartet. Komitas recorded this episode in his autobiography.

“I reached Berlin and, led by my friend (I did not know German), we arrived to see Joseph Joachim and to seek his advice.

At that time, this world famous violinist was the director of the Berlin (Imperial) State Conservatory.

Mr. Joseph Joachim interviewed me and then advised me to seek individual lessons, assigning me to Mr. Richard Schmidt, who accepted me in his music school and, after a long examination, took it upon himself to instruct me personally." (**Komitas Vardapet**, Studies and Articles, Book II, Yerevan 2007, pages 48-49, also pages 55, 60-61, 67).

Radecke – Albert Maria Robert Radecke (1830-1911) was a composer, conductor and musical director of the Berlin Conservatory (1871-1887). He was the Berlin royal opera conductor and a specialist in ecclesiastical music (see **François-Joseph Fétis**, *Biographie universelle des musiciens*, page 156).

At that – The Armenian և այն is misrepresented as և այլ (**"and others"**) in KL 2000 and KL 2007.

F<ather> Hussik lives in the house of a pastor in one of the villages nearby – He is referring to Hussik Zohrapyan, who had left for Germany with Komitas to receive higher education (see the letter dated 9 October 1895 addressed to Karapet Kostanyan and the corresponding notes).

13. <TO KARAPET KOSTANYAN>

The original is located at the MAL, KKF, 1090.

The first part of the letter has been published in KL 2000, pages 82-84, and then in KL 2007, pages 101-102.

The instructions for the performance of "The Fire of Your Love," attached to the letter (in Komitas' words, "I am sending it along with a guide to teaching it, so that they don't have a difficult time with it"), have been published for the first time.

From head teacher Richard Schmidt – Komitas has mentioned this episode in his autobiography (see **Komitas Vardapet**, Studies and Articles, Book II, Yerevan 2007, pages 48-49, also pages 55, 60-61, 67 as well as the letter dated 2 June 1896 addressed to Karapet Kostanyan and the corresponding notes).

Two times a week, on alternating occasions, I have lunch with my teachers - Margarit Babayan also mentions this in her memoirs.

"In 1896/7 a young Komitas went to Berlin to develop his talent. He quickly gained admission there to the highest music school in the Conservatory where Prof. Schmidt was a teacher. This name and the person associated with it must be loved by all of Komitas' friends and those who respect him, and here is why.

Komitas received a very humble allowance, while studying music was very expensive. All of the poor maestro's money went to renting a piano and organ, covering the payments for classes and university, not to mention his room and living expenses. He thus barely managed to eat one meal a day in a modest local tavern. His professor noticed that, as time went by, his student grew thinner and almost melted away. Finally, one day after class, he put aside his other tasks and followed our priest, entering that same tavern after him and watching his modest meal from afar. He then continued, following him until Komitas reached his quarters, and he acquainted himself with the landlady. By coincidence, Komitas' room was exactly one floor above the landlady's office. This wonderful professor spent the whole afternoon in the landlady's office and listened to the priest play the organ, then the piano, then sing, until he realized with horror that the young man would have no other means to eat that day.

Let us now leave the rest of the story to Komitas Vardapet's narration. "There was a knock on my door at 10 in the evening, and I was surprised to see my professor on the other side. 'You're here, dear professor?' Mr. Schmidt entered and started getting very angry, 'You rascal, paying me when you don't even have bread to eat. I hereby forbid you from paying me a single pfennig."

After that, our dear Komitas had to accept the professor's invitation to eat lunch at his house three times a week (emphasis by the editor – G.G.) and then go with him to the opera and other musical performances." ("Contemporaries on Komitas," Yerevan, 1960, pages 143-144).

The Fire of Your Love – This is probably a reference to the following section of the "Song for the Vespers" from the Hymnal –

May the fire of your love come down to the earth
And set our souls aflame,
The mystery of your heart cleansing our souls,
And the light of your knowledge shining,

Awakening us from the sleep of death,
Engulfing our minds in your flames,
So that we may, day and night,
Endlessly give you praise.

(See *Matenagirk Hayots*,[6] volume 8, Antilias, 2007, page 379).

14. <TO THE ADMINISTRATION OF THE GEVORGYAN THEOLOGICAL SEMINARY>

The original is located at the ANA, fn. 312, l. 1, f. 41.

It was first published in KL 2000, pages 46-47, then in KL 2007, pages 60-61.

Königlicher Professor und Musik-Direktor Richard Schmidt – Professor of the Royal Music School and Head Teacher Richard Schmidt (translated from German).

Harmonielehre – Harmony (translated from German).

Modulation der klassichen Meister – Modulations in the works of classical composers (translated from German).

Der strange Satz in der musikalischen Compositionslehre - Strict style of musical composition (translated from German).

Contrapunkt und Fuge im freien (modernen) Tonsatz einschliesslich Chorcomposition – Counterpoint and fugue in free (modern) style, including choral composition (translated from German).

Klavier – Piano (translated from German).

Musikgeschichte vom 16. Jahrundert an. Prof. Fleischer - History of music from the 16th century, taught by Prof. Fleischer (translated from German).

Musikwissenschaftliche Uebungen im Instrumenten-Museum. Professor Fleischer – Musical study exercises in the museum of musical instruments, Professor Fleischer (translated from German).

6 ["Armenian Manuscript"] – Translator's notes

Die Elemente der musikalischen Composition - Elements of musical composition (translated from German).

15. <TO THE ADMINISTRATION OF THE GEVORGYAN THEOLOGICAL SEMINARY>

The original is located at the ANA, fn. 312, l. 1, f. 41, p. 14.

It has been published for the first time.

1897

16. <TO KARAPET KOSTANYAN>

The original is located at the MAL, KKF, 1094.

It was first published in KL 2000, pages 84-86, then in KL 2007, pages 103-105.

Your letter – The letter has not been found.

In the diverse layers – The Armenian երկերի has been misrepresented as երկիրի (in the diverse countries) in KL 2000 and 2007.

Wandering – The Armenian բանդխողութեանս has been misrepresented as պանդխողութեանս in KL 2000 and 2007, because it was thought to have been an orthographical error on the author's part. In fact, Komitas is making a pun by combining the Armenian word for wandering (պանդխողութիւն) with the word for prison (բանտ). This has been represented in the translation by calling it "suppressive wandering" – a word for "suppressive" has not been used in the original Armenian version.

In this comedic sea – The origins of this expression come from Grigor Naregatsi's words, "The eyes, full of laughter from sea to sea" (see *Megheti Tznndyan*,[7] Armenian Manuscript, Volume 12, Grigor Naregatsi, Antilias, 2008, page 715).

Because, because – As written in the original. In KL 2000 and 2007, this has been reduced to one "because" (it was considered a careless mistake). Here, it is a stylistic repetition, used to emphasize a section of more significant meaning.

Fire of Your Love – See the letter dated 4 December 1896 addressed to Karapet Kostanyan and the corresponding notes.

7 ["Melody of Birth"] – Translator's notes

The food I eat is next to nothing - See the letter dated 4 December 1896 addressed to Karapet Kostanyan and the corresponding notes.

The 100 coins you had sent last time covered most of my debts – See the letter dated 31 December 1896 addressed to the Administration of the Gevorgyan Theological Seminary.

Holy Father Karapet – He is referring to Mother See Holy Etchmiadzin congregant Karapet Ter-Mkrtchyan.

I am sending you a small article for *Ararat* – He is referring to the article "Liturgical Singing in Ten and Six Voices," which was published in the February 1897 issue of *Ararat* (issue 2, pages 64-65. See also **Komitas Vardapet**. Studies and Articles, Yerevan 2005, Book I, pages 76-77, 469).

In KL 2000 (page 198) and 2007 (page 241), the "small article" that Komitas mentions has been mistakenly considered to be the piece titled "Armenian Ecclesiastical Music in the XIX Century," which was published three months later in the May issue of *Ararat* (no. 5, pages 221-225) and which is much bigger than the previous one in size.

To carefully copy out Samuel Anetsi's... from the manuscript library of Holy Etchmiadzin, issue number 1700 – Currently located at the MM, man. 1713.

The journal *Arevelk*... issue 5600 of the year 1896 – Komitas was interested in a piece published in that issue titled "A Newly Developed Textbook on Armenian Music" where the writer expressed the opinion that the author of the manuscript mentioned by Trdat Vardapet in the 1895 *Handes Amsorya* was Grigor Gapasakalyan, whose handbook on music titled "A Manual Called a Songbook" was published in 1794. Trdat Vardapet had found the manuscript in the library of the St. Daniel Monastery of Caesarea. The manuscript contained information on Armenian neumes and their significance.

See *Arevelk*, a political and national diary, Constantinople, 1896, issue 5600, *Handes Amsorya*, 1895, March, pages 65-68, April, pages 123-124.

17. <TO THE ADMINISTRATION OF THE GEVORGYAN THEOLOGICAL SEMINARY>

The original is located at the ANA, fn. 312, l. 1, f. 41, fol. 17a-18.

It has been published for the first time.

18. <TO KARAPET KOSTANYAN>

The original is located at the MAL, KKF, 1093.

It was first published in *Sovetakan Arvest*, 1962, issue 9, page 52, then in KL 2000, pages 86-87 and KL 2007, pages 106-107.

Geschichte der Musik im Mittelalter vom Beginn des Christenthums – History of Medieval Music from the Beginning of Christendom (translated from German).

Musikgeschichte Frankreichs und der Niederlande – History of Music in France and the Netherlands (translated from German).

Einführung in die Geschichte der Kirchenmusik – Introduction to the History of Ecclesiastical Music (translated from German).

Musikwissenschaftliche Uebungen in der Königl. Musikinstrumenten-Sammlung - Musical Study Exercises in the Royal Museum of Musical Instruments (translated from German).

Formenlehre – Musical form (translated from German).

Klavier (Uebungen) – Piano (exercises) (translated from German).

Moderner Tonsatz – Freestyle (translated from German).

Instrumentation, Orchestermusik – Instrumentation, orchestral music (translated from German).

Page 43, row 11 – ***Singakademie*** – Song academy (translated from German).

19. <TO THE ADMINISTRATION OF THE GEVORGYAN THEOLOGICAL SEMINARY>

The original is located at the ANA, fn. 312, l. 1, f. 41, fol. 34-35.

It has been published for the first time.

20. <TO THE ADMINISTRATION OF THE GEVORGYAN THEOLOGICAL SEMINARY>

The original is located at the ANA, fn. 312, l. 1, f. 41, fol. 37-38.

It has been published for the first time.

21. <TO KARAPET KOSTANYAN>

The original is located at the MAL, KKF, 1092.

It was first published in *Sovetakan Arvest*, 1962, issue 9, page 52, then in KL 2000, pages 88-89 and KL 2007, pages 107-109.

Aesthetik der Tonkunst. Prof. O. Fleischer – The Esthetics of Musical Art. Prof. O. Fleischer (translated from German).

Die Musik der alten Griechen. Prof. Bellerman – Ancient Greek Music. Prof. Bellerman (translated from German).

Allgemeine Geschichte der Musik. Friedländer – The General History of Music. Friedlander. (translated from German).

Musikinstrumentenkunde. Prof. O. Fleischer. – Musical Instruments. Prof. O. Fleischer (translated from German).

Musikwissenschaftliche Uebungen. Prof. O. Fleischer – Musical Exercises. Prof. O. Fleischer (translated from German).

Formenlehre – Musical form (translated from German).

Compositionlehre – Composition (translated from German).

Klavier – Piano (translated from German).

Stimmeinbildung - Harmony (translated from German).

22. <TO SIRAKAN TIGRANYAN>

The original is located at the A. Spendiaryan House Museum, with a copy at MAL, KF, 42.

It was first published abridged and with misrepresentations by R. Mazmanyan in the compilation "Nikoghayos Tigranyan. Articles, Memoirs, Letters." (Yerevan, 1981, page 164).

According to the postal stamp,[8] the letter was sent on 27 October 1897. The 10/12 written in the original (October-December) is an error, it should say 10/11 (October-November).

Today – R. Mazmanyan had misrepresented the Armenian այսօր as բիւր (**"a thousand, many"**).

I received... some of the musical pieces written by your brother, which you had sent me – Copies of N. Tigranyan's "Unlucky Days," "Moonlit Night" and "Come Home" are located in Komitas' library (MAL, KF, 759).

I have kept a copy – The Armenian օրինակն ինձ has been misrepresented by R. Mazmanyan as օրինակ.

The rest - The Armenian մնացեալները has been misrepresented by R. Mazmanyan as մնացածները.

Simple, natural - The Armenian պարզ, բնական has been misrepresented by R. Mazmanyan as պարզ-բնական.

Content - The Armenian բովանդակութեամբ has been misrepresented by R. Mazmanyan as ավանդութեամբ (**"tradition"**).

The discovery - The Armenian բացայայտութիւն has been misrepresented by R. Mazmanyan as բացատրություն (**"explanation"**).

My best regards to M<ister> Yevangulyants, as well as from... my landlady – This sentence was abridged in R. Mazmanyan's version.

---

8 [This and future references of "postal stamp" refer to the dates stamped on the envelope by the postal services of origin, transit and destination countries, not the collectible paper stamps usually glued on to top right corner of the envelope, which are simply referred to here as "stamps"] – Translator's notes.

23. <TO THE ADMINISTRATION OF THE GEVORGYAN THEOLOGICAL SEMINARY>

The original is located at the ANA, f. 312, l. 1, doc. 41, p. 46-47.

It has been published for the first time.

1898

24. <TO THE ADMINISTRATION OF THE GEVORGYAN THEOLOGICAL SEMINARY>

The original is located at the ANA, f. 312, l. 1, doc. 41, p. 49.

It has been published for the first time.

The receipt has not been found.

25. <TO KARAPET KOSTANYAN>

The original is located at the ANA, f. 312, l. 1, doc. 41.

It was first published in KL 2000, pages 89-90, and then in KL 2007, pages 109-110.

Geschichte der Musik des Mittelalters seit dem Anfang des Christenthums bis Franco von Cöln im 13. Jahrhundert – History of Music from the Acceptance of Christianity up to Franco of Cologne (XIII Century) (translated from German).

Deutsche Musikgeschichte (dritter Theil) von Händel und Bach an – History of German Music (Part 3), starting with Handel and Bach (translated from German).

Geschichte der Notenschrift – History of Notation (translated from German).

Musikwissenschaftliche Uebungen im Instrumentmuseum - Musical study exercises in the museum of musical instruments (translated from German).

Allgemeine Geschichte der Musik vom Beginn des 17. Jahrhunderts ab – General History of Music, starting from the XVII Century (translated from German).

Musikwissenschaftliche Uebungen (Erklärung ausgewählter musikalischer Kunstwerke) – Music Studies (Interpretation of Selected Music Works) (translated from German).

Instrumentation und Orchestersatz mit Vocal-, Chor- und Solo-Satz – Instrumentation, including Vocal, Choir and Solo Performance (translated from German).

A. Instrumentation:

a. Instrumentation für gewöhnliches Orchester
b. Instrumentation für das grosse symphonische Orchester
c. Das gewöhnliche Orchester in Verbindung mit Gesang in den niederen dramatischen Formen des Vaudeville.
d. Verbindung des symphonischen Orchesters mit der Vocalmusik in Oper und Orarotium.

A. Instumentation:
a) Instrumentation for a Regular Orchestra
b) Instrumentation for a Large Symphonic Orchestra
c) The Relation between a Regular Orchestra and Singing in the Dramatic Forms of Vaudeville.
d) The Relation between a Symphonic Orchestra and Vocal Music in the Opera and Oratory.
(translated from German).

B. Orchestersatz:

a. Das Orchester und seine Behandlung
b. Der Sologesang
c. Verbunder Instrumental-und Vocal-Satz.

B. Orchestra
a) Orchestra and its Usage
b) Solo Singing
c) The Combined Usage of Instruments and Vocal.
(translated from German)

26. <TO KARAPET KOSTANYAN>

The original is located at the MAL, KKF, 1096.

It was first published by *Sovetakan Arvest*, 1969, issue 11, pages 60, and then in KL 2000, pages 91-92 and KL 2007, pages 110-113.

Page 51., r. 5-12 –

1. ***Musikgeschichte des Mittelalters.* Prof. Fleischer**
2. ***Mozarts Leben und Werke.* Dr. Friedländer**
3. ***Musikgeschichte des 19. Jahrhunderts.* Prof. Fleischer.**
4. ***Das deutsche Lied.* Dr. Friedländer.**
5. ***Musikwissenschaftliche Uebungen.* Dr. Friedl**
6. ***Musikwissenschaftliche Uebungen.* Prof. Fleischer.**
7. ***Uebungen im Contrapunkt.* Prof. Bellerman.**
8. ***Ueber die Musik der alten Griechen.* Prof. Bellerman.**

1. History of Medieval Music. Prof. Fleischer
2. Mozart's Life and Works. Dr. Friedländer
3. History of XIX Century Music. Prof. Fleischer
4. German Lied. Dr. Friedländer
5. Music Study Exercises. Dr. Friedländer
6. Music Study Exercises. Prof. Fleischer
7. Counterpoint. Prof. Bellerman
8. On the Music of the Ancient Greeks. Prof. Bellerman (translated from German).

Instrumentationslehre und Orchestersatz – Instrumentation and Orchestra (translated from German).

That would last long - This has been misrepresented in KL 2000 and KL 2007 as "**that would suffice**" but in this case the phrase "that would last long" refers to the Harmonium, not the amount of money.

27. <TO THE ADMINISTRATION OF THE GEVORGYAN THEOLOGICAL SEMINARY>

The original is located at the ANA, f. 312, l. 1, doc. 41, p. 54.

It has been published for the first time.

28. <TO THE ADMINISTRATION OF THE GEVORGYAN THEOLOGICAL SEMINARY>

The original is located at the ANA, f. 312, l. 1, doc. 41, p. 54.

It has been published for the first time.

29. <TO MKRTICH I KHRIMYAN, CATHOLICOS OF ALL ARMENIANS>

The original is located at the ANA, f. 56, l. 17, doc. 22, p. 359.

It was first published in KL 2000, pages 75-76 and KL 2007, pages 92-93. For more about the letter see *Banber Hayastani Arkhivneri*, 1966, issue 2, page 159.

The massacres in Constantinople in 1896 – He is referring to the Hamidian massacres that occurred in the Ottoman Empire in 1895-96.

30. <TO KARAPET KOSTANYAN>

The original is located at the MAL, KKF, 1095.

It was first published in KL 2000, pages 93 and KL 2007, pages 113-114.

Based on what you wrote in your letter - The letter has not been found.

My predecessor would not have managed over 5 years – he is referring to Gevorg Chorekchyan, who was sent to Germany for musical training in 1889, during the time of Catholicos Makar.

1899

31. <TO KARAPET KOSTANYAN>

The original is located at the MAL, KKF, 1097.

It was first published in KL 2000, pages 93-94 and KL 2007, pages 115-116.

Oskar Fleischer – Oskar Reinhold Fleischer (1856-1933) omposer, organist, lecturer at the University of Berlin, Chairman of the Berlin branch of the International Music Society.

I am obligated to correspond with them regularly– Komitas published two articles in the journal of the Berlin branch of the International Music Society (see **Komitas Vardapet**, Studies and Articles, Book I, Yerevan 2005, pages 107-132, 473).

32. <TO THE ADMINISTRATION OF THE GEVORGYAN THEOLOGICAL SEMINARY>

The original is located at the ANA, f. 312, l. 1, doc. 41, p. 72-73.

It has been published for the first time.

33. <TO THE ADMINISTRATION OF THE GEVORGYAN THEOLOGICAL SEMINARY>

The original is located at the ANA, f. 312, l. 1, doc. 41, p. 70-71.

It has been published for the first time.

34. <TO KORYUN VARDAPET SAHAKYAN>

The original is located at the ANA, f. 56, doc. 378, p. 18.

It was first published in *Patma-banasirakan Handes*, 1966, issue 2, page 159, and later in KL 2000, page 97-98 and KL 2007, page 119.

Father Koryun – This is either the Armash-native priest Koryun Vardapet Yesayan, who was the conditional leader of Marash (*Ararat*, 1902, issues 10-11, page 1127, 1907, issue 2, page 141) or Koryun Vardapet Sahakyan, who resigned in 1906 (*Ararat*, 1906, issue 6-7, page 518). The latter is more probable, since the former did not serve the Holy See and could not fulfil the request that Komitas had made.

Khrimyan *Hayrik* had brought Koryun Vardapet to the Mother See, which is mentioned by Priest Gevorg Shakaryan in his memoirs. "**Koryun Vardapet of Arjak** – A student of the Haynkuysner Church, the son of an Armenian father and a Greek mother, an only child. He was thin and weak, he gained a regular education and became the deputy instructor and deacon of Haynkuysner. He went to Cairo to see his father, who had been living an immoral life there for 22 years. He returned to Constantinople and became the caretaker of a rich youth, then the holy Khrimyan took him under his wing as an acolyte and, when he became Catholicos, brought him to Holy Etchmiadzin, where he learned sufficient Classic Armenian and received the title of deacon. He benefited greatly thanks to Catholicos *Hayrik*, but because he was the son of an immoral father, he too took the same path and was dishonored, eventually being arrested by the Russian Government as a revolutionary, defrocked and exiled to the prisons of Siberia..." (**Priest Khosrov (Gevorg) Shakaryan**. *Memoirs* or *a Family Recording of the House of Shakaryan from Van*, manuscripts prepared for publication by Gurgen Gasparyan, Mother See of Holy Etchmiadzin, 2004, page 67).

Khoren *ef<fendi>* - The brother of Khrimyan *Hayrik*.

35. <TO KARAPET KOSTANYAN>

The original is located at the MAL, KKF, 1098.

It was first published in KL 2000, pages 95 and KL 2007, pages 115-116.

I had mentioned to you in my last letter that I would return to Holy Etchmiadzin in August – There is no such thing mentioned in the "last letter" (dated 19 March 1899) chronologically written to Karapet Kostanyan among the ones that were obtained. So the letter in question must have been written after 19 March and has not been found.

I recently gave two lectures with great success at the Berlin music school – Komitas gave his first lecture on 10 May 1899, and then repeated that lecture at the request of the Society on 14 June at the hall of the Schurvenka music center. The journal of the International Music Society had expressed wonder at that lecture (see **Komitas Vardapet**, Studies and Articles, Book II, Yerevan 2007, pages 57, 62-63).

Which will be published in August, will feature my article as well – He is referring to the article *Die Armenische Kirchenmusik* (Armenian Ecclesiastical Music), which was published in the journal *Sammelbände der internationalen Musik-Gesellschaft* not in August, but in the October-December issue (Leipzig, 1899, *Oktober-December*, pages 54-64).

Do not expect me at the Seminary before September – Komitas left Berlin for the Mother See of Holy Etchmiadzin on 4 September 1899 (see **Komitas Vardapet**, Studies and Articles, Book II, Yerevan 2007, pages 66).

36. <TO BABKEN VARDAPET KYULESERYAN>

The original is located at the MAL, KF, 3.

It was first published in KL 2000, page 44-45 and then in KL 2007, page 57-58.

The letter is a draft with multiple strikethroughs, which are represented in square brackets. There is no information about whether or not the letter was eventually sent to its addressee.

In KL 2007, the letter is dated **January** 1909, because the "Honorable Father" mentioned in the letter is considered to be Mattheos Izmirlian, to whom Komitas had sent a letter with the same request on 9 January 1909. "We are therefore certain that the letter addressed to Babken Vardapet was also written in the same time period," the notes say (KL 2007, page 229). In the letter, Komitas mentions "**A few years ago**, *(emphasis by the editor, G.G.)* the Prelate of Caesarea Honorable Bishop F<ather> Trdat Vardapet Palyan had found among the manuscripts of the St. Daniel Monastery [apparently with very interesting content] an old, Armenian manuscript about music, of which he had had a brief summary [very brief in nature, with mainly a list of the relevant headings] published in the *Handes Amsorya* journal." Komitas is referring here to Bishop Trdat Palyan's book *A Newly Developed Textbook on Armenian Music,* which was published in the March (issue 3, pages 65-68) and April 1895 (issue 4, pages 123-124) issues of *Handes Amsorya.* Thus, Komitas' reference to "**A few years ago**" indicates that the letter has been written "**a few years later**" following the publication of the *Handes Amsorya* issues, and 1909 could not have been "**a few years later**" (14 years). Notably, in his letter to Mattheos Izmirlian on 9 January 1909, Komitas mentioned this and said, "My Honorable Lord, among the manuscripts from the St. Daniel Monastery in Caesarea found **exactly 14 years ago** *(emphasis by the editor, G.G.)* there was a rulebook about Armenian neumes." So the letter addressed to Babken Vardapet could not be "written in the same time period." In his letter, Komitas also mentioned the agreement he had with Trdat Vardapet that the latter would bring the manuscript with him to the Mother See when he arrived at Holy Etchmiadzin to be ordained a bishop. Trdat Vardapet arrived at the Mother See to be ordained a bishop on 14 May 1899, was ordained on 27 May and left on 2 June (see *Ararat*, 1899, issue 5, pages 228-229), when Komitas was still studying in Berlin. Komitas returned to Holy Etchmiadzin in September 1899 and, seeing that Trdat Vardapet had not fulfilled his promise, wrote a letter to Babken Vardapet, most probably during September-October 1899.

A few years ago, the Prelate of Caesarea Honorable Bishop F<ather> Trdat Vardapet Palyan... published – For more on this see also the letter written to Karapet Kostanyan from Berlin on 15 January 1897 and the corresponding notes.

Copy - The Armenian ընդօրինակութիւնը has been misrepresented as ընդօրինակածը in KL 2000 and 2007. Komitas had shortened the Armenian suffix –ութիւն without using a period.

The Holy Father replied – The letter has not been found.

Be ordained as a bishop - The Armenian եպիսկոպոսանալու has been misrepresented as եպիսկոպոսն in KL 2000 and 2007.

I was studying in Germany - The Armenian ես Գերմանիայ ուս<ան>ում էի has been misrepresented as ես Գերմանիոյ ուս<ան>ում էի in KL 2000 and 2007.

My friends and students - The Armenian ընկերներից և աշակերտներից has been misrepresented as ընկերներին և աշակերտներին in KL 2000 and 2007.

I was forced to write once again - The letter has not been found.

He replied quickly and said that he would sell me the manuscript - The letter has not been found.

Please humbly kiss the H<oly> Right Hand of His Holiness – He is referring to the Patriarch of Constantinople Archbishop Maghakia Ormanyan. Babken Vardapet Kyuleseryan was the personal secretary of the Patriarch of Constantinople in 1897-99 and the General Abbott and Leader of the Taron region towards the end of 1899.

I am forced to support both myself on my annual 300 ruble salary and the large family of my poor paternal aunt – Komitas had regularly transferred money to his paternal aunt's family through the Constantinople Patriarchate (see the letters addressed to Maghakia Ormanyan).

1901

37. <TO NIKOGHAYOS TIGRANYAN>

The original is located at the A. Spendiaryan House-Museum.

It was first published with misrepresentations by R. Mazmanyan in the compilation "Nikoghayos Tigranyan. Articles, Memoirs, Letters." (Yerevan, 1981, page 164-165).

The letter was written in 1901, since the article *Armeniens Volkstümliche Reigentänze* ("Armenian Folk Dance") mentioned by Komitas had first been published in 1901 in the first issue of the journal *Zeitschrift für armenische Philologie* which Komitas had received the "other day" and "unable to wait any longer," had torn it out of the compilation and sent it to N. Tigranyan. *Interpunctionssystem der Armenier* was the title of the first sub-chapter in the article *Die Armenische Kirchenmusik* ("Armenian Ecclesiastical Music"). This article was published in 1899 in the journal *Musik-Gesellschaft* (see **Komitas Vardapet**, Studies and Articles, Book I, Yerevan 2005, pages 107-132, 473, 270-298, 496).

You – R. Mazmanyan misrepresented the informal քեզ in the letter as the formal Ձեզ.

Don't think - R. Mazmanyan misrepresented the informal Չկարծես in the letter as the formal Չկարծեք.

"...is a small extract from the big piece..." – The expanded version of the study "Armenian Folk Dance" has not yet been located.

Publish - R. Mazmanyan misrepresented the Armenian կտեսնէ in the letter as կտեսնի.

Dances - R. Mazmanyan misrepresented the Armenian պարերի in the letter as պապերի ("**...has no concept of our grandfathers/forefathers**").

Would be - R. Mazmanyan misrepresented the Armenian լինեն in the letter as լինին.

Anyway - R. Mazmanyan misrepresented the Armenian ինչ որ է in the letter as ինչեւէ.

Are - R. Mazmanyan misrepresented the Armenian են in the letter as է.

Keys - R. Mazmanyan misrepresented the Armenian ստեղիները in the letter as ստեղները.

...Will be printed in Paris is "Armenian Ecclesiastical Music in Eight Voices, its Locution and Keys" – The mentioned work was not printed in Paris. The author's German translation of the original article titled *Die Armenische Kirchenmusik II. Das Achttonsystem der Armenier* ("Armenian Ecclesiastical Music II: The Armenian Eight-Voice System") is located at MAL, KF, 647. It was first published in **Komitas Vardapet**, Studies and Articles, Book II, Yerevan 2007, pages 7-44, 465-466.

(The intonation of songs) - R. Mazmanyan misrepresented this as "the intonation of songs" in quotation marks instead of parentheses.

My studies - R. Mazmanyan misrepresented the Armenian պարապմունքներս in the letter as պարապմունքներիս.

Wellbeing - R. Mazmanyan misrepresented the Armenian քաջողջութիւն in the letter as քաջառողջութիւն (**"health"**).

Is - R. Mazmanyan misrepresented the Armenian է in the letter as եմ.

38. <TO HRACHYA ACHARYAN>

The original is located at MAL, Hrachya Ajaryan collection, 725.

According to the postal stamps, the letter was sent from Tiflis on 19 May 1901, and was received in Vagharshapat on May 21 (June 2, according to the old calendar).

The letter is written in Turkish using Armenian letters.

The original was prepared for publication and translation by Turkish studies scholar **Ani Avetisyan**.

This is one of the letters written to Hrachya Acharyan by Komitas, about which Acharyan had written in his "Memories from My Life" – "Once, he travelled to Germany. I asked him to send me a postcard with beautiful pictures from each city for the album I had compiled. I received 7 such postcards from different cities, which would have notes written on them such as 'Dear Hrachya, I have reached Vienna,' followed by the date and 'Komitas Vardapet.' Many years later, Ruben Terlemezyan received those 7 postcards from me, when he was compiling Komitas Vardapet's biography." (*Memories from My Life*, Yerevan, 1967, page 211)

Only one of those postcards has been preserved in the Hrachya Acharyan album kept at the Museum of Literature and Art, we could not find the remaining six in the Ruben Terlemezyan library either.

This postcard has been published for the first time.

39. <TO SARGIS KAMALYAN>

The original is located at MAL, SKF, 833.

The letter was first published by Gohar Aznavuryan in the journal *Sovetakan Arvest* (1962, issue 9, page 52), and then in KL 2000, page 175, and KL 2007, page 207.

According to the postal stamp, the letter was sent on 11 July 1901.

Komitas had jokingly written the name of the addressee on the postcard as "*An Herrn Surnatschi Kamalian*" (Mr. Zurna Player Kamalyan).

The new "Education Assembly" is already functioning – Gohar Aznavuryan wrote a note about this particular section – "In the summer of 1901, Komitas participated in the congress of the International Music Society in Berlin. He also gave a speech at the first meeting of the Armenian Students' "Education Assembly," speaking about Armenian folk songs, while also performing some of these songs," (*Sovetakan Arvest*, 1962, issue 9, page 52).

The cream of her face – the Armenian սեր երեսին is misrepresented in KL 2000 and KL 2007 as սէրն երեսին (the face of love).

40. <TO SARGIS KAMALYAN AND DEACON NERSES>

The original is located at MAL, SKF, 833.

The letter was first published in KL 2000, page 176, and KL 2007, page 208.

Komitas had jokingly written the name of the addressee on the postcard as "*Herrn Katschal Kamalian*" (Mr. Bald Kamalyan).

Deacon Nerses – He is probably referring to Nerses Ter-Mikaelyan, who later published *Das armenische Hymnarium* (The Armenian Hymn Book) in Leipzig in 1905 (*Ararat,* 1908, issue 10, pages 939-944).

From the pretty young lady sitting next to me – The text of the letter is followed by the "pretty young lady's" signature.

41. <TO SARGIS KAMALYAN>

The original is located at MAL, SKF, 829.

The letter was first published in *Sovetakan Arvest,* 1962, issue 9, page 5, and later in KL 2000, page 176, and KL 2007, page 208.

According to the postal stamp, the letter was sent to Berlin on July 15.

I am going to visit the musicians tomorrow – There is a note about this meeting, which occurred on July 15 ("tomorrow") according to Komitas, written by A. Chopanyan, "French maestros and musical scholars—Saint-Saëns, Charles Porte, Duval, Aubry—met Komitas Vardapet and got acquainted with his program, leaving in awe and encouraging him to continue his work" (*Anahit,* 1901, issues 6-7, June-July, page 144).

D<ea>c<o>n – G. Anzavuryan had read this word as the Armenian որպես ("as"), (the same misrepresentation occurs in KL 2000 and KL 2007), which is a mistake. The word appears in the margin of the postcard, where Komitas could have fitted the word որպես but the short form for "deacon" սրկի is clearly visible, with a sign of honor on top of it. The form սրկ is used to replace the full form of the word սարկաւագ, which would be in the genitive case here as սարկաւագի. Komitas is referring here to Deacon Nerses (see the letter addressed to S. Kamalyan on 12 July 1901 and the corresponding notes).

42. <TO SARGIS KAMALYAN>

The original is located at MAL, SKF, 831.

The letter was first published in KL 2000, page 176, and KL 2007, page 208.

According to the postal stamp, the letter arrived in Berlin on July 18.

This Sunday – that is, on July 21.

43. <SARGIS KAMALYAN>

The original is located at MAL, SKF, 832.

The letter was first published in KL 2000, page 177, and KL 2007, page 209.

According to the postal stamp, the letter arrived in Berlin on July 24.

On Sunday, I sang during H<oly> Mass - see the letter addressed to S. Kamalyan on 17 July 1901.

Our deacon Nerses - see the letters addressed to S. Kamalyan on 12 and 14 July 1901 and the corresponding notes.

The local musicians reacted positively to me - see the letters addressed to S. Kamalyan on 14 July 1901 and the corresponding notes.

Komitas had copied the section with the Armenian musical notes on the opposite side of the postcard, in the left corner of the picture.

44. <TO ARSHAK CHOPANYAN>

The original is located at the MAL, ACF, 3418.

The letter was first published in KL 2000, page 158, and KL 2007, page 191.

The letter is not dated. According to the postal stamp, the letter was sent on 1 August (1 Août). The phrase used in the letter "tomorrow, Friday, in the evening at 5" suggests that the letter was written in a year when the date August 2 ("tomorrow") was a **Friday**. August 2 was a Friday in 1901, 1907 and 1912. In 1912, Komitas was in Constantinople, in July-August 1907, Chopanyan was in Venice (while the postal stamp suggests that the letter was written and received in Paris), which suggests that the letter was written in 1901, when Komitas first visited Paris and made the acquaintance of Arshak Chopanyan.

The letter has therefore been dated 1 August 1901.

45. <TO ARSHAK CHOPANYAN>

The original is located at the MAL, ACF, 3386.

The letter was first published in *Patma-banasirakan Handes*, 1958, issue 1, page 247, and then later in KL 2000, page 120 and KL 2007, page 144.

The letter was written on Komitas' visiting card.

In KL 2000 and KL 2007, the date on which the letter was written was considered to be **29 December** 1901, while that is in fact the date on which it arrived in Paris (the postal stamp says Paris. 29.12.01). According to the date of the dispatch stamp (6 Дек 01), the letter was sent from Vagharshapat to Paris on 6 December 1901.

I received your note – The letter has not been found.

And the issue of Anahit. I am happy that you have praised me – He is referring to Arshak Chopanyan's article "Komitas Vardapet," where Chopanyan had written, "...and I think that he is the person necessary for Armenian music to radically purify itself from distortions and decline, and for it to introduce itself to European musicologists, and begin to occupy the place in world music that it deserves but has not yet achieved," (see *Anahit*, 1901, issue 6-7, page 142).

Your study on Narekatsi – He is referring to A. Chopanyan's article published in the November issue of the journal *Mercure de France* (see *Anahit*, 1901, issue 1, page 18, issue 12, page 292).

With M<ister> Manuk Abeghyan – The results of that study were later published in separate booklets. See **A Thousand and One Songs:** A Folk Songbook: The First Fifty, Vagharshapat, 1903, The Second Fifty, Vagharshapat, 1905.

1902

46. <TO MAGHAKIA ORMANYAN>

The original is located at the MAL, KF, 1701.

The letter was published in KL 2000, page 179, and KL 2007, page 211.

The letter was registered at the Armenian Patriarchate of Constantinople on 7 February 1902. On 24 February, the money was sent to Kutina, and on 4 March, a confirmation of receipt for the sum was received (see MAL, KF, 1701, page 2).

47. <TO VAHRAM MANKUNI>

The letter is located at the MAL, RTF, 82.

The letter was first published in KL 2000, pages 104-108, and then later in KL 2007, pages 126-132.

Completely – The Armenian լրապէս was misrepresented as լիապէս (which also has the same meaning – "completely") in KL 2000 and KL 2007.

Discussion of... Aram Bjshkyan's manual – "A Textbook of Armenian Ecclesiastical Notation." Aram Bjshkyan was the head of music at the *Soorb Astvatsatsin* Church in the Beşiktaş district of Constantinople who published a songbook for children in 1904 (*Ararat*, 1904, issue 4, page 329).

N. Tashchyan's textbook – He is referring to N. Tashchyan's volume called "Textbook on Armenian Ecclesiastical Notation" published in Vagharshapat, 1874.

48. <TO SARGIS KAMALYAN>

The original is located at the MAL, SKF, 828.

The letter was first published in KL 2000, pages 177-178, and then later in KL 2007, pages 209-210.

Khoren *effendi* – Khrimyan *Hayrik*'s brother (see the letter addresses to Koryun Vardapet Sahakyan on 19 May 1899 and the corresponding notes in this publication).

Yeznik – He is referring to Yeznik Vardapet Gyanjetsyan, with whom Komitas was ordained a monk on 11 September 1894 after graduating from the seminary, and then ordained a priest on 26 February 1895 (*Ararat*, 1894, issue 9, pages 289-291, 1895, issue, page 70).

Hussik – He is referring to Hussik Vardapet Zohrapyan.

My first songbook of folk music will be published next year – He is referring to the first volume of "A Thousand and One Songs," which was published in Vagharshapat in 1903.

From people familiar and unfamiliar – the Armenian ծանօթից եւ անծանօթից was misrepresented in KL 2000 and KL 2007 as ծանօթիդ եւ անծանօթիդ ("to people familiar and unfamiliar to you").

49. <TO PIERRE AUBRY>

The original is located at the Pierre Aubry collection kept at the Sorbonne University. The letter was provided to us by musicologist Armine Grigoryan, for which we express our profound gratitude. In a letter addressed to us, A. Grigoryan mentioned several interesting facts about this letter to P. Aubry. In particular, she wrote:

"1) The letter, in German, was located in Nikoghayos Tashchyan's book "A Textbook of Armenian Ecclesiastical Notation" (Vagharshapat, 1874).
2) Tashchyan's book belonged to Pierre Aubry. This is one of the books on Armenian music that Aubry's wife had donated to the Sorbonne library after her husband's death (in 1911).
3) The whole archive is currently located at the Bibliothèque de Musicologie; 3 rue Michelet, 75006 Paris.
4) Besides the books, the archive consists of manuscripts collected in two large envelopes. In 1952, the famous Romanian ethnomusicologist Constantin Braïloïu (1893-1958) coordinated and indexed Pierre Aubry's archives.

5) I have published Pierre Aubry's archives with the support of the French Ministry of Culture (*Edition critique de l'ensemble des manuscrits inédits de Pierre AUBRY sur la musique arménienne. Bourse de recherché; Ministère de la culture et de la communication (Direction de la Musique et de la Danse) avec le concours du* **C***entre de* **R***echerches sur la* **D***iaspora* **A***rménienne, PARIS, Octobre 1990).*"

Musicologist P. Aubry (1874-1910) and Archive Scholar/Paleographist Gaston Duval arrived in Etchmiadzin on 10 April 1901 to study Armenian ecclesiastical and folk music, and they stayed with Komitas, who gladly acquainted them with the results of his studies. P. Aubry wrote the following about those meetings and conversations: "Komitas was very helpful to us during the time we spent in Etchmiadzin, and I would have been very disappointed if I had not been able to meet him, because Mr. Meier had praised his knowledge of national ecclesiastical music very much in Paris. His constantly upbeat mood somewhat softens the impression left by his bony ascetic face. Nobody sings the folks melodies that he collected during his special trips like he does... His willingness to teach me Armenian music did not lose its sincerity for a moment... I often worked with Komitas in his quarters... He clarified all the difficult issues for me during long and interesting conversations. The things which he could not explain well were made understandable through song, and Komitas would gladly put aside his multiple explanations and express his thoughts through examples of song." (**M. P. Minasyan**, Pierre Aubry and Armenian Music, *Patma-banasirakan Handes*, 1968, issue 4, pages 201-202).

The letter is undated as far as the year is concerned, Komitas has only mentioned the month and day, and the place from which it was sent – **2/15 June, H. Etchmiadzin**. The letter could not have been written in 1901, because Komitas had already left for Germany at the end of May in that year and was not in Etchmiadzin in June. Besides that, in the letter Komitas gives his regards to Gaston Duval, as well as **his wife and daughter**, who had not accompanied him on that trip, and with whom Komitas had probably made their acquaintance during his first visit to Paris in mid-July 1901. His statements that "**My health is, in many respects, not very well**" and "**Despite all this pain, I am remaining here to work on these neumes. Perhaps**

I will be able to find explanations to these indecipherable neumes, in which case I will write to you again in September" suggest that Komitas had no plans to leave Etchmiadzin before September and had felt unwell at the beginning of June. A study of his biography reveals that Komitas had felt unwell in the beginning of June 1902. He mentions this on 1 June 1902, i.e. one day before writing this letter, in a letter he wrote from Etchmiadzin to Sargis Kamalyan – "**I have gone very pale, I need some rest. But my work is not allowing me a free moment**" – and he did not leave Etchmiadzin until the end of the year. Therefore, this letter was dated 1902, 2 June.

It has been published for the first time.

The German version of the letter has been prepared for publication and translated by musicologist **Artur Avanesov**.

50. <TO ARSHAK CHOPANYAN>

The original is located at the MAL, ACF, 3387.

It was first published in *Patma-banasirakan Handes*, 1958, issue 1, page 247, and then later in KL 2000, pages 120-121 and KL 2007, page 145. According to the postal stamp, the letter arrived in Paris on 16 December.

Your letter – The letter has not been found.

I am preparing to have them published – He is referring to the volume of the first fifty of "A Thousand and One Songs," which was published in Vagharshapat in 1903.

51. <TO MAGHAKIA ORMANYAN>

The original is located at the MAL, KF, 1702.

The letter was first published in KL 2000, page 179, and later in KL 2007, page 211.

It was registered at the Constantinople Patriarchate on 12 December. The money was sent to Kütahya, with a confirmation of receipt, on 20 December.

52. <TO THE ADMINISTRATION OF THE ARMENIAN DRAMA SOCIETY>

The original is located at the MAL, HMF, 384.

The letter was first published in KL 2000, page 98-99, and later in KL 2007, page 120-121.

The Armenian Drama Society – Founded in 1901 in Tbilisi through the efforts of Princess Mariam Tumanyan and Gabriel Sundukyan.

My **previous letter** – The letter has not been found.

The second reply from your administration – The letter has not been found.

1903

53. <TO ARSHAK CHOPANYAN>

The original is located at the MAL, ACF, 3388.

It was first published in in *Patma-banasirakan Handes*, 1958, issue 1, page 247-248, and then later in KL 2000, pages 121-122 and KL 2007, page 146-147.

I received your letter – The letter has not been found.

The *papa* Hambardzum you mentioned is Hambardzum of Armash – The Hambardzum of Armash is Hambardzum Cherchyan, about whom Komitas had written the following in his article "Armenian Ecclesiastical Music in the 19th Century"- "The third note writer was Hambardzum Cherchyan, who is teaching church singing and notation to this day at the Armash seminary. Yeghia Tntesyan had written the following about this, 'There may have been others who had taken on this task as well, but the notation conducted under the patronage of *amira* Karapet Palyan are the only ones known to us, which albeit an important piece of work, involves only one singer <and> one note taker, so it is the opinion of two <people> only, and does not have the critical angle that is necessary for a job of this kind. As one can immediately notice, the note taker has made

a few bold attempts to correct our melody from the Turkish one.' We agree with this opinion. We are in possession of some significant extracts from the notebook of his recordings, which allow us, as you will see, to confirm this writing by Tntesyan" (see **Komitas Vardapet** , Studies and Articles, Book I, Yerevan 2005, pages 88-89).

Coming to the folk songs gathered by M<ister> Poyachyan – He is referring to Russian-Armenian singer Galust Boyajyan, whose compilation of songs (*Chants Populaires arméniens*) was published in Paris in 1904. The lyrics of the ten songs included in the compilation were translated to French by Arshak Chopanyan, for which he had probably consulted with

Komitas on the folk nature of those songs. After the book was published, *Anahit* had written the following: "The pieces for piano accompaniment were composed by Mr. Auguste Sérieyx, one of the best students of the renowned Vincent D'Indy. Mr. Pierre Aubry, the well-known Armenologist and Musicologist, has written the foreword to the compilation. Mr. A. Fetvajyan has drawn a lovely Armenian-themed picture for the cover" (*Anahit*, 1904, issue 1, January, page 21). On 21 February of the same year, in front of a large crowd (consisting mainly of Europeans) at the hall of the École des Haute Études Sociales, Mr. Aubry gave a speech on Armenian music, after which Mr. Boyajyan, Mr. Lapani, Miss Reinalt and Ms. Silla sang the ten songs contained in Mr. Boyajyan's recently published compilation... On 26 March, Saturday evening, at the hall of the Union Chrétienne, Mr. Boyajyan gave a concert, where MR. Aubry once again gave a speech" (*Anahit,* 1904, issue 3, March, page 71).

In KL 2000 and KL 2007, **Galust Boyajyan** is mistakenly considered to be "editor and educator" **Byuzand Boyajyan** (pages 206 and 250).

If they have been gathered in Armenian villages and right from the pure mouths of the peasants, they will probably be accurate, although I might have doubts about the pronunciations in the songs. But if they have been collected in Tiflis or another city – This comment by Komitas results in an immediate reaction by Chopanyan in this section of his writing – "Mr. Boyajyan had personally collected these songs from the mouths of the Caucasian singers and he had written the notes as they were sung by the people" (*Anahit,* 1904, issue 1, January, page 21).

I expect to publish several folk songs - He is referring to the volume of the first fifty of "A Thousand and One Songs," which was published in Vagharshapat in 1903.

54. <TO ARSHAK CHOPANYAN>

The original is located at the MAL, ACF, 3389.

It was first published in *Sovetakan Arvest*, 1962, issue 9, page 53, and then later in KL 2000, pages 121-122 and KL 2007, pages 122-123.

According to the postal stamp, the letter was sent from Vagharshapat on 14 July 1903, and arrived in Paris on 6 August.

The first fifty folk songs are already done – See **A Thousand and One Songs**, First Fifty Songs, 1903. The rough draft of the compilation (with the handwriting of Komitas and M. Abeghyan) is located at the MAL, Manuk Abeghyan Fund, 11.

The ecclesiastical performance – According to Gohar Aznavuryan, "this is probably a reference to the official opening ceremony of the Armenian Church in Paris organized by the Armenian community there, which occurred in 1904 and an invitation for which was most probably sent to Komitas by Chopanyan" (*Sovetakan Arvest*, 1962, issue 9, page 53).

55. <TO MAGHAKIA ORMANYAN>

The original is located at the MAL, GKF, 21.

The letter was first published in the *Shogakhat* annual, 1970, pages 15-16, and then later in KL 2000, page 180 and KL 2007, page 212.

It was registered at the Constantinople Patriarchate on 27 October. The money was sent to Kutina, with a confirmation of receipt on 5 November.

1904

56. <TO ARSHAK CHOPANYAN>

The original is located at the MAL, ACF, 3390.

It was first published in *Patma-banasirakan Handes*, 1958, issue 1, pages 248-249, and then later in KL 2000, pages 123-124, and KL 2007, pages 148-149.

The enclosed letter – The letter has not been found.

To F<ather> Vramshapuh – He is referring to the abbot and spiritual leader at the Jean Goujon church Vramshapuh Kibaryan, the "enclosed letter" to whom has not been found. According to Armenak Shahmuradyan, before the opening ceremony of the Jean Goujon church, "a day earlier, Father Vramshapuh called the singers to a meeting and we came to a mutual agreement among ourselves on the distribution of the solo pieces" (**Armenak Shahmuradyan**, Yerevan, 1988, page 37).

The First Fifty. The second is already done – See **A Thousand and One Songs**, Second Fifty Songs, Vagharshapat, 1905.

57. <TO MARIAM TUMANYAN>

The original is located at the MAL, MTF, 455.

It was first published in *Sovetakan Arvest,* 1962, issue 9, page 53, and then later in KL 2000, pages 48-50, and KL 2007, pages 62-64.

Tumanyan's *Anush* – Komitas is referring to the second edition of the poem *Anush* included in the publication of the collection *Poems*, published with the sponsorship of Mariam Tumanyan in Tiflis in 1903. All the pages mentioned in the letter match the pagination of that edition. According to Mariam Tumanyan, she was the one who proposed the idea of converting *Anush* in to an opera by sending him this edition (*Tumanyan in the Memories of his Contemporaries*, Yerevan, 1969, pages 479-481). Komitas confirms this claim by M. Tumanyan in the letter ("happy to make your wish come true").

Please ask M<ister> Poet on my behalf – Academician Edward Jrbashyan, studying the circumstances of the composition of the libretto in the *Anush* opera, wrote, "It is not clear to what extent Tumanyan fulfilled Komitas' wishes. Only a copy of the 1903 edition has been preserved with multiple notes and additions by the poet, which are linked simultaneously to two issues – composing the opera libretto and preparing the poem for its separate publication in 1904 (see MAL, TF, 1354). Tumanyan divided the poem into four acts, mentioned the names of the characters, made a few contractions, added a few lyrical pieces, and compiled a glossary of words in dialect" (**Hovhannes Tumanyan**, A Comprehensive Collection of his Works in Ten Volumes, Vol. 3, page 521). The study of that copy shows that Tumanyan had begun working on converting the poem to a libretto, based on Komitas' instructions (see ibid., 352-353).

Reduce the old man's monologue – He is referring to the following section from *Anush* –

A dignified old man came and stood
Among the crowd of excited people
And calmly, pointing his finger towards the valley,
He said, as he shook his pipe:
"Last night, around midnight,
I had not yet fallen asleep,
My sleep is lost and my body is old,
I am left miserable in everything...
Yes, it was exactly at midnight,
That the dog suddenly got up from behind the wall.
"Hey, hey," I called, but nobody replied.
The dog went crazy, the dog went on...
"Oh, those happy days," I said to myself,
What I was then, and what I have become today?
I would sleep early at the pastures,
And jump up at the slightest of sounds...
So, I say, I was not even asleep,

It was the bitter midnight hour,
Two human shadows flickered,
Ran before the dog and went down there...

Add "the boy deserves it" – He is referring to the following section from the poem *Anush* –

"The boy deserves it, and we need to learn,
That is how one elopes with a girl."

Reduce the women's wailing (120), he can make use of the latest Ethnological Journal – He is referring to the examples of wailing by women mentioned in Yervand Lalayan's "Borjalu Village" published in the 1903 issue of the *Azgagrakan Handes* ("Ethnological Journal") – Mourning a Child, Mourning a New Bride, Mourning a Youth, Mourning a Literate Son, Mourning a Farmer, The Bride Mourns her Father-in-Law (see *Azgagrakan Handes*, 1903, pages 171-175).

To write once again the song of the mountain spirit and river waves that captures Anush after which she falls in the water (it should only be three stanzas, the fourth is already there – *Whoosh, whoosh*") (126-127) – He is referring to the following section of the poem *Anush* –

The river rushes, "Whoosh, whoosh"
Whirling and whirling,
Calling, "Come, Anush,
"Come, let me take you to your love..."

"Anush, oh Anush, come home, girl..."
Her mother calls from above, she calls,
The valleys are silent, so horribly quiet,
As the evil Debed murkily swirls.

Whoosh, whoosh, Anush, whoosh, whoosh, sister,
Whoosh to your love, to the man you love,
Whoosh, whoosh, Saro, whoosh, whoosh, brave man,

Whoosh to the mountains that you love...

The mother shouts across the valley – He is referring to the following section of the poem *Anush* –

And at the top of the valley, her hand on her brow,
She calls and calls her brave child now.

I am submitting articles to the academic journal of the International Music Society – After 1904, Komitas has had only one publication in "international academic journals" in 1907 in *La Mercure Musical*, where A. Chopanyan's translation was published of the article *La Musique Rustique Arménienne* ("Armenian Peasant Music") (see **Komitas Vardapet,** Studies and Articles, Book I, Yerevan 2005, pages 330-424, 501-502).

And Mr. T<igran> Nazaryants has also added to my task list recently – Komitas worked with Tigran Nazaryants in 1904 on the journal *Taraz* edited by the latter, editing three adapted academic articles - Wagner (*Taraz,* 1904, issue 8, pages 56-57), *Franz Liszt* (*Taraz,* 1904, issue 19, pages 173-174), Giuseppe Verdi (*Taraz,* 1904, issue 23, pages 208-209). See **Komitas Vardapet,** Studies and Articles, Book I, Yerevan 2005, pages 306-323, 500-501.

I am preparing textbooks with instructions from Arcbishop Vahram Mankuni – See the letter addressed to Vahram Mankuni on 14 March 1902. For the textbooks prepared by Komitas, see **Komitas Vardapet,** Studies and Articles, Book I, Yerevan 2005, pages 137-252.

I am editing the words to folk songs with M<ister> M<anuk> Abeghyan – He is referring to the editing work for the compilation "A Thousand and One Songs, The Second Fifty Songs."

58. <TO BARSEGH KORGANYAN>

The original is located at the MAL, KF, 1748.

It was first published in KL 2000, page 97, and then in KL 2007, page 118.

59. <TO PETROS TONAPETYAN>

The original is located at the MAL, KF, 1749.

It was first published in KL 2000, page 162-163, and then later KL 2007, pages 192-193.

Petros – This is probably Petros Tonapetyan, to whom Komitas gifted a photograph on 30 August 1903 with the following note, "A friendly memento from Komitas to Petros Tonapetyan, 30 August 1903. H. Etchmiadzin" (MAL, memento section, Komitas photograph collection, unprocessed).

The anniversaries of the Gevorgyan Seminary and the Catholicos Pontiff – He is referring to the 30th anniversary of the Gevorgyan Seminary and the 10th anniversary of Khrimyan *Hayrik* as the Armenian Catholicos.

60. <TO MAGHAKIA ORMANYAN>

The original is located at the MAL, GKF, 21.

It was first published in KL 2000, page 162-180, and then later KL 2007, pages 212.

In these publications, the date of writing was considered to be 14 December, while in reality that was the date of its registration at the Constantinople Patriarchate (see GKF, 21, the note of the registrar on the other side of the letter).

Upon studying the issue of how long letters sent from Etchmiadzin to Constantinople would take to arrive, we received the following information:

The letter sent by Komitas from Etchmiadzin on 10 January 1902 arrived in Constantinople on February 7 (28 days).

The letter sent by Komitas from Etchmiadzin on 22 November 1902 arrived in Constantinople on December 12 (20 days).

The letter sent by Komitas from Etchmiadzin on 8 October 1903 arrived in Constantinople on October 27 (19 days).

The letter sent by Komitas from Etchmiadzin on 18 August 1905 arrived in Constantinople on September 3 (16 days).

The letter sent by Komitas from Etchmiadzin on 9 January 1906 arrived in Constantinople on January 26 (17 days)(see MAL, KF, 1700, 1701, GKF, 21, 22, 23, 24).

Thus, letters from Etchmiadzin would arrive in Constantinople in 19 days on average and, based on the date that the letter was registered (14 December), one can assume that Komitas had sent it around November 24-25.

The money was sent to Kutina on 21 December, with a confirmation of receipt on 3 January 1905.

61. <TO ARSHAK CHOPANYAN>

The original is located at the MAL, ACF, 3391.

It was first published in *Patma-banasirakan Handes,* 1958, issue 1, pages 249-250, and then in KL 2000, page 124-125, and KL 2007, pages 149-150.

I had received the letter you wrote in reply – The letter has not been found.

The enclosed one, and I received the second enclosed item today – Based on the issues discussed in the letter, it seems that A. Chopanyan had sent Komitas the 1904 July-October issues of *Anahit* as "two enclosed items."

I handed over the first one personally to His Holy – He is referring to the Catholicos of All Armenians Mkrtich I.

The opening of the church by the Armenian community of Paris occurred without much ceremony – The consecration of the Armenian Church on Jean Goujon Street took place on 2 October 1904, on the occasion of which "no foreigners had been invited, although we know that many French people would have liked to be present at this event," wrote *Anahit,* "in order to once express their admiration of the Armenians by participating in this occasion and learning more about Armenian church music" (1904, issues 9-10, Sept-Oct, page 160). Regarding the reason that no foreigners were invited, *Anahit* wrote, "Perhaps the Armenian District Council of Paris had not wanted to extend such an invitation, considering that since they did not have a very good band, the foreigners might not be left with a good impression of the consecration ceremony." (ibid.)

M<ister> Maksutyan – He is referring to the French theater and movie actor Max Maksutyan (see PBH, 1958, issue 1, page 250), who had graduated from the Drama faculty of the Paris Conservatory in 1904 and had received first prize in tragedy for his performance of Triboulet's monologue (V. Hugo, *Le Roi S'Amuse*), for which Komitas was expressing his "amazement and the sincere joy." Reacting to this event, A. Chopanyan had quoted the gushing reviews of the French press about M. Maksutyan, and had written, "Maksutyan should never forget that he is Armenian, and now that he has given us the hope of a great future, his compatriots expect a lot more from him than foreigners do. One of the greatest services that an Armenian can render to his unfortunate nation is to prove the high levels of civilization of the Armenian people before the civilized world. Maksutyan proved that wonderfully on his first attempt. This young Eastern man, who came to Paris directly from Izmir, once again gloriously displaying the characteristics of his people—flexibility, hard work, love for art, the ability to grasp the highest beauty of the Western mind—beat his French competitors in the most difficult area for a foreigner to win – impeccable French pronunciation, and the faithful delivery of a French masterpiece" (*Anahit*, 1904, issue 5-6, June-July, page 124).

In KL 2000 and KL 2007, it is considered "more probable" that Komitas was referring to **Mesrop Vardapet Maksutyan**, who had defended a dissertation in Paris in 1911 on the topic of "The Dialect of Akna," but Mesrop Vardapet was not in Paris in 1904-1905; he was in Tavriz, because Khrimyan *Hayrik* had appointed him a deputy and inspector in the Diocese of Salmast and Urmia in 1904, and then leader of the state of Atrpatakan (see *Ararat*, issue 1, page 5, issue 3, page 200), from where he would send his translations of Persian literature to *Anahit* (Khayyam, Saadi, see the 1904-1905 issues of the *Anahit* journal). Moreover, Komitas would never refer to someone with a religious title using the word "Mister."

1905

62. <TO MARIAM TUMANYAN>

The original is located at the MAL, MTF, 456.

It was first published in KL 2000, page 50, and then later in KL 2007, page 64.

In her letter to Komitas dated 19 February 1905, Mariam Tumanyan informs him that the expenses of the concert would be borne by Mrs. Ghambaryan, who had sent Komitas a telegram on 25 February.

Mrs. Ghambaryan had asked for the concert lyrics by telegram – The telegram was sent on 25 February 1905. Komitas is referring to the following section of the telegram – "вышлите немедленно текст"[9]. The organizers of the concert that took place in Tiflis were the Armenian Women's Union. In his memoirs, Melkon Krishchyan had described his trip from Etchmiadzin to Tiflis in detail, writing, "We had been invited by the **Armenian Women's Union** of the Armenian aristocrats in Tiflis – Mrs. Ghambaryan (née Behbutyan), the Chairperson and her husband, Pavel (Poghos) Ghambaryan, director of the Tiflis Commercial Bank, brother of the renowned Prof. Ghambaryan of the Law Faculty at the Moscow University, and the parents of novelist Mariam Khatisyan and the future famous chemist of the Soviet Union Prof. Ghambaryan. Mrs. **N. Alibegyan** is the daughter of the novelist Mariam Khatisyan, sister of *Agha* Khatisyan and wife of the wealthy Alibegyan (niece of Mrs. Ghambaryan and my future relative). Mrs. **L. Ajemyan** from Moscow is the cousin of the Khatisyans. **Princess Behbutyan** (the wife of Mrs. Ghambaryan's brother), **Princess Yerkaynabazuk Argutyan** and her husband are the benefactors and sponsors of my unhappy classmate and literary critic Mambre Matenjchyan... Non-active member **Princess Tumanyan** is the sponsor of Hovhannes Tumanyan, and there are others as well. By inviting the Vardapet with his Gevorgyan Seminary Choir to Tiflis, the **Women's Union** had borne the whole cost of their travel as well as 3-4

9 ["Send the text immediately," translated from Russian] – Translator's notes.

days accommodation..." (**M. Krishchyan**, *Drowned Harp, Unextinguished Lantern*, Antilias, 1955, pages 122-123).

Will be presented with the lyrics, or the program – The editor allowed the publication of the concert program, which included both the performance program and the lyrics, on 29 March 1905 (see MAL, KF, 152).

63. <TO MARGARIT BABAYAN>

The original is located at the MAL, KF, 1339.

This letter was first published in parts in Margarit Babayan's memoirs *Komitas Vardapet Through his Letters* ("Mshakuyt," Paris, 1935, pages 154-155), and later in *Contemporaries on Komitas*, Yerevan, 1960, pages 116, KL 2000, page 13-14 and KL 2007, page 20-21.

I received your letter – the letter has not been found.

I am happy to send my friend Aubry 100 songs – Komitas met P. Aubry in March 1901 in Etchmiadzin (see the letter written to Pierre Aubry on 2 June 1902 and the corresponding notes). In one of the draft versions of his study "Armenian Peasant Music," Komitas wrote the following, "Recently, European musicologists have begun to pay attention, publish and disseminate Armenian folk melodies. The first person to take on this beautiful task was our sincere and loving friend, Pierre Aubry" (see **Komitas Vardapet**. Studies and Articles, Yerevan 2005, Book I, page 503). Pierre Aubry's plan to publish these 100 songs did not come to fruition, because the conditions he offered to Komitas were not to the latter's satisfaction.

I will go to Harich in a few days and spend the whole summer there – Komitas left for Harich with Yervand Ter-Minasyan on 28 June. Y. Ter-Minasyan wrote the following on that occasion, "After not having been in the homeland for so many years, I naturally had to visit our village, to relax with my parents and relatives. And that is what I did, but before I left Etchmiadzin, our dear friend Komitas had fallen ill with malaria and my friends had requested me to take him along to Ghpchagh, hoping that the clean air of the Aragats and perhaps a change of scene would cure him of that destructive disease. Of course, I took him along with pleasure, and he was truly cured, and after staying for 6 weeks in the monastery at Harich, he returned to his work in Etchmiadzin completely recovered. The life we spent together in Harich lasted from 28 June to 8-10 August (six weeks)" (see **Yervand Ter-Minasyan**, *Memories from My Life,* edited and with a foreword by Prof. Paruyr Muradyan, Yerevan, Magaghat, 2005, page 54).

The word you put in for me with M<ister> Mantashyan – He is referring to Alexander Mantashyan, but the intervention to which he is referring remains unclear.

It is utter chaos – He is referring to the situation created by the intercommunal conflicts between the Armenians and the Turks in 1905.

64. <TO MAGHAKIA ORMANYAN>

The original is located at the MAL, GKF, 22.

It was first published in *Shoghakat,* the 1970 annual, page 16, and then in KL 2000 and KL 2007.

The date of writing in KL 2000 and KL 2007 is mentioned as 18 November, which is the result

of misreading the text. The original mentions the Armenian letter Ը, which denotes the number 8, i.e. the month of August. The same is also noted on the stamp on the reverse side – "Dated 19 Aug<ust> <1>905."

The letter was registered at the Constantinople Patriarchate on 3 September, the money was sent to Kutina and a confirmation of receipt was received on 8 October.

65. <TO ARSHAK CHOPANYAN>

The original is located at the MAL, ACF, 3392.

It was first published by M. Muradyan (*Patma-banasirakan Handes,* 1958, issue 1, page 250), and then in KL 2000, pages 125-126 and KL 2007, pages 150-151.

The date of the letter's delivery is noted based on the postal stamp. According to the stamp, the letter arrived in Paris on 25 October.

Please translate the first fifty songs of *A Thousand and One Songs*, I will soon send the second volume, which has already been published – See *A Thousand and One Songs*: The Second Fifty, Vagharshapat, 1905.

For singing – The Armenian երգելու has been misrepresented as երգերու ("of the songs") in KL 2000 and KL 2007.

Descriptions - The Armenian նկարագրութիւններով has been misrepresented as փորագրութիւններով ("inscriptions") in KL 2000 and KL 2007.

1906

66. <TO ARSHAK CHOPANYAN>

The original is located at the MAL, ACF, 3393.

It was first published in *Patma-banasirakan Handes*, 1958, issue 1, page 251, and then later in KL 2000, pages 126-127 and KL 2007, pages 152-153.

Your letter – The letter has not been found.

The Second Fifty from *A Thousand and One Songs* – see *A Thousand and One Songs*: The Second Fifty, Vagharshapat, 1905.

67. <TO GAREGIN VARDAPET HOVSEPYAN>

The original is located at the ANA, f. 312, fol. 38, doc. 153.

It has been published for the first time.

68. <ARSHAK CHOBANYAN>

The original is located at the MAL, ACF, 3394.

It was first published in *Patma-banasirakan Handes*, 1958, issue 1, pages 251-252, and then later in KL 2000, pages 127-128, and KL 2007, pages 153-154.

The date and place of delivery is mentioned as on the postal stamp. Charlottenburg is a suburb of Berlin.

Came to Berlin to have my pieces printed – According to M. Muradyan, he is referring to the *Armenian Lyre* collection, which was published in 1907 in Berlin.

The articles I was going to send to Paris were with me too – He is referring to the study "Armenian Peasant Music," which was first published in *Anahit*, 1907, issue 3-5, 6-9, pages 70-73, 127-130. There are no samples of notes in the version published in *Anahit*. In the same year, a French translation of it by Arshak Chopanyan ("*La musique rustique arménienne*") was published as an expanded version (with sample notes added) in the journal *La Mercure Musical.*

69. <TO ARSHAK CHOPANYAN>

The original is located at the MAL, ACF, 3395.

It was first published in *Patma-banasirakan Handes*, 1958, issue 1, page 252, and then later in KL 2000, pages 128-129, and KL 2007, pages 154-155.

The last event planned for the spring has been moved to the fall – The event took place on 1 December 1906.

Copying my work is killing the time I have, especially copying the notational lines – He is referring to the task of copying the study on "Armenian Peasant Music," the final draft of which had been stolen in Rostov (see the letter dated 17 April 1906).

F<ather> Vramshapuh – He is referring to Vramshapuh Kibaryan (see the letter to A. Chopanyan dated 20 January 1904 and the corresponding notes).

70. <TO ARSHAK CHOPANYAN>

The original is located at the MAL, ACF, 3396.

It was first published in *Patma-banasirakan Handes*, 1958, issue 1, page 253, and then later in KL 2000, pages 129-130, and KL 2007, pages 155-156.

According to the postal stamp, the letter arrived in Paris on 28 May.

The performance - See the letter to A. Chopanyan dated 26 April 1906 and the corresponding notes.

According to the "List" – He is referring to the "List of Akna Folk Songs, Recorded by Komitas Vardapet" (Vagharshapat, 1895) in H. Janigyan's book "Antiques of Akna" (Tiflis, 1895).

Copying these songs is killing me - See the letter to A. Chopanyan dated 26 April 1906 and the corresponding notes.

71. <TO MARGARIT BABAYAN>

The location of the original is unknown. This section of the letter was first published by Margarit Babayan in her memoirs *Komitas Vardapet Through his Letters* (see "Mshakuyt," 1935, page 159). The original of the memoir is located in the M. Atmachyan collection at the MAL, from where it has been copied.

I am now currently engaged in the publication of the songs... So when the work is finished – According to M. Babayan, this letter was written on 14 July 1907 in Berlin, which is obviously wrong, since Komitas was not in Berlin on 14 July 1907, but rather in Paris (see the letters written to Arshak Chopanyan on 12 July 1907 and to Karapet Kostanyan on 16 July 1907 from Paris and the corresponding notes). On the other hand, according to M. Babayan, this letter was written after the publication of *Armenian Lyre*, which was published in Paris in **May** 1907 (see "Mshakuyt," 1935, page 159 and *Anahit*, 1907, issue 47, page 84), which is also a mistake, because Komitas' mention of "**when the work is finished**" suggests that this is a reference to work that is currently in publication and **not completed**. In July 1907, after *Armenian Lyre* was published, Komitas did not take on any other publication work, so M. Babayan is mistaken when she attributes the letter to 14 July 1907. In our opinion, the letter was not written in 1907, but rather in 1906, in Berlin on 14 July, when Komitas had arrived in Berlin and was preparing a collection of his songs and the final draft of the song samples in his study on *Armenian Peasant Music* to send to Arshak Chopanyan, because his previously prepared final draft had been stolen in Rostov (see the letter from Charlottenburg to Arshak Chopanyan dated 17 April 1906). We have therefore corrected the year of writing of this letter and denoted it as **1906**.

72. <TO MASTER MESROP TER-MOVSISYAN>

The original is located in the ANA, f. 312, fol. 38, doc. 3, p. 187-188.

It was first published by A. Adamyan (*Teghekagir Hasarakakan Gitutyunneri*, 1956, issue 9, page 106), and then by G. Harutyunyan (BHA, 1966, issue 2, page 162), who corrected the name of the addressee and the date when the letter was written (ibid., page 162-163)

I resigned from teaching at the Seminary at the end of last year, because I ended up with a powerful nervous illness – See the letter addressed to Margarit Babayan on 25 June 1905.

These chaotic times – G. Harutyunyan has the following interpretation for this phrase in the letter – "Truly, **not just in the Gevorgyan Seminary, but in several educational institutions throughout the Russian Empire, revolutionary fomentations were growing from 1905-1907**, and the struggle of the public masses against the Tsarist order was gaining pace everywhere. The **students of the Gevorgyan Seminary** had also been affected by the revolutionary ideas of the times. **A series of demonstrations were organized here in 1905-1906. The students were demanding a fundamental review** of the outdated subjects they were being taught, and an update of the **instruction** and teaching **methods** to match the spirit of the times. It is known that many of the rebelling students were expelled from the seminary. Komitas was well aware of all this. **He was very conscious of the fact** that, in those stormy times, **anybody in administration would not be able to create normal conditions** for the students and achieve their satisfaction to any degree" (BHA, 1966, issue 2, page 163).

Komitas' prediction soon came true. Yervand Ter-Minasyan wrote the following in his memoirs regarding the administration of Master Mesrop– "The month of August 1906 arrived, and we found out that Catholicos Khrimyan had given the position of administrator of the seminary to Mesrop Vardapet Ter-Movsisyan, who had achieved the title of Master in Petersburg with the support of Prof. Nik. Mar. But he too was unable to bring law and order into the lives of the emotional students, who continued their efforts to have their demands met and spent more time on those affairs than on serious learning. The new administrator could also not understand that the reason for the emotions and chaos was the result of the global rise of new intellectual and social phenomena, and not any personal or individual intervention. Unable to overcome these difficulties, Mesrop Vardapet Ter-Movsisyan also managed to get through the academic year somehow and then resigned from the administration of the seminary, which he had coveted so much earlier." the administrator of the seminary (**Yervand Ter-Minasyan**, *Memories from My Life,* Yerevan, Magaghat, 2005, page 58).

73. <TO MARGARIT BABAYAN>

The location of the original is unknown. This section of the letter was first published by Margarit Babayan in her memoirs *Komitas Vardapet Through his Letters* (see "Mshakuyt," 1935, page 155). The original of the memoir is located in the M. Atmachyan collection at the MAL, from where it has been copied.

A comparison of the preserved originals and the texts published by M. Babayan shows that the latter did not separate paragraphs in her versions of the letters, instead using an em-dash (—), and she also use parentheses to emphasize the first sections of pieces of text. While preparing this text, we have separated the body of Komitas' letter into paragraphs using these reference points from Margarit Babayan.

I have been invited officially once again to teach in Etchmiadzin – See the letter addressed to Master Mesrop on 18 July 1906. Based on this reference, the letter was probably written in the final ten days of July.

I am here – M. Babayan has added "**Berlin**" in parentheses as a reference here.

These seven years – Komitas began teaching at the Gevorgyan Seminary in 1899, after graduating in Berlin.

74. <TO ARSHAK CHOPANYAN>

The original is located at the MAL, ACF, 3397.

It was first published in *Patma-banasirakan Handes*, 1958, issue 1, pages 253-254, and later in KL 2000, page 160-162 and KL 2007, page 156-158.

"Armenian Peasant Music" – See **Komitas Vardapet**, Studies and Articles, Book I, Yerevan 2005, pages 330-424, 501-515.

I have also given them to a skilled poet to translate into German – It is unclear to whom he is referring.

I have dedicated this work to M<ister> A<lexander> Mantashyan – See the dedication note here - **Komitas Vardapet**, Studies and Articles, Book I, Yerevan 2005, page 330.

We will consult in detail about the concert and lecture arrangements in September – The year in which the letter is written has not been mentioned. The concert and lecture mentioned here that were "moved to the fall" took place on 1 December 1906. Thus, the letter was written in 1906.

75. <TO SPIRIDON MELIKYAN>

The original is located at the MAL, SMF, 225c.

It was first published in **Spiridon Melikyan**, Articles, Memoirs, Letters, Documents, compiled by Satenik Melikyan, Alexander Tadevosyan, Yerevan, 1964, page 155, and then in KL 2000, page 114.

In these two publications, the year in which the letter was written was considered to be 1908, while in KL 2007 (page 138), the letter is dated July 1907. Both attributions are wrong. Firstly, Komitas had not been in Paris in 1908, and second, a "06" is clearly visible on the postal stamp, which suggests that the letter was written in 1906 (it is unclear why the editor of KL 2007 changed the date of 1908 to July 1907). Because the stamp was removed from the postcard, part of the postal stamp, where the month that the letter was sent would have visible has been damaged, leaving only a "23" as the date. Since Komitas mentions in the letter that in two days he will be moving to the Armenian Church located on Jean Goujon Street, and he mentions to Sofia Babayan in his 2 October 1906 letter "I am in Paris already and residing at the Armenian Church, Rue Jean Goujon, 15", the letter was written before 2 October 1906, in the month of September (on 23 September, according to the postal stamp). We have therefore dated this letter 23 September 1906.

The letter has been sent to Berlin, where Spiridon Melikyan was studying in 1906.

Stepan – Spiridon Melikyan's spiritual name.

76. <TO SOFIA BABAYAN>

The original is located at the KF, 1344.

It was first published in *Sovetakan Arvest*, 1970, issue 2, page 63, and later in KL 2000, page 43 and KL 2007, page 56. The letter is dated based on the postal stamp that reads 2.10.06.

Mrs. Babayan – Sofia Babayan was Avetik Babayan's wife.

I am extremely busy with the pieces that I have to submit for publication – He is referring to his study on "Armenian Peasant Music," the final section of which was published in the June-August joint issue of *Anahit*.

The young ladies – He is referring to Shushik and Margarit Babayan.

This Sunday is the festival of the church - He is probably referring to the second anniversary of the consecration of the Armenian Church in Paris (the church was consecrated on 2 October 1904). See his letter to A. Chopanyan dated 30 December 1904 and the corresponding notes.

77. <TO ARSHAK CHOPANYAN>

The original is located at the ACF, 3398.

It was first published in KL 2000, page 43, and KL 2007, page 56.

The letter is dated based on the postal stamp that reads 20-10.06.

***Zurna* player** – According to Garegin Levonyan, "And he often had a phrase he liked to use, with which he honored his closest friends and students – '*zurna* player.'" (*Contemporaries on Komitas*, Yerevan, 1960, pages 149).

The program – Komitas presents the program of the upcoming concert, which took place on 1 December 1906.

78. <TO MARGARIT BABAYAN>

The original is located at the MAL, KF, 1341.

It was first published in KL 2000, page 15, and KL 2007, page 22-23.

According to the postal stamp, the letter was sent on 23 October. The letter is written on a pneumatic card.

Your letter – The letter has not been found.

Archbishop Sukias – He is referring to Etchmiadzin congregant, philologist, and pedagogue Archbishop Sukias Parzyan (1837-1914).

The singers' parts need to be lithographed – Komitas uses the Armenian word քարտոիպ to refer to lithography. This is a smooth printing technique where a stone surface plays the role of the printing mold. See a sample of the printed booklet at the MAL, KF, 624.

"*Msho shoror*" that our talented and dear Miss Shushik must play – On 1 December, in the preparatory period before the concert, Komitas arranged "*Msho shoror*" which was to be performed by M. Babayan's sister Shushik Babayan. In her memoirs, M. Babayan wrote, "And he was adapting the dances of Mush to my sister's piano..." (*Contemporaries on Komitas*, Yerevan, 1960, pages 140).

Laloy – He is referring to Louis Laloy (1874-1944), the French musicologist.

May the head doctor hear these words – He is referring to M. Babayan's father, Doctor Avetik Babayan.

79. <TO ARSHAK CHOPANYAN>

The original is located at the MAL, ACF, 3399.

It was first published in KL 2000, pages 131-133, and then in KL 2007, pages 160-162.

The letter is dated based on the postal stamp that reads 26-10.06.

Mughunyan – He is referring to Hovakim Mughunyan. See the letter to A. Chopanyan dated 12 July 1907 and 5 August 1908, as well as the corresponding notes.

I couldn't send it to you – This version of the program that Komitas has sent served as the basis for the publication of the concert program (see and compare MAL, KF, 1458).

80. <TO KARAPET KOSTANYAN>

The original is located at the MAL, KKF, 1099.

It was first published in *Sovetakan Arvest*, 1962, issue 9, page 53, and later in KL 2000, pages 131-133 and KL 2007, pages 116-117.

The top right corner of the original letter contains the text "1906, XI-XII" written in another handwriting. Because the Father Nahapet mentioned in the letter died on 1 October 1906, and the concert took place on 1 December 1906 (which, Komitas mentions here "is now ready"), the letter has been dated November 1906.

The Paris concert is now ready – He is referring to the 1 December concert, which has been described by *Anahit* - "Upon the initiative and through the efforts of the Armenian Union of Paris, an Armenian concert took place on 1 December, a Saturday evening, in the *Salle des Agriculteurs*. The evening was a glowing success thanks to the valuable support of renowned musician Komitas Vardapet. Komitas Vardapet, whose name is known to the readers of ***Anahit*** through the article that we have dedicated in these pages to his talented activities, agreed upon the request of the Armenian Union of Paris to compile the concert program consisting of pieces he has notated, and he directed the choir.

"The selected pieces consisted of folk music such as **The Braves of Sipan, Blow the Wind, Mount Alagyaz is Cloudy, The Ash Tree at our Door, The Rain Came Rushing Down, You are a Plane Tree, Don't Bend, Come, Come, Dear Ox, Spin, Dear Ox, Apricot Tree, My Handsome Love, It Is Spring, It Has Snowed, Crane, The Sweet Moon, It is Cloudy, but No Rain Comes, *Habrban, Keler, tsoler,* My Love, Over the Mountains, I Saw the Light Last Night, Lullaby (of Akna), Pull hard** and ecclesiastical music such as **The Lord's Prayer, Mother of God, Lord Have Mercy, Remember, Deep Mystery, *Havik mi paytzar tesi,* O Wondrous, Don't be Angry, River, The Sound Today of the Father.**

Among these, "Blow the Wind," "You are a Plane Tree," "Mother of God," "*Havik*," "Lord Have Mercy," "It Is Spring, It Has Snowed," "Crane," "My Handsome Love," "The Sweet Moon," solo, (some accompanied by the piano or the choir), the duet "*Habrban*," and the songs sung in a single voice - "Mount Alagyaz is Cloudy," and "*Keler, tsoler*" gave Paris society an idea of Armenian music as the Armenian people have created it and sing it, while the other pieces, arranged for four voices while maintaining an intact identity, led to an understanding of both Armenian music and Komitas Vardapet's personal, beautiful talent. Miss Margarit Babayan, Messrs. Mughunyan and Shahmuradyan sang wonderful solos, while Miss Shushik Babayan played "*Msho Shoror*" and all the dance tunes from Yerevan skillfully on the piano. Komitas Vardapet sang as well, in a way that only he can, performing **Mother of God** and ***Havik***. The public greeted these pieces with abundant applause and demanded an encore of 5-6 of them. The choral songs were performed by a choir that consisted of singers who had participated in the performances in Lamoureux and Cologne.

Mr. Chopanyan gave a lecture on Armenian music and poetry.

The hall was full of people, more than half of whom consisted of Europeans. There were some well-known people among the attendees, such as Opera Director Gailhard, the famous musician Burgo du Coutré, Conservatory instructor Duvernoix, the poet Maurice Bouchor, sculptor Delarue-Mardrus, *Oror* newspaper employees Messers. Paul Kieux and Paul Suchon, Pierre Kilar, Louis Dumure, several representatives of French and foreign newspapers, representatives of French nobility like Princess de Polignac, Princess Sistria, Viscount d'Umier, Meier, Machler, and so on.

This concert caused profound joy to the assembled Armenians and left an indelible impression on the Europeans who attended." (1906, issue 10-11-12, page 240).

Read the news of Father Nahapet's death – He is referring to Bishop Nahapet Nahapetyan, who passed away on 1 October 1906 at the age of 58. According to Gohar Aznavuryan, "Nahapet (also known as Arshak) Nahapetyan was a scientist, pedagogue, and had served for many years at the Gevorgyan Seminary and the Nersisyan School of Tiflis as an administrator and teacher" (*Sovetakan Arvest*, 1962, issue 9, page 53).

If there was ever an unlucky man in the world, it was him – In an article (*Ararat*, 1907, issue 1, pages 44-50) about Father Nahapet, Garegin

Hovsepyan concluded on the same note, “Whatever work he has engaged in or position he has occupied, he has left a characteristic impression on everything - exemplary discipline, responsibility, integrity and purity. However, **he was one of the unlucky people in this world** (emphasis by the editor – G.G.); even these qualities would cause his opponents and enemies to grind their teeth. And he had many enemies, most of whom were unknown to him, people who had not met him face to face, even though he had a reputation of being sweet and humble. Nobody has been subject to such unjust gossip and persecution as he had; it was in the midst of this persecution that he passed away” (ibid., page 50).

81. <TO MARGARIT BABAYAN>

The original is located at the MAL, KF, 1342.

It was first published in parts by Margarit Babayan (“Mshakuyt” 1935, pages 156-158), and then later in KL 2000, pages 15-18 and KL 2007, pages 23-26.

According to the postal stamp, the letter reached its addressee on 6 December 1906 (6.12.06). However, at the end of the letter, after its main body, Komitas mentions the date as **1906. Dec. 8 Paris**. This suggests that Komitas had sent that final page of the letter, with the post scriptum, after he had posted the rest of the letter. The ink on that page is of a different shade than the ink used on the rest of the letter. Unless Komitas had made a mistake in writing **December 8** instead of **December 6**, the only assumption to be made is that the final page was written later, after two days, during one of the meetings he had with Margarit Babayan. The date of the rest of the letter should be based on the postal stamp – 6.12.06.

Your letter – The letter has not been found.

People believe bad news more – He is probably referring to the following statement he made in his letter to K. Kostanyan in November 1906 - “There is news going around that I have left or plan to leave the priesthood – this is the worst kind of gossip, at the very least”.

Another sketch in the same style as this one has also been preserved in the MAL Komitas Fund (1658).

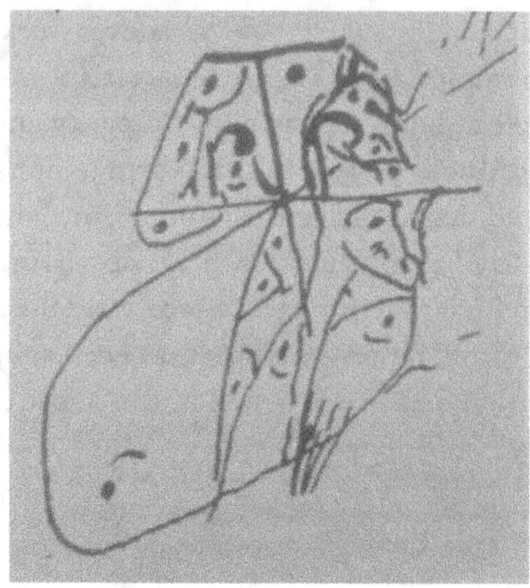

Have you no home? - The Armenian original բուն is misrepresented as բան ("**thing**") in KL 2000 and KL 2007.

82. <TO ARMINE MELIKYAN>

The location of the original is unknown.

The letter was first published by Robert Atayan (*Garun*, 1969, issue 11, page 19). The letter is addressed to Armine Melikyan, the daughter of the treasurer of the Armenian Union of Paris Hambardzum Melikyan. Considering Atayan's comment that "even someone with a good knowledge of *grabar* would have difficulty understanding this unnaturally complicated 'command,'" we have added a modern Armenian translation of the letter immediately following it. According to Atayan, this letter was written in 1913, which is not very likely, since the Melikyans lived in Paris and Komitas was in Constantinople in 1913, and would probably not send his coat to Paris for repairs. It is more likely that the letter was written at the end of 1906, when Komitas had left for Paris to organize a big concert (which took place on 1 December), because he refers in the letter to a "first 40-day mourning period" that would "last up to December 7 of this year." This was probably the coat that Komitas wore in Berlin when he was a student, i.e from 1895 onwards, and in which he has been photographed in Berlin in 1898.

Our dear Arkayan family – Matching the spirit of the letter, Komitas has wittily translated the name of the Melikyan family into "Arkayan" (*melik* is a word used in the Middle East for "king," the pure Armenian translation of which is "*arka*").

Make it wearable again... - There is text missing in this part of the letter, but the absence of the original makes it impossible to fill this gap.

83. <TO MARGARIT BABAYAN>

The original is located at the MAL, KF, 1343.

It was first published in KL 2000, page 40 and KL 2007, page 26.

Considering Komitas' suggestion to "let Shushik come on Friday morning" (i.e. on 21 December), we have dated the letter 17-20 December 1906 (the beginning of the week).

When the gown is blessed – The tradition of blessing the wedding gown before a wedding ceremony.

The priest – He is referring to Vramshapuh Kibaryan.

Zorayan – This is misrepresented as **Zorakan** in KL 2000 and KL 2007.

The wedding will be at 2 o'clock on Saturday, the 22nd – He is referring to the wedding of Shushik Babayan and Louis Laloy.

Let Shushik come on... to confession, and get communion – S. Babayan's father, Avetik Babayan, mentions this event in his letter to Tiruhi and Karapet Kostanyan dated 30 December 1906 (see MAL, KKF, 691/177, and also KL 2007, page 220). When quoting the relevant section from this letter, the editor of KL 2007 has misrepresented a word used by Avetik Babayan—քեօչակութիւն (read "keochakutyun")—as քեօփակութիւն (read "keopakutyun") (although the original letter by A. Babayan clearly uses the letter չ instead of the letter փ). The resulting sentence was "**That rascal did a lot of *keopakutyun*,**" followed by an explanation that "the word '*keopakutyun*' used by Avetik Babayan in this context should be understood as 'mischief,' because Komitas "had been very cheerful by nature and loved a good joke, and was thus very different from the image created about him by later generations" (KL 2007, page 220). This suggests that when conducting the confession and communion ceremony, Komitas had "**done a lot of *keopakutyun***" or mischief, because he was "very cheerful by nature and loved a good joke." The fact that Komitas was cheerful and loved joking around has been confirmed by the memoirs of his contemporaries, but the suggestion that he had been mischievous of "done a lot of *keopakutyun*" during a sacred ceremony is **simply a judgment based on a misreading of the original text**. On the other hand, the phrase "doing a lot of *keopakutyun*" has been used to mean "talking a lot, giving a long speech, preaching, talking too ceremoniously." The origins of the word lie in the Turkish "***keochak***" which means "moving, in motion, dancing." Notably, later in the same letter, when describing the wedding ceremony, A. Babayan uses this word once again, this time in a different context – "...so we saw what a Catholic wedding ceremony looks like, with music and everything – describing it would take too long. It is similar to ours, but there is more ***keochakutyun*** and ballet-like movement, the girl's father must take the hand of the boy's mother and move from place to place, while the boy's father must take the hand of the girl's mother and do the same, and then there were other symbolic actions between the in-laws like this one." In this case, the word is used to mean "to stretch out, to be more priestly than necessary."

Below, we present a few extracts of the letter from Avetik Babayan, preserving the spelling used in the original.[10]

"30.XII.06

<...> The "Engagement" ceremony took place a week earlier, occurring at the office of the municipal administration, and it was very similar to our "Engagement" tradition. We went to the municipal office, and the groom and in-laws were waiting for us there. They took us into a large hall and sat the bride and groom together, and the parents sat next to their children. The mayor entered and we had to all stand up. He sat down, and they nodded towards us to say that we could sit as well. He read out their laws and, after asking the bride and groom whether they approved of each other, brought forward the rings, which had been previously given to him on a silver tray,

10 [A. Babayan spells some words as they would be spoken in a dialect, rather than using traditional Armenian spelling] – Translator's notes

for each to put on the other's finger. He congratulated us and let us leave. We were all very happy that the thing ended so quickly. <...> On the first day, Shushik went to Holy Father Komitas for confession. That rascal did a lot of *keochakutyun*, but he conducted the confession so seriously, with such detailed explanation, that Shusho's heart had nearly broken and she had ended up in tears. She came back home with a special heavenly light within her. On Saturday, at around 10 a.m., a large group from the in-laws came to pick the four of us up, to take us to the Catholic Church, where the groom and the in-laws had gathered <...> so we saw what a Catholic wedding ceremony looks like, with music and everything – describing it would take too long. It is similar to ours, but there is more ***keochakutyun*** and ballet-like movement, the girl's father must take the hand of the boy's mother and move from place to place, while the boy's father must take the hand of the girl's mother and do the same, and then there were other symbolic actions between the in-laws, like this one. The ceremonies occur in the "sacrisite"[11] in a very mystical manner. Tired from all that, we went to the in-laws' place for breakfast and, at exactly 2½ we went to the Armenian Church. The groom's friends had gathered there – professors from the Sorbonne and a couple of musical celebrities. From our side, there was A<lexander> Iv<anovich> Mantashyan, Mr. Hamb<ardzum> Melikyan with his wife and Mr. Arsh. Chopanyan as the cross-bearer. Somehow, our previous mayor, Gegham Ter-Petrosyan, had heard the news and had also come to the church. And the number of French guests kept increasing with time. Komitas Vardapet conducted the wedding ceremony (officiating alongside Father Vramshapuh of that church and the acolyte), in glorious vestments. The choir consisted of Greta <he is referring to Margarit Babayan – G.G.> and her students Shah-Muradyan and Mughunyan (the best singers). Greta sang the first hymn solo, and then the choir joined in (with Komitas accompanying them as well), and then they went up the altar during the hymn "Be Happy." All the ceremonies – passing the wine glass and drinking from it, bearing the cross over their heads, tying the *narod*[12] and so on, all accom-

11 [A. Babayan uses this very word, spelled out in Latin script, and placed in quotation marks. Perhaps he is referring to the "sacristy"] – Translator's notes.

12 [A thread tied around the foreheads of the bride and groom during Armenian wedding ceremonies] – Translator's notes.

panied by that wonderful singing, left a huge and beautiful impression on our French guests, as they all later confessed, when they came with us for a cup of tea of champagne after the church. Mother had prepared a large table in our dining room full of sweets and sandwiches, brightly lit as we do during the New Year. More than 40 people poured into our small apartment, we emptied many bottles of champagne, and when I grew more excited, I gave the following speech in French, which I am mentioning here especially for Tuto <he is referring to his sister, Tiruhi Kostanyan – G.G.>, translated: "Ladies and gentlemen, although it is difficult for me to give a speech before such esteemed representatives of French society because I do not speak your language well, but when a person's heart is full of emotion, in such circumstances, words start to flow even from the mouth of a mute person. Someone told me (I gestured towards the groom) that it would be very difficult for my spouse and me to gift the most beautiful **flower** of our Armenian nation to a foreigner, a Frenchman. Yes, that is difficult for us to do. But am I not receiving from your nation in exchange a sweet **fruit** that is ripe and educated in every way? God has not given me any male children, but he has been kind enough to compensate for that by giving me two boys who are lovely in all aspects and deserving, from one of the greatest nations in the world. And I have to obey His sacred will and gratefully accept His two gifts – Charles Carbonel and the newlywed Louis Laloy. But do you know, ladies and gentlemen, what "Louis" means in Armenian? If we pronounce all the letters, then it is "*luys*" or *la lumière*![13] So (hugging the groom), I kiss you, dear *Luys*, and hand over to you and your noble family the flower of my life, hoping that on your part, you will allow our nation to partake in your people's light—your great civilization!!!—as much as possible. Tutik *jan*, can you imagine the excitement this speech of mine caused among the guests? Glasses upon glasses were emptied and Shushik was inspired to immediately begin the "*uzundara*" dance,[14] accompanied by Greta on the piano. After that, following some Armenian songs in Mughunyan's wonderful tenor, Father Komitas sang *horovel*,[15] which enchanted me, the whole thing

13 [Avetik Babayan uses the French word for "light" here] – Translator's notes.

14 [A bridal dance] – Translator's notes.

15 [A folk song traditionally sung by farmers when tilling the land] – Translator's notes.

is composed with such amazing skill, it has been taken from various places and put together with characteristic harmony. Thus our wedding ended, in such a good and happy way. They left around 7 and we remained without our Shushik...

Tuto *jan*, do you understand that the words I addressed to our new groom were not just flattery? If you were to see the efforts he made and sacrifices he went to in order to gain Shushik's approval, he went through so much difficulty before he got the parents' agreement. If you were to know this, you would also say that he deserved the flower that he received, in exchange for such a lasting and strong love... If you see know how much he respects and loves Mother and me - almost as much as Shushik does. Three or four days ago, I went to attend a lecture he was giving at the Sorbonne (University) – he spoke with such wonderful oratory skills and explained the history of art, there were more than two hundred people in the audience, while other professors gather crowds of only 15-20 people in that department. My heart was full of glory in his lecture hall. I am already dreaming about how he will travel with Shushik to the Caucasus next summer, how he will hear our bards in our Alexandropol,[16] and study the melodies that they sing, and so on <...>"

84. <TO ARSHAK CHOPANYAN>

The original is located at the MAL, ACF, 3400.

It was first published by Gohar Aznavuryan in the journal *Sovetakan Arvest* (1962, issue 10, pages 53-54), and then in KL 2000, page 133 and KL 2007, page 162.

The letter is dated based on the postal stamp on the day it was sent – 22.12.06.

Bring the notebooks with you to church – He is referring to the Armenian Church on Jean Goujon Street, where Komitas was residing.

So that I copy the *Mercure Musicale* article – He is referring to the article by Louis Laloy on the 1 December concert, published in the 15 December

16 [The city of Gyumri in modern Armenian] – Translator's notes.

issue of the *Mercure Musicale*. Arshak Chopanyan translated that article and had it published in the January 1907 issue of *Anahit* (pages 27-29). The article wrote the following about Komitas, in particular – "...and Komitas Vardapet, who had the courage to come and direct the choir and sing melodies himself, was faced with such powerful emotion through the Virgin, that he nearly reduced everyone to tears, and the audience gave him an ovation[17] for this. Nothing was more moving than seeing him bow before the clapping audience, sweetly and majestically, under his high black cowl, and then sitting once again before the Mustel organ and repeating the final refrain, singing it in a low voice, lost in the mysteries of that pain, emphasizing an earthly compassion and thoughtfulness that make a godly presence felt."

In her notes on this section, G. Aznavuryan wrote, "*Mercure Musicale* was the official journal published in Paris by the International Music Society, and in which Chopanyan's French translation of Komitas's article with the title 'The Expansion and Development of Folk Melodies: The Role of the Parish School in the Times of Catholicoses Gevorg IV and Makar: Song Writing and Singing' had been published in December 1906 (after the concert in Paris on 1 December)" (*Sovetakan Arvest*, 1962, issue 10, pages 53-54), and the same is repeated in KL 2000 (page 208) and KL 2007 (page 253).

However, no such article was published in the *Mercure Musicale* in 1906, neither in the December issue nor in any of the other months. Arshak Chopanyan had translated and published Komitas' study on "Armenian Peasant Music" in issue no. 5 of *Mercure Musicale* in 1907 (pages 472-488). The title mentioned by G. Aznavuryan ("The Expansion and Development of Folk Melodies: The Role of the Parish School in the Times of Catholicoses Gevorg IV and Makar: Song Writing and Singing") constituted the sub-sections of this article that had been published by the journal *Anahit* not in 1906, but rather in 1907 (issues 3-5, 6-9, pages 70-73, 127-130). See **Komitas Vardapet**, Studies and Articles, Book I, Yerevan 2005, pages 330-423, 501-502.

I will meet you on Sunday – i.e. on 23 December.

17 [The author uses the French word "ovation" (spelling it out in Armenian letters within quotes as "ovasyon")] – Translator's notes.

1907

85. <TO ARSHAK CHOPANYAN>

The original is located at the MAL, ACF, 3401.

It was first published in KL 2000, page 133, and in KL 2007, page 162.

The letter is dated based on the postal stamp on the day it was sent.

I told the priest – He is referring to Vramshapuh Kibaryan.

It would be Saturday, not Friday – i.e. On January 12, not 11.

86. <TO MARGARIT BABAYAN>

The original is located at the MAL, KF, 1345.

It was first published by Margarit Babayan in "Mshakuyt," 1935, pages 158-159, and then in KL 2000, pages 19-20 and KL 2007, pages 26-27.

The letter is dated based on the postal stamp on the day it was sent – 7-2.07.

Pelléas and Mélisande – He is referring to the opera written by Claude Debussy (1902) based on Maurice Maeterlinck's Symbolist drama (1892) of the same name.

Amen – In the original, Komitas had written this word in much larger letters than the rest.

Melikyan's – He is referring to Hambardzum Melikyan.

I received an invitation for two from Davidov today – Sasha Davidov's (Arsen Karapetyan, 1850-1911) concert took place on 8 February (*Sovetakan Arvest*, 1970, issue 3, page 52).

Missing you vely much, Hello – Komitas had written these words in considerably larger block letters.

87. <TO MARGARIT BABAYAN>

The original is located at the MAL, Marie Atmachyan fund, unprocessed.

It was first published in KL 2000, page 21 and KL 2007, pages 28-29.

The letter is dated based on the postal stamp on the day it was sent – 15-2.07. Margarit Babayan gifted the letter to Marie Atmachyan on 6 October 1954 with the following note, "A heartfelt gift to my dear student and wonderful poet Marie Atmachyan."

The Priest's – He is referring to Vramshapuh Kibaryan.

Wrote to them today – The letter has not been found.

88. <TO ARSHAK CHOPANYAN>

The original is located at the MAL, ACF, 3402.

It was first published in KL 2000, page 134, and KL 2007, page 163.

The letter is dated based on the postal stamp on the day it was sent – 8-3.07.

Demets – E. Demets, the publisher of Komitas' collection *Armenian Lyre*. The collection was published in May 1907.

Monday – i.e. 11 March.

89. <TO MARGARIT BABAYAN>

The original is located at the MAL, KF, 1340.

It was first published in KL 2000 (page 190), according to a note by the Margarit Babayan Fund, and then in KL 2007, page 228.

Komitas has written the letter in code, using a sequence of vertical, horizontal and curved lines written separately, on both sides of the same sheet, such that the text can be read only using the combination of these lines. A reading of the text shows that there is only one mistake in the letter as originally read by Margarit Babayan – Komitas had written "***Luys Zurna***" and not "***Luys Laloy***".

Based on the content of the letter, Komitas must have written it in the beginning of April 1907, because A. Babayan, S. Babayan and Louis Laloy gave a joint charity concert on 16 April 1907 to benefit the starving Armenians. Komitas had refused to participate in this concert, following Vramshapuh Kibaryan's advice (see the letter addressed to Margarit Babayan on 15 February 1907). *Anahit* published the following commentary on that concert – "On the evening of 16 April, a concert of folk music took place in the Salle Pleyel, organized by Miss. M. Babayan, and Mrs. S. Babayan-Laloy. Miss. M. Babayan sang around twenty Armenian, French, Greek and Russian folk songs, and Mrs. S. B.-Laloy played dance tunes from those four nations on the piano.

The audience, consisting mainly of invited Europeans, reacted warmly to the two talented musical scholars. The Armenian music proved particularly popular; the critic's articles which later appeared in the music press spoke very highly of it. Mr. Louis Laloy gave a skillful speech presenting a comparative study of the folk music of those four nations. The Babayan sisters donated the proceeds from the concert, 50 fr., to the Armenian Union of Paris, in order for it to be sent to the starving Armenians" (1907, issue 5-6, page 96).

Luys Zurna – He is referring to Louis Laloy.

90. <TO HRIPSIME YENGIBARYAN>

The original is located at the MAL, KF, 1707.

The letter has three authors: Armen – Hripsime Yengibaryan's brother, Margarit Babayan and Komitas Vardapet. Komitas and Margarit Babayan wrote on the side of the postcard with the picture. Armen Yengibaryan's "We will probably not go anywhere in the summer" and Margarit Babayan's "Aren't you planning on coming in the summer?" suggest that the postcard has probably been sent in the spring of 1907. Based on the contents of the letters sent by Komitas to H. Yengibaryan on 7 May 1907 from Zurich and 11 June 1907 from Paris, one should assume that this joint letter was sent in April 1907.

It has been published for the first time.

Do you like this picture – The picture shows a mermaid being pecked by a stork.

91. <TO ARSHAK CHOPANYAN>

The original is located at the MAL, ACF, 3403.

It was first published in KL 2000, page 134 and KL 2007, page 163.

The letter has been dated and the location of the author has been mentioned based on the postal stage – 7.V.07, Zurich.

92. <TO HRIPSIME YENGIBARYAN>

The original is located at the MAL, KF, 1708.

It was first published in KL 2000, page 48 and KL 2007, page 62.

The letter has been dated and the location of the author has been mentioned based on the postal stamp – 7.V.07, Zurich. KL 2000 does not mention the city from which the letter was sent, while KL 2007 mistakenly notes it as Paris.

Our Varduk has written to me – The letter has not been found.

I'm going to come over with these people soon – He is referring to the postcard picture, which depicts mountain climbers holding staffs.

93. <TO ARSHAK CHOPANYAN>

The original is located at the MAL, ACF, 3404.

It was first published by Gohar Aznavuryan (*Sovetakan Arvest*, 1962, issue 10, page 54) and then in KL 2000, pages 134-135 and KL 2007, page 164).

The letter has been dated and the location of the author has been mentioned based on the postal stage – 22.V.07, Genève.

I sent an open letter to Shahmurad – The letter has not been found.

The concert will take place on June 1 – *Anahit* wrote the following about this concert – "To benefit the starving people of Van, the Armenian students of Geneva organized an Armenian Music Concert on 1 June in the large hall of the city Conservatory, sponsored by well-known Armenophile Leopold Favre. The students had invited Komitas Vardapet to organize the choir and direct the concert. A. Chopanyan was also invited to give a speech on Armenian music and poetry, as was Mr. Shah-Muradyan, who added to the sheen of the concert with his powerful voice. Other participants in the concert included Mr. Sheridchyan, an attractive and nuanced baritone, and Mrs. Sheridchyan, a gloriously talented pianist. The choir consisted of male and female Armenian students, who were supported by a few music-loving Armenians and Russian students. The concert was a big success. The *Journal de Genève*, *Tribune de Genève* and *La Suisse* newspapers dedicated warmly positive articles to the event. The proceeds came to around 2000 fr. Mr. Favre, enthusiastic in his most noble music loving and philanthropic emotions, decided to cover all the costs of the concert personally, such that all of the proceeds were sent to Van" (1907, issue 6-9, page 160). The Komitas Fund at the MAL has a copy of the concert program (KF, 1467).

94. <TO SPIRIDON MELIKYAN>

The original is located at the MAL, SMF, 225b.

It was first published in **Spiridon Melikyan**, Articles, Memoirs, Letters, Documents, compiled by Satenik Melikyan, Alexander Tadevosyan, Yerevan, 1964, page 155, and then in KL 2000, page 113-114 and KL 2007, page 138.

The letter was sent to the address of Prof. Richard Schmidt, to be handed to Spiridon Melikyan (An Herrn Prof. Richard Schmidt (für Herrn Stephannos)). Spiridon Melikyan was studying at Richard Schmidt's music school.

The concert in Geneva also went very well – See the letter addressed to A. Chopanyan on 22 May 1907 and the corresponding notes.

I am going to Lausanne and Berne tomorrow to give lectures. Then, I will return to Geneva to lecture again, and then to Paris, from where I will go to Italy – Komitas left for Lausanne on 3 June, gave a lecture in Berne on 5 June, returned to Geneva on 6 June, and left for Lausanne again on 7 June, where he participated in the event called "Armenia" organized by the Armenian students there. He then returned to Berlin, then Paris, from where he left in mid-June for Italy with A. Chopanyan.

95. <TO MARGARIT BABAYAN>

The location of the original is unknown. A typed copy of the letter is located at the MAL, KF, 1507.

It was first published in KL 2000, page 20 and KL 2007, pages 29-30. The following note is written at the bottom of the typed copy of the letter – "M. Babayan's note on the reverse side of the letter – 'A heartfelt gift for Gegham Atmachyan's 'A. Sema' collection. Margarit Babayan, 6 Oct. 1954, Paris.' The letter was gifted to Vazgen I. It was provided to us for the purposes of copying by R. Atayan. 1964/1."

The concert in Geneva was marvelous - See the letters addressed to A. Chopanyan on 22 May 1907 and Spiridon Melikyan on 2 June 1907 and the corresponding notes.

We will leave on Sunday or Monday, and come to Paris – According to K. Samuelyan's "Annals," Komitas left for Berlin after the 7 June concert in Lausanne (37 days later), from where he wrote two letters dated 14 July and 15-20 July to Margarit Babayan, and from 15-20 July Komitas went to Venice, Italy from Paris, where he stayed at one of the hotels on Saint Mark's Square (July 20-25) and a meeting with Komitas Vardapet took place at the Congregation hall around 25-30 July. Komitas' speech at the Murad-Rafaelyan School took place, according to K. Samuelyan, in the period between 25 July and 15 August, after which Komitas left for Geneva on 15-16 August, then to Lausanne on 17 August, from where he wrote a letter to Karapet Kostanyan and, on 19 August, he returned to Paris and wrote a letter from there to Arshak Chopanyan (*Sovetakan Arvest*, 1970, issue 5, pages 53-54).

But a study of the letters written by Komitas in this period and press publications from this time shows that there is some obvious confusion here, which has resulted in a number of chronological inconsistencies that has been repeated in a number of later publications on Komitas.

Komitas wrote this letter on 7 June 1907, which was a **Friday** based on a calendar of 1907. So Komitas, as he mentions himself, "**will leave on Sunday or Monday, and come to Paris**," i.e. on 9 or 10 June. The postal stamp of the letter addressed to Hripsime Yengibaryan on 11 June 1907 confirms that Komitas was already in Paris **on 11 June**.

In his letter to Arshak Chopanyan, written from Paris on 12 June, Komitas says that it "is the second day that I am in Paris," i.e. from **10 July**. Thus, Komitas left Venice on 8 July, since he stayed for a day on Geneva on the way to Paris at the house of Melik Haykazyan (on 9 July), he stayed for a night at the Nalbandyans' house in Geneva (on 10 July), and arrived in Paris on 10 July 1907 (compare this to Komitas' 12 July letter to Arshak Chopanyan – "Dear Arshak, I stayed for a day in Geneva. I had lunch with the Melik-Haykazyans... I stayed for one night in Lausanne at the Nalbandyans' house, they were very hospitable, we played music and sang; today is the second day that I am in Paris"), from where he had written the details of his return in his letter to Arshak Chopanyan. Thus, Komitas' trip to Italy took place in the period between 11 June and 10 July.

The reason for the chronological confusion is a misreading of the location for the letter to Karapet Kostanyan, written on 16 July 1907 in Paris, and a misrepresentation of the letter's date. The fact is that a different handwriting had added the text "17 Aug. 1907" to the top of the letter, and next to that is the word "Lausanne" once again in handwriting different from that of the letter body. Following the wrong date suggested by this note, Gohar Aznavuryan (*Sovetakan Arvest*, 1962, issue 10, page 54), dated the letter as 17 August, written from Lausanne, which was then reflected in K. Samuelyan's Annals and the published copies of the letter. However, according to the postal stamp (16-7.07, i.e. 16 July 1907), the letter was sent from Paris (from the Armenian Church on Jean Goujon Street, where Komitas was residing) on 16 July 1907 and, according to the receipt stamp (17.VII.07, i.e. 17 July 1907), the letter arrived in Lausanne on 17 July 1907 (see the address to which the letter was sent – *Suisse. Monsieur Karapet Kostanian. Poste restante. Lausanne. Etp. Komitas V. Paris, Jean-Goujon, 15*). In that letter, Komitas states that he "returned from Italy and received the letters you had sent. In Lausanne, Kajberuni had not turned up at my hotel at the appointed time; I looked for him but could not find him. Perhaps he had then looked for me. In a word, we did not come across each other, and he had not given me your address, so I had to leave without seeing you, regretfully."

Based on the information provided by the postal stamps, we have dated that letter to Karapet Kostanyan as 16 July 1907.

Now what remains to be understood is when Komitas left for Venice with Arshak Chopanyan, and how much time he spent in Italy. In the letter to Karapet Kostanyan, Komitas mentions that he "**worked for 3 weeks at the monastery in Venice**" and in the "Autobiography" dated 5 June 1908, he wrote, "I stayed in Italy for one month and reached up to Rome" (**Komitas Vardapet**. Studies and Articles, Book II, Yerevan 2007, pages 52). Komitas mentioned some details of his visit to Rome in one of his interviews. "Having reached Italy, I sought the Pope and he opened the museums before me with great hospitality; I found and studied many things there," (*Jamanak*, 1910, issue 584, page 1). Thus, Komitas' trip to Italy lasted around **one month**, of which he spent three weeks in Venice. As we saw earlier, Komitas was already in Paris on 10 July, so he must have left for Venice with Chopanyan on 12 June at the latest, having reached Paris from Geneva on 10 June (from where he wrote Hripsime Yengibaryan a letter on 11 June), and his meeting with the Congregants occurred after **13 June**. The fact that Komitas' meeting at the Congregation Hall occurred in **June** is also confirmed by the author of the article in *Bazmavep* on the lecture and concert organized by Komitas at San Lazzaro island, who says the *following* in the description of this event – **"It is a June evening** *(emphasis by the editor, G.G.)*. A club of Mekhitarists has come together in the San Lazzaro Hall" (*Bazmavep*, 1907, issue 6-8, page 369), as well as by Ghevond Tayan, in an article dedicated to the life and work of Komitas – "Komitas V.'s visit to Venice, which he mentions, took place in June 1907" (*Bazmavep*, 1936, issue 1-2, page 8).

In order to avoid this chronological confusion, K. Samuelyan dated the letter sent to Arshak Chopanan on 12 July 1907 (according to the postal stamp) as 19-20 August, and moved all the biographical data and episodes from July to August 1907. This mistake in K. Samuelyan's Annals was repeated in a number of later books published about Komitas (see, for example, KL 2007, page 243, 260, **C. G. Batikyan**, *Komitas as he was*, Yerevan, 2002, page 196, and so on).

96. <TO HRIPSIME YENGIBARYAN>

The original is located at the MAL, KF, 1707.

It was published for the first time in KL 2000, page 48 and in KL 2007, page 62.

These two publications do not mention the month or day on which the letter was sent. According to the postal stamp, the date was 11.6.07, i.e. 11 June 1907, from Paris to Geneva. The postcard bears the following address – "*Mademoiselle H. Enguibarian, 19^{I} Rue de Carouge, Genève. Etp. Komitas Wardapet, 15, Rue Jean Goujon, Paris.*"

97. <TO ARSHAK CHOPANYAN>

The original is located at the MAL, ACF, 3405.

It was first published by M. Muradyan in *Patma-banasirakan Handes*, 1958, issue 1, pages 255-256, and then in KL 2000, pages 135-137 and KL 2007, pages 164-166.

The letter was sent to the address of the Murad-Rafaelyan School in Venice, to Father Poturyan. On a postcard, Komitas had written "Please hand this to A. Chopanyan." According to the postal stamp, the letter was sent on 12.7.07, i.e. 12 July 1907 from Paris. See also the letter addressed to M. Babayan from Lausanne on 7 July 1907 and the corresponding notes.

I stayed for a day in Geneva - See the notes related to the letter addressed to M. Babayan on 7 July 1907.

I had lunch with the Melik-Haykazyans – According to M. Muradyan, "he is probably referring to the family of lawyer Melik-Haykazyan" (*PBH*, 1958, issue 1, page 256).

Starting with Malumyan – According to M. Muradyan, he is referring to the public figure and journalist, ARF[18] activist Khachatur Malumyan (E. Aknuni) (1863-1915).

18 [The Armenian Revolutionary Federation, also often referred to as the *Dashnaktsutyun*, an Armenian political party active in the Diaspora] – Translator's notes.

I couldn't find M<ister> Kostanyan either, because Kajberuni, the student who knew his address – According to KL 2007 (page 243), "this is probably a reference to Gabriel Ter Hovhannisyan (Kachberuni, 1837-1920), who was a doctor and had published articles in the press as well as travel notes." However, it is much more probable that Komitas was referring to Gevorgyan Seminary alumnus Hayk Ter Astvatzatryan, who had published articles under the pen-name "Kachberuni" in *Ararat*, because Gabriel Ter Hovhannisyan was in Baku in 1907, not in Lausanne. Moreover, it is difficult to imagine Komitas using the word "student" to refer to the 70-year old Gabriel Ter Hovhannisyan.

I stayed for one night in Lausanne at the Nalbandyans' house – According to M. Muradyan, "he is referring to the family of the renowned astronomer and later the manager of the Central School in Constantinople Martiros Nalbandyan" (*PBH*, 1958, issue 1, page 256), who published the illustrated monthly journal *Gitutyun*[19] in Lausanne (1904-1905) and then in Paris (1908-1909) (a publication of the Lausanne Haykazyan School). See the Armenian press, compiled manuscript collection, 1794-1980, Yerevan, 1986, page 58.

Today is the second day that I am in Paris - See the notes related to the letter addressed to M. Babayan on 7 July 1907.

I saw Sherichyan in Geneva – The Sherichyan spouses also participated in the 1 June 1907 concert in Geneva benefitting the starving Armenians of Van. "Other participants in the concert included Mr. Sheridchyan, an attractive and nuanced baritone, and Mrs. Sheridchyan, a gloriously talented pianist" (*Anahit,* 1907, issue 6-9, page 160).

Favre has gone to his summer house – Leopold Favre was the sponsor of the Geneva concert (*Anahit,* 1907, issue 6-9, page 160), about whom *Ararat* wrote the following – "This concert was organized with the sponsorship and financing of Armenophile nobleman Leopold Favre, who is not only familiar with the Armenian language, but has personally travelled to Armenia, and as the head of mission, he had come to the aid of our Turkish-Armenian brothers" (*Ararat*, 1907, October, page 909).

Demets - the publisher of Komitas' collection *Armenian Lyre* (Paris, 1907).

The Prince – According to *Bazmavep*, the Venice concert was also attended by Prince Boris Arghutyants. "It was presided upon by His Excel-

19 ["Science"] – Translator's notes.

lency Abbot Kyureghyan. Next to him sat a young Armenian nobleman, Prince Boris Arghutyants, who was our guest on that day by a lucky coincidence" (*Bazmavep*, 1907, issue 6-8, page 369).

The Hovakimyans – On 8 March 1907, the members of the *Masis* Armenian club in Paris decided to found an organization with the name "Armenian Union of Paris." A committee was created to compile the statute of the organization and one of the members of that committee was M. Hovakimyan (see *Anahit*, 1907, page 92).

I saw Armenak – He is referring to Armenak Shahmuradyan,

Ipekyan – He is referring to Gaspar Ipekyan,

Poor Mughunyan died and was buried a week ago, may the sun keep shining down on you – Hovakim Mughunyan's obituary was published in *Anahit*, 1907, issue 6-9, page 160. H. Mughunyan died at the age of 23, at 6 in the morning on 28 June 1907 (*Bazmavep*, 1907, issue 9, page 412).

Melikyan has gone to Baku – He is referring to the treasurer of the Armenian Union of Paris, Hambardzum Melikyan (see *Anahit*, 1907, page 62).

M<ister> Norayr – He is probably referring to the author (signed "Norayr") of the article "The National Ecclesiastical Concert and Clergymen in the Theater" published in issue 12 in 1905 of the *Taraz* weekly. The article was dedicated to the concert organized by Komitas on 1 April 1905 in the hall of the Tiflis Artistic Society.

98. <TO KARAPET KOSTANYAN>

The original is located at the MAL, KKF, 1100.

It was first published by Gohar Aznavuryan (*Sovetakan Arvest*, 1962, issue 10, page 54), and then in KL 2000, pages 96-97 and KL 2007, pages 117-118.

In KL 2000, the date and place of writing of the letter are considered to be 17 July 1907 in Lausanne, while in G. Aznavuryan's publication and in KL 2007, this is considered to be 17 August 1907 in Lausanne. The date when the letter was sent is wrong in both cases. According to the postal stamp, the letter was sent from Paris on 16 July 1907 (see the notes related to the letter addressed to M. Babayan on 7 July 1907). On the envelope, Komitas had written:

"Suisse
Monsieur Karapet Kostanian
Poste restante
Lausanne
Etp. Komitas V. Paris, Jean-Goujon, 15"

The postal stamp bears the date 16.7.07 (i.e. 16 July, 1907) and the letter was stamped at the post office in Lausanne with the date 17.VII.07 (17 July 1907). The compilers of KL 2007 have repeated the error made by Gohar Aznavuryan and K. Samuelyan's "Annals" by writing "Around 20-25 July 1907, Komitas left with Arshak Chopanyan for Italy (Venice) and then arrived in Lausanne on 17 August, where he wrote this letter" (KL 2007, page 243).

Received the letters you had sent – The letters have not been found.

Kajberuni had not turned up at my hotel at the appointed time - See the notes related to the letter addressed to M. Babayan on 7 July 1907.

I worked for 3 weeks at the monastery in Venice - See the notes related to the letter addressed to M. Babayan on 7 July 1907.

In one of the hotels on S<aint> Mark's square along with M<ister> Chopanyan - See the notes related to the letter addressed to M. Babayan on 7 July 1907.

Go to the Caucasus in a month – Komitas returned to the Caucasus two and a half months later, 30 September (see *Ararat*, 1907, October, page 906).

99. <TO MARGARIT BABAYAN>

The original is located at the MAL, KF, 1346.

It was first published in parts by Margarit Babayan in her memoirs *Komitas Vardapet Through his Letters* (see "*Mshakuyt,*" 1935, page 159-160).

Taking into consideration the phrase "I am leaving here on October 1" and the fact that, according to M. Babayan, the letter was sent from Berlin, we have dated the latter in the beginning of September 1907, because in his letters to V. Mankuni on 10 September and Arshak Chopanyan on 25

September, when the date of his departure is already clear, Komitas says **"I will come to Holy Etchmiadzin in a few days"** or **"I will leave in the coming days."**

These letters addressed to V. Mankuni and M. Babayan were written on paper with a light green tint, and having the same size and thickness, using the same blue ink, all of which suggest that the letters were written in the same period.

Your letter – The letter has not been found.

Lusik – According to Margarit Babayan's notes, Komitas is referring to Louis Laloy – "Mr. Louis Laloy, renowned musicologist and critic" (*"Mshakuyt,"* 1935, page 160). In other letters, Komitas refers to Loius Laloy as "Luys," modifying the French spelling of the name Louis.

If the same songs are deemed worthy of a second edition – He is referring to the collection *Armenian Lyre*; Louis Laloy (Lusik) had made a few comments about some of the songs that had been included in it.

Boldly – the original uses the Armenian յամարձակ instead of համարձակ, which is a case of misspelling.

There is no space left – i.e. to continue the letter. This section of the original is written at the end of the fourth page. Komitas left a few lines to pass on his regards.

Armenuhi and the Doctor – Armenuhi Babayan, Margarit Babayan's sister and a painter (1876-1971). **The Doctor** – he is referring to Avetik Babayan.

I am leaving here on October 1 – Komitas returned to Etchmiadzin on 30 September. This section is written in the margin of the first page, perpendicular to the body of the letter.

100. <TO ARSHAK CHOPANYAN>

The original is located at the MAL, ACF, 3406.

It was first published in *Patma-banasirakan Handes,* 1958, issue 1, page 266, and then in KL 2000, page 137 and KL 2007, pages 166-167.

The letter is dated according to the postal stamp 9.9.07, Charlottenburg.

I received a letter and some money from the Prince – See the letter written to A. Chopanyan on 12 July 1907 and the corresponding notes. The letter sent by Prince Boris Arghutyan to Komitas has not been found.

101. <TO VAHRAM MANKUNI>

The original is located at the MAL, KF, 1446.

It was first published by A. Chopanyan (*Anahit*, 1933, issue 3-6, pages 228-229). According to Chopanyan, V. Mankuni sent Komitas an "Armenian mass arranged for three voices (which was probably the work of B. Chilingiryan)."

I receive/d the notebook and letter – the letter has not been found.

I will come to Holy Etchmiadzin in a few days – Komitas arrived in Etchmiadzin on 30 September 1907.

102. <TO ARSHAK CHOPANYAN>

The original is located at the MAL, ACF, 3407.

It was first published by *PBH*, 1958, issue 1, pages 266-267, and then in KL 2000, page 159, and KL 2007, pages 191-192.

The letter is undated. It was written in Berlin in September 1907, because Komitas was writing about returning his comments regarding the notebook sent by the Music Examination Committee in Constantinople (he is referring to the letter he wrote to the Constantinople Music Examination Committee Chairman Vahram Mankuni on 23/10 September 1907). Taking into consideration the phrase "I received the third telegram. They're calling me, I will leave in the coming days," and the fact that Komitas arrived in Etchmiadzin from Berlin on 30 September 1907, the letter must have been written in the period between 11 and 27 September 1907. The dispatch date stamped on the envelope has been cut out of the top right corner along with the postal stamp, while the stamps of receipt visible in the lower right and left sides confirm that the letter arrived in Paris on 26 September 1907. Komitas wrote the return address on the reverse side of the envelope – "Charlottenbourg, Kant str. 116[I]. l." Considering the fact that letters from Berlin would get to Paris in one day, we have dated this letter 25 September 1907.

The first publisher of this letter, M. Muradyan, has written the following note after the main text, "The envelope bears the text – 26 Sept. 1914, Scharlottenburg," [sic] but the original of this letter at the A. Chobanyan Fund of the MAL does not have a visible date of dispatch and it could not have been written in 1914, because Komitas was in Constantinople in September 1914.

The letter is written in the same ink and on paper of the same color and size as the ones written to V. Mankuni on 10 September 1907 and M. Babayan on 25 September.

I received the third telegram – the telegram has not been found.

Gevo – It is not clear to whom Komitas is referring.

Manuelyan – He is referring to the microbiologist **Yervand Manuelyan**, who became the director of the Pathological Histology and Microbiology Laboratory at the Pasteur Institute in Paris in 1902. He is the author of around 100 research articles related to aging, rabies, alcoholism, and hereditary syphilis. He was an active participant in Armenian community activities in Paris (see *Renowned Armenian Physicians*, Book I, Yerevan, 2002, pages 111-112).

Edgar – He is referring to painter Edgar Chahine (see also the letter he wrote to A. Chopanyan on 15 April 1909).

103. <TO GAREGIN LEVONYAN>

The original is located at the MAL, GLF, 1510.

It was first published in KL 2000, pages 71-72, and then in KL 2007, pages 86-87. Based on the content of the letter, it was written when the journal *Gegharvest* was not yet being published and Garegin Levonyan had just told Komitas Vardapet about his intention to start publishing a journal, the first batch of which was printed in 1908. Garegin Levonyan wrote about his memories around the publication of *Gegharvest* in his memoirs about Komitas (see "Contemporaries on Komitas," Yerevan, 1960, page 152).

I received your letter – The letter has not been found.

I had already spoken to you about the cultural journal when I was in Tpghis – Garegin Levonyan and Komitas Vardapet met in Tiflis in the summer of 1905, when the latter had gone there for medical treatment. "The next time I saw Komitas was in the summer, in Tiflis," wrote Garegin Levonyan, "He had come to be treated. He would often come over to our place, and he remembered our family members quiet well from Sanahin" ("Contemporaries on Komitas," Yerevan, 1960, page 153). The idea to publish a cultural journal had probably first been developed that summer of 1905, because on 25 February 1906, G. Levonyan wrote a letter to the administration of the Gevorgyan Seminary, requesting a statement that would allow him to complete the necessary documentation. "With the objective of publishing a cultural journal with my colleague F. Komitas Vardapet in the coming fall in Etchmiadzin," G. Levonyan wrote, "We are asking whomever it concerns for the necessary permission. We ask you, honorable administrator, to provide a statement certifying my four years of service at the Seminary, which we will send along with our other documents to the Governor of Yerevan" (ANA, f. 312, l. 1, doc. 151).

I would even be happy to contribute music-related material from time to time – The first issue of *Gegharvest* published in 1908 contains the song "I cannot" recorded and arranged by Komitas (page 100-101) and the second issue has "*Hoy, nazan im*" (pages 146-150).

I have only taken on choir lessons at the Seminary, and general musical history for Grade 1 – This reference suggests that the letter was written after Komitas' return from Europe to Vagharshapat, in October 1907.

Mesrop – He is referring to the economic officer at the Gevorgyan Seminary, Mesrop Abovyan.

He is withholding money from your salaries – Garegin Levonyan worked as an art teacher at the Gevorgyan Seminary from 1902 to 1907 (see "Contemporaries on Komitas," Yerevan, 1960, page 149). This reference also suggests that the letter was written in 1907.

104. <TO MARGARIT BABAYAN>

The original is located at the MAL, KF, 1349.

It was first published in parts by "Mshakuyt," 1935, pages 161-163, and then in KL 2000, pages 40-43 and KL 2007, pages 32-35.

The Holy's unexpected death – He is referring to Khrimyan *Hayrik*, who passed away on 29 October 1907. The death of Catholicos Mkrtich I was unexpected, because "Up to the day immediately preceding his death, His Holiness did not have any infirmity, besides the weakness that comes with old age, so **the news came as a surprise** (emphasis by the editor – G.G.) when it spread in the congregation on 28 October about the perilous situation regarding his health" (*Ararat*, 1907, October-November, Page 1).

With me having just arrived here – Komitas had returned from Germany to the Mother See a month earlier, on 30 September 1907.

The burial mass in time for the ceremony – 6 November had been appointed as the date for Mkrtich I's burial (*Ararat*, 1907, October-November, page 10).

For a full 3 weeks after the burial, I could not come to my senses. Today, although my hands are trembling, I want to nevertheless attempt this difficult writing – Taking this reference into consideration, we can suggest that this letter was written on 27 November 1907.

Schröder Conzert Flügel – This piano had been gifted to Komitas Vardapet by A. Mantashyan.

The letter to dear Shushik – The letter has not been found.

Grandpa – He is probably referring to Avetik Babayan, who had arrived in Etchmiadzin for the Catholicos' burial.

Father Garegin – He is referring to Garein Vardapet Hovsepyan.

The Hovhannisyans – He is referring to Hovhannes Hovhannisyan.

Bastin – He is referring to the Grand Opera conductor in Paris, Maurice Bastin.

Dear J. Périer – Jean (Alexis) Périer (1869-1954), French singer and actor. He played the role of Pelléas during the first performance of Claude Debussy's opera Pelléas and Mélisande (30 April 1902, Opera Comique). Mélisande was played by Marie Garden.

I received their open letter – See the "open letter" sent by Maurice Bastin and Jean Périer.

1908

105. <TO MAGHAKIA ORMANYAN>

The original is located at the MAL, GKF, 23.

It was first published in KL 2000, page 181, then in KL 2007, page 213.

In KL 2000 and 2007, the date the letter was sent is mentioned as 26 January, while that is actually the date on which the letter was registered at the Constantinople Patriarchate, according to the registration stamps (see GKF, 23, page 2). Since letters from Etchmiadzin took on average 19 days to reach Constantinople (see the letter written to Maghakia Ormanyan on 24-25 November and the corresponding notes) and based on the letter's registration date (26 January), this letter had been sent by Komitas around 7-8 January.

The money was sent to Kutina and a confirmation of receipt was received on 12 February 1908.

106. <TO GAREGIN LEVONYAN>

The original is located at the MAL, GLF, 1511.

It was first published in KL 2000, page 70, and then in KL 2007, page 87-88.

The letter was written before the publication of issue 1 of *Gegharvest* (April 1907). In the December issue of *Ararat*, there was an announcement published which said "In the beginning of 1908, a literary, artistic, musical journal with illustrations *GEGHARVEST* will be published in Tiflis" (page 1126). The journal program has a separate point stating "7. Musical pieces – a. ecclesiastical music, b. worldly music, c. folk and peasant songs and dance music" (ibid., page 1127). Since the establishment of the journal had already been confirmed, Komitas fulfilled his promised and sent material to *Gegharvest* for publication.

I am sending you what I have promised – He is referring to these words he wrote to Garegin Levonyan in his October 1907 letter: "I would even be happy to contribute music-related material from time to time".

You probably know the lyrics better, since this song is from your parts – He is referring to the song "I cannot" which was published in the first issue of *Gegharvest* (1908, pages 100-101). **this song is from your parts** – Komitas wrote the song in the Shirak region, where Garegin Levonyan was born in Alexandropol.

107. <TO GAREGIN LEVONYAN>

The origivnal is located at the MAL, GLF, 1512.

It was first published in KL 2000, page 69 and then in KL 2007, page 88.

Evening – The Armenian իրիկուն is misrepresented in KL 2000 and 2007 as երեկո.[20]

The first issue of *Gergharvest* that you had published – See the notes for the previous letter.

Do you have my song printed separately? - See the notes for the previous letter.

108. <TO HOVHANNES TUMANYAN>

The original is located at the MAL, TF, 754.

It was first published in *Sovetakan Hayastan*, 1969, issue 272, and then in *Tumanyan: On Art*, Yerevan, 1969, pages 191-192 and *Tumanyan: Studies and Publications*, Vol. 5, Yerevan, 1988, pages 325-326.

I did not get to see you when I was in Tpghis – Komitas was in Tiflis in February 1908 (see MAL, KF, 175, the photograph is captioned "1908. 12/2. Tpghis").

---

20 [Both words mean the same – "evening"] – Translator's notes.

I began a long time ago and have written quite a few things for your "Anush" – See the letter to Mariam Tumanyan written on 22 January 1904 and the corresponding notes.

Shant – He is referring to Levon Shant,

Tell Stepan to send me a few copies if he can of the "Partridge's song" that I wrote – "The Partridge's Song" was published as an appendix in the April issue of the journal *Hasker*, published by Stepan Lisitsyan.

109. <TO GAREGIN LEVONYAN>

The original is located at the MAL, GLF, 1513.

It was first published in KL 2000, pages 69-70 and then in KL 2007, page 88.

I received *Gegharvest* and the songs – He is referring to the first issue of the journal *Gegharvest* and separately printed copies of the song "I cannot" which had been printed in that issue. Garegin Levonyan has fulfilled Komitas' request: "Do you have my song printed separately? If yes, please me a few copies of that as well" (see the letter written to G. Levonyan on 24 May 1908).

Levon – It is not clear to whom Komitas was referring.

I have prepared "*Hoy nazan im*" for three male voices and I will copy it today or tomorrow – The song was published in the second issue of *Gegharvest* (1908, pages 147-150).

Especially one about neumes, since my study has not yet been completed – Komitas' study on neumes did not survive to our times. For sections of it that have been preserved, see **Komitas Vardapet**, Studies and Articles, Book II, Yerevan 2007, pages 321-461).

110. <TO HOVHANNES TUMANYAN>

The original is located at the MAL, TF, 755.

It was first published in *Grakan Tert*, 1936, issue 13, and then in ***Tumanyan:*** *On Art*, Yerevan 1969, pages 192-193.

If you prefer Dilijan, fine – Tumanyan had probably expressed this wish in a letter that has not been found.

Composing the libretto – See the letter to Mariam Tumanyan dated 22 January 1904 and the corresponding notes.

111. <TO HOVHANNES TUMANYAN>

The original is located at the MAL, TF, 756.

It was first published in *Sovetakan Arvest*, 1962, issue 10, page 55.

Liparit – He is probably referring to writer and literary scholar Liparit Nazaryan.

You aren't going to Dilijan – See the previous letter.

You would be going to your village[21] – In July 1908, Tumanyan sent his family to Dsegh for vacation, while he remained in Tiflis. See the letter sent by Hovhannes Tumanyan to Avetik Isahakyan on 2 July 1908 (**Hovhannes Tumanyan**, Compilation of Works, Vol. 10, Yerevan, 1999, pages 41-42).

I will wait until the 10th of the month, after which I will leave, probably for Tpghis, I have a few things I need to print – Komitas had intended to go to Tiflis to publish the solo version of *Armenian Lyre* (see the letters to M. Babayan dated 2 July 1908, to A. Chopanyan dated 5 July 1908 and 5 August 1908, and the corresponding notes.

112. <TO MARGARIT BABAYAN>

The original is located at the MAL, KF, 1347.

It was first published in parts by **K. Samuelyan**, Annals, *Sovetakan Arvest*, 1970, issue 6, pages 54-55, and then in KL 2000, pages 23-24 and KL 2007, pages 35-37.

21 [Tumanyan was from the village of Dsegh, now in the Lori region of modern Armenia] – Translator's notes.

I gave 5 concerts and 6 lectures – During 1908, until the month of July, Komitas gave concerts in Igdir on 4 January, in Vagharshapat on 20 February, in Yerevan on 22 February, as well as in Baku on 1 and 4 April. The concerts were accompanied by lectures. (see **K. Samuelyan**, Annals, *Sovetakan Arvest*, 1970, issue 5, pages 58-60, issue 6, pages 52-54).

I have begun the publication of the solo *Armenian Lyre* – See the letters written to A. Chopanyan on 5 July 1908 and 5 August 1908, and the corresponding notes.

Deacon Stepan, who was studying in Berlin, graduated this year and will come to Holy Etchmiadzin in August – After Deacon Stepan (Spiridon Melikyan) returned to Etchmiadzin, he presented a statement of resignation from celibate priesthood and, through a decision of the Synod on 29 January 1909, he was freed of his spiritual duties (see **Spiridon Melikyan**, Yerevan, 1964, pages 182-184). In the memoirs she wrote later, Spiridon Melikyan's wife Satenik Melikyan described the meeting between the teacher and his student at the station in Etchmiadzin in the following way:

"Komitas was pacing impatiently on the platform. He had come to meet his student who had just finished his studies in Berlin. Spiridon's brother Garnik was also at the station. The train approached, whistled and sighed to a stop. Spiridon emerged from the passenger car, saw his beloved teacher immediately and embraced him. Then the brothers kissed each other. There were two carriages waiting at the station – Komitas had arrived in one, Spiridon's brother had come in the other. They had to arrange the luggage. But which carriage would they use? Komitas proposed his, but Spiridon objected.

'Holy Father, Garnik will take the luggage in his carriage, and I will ride in yours. We will go to Etchmiadzin, straight to our house.'

'I don't understand, what have you decided? Where will you live, what's on your mind?'

And it became clear to Komitas that Spiridon had decided not to return to the monastery and to give up his spiritual life. Of course, Spiridon had made the right decision, but on the other hand, it was difficult to leave Komitas on his own...

And there was the entry to the monastery, the start of the forest.

Komitas stopped the carriage and once again asked, 'Spiridon, what is your final decision?'

Spiridon repeated his words.

'Lucky you, poor me,' Komitas said" (ibid., pages 108-109).

Plan [plan] – Komitas had erased the repeated word in the original.

After the election of the Catholicos – The election of Catholicos Mattheos II Izmirlian took place on 1 November 1908.

113. <ARSHAK CHOPANYAN>

The original is located at the MAL, ACF, 3409.

It was first published in *Patma-banasirakan Handes*, 1958, issue 1, pages 256-257, and then in KL 2000, pages 138-139, KL 2007, pages 169-170.

In KL 2000, the letter is dated "1908, 5 February" which was changed according to K. Samuelyan's "Annals" to "1908, 2-5 July" in KL 2007 (*Sovetakan Arvest*, 1970, issue 6, pages 55). The first publisher of the letter, M. Muradyan, described the date referenced by the postal stamp – "on the envelope – 5.2.08" (5 February, 1908 – see *PBH*, 1958, issue 1, page 257), which was a case of misreading (the "7" was taken for a "2"). The postal stamp clearly shows the date of dispatch as "5.7.08" and we have therefore dated the letter as 5 July 1908.

I have given five concerts and lectured six times – See the letter dated 2 July 1908 to M. Babayan and the corresponding notes.

I have prepared and begun the publication of the solo "Armenian Peasant Lyre" – See the letter dated 5 August to A. Chopanyan and the corresponding notes.

My first student, Deacon Stepan, has graduated in Berlin and will come to Holy Etchmiadzin in August - See and compare with the letter dated 2 July 1908 to M. Babayan and the corresponding notes.

Seriously pursuing education, which is our only salvation and the platform to build our lives in the future – See and compare with the letter dated 5 August to A. Chopanyan and the corresponding notes: "we have to start now and <turn> quickly towards studying, so that we can resist the pressure".

Gevo – It is not clear to whom Komitas is referring.

The Gevreks – This is misrepresented in KL 2000 and 2007 as **the Gevleks.** In 1906, Komitas was photographed with A. Gevrek at the summer house (see **Toros Azatayan**, Komitas Vardapet, Constantinople, 1931, page 69).

The Hovakimyans – He is referring to the founding member of the Armenian Union of Paris, M. Hovakimyan (see *Anahit*, 1907, page 92).

Yervand Manuelyan – See the letter dated 25 September to A. Chopanyan and the corresponding notes.

I sent a letter to Melikyan as well – He is referring to the treasurer of the Armenian Union of Paris, Hambardzum Melikyan (see *Anahit*, 1907, page 92). The letter has not been found.

114. <TO ARSHAK CHOPANYAN>

The original is located at the MAL, ACF, 3408.

It was first published by Gohar Aznavuryan (*Sovetakan Arvest*, 1962, issue 10, page 54) and then copied in KL 2000, pages 140-142 and KL 2007, pages 167-169.

When the stamp was cut out from the top right corner of the envelope bearing this letter, part of the letter was removed with it, as a result of which the text is partially missing. G. Aznavuryan published the letter with her own version of the missing text, which we have preserved here, adding our own corrections (as our own restored version), based on the content.

G. Aznavuryan, and following her example, K. Samuelyan, dated this letter 5 February 1908 (1908, 5. II, Tpghis), which is unlikely, because the letter speaks of the constitutional order established in Turkey after the revolution by the Young Turks (see the final paragraph of the letter). Those events occurred in Turkey in July 1908. The first page of the letter bears the text **"1908. 5 Au<...>"** (with the remaining having been cut of) and since Komitas would write the names of the months using capital letters, as the generally accepted orthography of the time required,[22] that "**Au**"[23] could only be the start of the word "August." G. Aznavuryan mistook that capital "**O**" for the Roman numeral **II**. Komitas has never used Roman numerals

22 [In modern Armenian, the names of the months do not begin with capital letters] – Translator's notes.

23 [In the original Armenian version, this is the letter **O** from the month Oqnuunnu] – Translator's notes.

to date his letters. Komitas had mentioned his return address in Etchmiadzin on the envelope but, according to the postal stamp, he had posted the letter from Tiflis on 7 August 1908. During this period, Komitas was busy with the publication of the solo compositions in "Armenian Peasant Lyre," printed in separate notebooks, which he had mentioned in his letters dated 2 July 1908 to M. Babayan and 5 July 1908 to A. Chopanyan ("I have begun the publication of the solo *Armenian Lyre*," "I have prepared and begun the publication of the solo "Armenian Peasant Lyre" in sets of ten") and, for the purposes of arranging that publication, he had written a request on 31 July to the acting Catholicos Archbishop Gevorg Surenyants for a one-month vacation, to travel for personal reasons and go to Tpghis, which he mentions in this letter as well ("I came to Tphgis <to> print my s<ongs>").

<On the day> I received your letter – The letter has not been found.

I got a letter from Shahmurad - The letter has not been found.

<Mughun>yan, despite all the chances <he had> - He is referring to the good reputation Mughunyan had in the salons of Paris and his contacts in wealthy society. *Bazmavep* wrote the following in this regard: "In Paris, a young Armenian singer has fallen victim of tuberculosis, Hovakim Mughunyan, who had often been applauded for his sensitive and touching voice in the salons frequented by ambassadors and famous people" (1907, issue 9, page 410), "He rose to the stages of the largest salons in Paris through Marquise St. Paul" (ibid., page 411).

<Shahmu>rad's – According to G. Aznavuryan this is "**Shahmuradyan**" but this is a mistake. This part of the letter refers to their **voices**, not to them individually.

You cannot make up for the fact that you did not come – See and compare the letter dated 5 July 1908 to A. Chopanyan – "We were very sad to hear you cannot come..." (page 143, r. 16-23 of this publication). Chopanyan arrived in Etchmiadzin in October 1908 as a delegate during the elections of the Catholicos, and was hosted by Komitas.

Our country is free as well – He is referring to the revolution by the Young Turks in 1908 and the overthrow of the Hamidian regime.

Betray. <...> I have (old calendar) <...> - According to G. Aznavuryan, this line "has been damaged badly and is illegible."

115. <TO GAREGIN LEVONYAN>

The original is located at the MAL, GLF, 1514.

It was first published in KL 2000, page 70, and then in KL 2007, page 89. The editor of KL 2007, following K. Samuelyan "Annals" (*Sovetakan Arvest*, 1970, issue 6, page 57), considered the date of the letter to be 22-25 December. However, the postal stamp on the other side of the postcard, the letter was sent from Etchmiadzin on 22 December (22.12.08 Эчмиадзинъ), so it must have been written no later than 22 December. It arrived in Tiflis, once again according to the postal stamp, on 24 December (24.12.08, Тифлисъ).

Zurna player – See the letter written to A. Chopanyan on 20 October 1906 and the corresponding notes.

16 copies of *Gegharvest* – He is referring to the second issue of the journal *Gegharvest*, published in 1908, where the article "Komitas Vardapet" (pages 125-128) was published, authored by **Shavarsh** (Garegin Levonyan's pen name), as was the song written and arrange by Komitas, "*Hoy Nazan Im*" (pages 146-150). Studies have shown that the author of the article had a copy and made use of the "Autobiography" written by Komitas on 24 July 1908 (see and compare **Komitas Vardapet**, Studies and Articles, Book II, Yerevan 2007, pages 54-58).

I carried... and brought – Komitas had brought the issues of *Gegharvest* from Tiflis, where he had gone to organize a concert to benefit the Armenian Benevolent Society of the Caucasus. On 10 December, Komitas was photographed in Gevorg Bashinjaghyan's Tiflis studio with Hovhannes Tumanyan, Ghazaros Aghayan, Avetik Isahakyan, Arshak Chopanyan, Vrtanes Papazyan and Gevorg Bashinjaghyan.

Old man Kochar – He is probably referring to Gevorgyan Seminary instructor Karapet Kocharyan.

116. <TO MATTHEOS IZMIRLYAN>

The original is located at the MAL, KF, 8.

It was first published in KL 2000, pages 55-57 and then in KL 2007, pages 70-72.

According to the editor of KL 2007, "the continuation of the letter has not been found." However, the space remaining for two-three lines on the final page of the letter, the partial corrections on the draft copy, as well as the fact that the letter is not signed, all suggest that Komitas Vardapet **never continued** writing the letter and did not send it to the addressee in Constantinople.

Considering the date mentioned in the letter for the statement of the Religious Assembly of the National Central Administration, **29 November**, the time taken for letters to arrive from Constantinople to Etchmiadzin (19 days on average), and Komitas' statement about his "sacred duty to respond immediately," we have dated the letter 20-21 December 1908.

The comments made in the letter about Armenian ecclesiastical music and singing the mass have been presented in greater detail and with more justification by Komitas in his article "Armenian Ecclesiastical Music in the 19th Century" and his lecture titled "The Characteristics of Armenian Ecclesiastical and Folk Music: The Influence of Foreign Music on Armenian Ecclesiastical and Bard Music" (see **Komitas Vardapet**. Studies and Articles, Yerevan 2005, Book I, pages 78-89, Book II, Yerevan, 2007, Pages 188-193).

I received... and read it with indescribable emotion in my heart – The letter has not been found.

117. <TO ARSHAK CHOPANYAN>

The original is located at MAL, ACF, 3410.

It was first published in KL 2000, pages 139-140, and then in KL 2007, pages 170-171.

The letter was sent to Hovhannes Tumanyan's address – "Г-ну Ионаесу Туманянцу, Тифлис, 44 Бебутовская 44."[24] Below the address, Komitas had written, "**Hand this to *zurna* player old man Arshak Chopanyan**."

According to the postal stamp, the letter arrived in Tiflis on 29 December.

It seems like you have found a warm place to stay – He is referring to Hovhannes Tumanyan's hospitality.

24 ["To Mr. Ioanes Tumanyants, Tiflis, 44 Bebutovsyaka 44"] – Translator's notes

I called the photographer and he made this very good offer considering your dedicated service to your homeland through your art – In a letter written to Catholicos Mattheos Izmirlyan, A. Chopanyan explains the purpose for his request to Komitas regarding the photographs, "...I have prepared an extensive volume in French about ancient Armenian poetry (Khorenatsi, Yeghishe, Narekatsi, Shnorhali and so on), I have translated many beautiful passages with references. This will be the most important of my publications. **I want to illustrate this book with a number of photographs and samples of Armenian art.** That is why I had instructed for 15-20 photographs to be taken of a number of items located in Etchmiadzin (a painting, curtain, sculpture, and so on) as well as illustrated ancient manuscripts. Komitas Vardapet has taken on the task of having the pictures taken and sending them to me and has convinced photographer M<ister> Datyan to prepare the pictures for a cheap price (because resources are limited). **Komitas Vardapet has informed me that most of the photographs are ready, but he has not yet sent them, because he has not been able to have pictures taken of any manuscripts.** I would be profoundly grateful to you if you would issue the necessary command for the pictures of the manuscripts to be taken and sent to me as quickly as possible" (MM, M. Izmirlyan archive, fol. 14, doc. 523).

The A. Chopanyan Fund at the MAL contains several photographs of church items and illustrated manuscript pages not just from the manuscript library at Ecthmiadzin, but also from Jerusalem, Venice and other archives (MAL, memoir section, ACF, unprocessed).

Minas Berberyan said that... despite the teachers' complaints – In 1907, through an edict by Catholicos Mkrtich I, Minas Berberyan had been appointed the administrator of the Gevorgyan Seminary (*Ararat*, 1907, issue 9, page 747, 781-782).

Father Nerses Vardapet Karakhanyan – He is probably referring to the Armenian prelate in Mush, Nerses Vardapet Kharakhanyan, who was ordained a bishop on 25 October 1909 (*Ararat*, 1909, issue 9-10, pages 810-814).

The camel came – According to the reference made in a letter to A. Chopanyan dated 30 October 1909, Komitas referred to Master Mesrop Ter-Movsisyan as "the camel" – "Having heard this, the camel Mesrop Vardapet".

Karagyans – It is not clear to whom Komitas is referring here.

1909

118. <TO MATTHEOS IZMIRLYAN>

The original is located at the MAL, GKF, 24.

It was first published in KL 2000, pages 55-57, and then in KL 2007, pages 72-74.

In my official reply – He is possibly referring to another version of the incomplete letter dated 20-21 December 1908, which has not been found.

The rules and laws regarding ancient Armenian neumes, and I compiled a music textbook – There are a number of writings and extracts from various sources on the study of neumes kept at the Komitas Archives of the MAL, but the "music textbook" referred to by the author has not been found (see **Komitas Vardapet**, Studies and Articles, Book II, Yerevan 2007, pages 321-461, 507-563).

Father Trdat Palyan had found a rulebook about Armenian neumes among the manuscripts of Caesarea's S<aint> Daniel Monastery... to receive and study that manuscript have yielded no results – See the letters written to Karapet Kostanyan on 15 January 1897 and Babken Vardapet Kyuleseryan in September-October 1899, as well as the corresponding notes.

I even asked the deceased Catholicos – He is referring to Catholicos Mkrtich I (who passed away on 29 October 1907).

I request you to issue instructions – Regarding Komitas' letter, the following was noted during the minutes of the Religious Assembly meeting dated 27 January 1909:

"The Assembly decided during the Jan. 27 meeting to send a note of gratitude to F. Komitas Vard. for his selfless and hardworking efforts aimed at the improvement of Armenian ecclesiastical music. At the same time, F. Komitas Vard. should be informed that a copy will be sent to him of the rulebook about Armenian neumes found among the manuscripts of the St. Daniel Monastery by Archbishop Trdat 14 years ago. In addition, the Assembly found it suitable to request a copy of the Armenian notation textbook prepared and published by him. The Assembly also decided to write to the Holy Leader of Caesarea so that a copy or photograph of the manuscript requested by F. Komitas Vard. is sent to that Vardapet in Etchmiadzin urgently" (see MAL, GKF, 24, page 6).

119. <TO GHEVOND TAYAN>

The location of the original is unknown.

This letter was first published by Ghevond Tayan in the article "Komitas Vardapet" (*Bazmavep*, 1936, issue 1, pages 9-10). Regarding the circumstances in which he came to receive this letter, G. Tayan wrote, "And I was one of the 'unfortunate' ones, who was in St. Xenon for my annual vacation and was waiting for his arrival based on a piece of news I had received earlier, but we were all left disappointed at the last moment, because the Vardapet had been forced to hasten his departure to Paris.

To be honest, I have to say that it was difficult for me to come to terms with this arrangement by the V., and it seems like the desire to have 'revenge' grew within me for this reason. I waited for some time to pass, for the Musician to return to Etchmiadzin with his laurels of victory.

And around a year and half went by.

I recall that in my first letter, I had told him about my great appreciation for his honorable self and his work, and then mentioned the pain and disappointment I had felt in the past when I had missed his lectures. Then I asked for the list of his published works, so that I could make use of them. And in the end, I did not hide my desire to have a sample of his songs, about which I had heard such good things.

It is impossible to describe the pleasure I felt when one day I received a reply from Etchmiadzin written and signed personally by Komitas V. My admiration for that noble soul grew immensely when I saw that the fourth page of the letter bore a song penned and recorded by him, ***'Akh Maral jan.'***"

Attached to the letter, Komitas Vardapet had sent the notes for "*Akh Maral jan,*" which G. Tayan published in the article (Ibid., pages 12-13).

Your letter full of interest – The letter has not been found.

I am indeed going at the end of the spring to Constantinople and then to Jerusalem and Egypt – Komitas left for Constantinople one year later, at "the end of spring" in 1910.

I have the Armenian mass arranged in 7 different kinds of polyphony, but it has not been published – G. Tayan published a copy of this section of the original letter in his article (Ibid., page 30).

A collection of folk songs will soon be published – He is referring to the solo publication of "Armenian Lyre" in separate booklets (see the letters to M. Babayan dated 2 July 1908, to A. Chopanyan dated 5 July 1908 and 5 August 1908).

120. <TO SIRANUSH>

The original is located at the MAL, SF, 225.

It was published for the first time in *Grakan Tert*, 1936, issue 9, and then *Hayreniki Dzayn*, 1969, issue 46, KL 2000, pages 163-164, KL 2007, pages 193-195.

The 35th anniversary of Siranush's theatrical career was celebrated in Baku in 1909. The MAL Komitas Fund has a photograph (no. 255) of Siranush gifted to Komitas with the following text, "To honorable Father Komitas with profound respect, in exchange for beautiful and valuable memories." The "**beautiful and valuable memories**" is probably a reference to this letter written by Komitas.

Cleared a straight and narrow path – K. Samuelyan had edited this Armenian phrase "ճանապարհ հորդեցիք" and made it "ճանապարհորդեցիք" (resulting in the meaning that Siranush had "travelled" straight for 35 years), while the editors of KL 2000 and KL 2007 had corrected Komitas' orthographical "error" and changed the Armenian հորդեցիք to յորդեցիք, suggesting that the word originated from the Armenian "յորդ." According to the Haykazyan dictionary "յորդել" means "to overflow, to run over, to flow" (which would mean that Siranush had "poured" a path for 35 years.). But in reality, there are not mistakes or typos here. Komitas had used the word "հորդել" with its regular meaning. According to the Haykazyan dictionary, the verb "հորդել" means to "prepare, smooth, clear, open." Take for example the phrases from the book of Isaiah "Build up, build up, prepare the way" (Is 56:14) and "prepare the way" (Is 62:10) which both use the verb "հորդել" in the Armenian translation. There are also many other cases in which the phrase "ճանապարհ հորդել" has been used to mean "to clear a path" (see *Nor Bargirk Haykazyan Lezvi*, Vol. 2, Venice, 1837, page 124, 371).

121. <TO MARIAM TUMANYAN>

The original is located at the MAL, MTF, 457.

It was first published in *Sovetakan Arvest*, 1962, issue 10, page 55, and then in KL 2000, pages 50-51, and KL 2007, pages 65-66.

For our concert – Komitas gave two concerts when he went to Tiflis, "one was in the presence of the king's deputy, who had come with his whole delegation particularly to hear the Armenian folk songs performed by me and my choir, for the benefit of the Caucasus Benevolent Society, and the second was in the royal Theater, where I directed the Armenian segment of the international ecclesiastical music concert to benefit the poor families of the fallen soldiers from the last Russian wars" (see the letter to Ghevond Tayan written on 12 July 1909). In this case, Komitas is referring to the first concert, because two days later, on 14 February 1909, he writes in his letter to M. Tumanyan "I have decided not to participate in philanthropic events anymore because they only end up exploiting me." Komitas did, nevertheless, participate in that concert, which took place in the period between 25 February and 2 March, before the concert on 3 March.

I received the illustrated notebooks for children – He is referring to the illustrated children's booklets that Mariam Tumanyan had published. "Tumanyan had collected many tales and legends, and we decided this time to take on the publication of an illustrated children's booklet," M. Tumanyan wrote in her memoirs (*Tumanyan in the Memories of his Contemporaries*, Yerevan, 1969, pages 482).

122. <TO MARIAM TUMANYAN>

The original is located at the MAL, MTF, 458.

It was first published in *Sovetakan Arvest*, 1962, issue 10, page 55, and then in KL 2000, pages 51-52, KL 2007, pages 65-66.

I received your letter – The letter has not been found.

Sent you a telegram – The telegram has not been found.

The theater has already been reserved – He is referring to the Royal Theater of Tiflis, where a spiritual music concert was held on 3 March.

I have decided not to participate in philanthropic events anymore – See the letter written to M. Tumanyan on 12 February 1909 and the corresponding notes.

Our Hovhannes was not set free – Hovhannes Tumanyan was arrested and imprisoned in December 1908.

"Anush" is moving forward – See the letter written by Komitas to Mariam Tumanyan on 22 January 1904 and the corresponding notes and *Tumanyan in the Memories of his Contemporaries*, Yerevan, 1969, pages 479-481.

123. <TO HOVHANNES ARSHARUNI>

The original is located at the MAL, KF, 1.

It was first published in KL 2000, pages 12-13 and then in KL 2007, pages 18-19.

The letter is a draft; deleted words are presented in square brackets. It is not clear whether or not Komitas sent the letter.

For an explanation of the motivation behind the writing of this letter, see the letters written to Mattheos Izmirlyan on 20-21 December 1908 and 9 January 1909, as well as the corresponding notes.

I have not yet received a copy of the manuscript on music from the St. Daniel Monastery of Caesarea – On 27 January 1909, the Religious Assembly had decided to "write to the Holy Leader of Caesarea so that a copy or photograph of the manuscript requested by F. Komitas Vard. be sent to that Vardapet in Etchmiadzin urgently". Bishop Trdat had apparently not acted on the Assembly's decision. Later, in an interview with Komitas led by conductor Levon Cherrahyan, published in the daily *Jamanak* in 1910, the former once again refers to this issue and to the interpretation of neumes, saying, "There are photographs of old Armenian neumes in the Soorb Karapet monastery of Caesarea, in Bishop Trdat's possession. I wrote to the Holy Father, who was a priest then, to send me those photographs, but my requests fell on deaf ears. I wrote to the national administration after that, to the Patriarch of the time, his replacement and failed in the end to achieve my objective because the prelate of Caesarea wanted to sell the manuscripts for 300 rubles, a price which I had to reject, since I did not have the money. So I decided to go to Europe and having reached Italy, I sought the Pope and he opened the museums before me with great hospitality; I found and studied many things there. I went to other cities as well – Berlin, Paris, and then Switzerland. But they were all illegible. I needed old dictionaries to read then and that immense task greatly exhausted me. But, after a lot of searching, I finally managed to achieve my objective, and now there are now secrets left for me about Armenian music," (*Jamanak*, 1910, issue 584, page 1).

Copy – The Armenian ընդօրինակություն has been misrepresented in KL 2000 and 2007 as ընդօրինակքը. Komitas has written the suffix "-ություն" in contracted form.

124. <TO ARSHAK CHOPANYAN>

The original is located at the MAL, ACF, 3411.

It was first published in *Patma-banasirakan Handes*, 1958, issue 1, pages 257-259, and then in KL 2000, pages 12-13 and KL 2007, pages 172-176.

I have received your letters – The letters have not been found.

I can have the remaining two pictures taken at the Gayane monastery, and then send you 80 photographs – See the letter written to A. Chopanyan on 23 December 1908 and the corresponding notes.

F<ather> Garegin – He is referring to Garegin Vardapet Hovsepyan.

Because the camel - According to the reference made in a letter to A. Chopanyan dated 30 October 1909, Komitas referred to Master Mesrop

Ter-Movsisyan as "the camel" – "Having heard this, the camel Mesrop Vardapet".

As for the ones that F<ather> Garegin was supposed to photograph, they are linked to very random obstacles, because the camel is citing a number of obstacles. I suggest that we leave that for the moment until the Catholicos comes – He is referring to Catholicos Mattheos Izmirlyan, who had left for a tour (Constantinople, Russia, Georgia) after his election (on 1 November 1908) and returned to the Mother See on 28 July 1909 (*Ararat*, 1909, supplement, page 83-85). Chopanyan followed Komitas' advice and wrote a letter to Mattheos Izmirlyan in June (see the letter written to A. Chopanyan on 23 December 1908 and the corresponding notes.

Gal<lic> - French.

Instead of four (4) Napoleons – *Napoleon d'or* – A French gold coin, which was issued starting from 1803.

The Locum Tenens – the Locum Tenens at that time was Archbishop Gevorg Surenyants.

His thieving vassal Archbishop Hussik – He is referring to Archbishop Hussik Movsesyan. According to M. Muradyan, "Komitas called him a thief for embezzling the church's money" (*PBH*, 1958, issue 1, page 259).

Surenyan and company have decided to turn everything upside down before the Catholicos arrives, come what may. They want to disgrace Berberyan, F<ather> Garegin, Yervand, Hussik and Komitas Vardapet with disgusting lies – The situation at that time at the Mother See and the consequent events that unfolded have been described in detail by Yervand Vardapet (Yervand Ter-Minasyan) in his memoirs.

"Minas Berberyan was a very friendly, loving and humorous individual; we soon grew close and began to live and work together like brothers. It was only in 1909 that some discontent began to appear again among the students towards the administrator and **in the month of March and April, Minas Berberyan was arrested through the order of the Tsarist government as a person belonging to the Dashnaktsutyun party** and he was expelled from Etchmiadzin, although he had never had anything to do with that party and its activities.

In any case, the calm life of the seminary was once again troubled, **the students began to put forth demands, boycott the examinations at the**

end of the year and cause disorder, such that the temporarily appointed administrator Manuk Abeghyan and the whole faculty did not know how to resolve the difficult situation that had developed, **especially since the Catholicos' deputy Archbishop Gevorg Surenyan, urged on by those surrounding him, was not reigning in the students' disarray; instead, his decisions and scolding of the faculty encouraged the disorderly students.** Things reached a point where the whole faculty resigned their positions, all except for one – Stepan Kanayan, who was the only supporter the deputy had among the faculty, and was appointed temporary administrator of the seminary during the summer months of 1909. Surenyan happily accepted the resignation of the faculty and dismissed them. The faculty prepared a written complaint and requested their supporters Yervand Vardapet, Hovhannes Hovhannisyan and N. Kyurdyan to personally present the complaint to the newly elected Catholicos of All Armenians Mattheos II Izmirlian, who was due in Etchmiadzin in those summer months.

And Catholicos Mattheos did indeed arrive in Etchmiadzin, heard the complaint of the seminary representatives about the irregularities and disorder that had occurred, but did not follow up on it and, in two months, he invited the well-known *Dashnak* activist Sirakan Tigranyan to bring together the new members of the faculty, excluding many people from the previous group. I too was excluded from the seminary along with them. Understandably, I took this as a horrible blow and I was in a state of dilemma and anxiety about what I was to do in Etchmiadzin if I could no longer be a teacher at the seminary" (Yervand Ter-Minasyan, *Memories from My Life*, Yerevan, 2005, pages 66-67).

I resigned for a whole month – Komitas presented his resignation during the 1908-1909 academic year because the budget sheet drawn up by Archibishop Gevorg Surenyants did not include Komitas' work as conductor of the four-voice choir and reduced his salary of 600 rubles (ANA, f. 212, fol. 27, doc. 250, page 25). Referring to this episode, A. Adamyan wrote, "The minutes of the extraordinary meeting held on 18 February 1909 by the Pedagogical Council of the Gevorgyan Seminary are valuable; they show that during the 1908-1909 academic year, the seminary administrator presented a budget sheet to the Locum Tenens, who did not approve it, resulting in a new budget sheet that did not include Komitas' position as conductor of the four-voice choir, and also left out the salary increase of those seminary teachers who had served for more than five years, the salary of the manuscript library manager, some other economic expenses and so on.

"The Deputy's budget that has been mentioned led to complaints and protests among the seminary faculty. The faculty complained in particular about the deletion of Komitas' work as director of the choir. Komitas, claiming that the deputy did not appreciate the subject he taught and the work he did, resigned from working at the seminary. In this regard, the minutes have the following note,

'...F. Komitas said that he felt dishonored and was resigning from working at the seminary from that very day, because he noticed that the Locum Tenens felt that his presence at the seminary was unnecessary, and that he would pay back the salaries he had received (according to the newly approved budget) from the congregational payments.

"Considering his strange and incomprehensible behavior by the Locum Tenens against the seminary and its teaching staff, the whole faculty decided unanimously that, while they considered the Administrator's concern about the expected dissatisfaction from the students regarding the inexplicably reduced budget, the sole responsibility for that lay with the Locum Tenens and his 'personal council.' Regarding the changes to the faculty salaries, the teachers stated that they could not accept the reduction in their payments and demanded their full salaries as promised to them at the beginning of the academic year. And because the teachers had not been receiving salaries despite several verbal and written requests, the pedagogical council decided to make a conclusive request of the Administrator to pay in full for the months of November, December, January and February by 22 February at the latest, otherwise they would be forced to seek measures that would be unpleasant for them all.

"The Administrator and the faculty were unanimous in their expression of warm commiserations to F. Komitas and asked him to wait before putting things into motion. F. Komitas said with regret that he considered it impossible to change his decision, because there was no way he could ignore the offense to which he had been subjected" (*Teghekagir Hasarakakan Gitutyunneri*, 1956, issue 9, pages 108-109).

We are now even more convinced and our consciences are clear that all that talk was slander directed against Ormanyan – During the

1908 revolt, on 16 July, the protesters stormed the Constantinople Patriarchate and forced the Patriarch, Maghakia Ormanyan, to resign, which he immediately did. After that, a series of claims were presented against Ormanyan, suggesting that he had displayed inaction during the time of the Hamidyan regime that was not in the interests of their nation, and that he had led a "servile policy" and so on (for more on this, see **H. C. Siruni**, Ormanyan and his Times: The Accused and his Crimes, *Etchmiadzin*, 1961, issue 12, pages 30-44). "Ormanyan's case" was discussed for years in the Armenian press. In the National Assembly session dated 14 December 1912, Krikor Zohrab described the position against Ormanyan in the following words,

"Many accusations have been brought forward against Holy Father Ormanyan, but nobody said that Holy Father Ormanyan had abused resources or embezzled money. The biggest of the charges placed against him was that he followed the Ottoman Government with a servile policy.

After the Massacres, Holy Father Ormanyan became the Armenian Patriarch and followed a policy of conciliation until the end. Perhaps this is not a policy that everybody approves, but it was obligatory considering the prevalent conditions in those times. Also, conciliation is a policy we have been following for millennia. Armenian history is the history of submission. Many of the nations with whom we have been contemporaries are now wiped off the face of the earth, but we still exist - we owe this to that policy and this is why the Armenians have managed to live under many rulers (**Krikor Zohrab.** A Collection of Works in 4 Volumes, Compiled by Albert Sharuryan, additional volume with two books, Book 2, Vol. 6, page 225).

The issues related to schools and the estates will come up again – Benik Vardapet Ter-Yeghiazaryan wrote the following about the anti-Armenian policy of Russian from 1895 to 1905 - "In 1895, the Tsarist authorities vengefully closed down the Armenian national church schools, and strengthened the propaganda of Russian missionaries in Armenian villages with the objective to convert the Armenians. Afraid of an even greater display of vengeance by the Tsar, the Catholicos in Etchmiadzin ignored the advice of Bishop Nahapet and, at prosecutor Kanzeli's suggestion, allocated the best piece of land in Vagharshapat for the construction of a grand

Russian church, which would be a competitor to the Mother See in Etchmiadzin and would aim to proselytize. In 1903, he grabbed all the estates of the Armenian Church, the buildings and property it owned in various cities, and ordered Etchmiadzin to present ordered lists to the Tsarist authorities' committees of all the estates, property and finances (My Memoirs, MAL, KF, 77, pages 114-115).

The leadership has decided to erase the institution called the *Dashnaktsutyun* at any cost – He is referring to the mass arrests undertaken by the last Tsarist government in 1908 as part of the "*Dashnaktsutyun* case."

My concert has been cancelled – It is not clear to which concert he is referring.

We Armenians excelled against everyone at the spiritual music concert – He is referring to the 3 March 1909 concert (see the letters to Mariam Tumanyan dated 12 and 14 February 1903).

They called me by telegram – The telegram has not been found.

So that I can go to my home town for a few months and rest in the springs – Komitas arrived in his homeland of Kütahya in July 1910.

We received news of the confirmation by telegram, but the official edict has not yet arrived – He is referring to the edict by Nikolai II confirming Mattheos II Izmirlian as Catholicos, which was received in Etchmiadzin on 28 April 1909 (*Ararat*, 1909, issue 5-6, page 415).

I found the key to the old Armenian neumes and I began to read the simple melodies – See and compare the letter written to Hovhannes Arsharuni on 19 March 1909.

Not mourning like Khorenatsi – See Movses Khorenatsi, Armenian History, Part Three, Chapter 68.

Please hand the enclosed song to Shahmurad – It is not clear which song Komitas had sent.

Except for the Babayans – He is referring to Margarit and Shushik Babayan.

To my dear Hovakimyan family – See the letter dated 12 July 1907 to Arshak Chopanyan and the corresponding notes.

Yervand Manuelyan - See the letter dated 5 July 1908 to Arshak Chopanyan and the corresponding notes.

Chahine - He is referring to painter Edgar Chahine.

Polat – KL 2000 and 2007 has misrepresented this as **Polar**. He is referring to engraver Tigran Polat (1874-1950).

Gevo – It is not clear to whom Komitas is referring.

Garib – He is referring to Onnik Garibyan, a spectacle seller from Constantinople.

125. <TO GHEVOND TAYAN>

The location of the original is unknown.

This letter was first published by Ghevond Tayan in the article "Komitas Vardapet" (*Bazmavep*, 1936, issue 1, pages 10-11).

Your soulful letter – The letter has not been found.

I had been summoned to Tpghis to conduct the Armenian concerts there - one was in the presence of the king's deputy... the second was in the royal Theater – See the letters written to Mariam Tumanyan on 12 and 14 February 1909 and to Arshak Chopanyan on 15 April 1909, as well as the corresponding notes.

One was in the presence of the king's deputy – He is referring to General Vorontsov-Dashkov, who served as the King's deputy (Governor General) in the Caucasus from 1905 to 1915.

When I returned to Holy Etchmiadzin – Komitas returned to Etchmiadzin on 4 March (see **K. Samuelyan**, Annals, *Sovetakan Arvest*, 1970, issue 6, page 60). Ghevond Tayan mentions the fact that he "**hastened to thank him**" *(emphasis by the editor, G.G.)* for the letter Komitas wrote on 12 February 1909 (*Bazmavep*, 1936, issue 1, page 10), meaning that the letter addressed to Komitas had been sent on 13 February, and Komitas received it at the Mother See on 4 March, but delayed his reply, waiting for the photograph he had ordered in Baku (see the next note).

I ordered a photograph of myself in Baku so that I would not leave your requests unfulfilled, and it ended up late – According to Ghevond Tayan, "I availed of the Vardapet's generosity this time as well and asked for a photograph of him" (*Bazmavep*, 1936, issue 1, page 10). In the 1909 issue of the journal *Geghuni* (page 56), Ghevond Vardapet published both the photograph and the original notes of "*Akh, Maral jan*" which he had received with the letter dated 2 June 1909. On the reverse side of the photograph, according to Tayan, Komitas had written the following note, "To hon. F. Ghevond Vard. Tayan – a memento of friendship – Komitas Vr. – 1909 12/6 – Holy Etchmiadzin" (*Bazmavep*, 1936, issue 1, page 11, footnote).

Something which is badly understood and unappreciated among us – According to Ghevond Tayan, "He is referring, of course, to the opposition that existed towards him right then, in 1909, at the monastery in Etchmiadzin, which had even led to a reduction in his salary by His Grace Surenyan, the deputy of the Catholicos."

126. <TO ARSHAK CHOPANYAN>

The original is located at the MAL, ACF, 3412.

It was first published in *Patma-banasirakan Handes*, 1958, issue 1, page 260.

There was a delay with sending the photographs; I had mentioned the reasons in my previous letter... Father Garegin will send some soon as well... The other day, His Holy summoned the camel and ordered him to facilitate the whole process – See the letters written to Arshak Chopanyan on 23 December 1908 and 15 April 1909, as well as the corresponding notes.

Father Garegin – He is referring to Garegin Hovsepyan.

His Holy summoned the camel – This means that Catholicos Mattheos II summoned Master Mesrop Ter-Movsisyan.

And gaining attention... - The ellipsis was present in the original.

Like Surenyan – He is referring to Catholicos Locum Tenens Archbishop Gevorg Surenyants.

Recently, he summoned me and we had a long talk. He also called Yervand and Hussik – In his memoirs, Yervand Ter-Minasyan wrote about these meetings, the conversations and the events that followed –

"In the summer, the Catholicos of All Armenians Mattheos II arrived in Etchmiadzin and, because it was unbearably hot in Etchmiadzin, he left immediately for the patriarchal summer house in Byurakan and started dealing with his duties. The arrangements that he made for the Gevorgyan Seminary have already been mentioned above in their rightful place, and as for the issue that is of interest to me, the Catholicos welcomed me in a loving manner, had a pleasant conversation with me, but later, it seemed, he forgot about my issue and did not give any instructions about it. And when I expressed my desire in writing in the weeks that followed, hoping to finally see the conflict that had arisen been the deputy Surenyan and me resolved, Catholicos Mattheos II Izmirlyan summoned my teacher supreme Vardapet Karapet and instructed him to form a tribunal of Etchmiadzin congregants to examine the Deputy's arguments and mine in order to decide which of our two sides justice favors, and then to report to him. Supreme Vardapet Karapet had convinced the Catholicos that such an initiative was not the most suitable approach, because the case might end up like a Medieval Inquisition, which would then be the subject of rumors and criticism by the press, without finding a solution to the problem. They let the issue slide just like that, and I never received an answer.

I understood that there was nothing left for me to do but to give up my spiritual calling and leave Etchmiadzin" (**Yervand Ter-Minasyan**, *Memories from My Life*, Yerevan, 2005, pages 90-91).

23 August, the day he was sent on exile – Catholicos Mattheos II's ordination ceremony took place on 13 September 1909, not on 23 August "the day he was sent on exile" (*Ararat*, 1909, issue 9, page 702).

His Holy was visited by the Governor of Yerevan – He is referring to the Governor of Yerevan Count Tiesenhausen. *Ararat* has published a report on this meeting. "The Governor of Yerevan, Count Tiesen-Hausen arrived at the Mother See on 10 July accompanied by Mr. Thaddeos Kalantaryan, to visit the Holy Patriarch and, after having breakfast in the Patriarchate, he returned to Darachichag the same day" (1909, issue 7-8, page 537).

I will probably go to Constantinople and my homeland after the ordination – Komitas arrived in his birthplace, Kütahya, in June 1910.

127. <TO MATTHEOS IZMIRLYAN>

The original is located at the MAL, RTF, 83.

It was first published with editing to the punctuation by Toros Azatyan (**Komitas Vardapet,** Constantinople, 1931, page 98(. According to T. Azatyan, "This valuable piece has been provided by musicologist Mr. Nerses Khyudaverdyan."

Nerses Khyudaverdyan was the choirmaster at the Holy See of Jerusalem.

Hesitation – T. Azatyan had misread and changed the original Armenian վարանանք to վարանմունք, another version of the same word.

Release me of my oath to the Congregation at Holy Etchmiadzin – Komitas uses the Armenian word ուխտ (pronounced "ukht," meaning "oath") which may be a pun or a poke at Master Mesrop Ter-Movsisyan, whom he referred to in his letter to A. Chopanyan as Ուղտ (pronounced only slightly differently – "ught," meaning "camel").

128. <TO MARGARIT BABAYAN>

The original is located at the MAL, KF, 1348.

The letter was written by A. Shahmuradyan. Komitas wrote his text on the reverse side of the postcard, on the picture.

It has been published for the first time.

129. <TO ARSHAK CHOPANYAN>

The original is located at the MAL, ACF, 3413.

It was first published in *Patma-banasirakan Handes*, 1958, issue 1, pages 261-264.

According to the postal stamp, the letter was sent from Etchmiadzin 7 days after it was written, on 7.11.09, i.e. 7 October 1909.

I have received your letters – The letters have not been found.

You have probably already received the photographs, I had the ones prepared by Father Garegin sent some time ago as well – See the letters written to A. Chopanyan on 23 December 1908, 15 April 1909 and 14 July 1909, as well as the corresponding notes.

Father Garegin – He is referring to Garegin Hovsepyan.

I returned from Tpghis yesterday. I had gone for the burial of Mrs. Mantashyan – Darya Mantashyan's burial took place on 26 October 1909.

Sirakan Tigranyan, who was the editor of the newspaper *Horizon*, was brought to Holy Etchmiadzin – Sirakan Tigranyan was Nikoghayos Tigranyan's brother.

The camel... pushed himself up to the title of Bishop – Master Mesrop Ter-Minasyan was ordained a bishop on 25 October 1909 (see *Ararat*, 1909, issue 10-11, pages 812-813).

The congregation has not chosen him, nor does he have a document from the people – *Ararat* had the following explanation for the ordination of Mesrop Vardapet as a bishop, "Four of the eight members of the Synod must be bishops or archbishops, but there were only three archbishops in the Synod. His academic reputation, the positions he had held and his literary achievements were enough to have justified His Grace Mesrop's ordination as a bishop a long time ago, and being appointed a member of the Synod finally gave him the right to become a bishop" (ibid.)

(Through Mesrop, Sirakan Tigranyan and Babken) dismissed the old faculty which was seeking to protect patriarchal rights and the interests of the church... The poet Hovhannisyan and the others have been left out – See the letter to Arshak Chopanyan on 15 April 1909 and the corresponding notes.

He had summoned Benik Vardapet and ordered him to prepare to leave for Yerevan as a deputy – He is referring to Benik Vardapet Ter-Yeghiazaryan.

Muradbekyan Vardapet – He is referring to Khoren Vardapet Muradbekyan, who later became Catholicos of All Armenians Khoren I (1932-1938). Khoren Vardapet was appointed deputy prelate of Yerevan and confirmed in his position on 29 December 1909 by a patriarchal edict (see *Ararat*, 1909, issue 12, page 909).

Evildoing – M. Muradyan has misread the Armenian չարարար as չարարատ ("full of evil"). The handwriting in the original shows clearly that the word ends in արար. In KL 2000 and 2007, this has been misread and misrepresented as զարարար, but no such word exists in the Armenian language. The Haykazyan dictionary defines չարարար as "someone who acts with evil intentions, an evildoer" (*Nor Bargirk Haykazyan Lezvi*, vol. 2, Venice, 1837, page 570).

From Bishop Yeremia – Benik Vardapet wrote the following about the period when Bishop Yeremia was Locum Tenens, "After the death of the martyr Catholicos Makar, the image, direction and spirit of the Etchmiadzin congregation immediately changed when, contrary to the rules and traditions of Etchmiadzin, senior Synod member Archbishop Yeremia became the Catholicos Locum Tenens, with the power of a Synod prosecutor. A Locum Tenens was supposed to be appointed by the Catholicos himself through a special edict while still alive and the appointee was obliged after the Catholicos' death to govern Etchmiadzin without deviating from the rules and without making any changes or innovations, handing it over to the newly elected Catholicos in the same state as he received it from the deceased Catholicos," (*My Memoirs*, MAL, KF, 77, page 35). According to Benik Vardapet, that forced appointment was due to certain political objectives pursued by the Tsarist government, which was clearly stated in the program presented by Prosecutor Kanzeli, the head of the Caucasus government, and the Tsarist Minister of Internal Affairs, "Etchmiadzin has two important institutions, which should each be given separate attention – the Seminary and the Synod. Until now, the education and training of the Seminary students had been entrusted to Armenian patriots, including Catholicos Makar. Several of the students taught by these teachers have already become seminary monks and have entered the monastery. If their number continues to grow, and it most certainly will, the Tsarist policy will face difficulties in the future. I therefore find it desirable to have all the teachers at the Seminary dismissed and replaced by teachers who are in the interests of the Tsarist authorities. The bishops surrounding Catholicos Makar should be scattered and exiled, replaced by 'the monks who have been trained by Archbishop Aristakes Sedrakyan,' who are faithful to the Tsarist authorities" (ibid., page 62-63). Archbishop Yeremia sent a number of undesirable congregants away from Etchmiadzin, dismissed the quality faculty at the seminary and so on. Traditional order was restored in Etchmiadzin only after the election of Catholicos Khrimyan (ibid., page 38).

Father Karapet – He is referring to Karapet Vardapet Ter-Mkrtchyan.

Archbishop Hussik was elected editor of *Ararat* – Archbishop Hussik Ter-Movsisyan was appointed editor of *Ararat* through a patriarchal edict dated 31 October 1909 (*Ararat*, 1909, issue 10-11, pages 775-776).

He has not called His Holy by the title of His Holiness, but rather as saintliness, reducing him to the level of a bishop – He is referring to the congratulatory telegram sent by Nikolai II on the occasion of the ordination of the Catholicos of All Armenians. *Ararat* did not publish the text of the telegram, stating, "A number of congratulatory telegrams have also been received, which we could not place in this issue due to lack of space" (1909, issue 9, page 717).

To come... - The ellipsis was present in the original.

130. <TO ALEXANDER MYASNIKYAN>

The original was located in the possession of Ashot Hovhanniyan. A photocopy is kept at the MAL, KF, 1583.

It was first published in *Sovetakan Arvest*, 1956, issue 2, page 9.

I received your letter yesterday – The letter has not been found.

I had gone to Tpghis for the funeral of Mrs. Mantashyan – See the letter written to A. Chopanyan on 30 October 1909 and the corresponding notes.

131. <TO THEODIK>

The location of the original is unknown.

The letter was first published by Theodik (Theodos Lapchinyan) (*Amenun taretsuytsy*, 1911, page 2): In the beginning of December 1909, Theodik sent the next almanac, the one for 1910, to Catholicos Mattheos II

Izmirlyan at the Mother See and, on 24 December, he received the following letter from him:

“Dear Theodik, I submitted the li<terary> and artistic volume you have weaved freely in your independent style to the appreciation of my mind and my eyes. My mind was satiated with pleasure by the varied and wise content, and my eyes gained satisfaction with pleasure through its beautiful pictures. Your taste, selection and creative talent deserve praise. I wish you success in all your efforts, with blessing” <...>

Catholicos Mattheos II

(Theodik, *Amenun Taretsuytsy*, 1911, page 2).

Theodik replied to this letter on 17 January 1910,

“Holy Patriarch,

Having received with great joy the blessed letter by your Holiness dated 24 Dec. 09, I felt relieved of a year’s hard work, enjoying in relaxation its precious contents. The accepted word ‘Thank you’ seems like too little to express my feelings of gratitude for the appreciative lines that your Holiness’ letter contained regarding the 1910 almanac.

Even as a young boy, I had always felt admiration for the name Izmirlyan and the noble clergyman who bore it. My humble self should be able to use your lines a source of unending encouragement to keep this future pen working, and overcome every obstacle to apply even more care for the preparation of the 1911 *Amenun Taretsuyts*.

How great my excitement would have been if I had known earlier that I would soon come to possess a photograph of our dear Armenian Catholicos with his Patriarchal See (the latter also photographed separately), which would serve to glorify introductory page of volume 6 in the Almanac.

Gathering my boldness to reply to the ‘P.S.’ of the letter I have received, I will add that the sentence “Be everything to everyone” was taken from the journal *Handes Amsorya* [*Amenuyn Taretsuytsy*, 1910, page 9, row 37]. As a philologist, I had used those words simply to fill the page opposite your photograph, and did not expect it to be interpreted in any other way, because of its neutrality.

Earlier, F<ather> Komitas Vardapet had instructed me to print pictures of your time a) as a priest, b) as Bishop, c) as Prelate in Egypt separately from my Almanac on glossy paper, and I sent 10 copies of each a few weeks ago to Holy Etchmiadzin, and you must have received them by now.

Your humble maid, Arshakuhi Theodik—who returned recently to Constantinople from Cilicia, where she had been sent by the Patriotic Armenian Women's Society and had opened schools in various locations for Armenian orphan girls—also adds her heartfelt congratulations to mine, and both of us wish that we are one day rewarded by a visit to Holy Etchmiadzin personally to place our admiring kisses on your Holy Right Hand, as a guarantee of our boundless service and awe, and to present our prayers and wishes to Your Holiness in person, that you may live in good health on the Patriarchal throne, filling Etchmiadzin and its surroundings with grace and philanthropy...

Your humble son
Theodik

Iskender, 8 January 1910"
(MM, M. Izmirlyan Fund, fol. 14, doc. 579)

Komitas' letter had also been sent in December 1909 (the composer was already in Constantinople in December 1910), and Theodik, as promised (see the letter addressed to the Catholicos) sent the 1911 Almanac along with the letter to the Catholicos.

132. <TO ANTON MAYILYAN>

The original is located at the MAL, KF, 43.

It was first published in KL 2000, page 102 and then in KL 2007, pages 124-125.

I received your open letter – The letter has not been found.

Getting an article ready was impossible – According to KL 2007, "This is a reference to an expected contribution from Komitas in the form of his study on 'Armenian Peasant Dances' to be printed in the first issue of the journal published by Mayilyan" (page 245), while the letters refers more to generally "getting an article ready" for the new journal, i.e. contributing with new material, and not to a specific article. Komitas had not sent any new articles to Anton Mayilyan's journal *Tatron yev Yerajshtutyun* later either, choosing rather to translate and send to Mayilyan the article "*Armeniens Volkstümliche Reigentänze*" ("Armenian Peasant Dances") published in the first issue of *Zeitschrift für armenische Philologie* in 1901. Komitas edited and corrected some sections of the article in his translation (see **Komitas Vardapet**. Studies and Articles, Book I, Yerevan 2005, pages 270-292, 496).

133. <TO MATTHEOS IZMIRLYAN>

The original is located at the ANA, fn. 57, l. 2, f. 2281, fol. 4-5

It was first published by G. Harutyunyan (*Banber Hayastani Arkhivneri*, 1966, issue 2, pages 164-166), who presented the circumstances in which the letter was written in the following way – "On 27 November 1909, the chancery at Etchmiadzin, under instructions from the Catholicos, handed Komitas handwritten copies of Ruben Ghorghanyan's work 'Singing the Holy Mass: A Simple Arrangement for 4-Voice Choirs in Schools and People's Churches.' Ghorghanyan <...> had presented, along with the piece, positive feedback from a number of well-known scholars in Russia – the renowned musicologist professor Ipolitov-Ivanov, the director superior of the choir at the Russian Synod of Moscow and the ecclesiastical singing school professor S. Kruglikov, as well as editor of the Petersburg Music Journal and musicologist at the Petersburg Conservatory M. Goylison. <...> Having received Komitas' report, the chancery sent back Ghorghanyan's work on 13 December of the same year, accompanied by the following note.

'Through the kind order of the Patriarch of our nation, this chancery is returning, along with this note, the notebook for church singing composed by you and presented to His Holiness on 15 November, and is informing you that, according to the opinion of music expert F<ather> Komitas Vardapet, these mentioned pieces cannot be sung in churches.'" (ibid.)

Semitones – The Armenian կիսաւորների has been misrepresented as կիսաւորաների ("semi-sectors") in KL 2000 and 2007.

134. <TO RUBEN GHORGHANYAN>

The location of the original is unknown. This section of the letter was first cited in the letter sent by Ruben Ghorghanyan to the Chancery at the Mother See of Holy Etchmiadzin (ANA, fn. 57, l. 2, f. 867, pages 8-11).

It has been published for the first time.

Musicologist R. Ghorghanyan, having received the letter dated 13 December 1909 from the Chancery at the Mother See of Holy Etchmiadzin (see the letter to Mattheos Izmirlyan dated 11 December 1909) and the piece he had presented for publication, had written to Komitas to ask for an explanation for the rejection, as the letter written to the Chancery on 28 January 1910 shows. After receiving a reply from Komitas, some sections of which he cited, the musicologist does not reply to Komitas but rather writes the Mother See Chancery a letter, which we are presenting here in full, , preserving the spelling and punctuation used in the original.

"To the Chancery of the Catholicos of All Armenians
At Holy Etchmiadzin

Ruben Ghorghanyan, Yekaterinodar, Kuban Region.
(Postbox N 10)

Statement

Following letter N539 sent to me by the Chancery on 13 Dec<ember> of the y<ear> <1>909, while I have accepted the sacred decision of the Holy Patriarch with complete reverence, I nevertheless allow myself to inform the Chancery of my objection for the following two reasons, which are simultaneously the responsibility of your esteemed Organization, as an advisory body and the one reporting on this issue to the Holy Pariarch.

First, in letter N539 mentioned above, your Chancery has cited the negative opinion of Father Komitas but has not mentioned the main explanations for his feedback as all such, even state, institutions do in general, and for musical pieces in particular (for example, the Conservatory, the Palace Capella, music societies and so on).

Second, despite the fact that my work needed review, this review was organized inadequately, by handing the piece to an individual—perhaps very capable and reputed—without my prior consent. Thus, both the task is left incomplete, and I have been treated inappropriately.

Your Chancery can never justify the circumstances in which, due to local conditions, no suitable solution or approach has been found to treat my case differently, firstly, because while I have been able to receive the main explanations mentioned above (naturally, after directly writing to the examining Father), your Chancery could have done the same, both to review his explanations and to relay them to me.

In the second case, the Chancery could also have organized the musical review body (committee) I requested outside of Etchmiadzin, through a higher education institution for music for example (in Russia or abroad), appointing a representative there, or presenting that body with your written comments and explanations. And if your Chancery does not recognize, or does not want to recognize, any experts in these issues beyond the walls of Etchmiadzin, all that was left to do was seek my consent to submit the work to the decision of this or that individual, or to retract my initial request.

Coming to Father Komitas' letter, I find it necessary to state

Firstly, a) considering his position, as an official in this situation, I consider his letter an official reply, complementing letter N593 from your Chancery.

b) Considering that your Chancery is probably not knowledgeable in the specialized musical topics covered in the letter, and being left without the opportunity to rebut the explanations through a theoretic point of view, I will satisfy myself by doing so through a general view of the subject.

c) I am presenting my explanations and council below to your Organization by considering the issue only from a point of view of principle.

In the letter I mentioned from the examining Father, despite its expansiveness, I could unfortunately not find a direct answer to the question I had posed – which are the mandatory general, principle requirements that are necessary for Armenian polyphonic ecclesiastical compositions? Instead of this, there were many ill-exposed and even self-contradicting comments.

I am citing the most essential of the explanations received –

a) The melodies are foreign and do not match the style and spirit of Armenian spiritual music.

Since the melodies have been taken partially from the ones currently used freely in our churches, and partially from publications printed by Etchmiadzin, my humble self finds this explanation irrelevant.

b) The rhythm has been disrupted. There are foreign accelerations and excesses, which do not originate in the basic spacing rules of our language.

If we were to allow this comment to be true for one minute, then that should be true for the composer (the creator) of that music, not the arranger, otherwise the same comment can be made for the compositions by Yekmalyan.

c) The harmonization does not have a common style, a common unity, and does not match the style of music.

This objection, as one of individual perception, ability and even taste (and we know that one can't argue when it comes to taste) is simply an **assessment** of the actual work and, since the music and harmonization rules have not been violated, blocking it means infringing upon other's tastes, and does not make for objective reasoning.

The remaining points are general ones about the study of music, the objective of art, the preparation of art and so on, and are very true for original (composed) pieces and not for applied (harmonized, as I have done) works. But let me return to my case, in order to simply show the contradictions.

'Language is the pulse of music. Armenian language and music have rules that are characteristic to them. The German Mozart and Weber, the German Beethoven and Wagner, and others **are all separate interpreters** of their mother tongue. The borders of the musical sea created by any musician are **unstable** – the closer you get to the border, the further away and more expansive it becomes. **We have not yet understood** and probed Beethoven and Wagner. Composers should not accommodate public desire, he should not sacrifice something beautiful for the sake of the miserable situation in everyday life. Polyphonic singing is weak in our tradition because of **our**

elementary musical ignorance, because our polyphonic hearing **has not developed** well <...>'

I repeat – these criticisms should be made to the artist, the composer, but not to my humble self, who has never had the audacity to make a name for himself as a composer. My works are mostly humble pieces and have been written with a specific purpose – to give our artistically unprepared choirs, and especially society in general, pieces that are easy to comprehend and sing at any time or place. Perhaps they are not free of imperfections, but they are open to everybody.

In the churches of all the Christian, cultured and artistic nations, alongside even ingenious music, there exists a more practical version that has been adapted to society and so on, based on the requirements of everyday life.

But even when reviewing the music on one's own, how is it possible to ask the person who wrote it to feel like it expresses his emotions and particularly (from a technical point of view) to act simultaneously like a language interpreter, all identical, monotonous and monotypic because even the titans of music are, according to the examining Father's comments, separate from each other and the borders of the musical sea are unstable and unreachable.

I am not denying at all that the musicologist should not adapt to the wishes of the masses and sacrifice something beautiful and majestic, but I do not believe that this is the role I am fulfilling. And if Etchmiadzin has taken on this role for itself, how is it that it not just done nothing in that area so far (I am referring to polyphonic singing), but It has also allowed in the last 15-20 years for its churches to fully corrupt solo singing and has remained in the current situation that is very, very far from artistic reality? If Etchmiadzin is interested in the purity and originality of our national spiritual music, how is it that the churches that belong to it use foreign music (Weber) or the bad quality compositions of Seminary choirmasters? Is the Divine Service always and at all times rendered artistically (from the point of view of singing) in Etchmiadzin and in all its churches? I think that there are also practical requirements—like during full-day services, long masses, and on other days—when the artistic is definitely sacrificed in the name of the practical. From the artistic point of view, which is the more dangerous? Allowing the churches to sing a plain, but acceptable for all times and places, polyphonic version or to prefer either a solo that is unbearable to the point of disgust in some parts, or a polyphonic version that is artistic but too complicated to be understood in many places? Does Etchmiadzin make decisions based on the artistic, when two of its congregant musicians, one of them in Etchmiadzin itself, the other in Nor Nakhijevan *(he is referring to Komitas and Gevorg Chorkchyan – G.G.)* never use the Yekmalyan mass that has been approved by Etchmiadzin itself. If we are ignorant in elementary music, how is it that we can comprehend only ingenious and perfect musical compositions?

In the letter mentioned above, I was suggested, among other things, to study the rules of harmonization for our melodies. But it seems to be forgotten that those rules are derived from the works of classic composers, and not the other way around.

The artistic demands of any society depend on the level of artistic development of that society and how cultured it is. And if that society is on the lower levels of being cultured, no matter how much it is nurtured, ingenious pieces of music will remain incomprehensible to it, because societal musical education occurs step by step. Aren't the complaints well known about the corruption of Yekmalyan's simple mass?

How, for example, can one explain the fact that the Russian people, who are not far beyond us in terms of culture, have polyphonic singing even in the church villages; although it is simple, it is tidy and pleasant. It can only be explained by the perfect adaptation of that singing. This "sacrifice" of the artistic is done by the Church there (both here in Russia, and abroad) giving society an easily arranged (yes – brief, simple and comprehensible to all) piece of music. Besides this, there is never an obstacle regarding the use of thousands of similar works and compositions, many of which gain their rightful place through performance, and some of which disappear with the latest requirements of changing times.

If Etchmiadzin is truly charged with the musical education of our people in general, and the supervision of our spiritual music in particular, then this needed to be demonstrated through action and not just through caretaking. Opportunities should have been given for each individual to work in this area, thus creating competition and progress. Bad and defective pieces of music will remain unused even without a caretaker, while this tendency to "block" has truly "contradicted our church's (free) spirit" and could have already caused some losses.

These are my explanations and my council, which (although respectful of the character and work of Father Komitas, who examined my arrangements) I cannot help but present as a matter of principle to your Chancery, with the view to report it in the future (whenever the opportunity arises) to His Holiness, whose holy right hand I kiss and remain, a humble son

Ruben Ghorghanyan
28 January of the year 1910
Yekaterinodar"
(ANA, fn. 57, l. 2, f. 867, p. 8-11).

The Chancery of the Mother See, having received R. Ghorghanyan's letter, sent a copy of Komitas' explanatory letter to Mattheos Izmirlyan, with the following note attached.

"13 February 1910
Holy Etchmiadzin

Respected Mr. Ruben Ghorghanyan

Having reported to the Patriarch of our nation about your letter dated 28 January of this year, in which you expressed dissatisfaction about the rejection of the music you had arranged without any explanation, an order was issued to send you a copy of the statement dated 11 December 1909 written by Komitas Vardapet, who had examined your work." (ANA, fn. 57, l. 2, doc. 867, p. 12).

135. <TO MARGARIT BABAYAN>

The location of the original is unknown.

This section of the letter was first published in Margarit Babayan's memoirs *Komitas Vardapet Through his Letters* ("Mshakuyt," Paris, 1935, page 161). The original of the memoirs is located at the MAL Mari Atmachyan fund, from where it has been copied. The letter has been dated by Margarit Babayan.

I go out and roam about here and there like a tiger, on my own, in my garden and on my roof – Manuk Abeghyan had described Komitas' quarters and garden in his memoirs – "And then Komitas, who also liked to spend time on his own earlier, started to grow melancholic and sad without, however, reducing his relentless work. He was growing bored of Etchmiadzin. There is a wrong opinion going around that he was treated badly there. That is not true at all. On the contrary, he was treated with great respect and love in general, and not just by his friends, but also by others. And it was not just that. They were very forgiving of him in certain respects and were not demanding of him as an artist. But he was also highly responsible. Even the elderly congregants respected and liked him. One of them, for example, Bishop Hovhannes Shirakuni, gifted him a thousand rubles to buy a grand piano. They had allocated him an apartment at the very beginning which was old, it was true, but very suitable in its completely isolated location. Its upper floor consisted of three rooms and a corridor, while the lower floor had the kitchen and cellar and, most importantly, a garden with cherry, *malachay* pear, and other fruit trees. A stream would constantly flow through the garden. A powerful elm tree rose in the middle of it and benches, tables and chairs where arranged below it, in its abundant shade. There were always people there during favorable weather, they would come there to relax, because beyond Komitas' garden, on the other side of the fence, there was the village boulevard with its thick tree cover. These people did not bother Komitas, who would rehearse upstairs, playing music and singing. He would come downstairs when he too wanted to rest. He would always lovingly welcome his regular guests, which he would sometimes also offer the Turkish coffee he made himself, poured into small cups. He would also often sit alone under that elm tree or potter about in his garden, where he would plants herbs and root plants in the free spaces, especially blackcurrants, which he would grow with his own hands and then pluck." (**Manuk Abeghyan**, Works, Vol. 7, Yerevan, 1975, pages 437-438).

The fact that Komitas' garden was a popular gathering spot for the Etchmiadzin congregants has also been confirmed by Yervand Ter-Minasyan – "We would all have lunch or dinner together either in Hussik Vardapet

Zohrabyan's apartment, or in Komitas', where we would be in the shade of the marvelous elm tree in the garden next to Komitas during the months of summer and fall'" (**Yervand Ter-Minasyan**, *Memories from My Life,* edited and with a foreword by Prof. Paruyr Muradyan, Yerevan, Magaghat, 2005, page 66). "Two months later, in September 1908, when my book 'The Relations of the Armenian Church with the Assyrian Churches' was published, and I gifted him a copy, I received a nice lamb from Khachik Vardapet the following Sunday, which we (our whole group) enjoyed along with him at our lunch spot in Komitas' garden" (ibid., page 85-86).

Shushik – He is referring to Shushik Babayan.

1910

136. <TO ARSHAK CHOPANYAN>

The original is located at the MAL, ACF, 3414.

It was first published in KL 2000, page 152, and then in KL 2007, page 183.

I received your letters – The letters have not been found.

The photographer was not here... we will send everything that you wanted – See the letters written to A. Chopanyan on 23 December 1908, 15 April 1909, 14 July 1909, 30 October 1909, as well as the corresponding notes.

He did not have large pieces of glass – Photography equipment at the end of the 19th and the beginning of the 20th centuries used different sized pieces of glass coated with photosensitive chemicals, which would then produce the negative of the photograph. The Arshak Chopanyan Fund at the MAL has small pieces of glass negatives of this kind (memoir section, ACF, unprocessed).

I will be coming for a month to your honorable parts – KL 2000 and 2007 have misrepresented the Armenian word Ձերապատիւ ("your supremely honorable") as գերապատիւ ("supremely honorable"). Komitas has used a bit of linguistic humor to create a new word by merging Ձեր ("your") with գերապատիւ ("supremely honorable").

137. <TO MATTHEOS IZMIRLYAN>

The original is located at the MAL, KF, 38.

The letter is a draft and it is not clear whether or not it was sent.

It was first published in parts by K. Samuelyan' "Annals" (*Sovetakan Arvest*, 1971, issue 1, pages 51-52, hereinafter KS) and then in KL 2000, pages

61-64 and KL 2007, pages 78-83. Both publications are replete with errors, and we present a few of them below.

Kind consideration – The Armenian բարեհայեցողութիւն has been misrepresented in KL 2000 and 2007 as բարեհայեցողութեան.

One can see - The Armenian պատկերացնում են ("one can see") has been misrepresented in KS as պատկերացնում եմ ("I can see").

Singing - The Armenian երգեցողութեանց has been misrepresented in KS as երգեցողութեանը.

Page 179, r. 11 – **songs** - The Armenian երգերն has been misrepresented in KS as երգերը.

Are almost all foreign in origin and consist of tasteless melodies – Komitas has spoken on this issue and raised it on several occasions in his articles and studies (see **Komitas Vardapet**. Studies and Articles, Book I, Yerevan 2005, pages 55-172).

Turkish-Arab-Greek - The Armenian տաճիկ-արաբ-յոյն has been misrepresented in KS as տաճիկ, արաբ, յոյն.

Persian-Arab - The Armenian պարսիկ-արաբ has been misrepresented in KS as պարսիկ, արաբ.

Old Jugha – Misrepresented in KS as **old Jugha**.

Even more – The Armenian աւելին կասենք has been misrepresented in KS as աւելին, կասենք.

Search for it and learn – The Armenian որոնել, սովորել has been misrepresented in KS as որոնել սովորել ("to learn how to search").

No common mother tongue - The Armenian մի ընդհանուր՝ մայրենի has been misrepresented in KS as մի ընդհանուր մայրենի.

Community spirit - The Armenian անհատական համայնքի has been misrepresented in KS as անհատական հաճոյքի ("individual enjoyment").

Borrowed – The Armenian մուրացածոյ has been misrepresented in KL 2000 and 2007 as մոխրացած ("ashen"), which deprives the sentence of the meaning the original text aimed to have.

Is - The Armenian ներկայացնում has been misrepresented in KS as ներկայանում.

National-musical - The Armenian երաժշտական-ազգային has been misrepresented in KS as երաժշտական ազգային.

Arteries - The Armenian զարկերակներ ("arteries") has been misrepresented in KS as պատկերացումներ ("images").

Melodies— - The Armenian եղանակներ՝ has been misrepresented in KS as եղանակներ.

Have now been condemned - The Armenian դատապարտուել են has been misrepresented in KS as դատապարտել են ("have condemned").

Loss - The Armenian կորստի has been misrepresented in KS as կորուստի.

Decline - The Armenian անկման has been misrepresented in KS as անկմանը.

Unsuitably - The Armenian անյարիր has been misrepresented in KS as անխտիր ("without exception").

Extracts - The Armenian քաղուածոյ has been misrepresented in KS as քաղածոյ.

Innovations - The Armenian նորամուծումներն has been misrepresented in KL 2000 and 2007 as նորամուծութիւններն.

Educate and purify, by instilling a feeling of spiritual music – This sentence is punctuated differently in KL 2000 and 2007, distorting the meaning to a certain extent.

Lead to a decline and will drown out - The Armenian անկումն կը պատրաստէ եւ կը խորտակէ has been misrepresented in KL 2000 and 2007 as անզամ է՛ւ կը պատրաստէ է՛ւ կը խորտակէ ("which both leads to it and drowns it").

Soft - The Armenian քնքոյշ has been misrepresented in KS as քնքուշ.

Through - The Armenian միջոցաւ has been misrepresented in KS as միջոցով.

No matter how much - The Armenian ինչքան էլ has been misrepresented in KS as որքան էլ.

Page 181, r. 8 – **what remains** - The Armenian մնացածը has been misrepresented in KS as անյայտացածը ("what has vanished").

Basis - The Armenian հիմք has been misrepresented in KL 2000 and 2007 as գովք ("praise"), making the sentence in the original meaningless.

And so on - The Armenian եւ այլն has been misrepresented in KL 2000 and 2007 as եւ այլի.

Experienced - The Armenian փորձուած has been misrepresented in KS as կրթված ("educated").

Choir - The Armenian դպրութեան has been misrepresented in KS as դպրութեանը.

Children - The Armenian երեխաների has been misrepresented in KL 2000 and 2007 as եղանակների ("melodies"), making the sentence in the original meaningless.

The Mother Choir of the Mother Church of the Mother See - KL 2000 and 2007 editions have separated this using commas into "The Mother Choir of the Mother Church, the Mother See" which makes the original meaningless (the Mother See and the Mother Church do not have separate choirs, this is a series of substantives, not a list).

Choirmasters - The Armenian դպրապետներ has been misrepresented in KS as դպրապետների and as դպրոցների ("schools") in KL 2000 and 2007.

Each - The Armenian իւրաքանչիւր has been misrepresented in KL 2000 and 2007 as եղանակներ ("melodies"), making the sentence in the original meaningless.

Daughter - The Armenian դուստր has been misrepresented in KL 2000 and 2007 as տարբեր ("different"), making the sentence in the original meaningless.

Personally - The Armenian անձնապէս has been misrepresented in KS as ամբողջապէս ("completely") and as անմիջապէս ("immediately") in KL 2000 and 2007.

As I can - The Armenian իմովսանն has been misrepresented in KS as կամովս ("willingly").

As much effort - The Armenian չան գործել has been misrepresented in KS as աննկուն գործել.

Given - The Armenian տրուեն has been misrepresented in KS as տրուէին.

Serving - The Armenian ուխտել եմ has been misrepresented in KS as եւ սկսել եմ ("and I have started") and as ու ստացել եմ ("and I have received") in KL 2000 and 2007, making the sentence in the original meaningless.

Golden - The Armenian ոսկի has been misrepresented in KS as աւելի ("more").

My heart - The Armenian սրտիս has been misrepresented in KL 2000 and 2007 as արդէն ("already"), making the sentence in the original meaningless.

Despair - The Armenian յուսահատութիւն has been misrepresented in KS as յոռետեսութիւմ ("pessimism").

Sieging - The Armenian պաշարէ has been misrepresented in KL 2000 and 2007 as պաշարել.

Almighty - The Armenian ամենակարող has been misrepresented in KL 2000 and 2007 as ամենաիսկական ("most real").

Right - The Armenian Աջոյն has been misrepresented in KL 2000 and 2007 as Աջոյ.

138. <TO THE EDITORIAL BOARD OF *TACHAR*>

The location of the original is unknown.

It was first published in *Tachar*, 1910, issue 10, page 311, under the title "The Meaning of Hymnal Neumes" (see **Komitas Vardapet**, Studies and Articles, Book II, Yerevan 2007, pages 69-70).

Honorable Editor – He is referring to the editor of *Tachar*, Garegin Vardapet Khachatryan.

F<ather> Abraham Epeyan is proposing – He is referring to the following section of Priest Abraham Epeyan's article "Hymnal Neumes" – "On this occasion, I cannot forget to mention the renowned musicologist of Holy Etchmiadzin, his grace F. Komitas Vardapet, whose study on hymnal neumes and musical skill are known to all. This is especially true since some newspaper recently wrote that he will be giving public explanations on this topic. As a follower of music and an admirer of our precious ecclesiastical music in particular, and as someone who desires to acquaint oneself with it even more properly and effectively, I humbly ask in public for this holy clergyman to produce his theories on hymnal neumes as well as on ecclesiastical music and signing within the pages of the religious newspaper ***Tachar***

through which he will provide boundless contentment not just to us, but to all music lovers and especially those who desire the regulation and development of our ecclesiastical music" (see *Tachar*, 1910, issue 6, page 188).

139. <ANTON MAYILYAN>

The original is located at the MAL, KF, 32.

It was first published in parts by K. Samuelyan' "Annals" (*Sovetakan Arvest*, 1971, issue 1, page 52) and then in KL 2000, pages 102-103 and KL 2007, pages 125.

I am sending you my small study on "Armenian Peasant Dances"... not yet been published in Armenian – See the letter to Anton Mayilyan dated 3 December 1909 and the corresponding notes.

First issue of the journal *Tatron yev Yerajshutyun* and its supplements – Along with the first issue of *Tatron yev Yerajshtutyun*, Anton Mayilyan sent his subscribers two supplements – 1) "Children's songs" by A. Mayilyan and 2) "Dramatic Poetry" by V.T. Abr. (see *tatron yev Yerajshtutyun*, 1910, issue 1, page 1).

The promotion of the Adamyan sisters is good news – He is referring to Heghine (1881-1960) and Yevgine (1883-1945) Adamyan, an article about whose activities was printed in *Tatron yev Yerajshtutyun*, which stated in particular, "Recently (during 1909), in the centers of European music like Vienna, Geneva, Berlin, Dresden, Leipzig, Copenhagen, München, Stuttgart, two Armenian young ladies—the sisters Heghine and Yevgine Adamyan from Baku—have created a lot of furor with their impressive skills. They studied at the Geneva Conservatory and now, from 1904 to 1908, thanks to the private care of Martin Krause, the renowned musician and pedagogue at the Berlin Conservatory, they have each grown into a talented individual and have attracted the attention of all the well-known and capable forces in the music sector of the famous cities of Europe, coming to deserve their warm praise. We have come across a brochure (in German) which summarizes the critical reviews of all the performances of these famous Armenians over the last year. That booklet also has a picture of the Adamyan sisters. What admiration and praise is lavished on their musical talent by sixty two (62) famous newspapers and specialized musical journals" (*Tatron yev Yerajshtutyun*, 1910, issue 1, pages 4-5).

Who is that G. Verdyan who is attacking so mercilessly the mild song of the sorrowful Armenian villager? – He is referring to the review of the event dedicated to Goghtan[25] at the Baku Philanthropic Hall on 30 January, published in joint issues 1-2 of *Tatron yev Yerajshtutyun*, where the author says in particular,

"The third part consisted of a concert, or rather, a conglomerate of dissonance.

The oriental orchestra consisted of a range of instruments with European and oriental timbres and sounds that did not reconcile well with each other, and that corrupted the Armenian melodies and the achievements of Armenian musicians like K. V.'s "Over the Mountains" that was played as if it were Mr. G. Verdyan's "Meyramo."

According to the program, all the musical pieces played had been composed by Mr. G. V. Perhaps the tasteless harmonization and orchestration of some of the melodies was the work of that person, but not the music.

For the sake of music itself, we request Mr. G. V. not to use the name of music among circles that live far from real art" (ibid., pages 22-23).

140. <TO ANTON MAYILYAN>

The original is located at the MAL, KF, 33.

It was first published in parts by K. Samuelyan' "Annals" (*Sovetakan Arvest*, 1971, issue 1, page 53) and then in KL 2000, pages 104 and KL 2007, pages 126.

K. Samuelyan dated the letter as April-May 1910, probably considering the date for the previous letter written by A. Mayilyan (22 March 1910), and the fact that the letter was written from Etchmiadzin, i.e. before Komitas left for Constantinople (20 May 1910).

25 [A region in the south of Armenia] – Translator's notes

The uncomfortable situation in which my proposal – He is referring to the his request in the letter dated 22 March 1910 regarding the printing of the copies of his article on "Armenian Peasant Dances" as relayed in the following section – "I only ask that, if it not an inconvenience to you, you take the initiative and have as many copies as you can printed". It seems like A. Mayilyan has not managed to preserve the layout of the article.

141. <TO MATTHEOS IZMIRLYAN>

The original is located at the ANA, fn. 57, l. 2, doc. 2282, p. 1-3. A draft copy of the original is located at the MAL, KF, 35.

The letter was first published in *Banber Hayastani Arkhivneri*, 1966, issue 2, pages 168-170, and then reprinted in KS, 1971, issue 1, pages 53-54, KL 2000, pages 64-67, KL 2007, pages 83-85.

According to K. Samuelyan, this letter/report was the final version of the letter/report begun on 12 January 1910 (see KS, 1971, issue 1, pages 53 and also this publication). The upper right corner of the letter contains the note "Important and mandatory, but requires great capital, which needs to be raised."

The differences between the final version (ANA, fn. 57, l. 2, doc. 2282, p. 1-3) of this letter and its draft (MAL, KF, 35) are presented below.

Which has – the Armenian եւ այն is not present in KF 35: In KL 2000 and 2007 it is misrepresented as եւ այլ ("and other").

Singing – KF 35 – [melodies]

Relegated – KF 35 – relegated to positions of secondary importance and even fully to the background, [with the word 'hymn' taking on a meaning lacking respect, which is sad, and]

Which - the Armenian որով is որ in KF 35.

Reducing in number every day – KF 35 - reducing in number every day [while]

And – KF 35 – [or]

And – the Armenian ու is եւ in KF 35.

Theoretical - In KL 2000 and 2007, the Armenian զտեսութիւն is misrepresented as չտեսություն ("greed").

Energetic – KF 35 [energy]

All clergymen – KF 35 – **all clergymen involved in spiritual music**

From oblivion – KF 35 from oblivion [the abyss]

Print – KF 35 [have published]

Doing – KF 35 [making the use of]

Make – KF 35 [establish as mandatory]

Select... using strict criteria – KL 35 using strict criteria, select

In their appointments – KL 35 [only]

And care of – KF 35 [report to]

Certified instructors – i.e. having a certificate.

First – KF 35 [the very] first

Twenty four – KF 35 [at least] twenty four [excellent singers]

In order to have – KF 35 [for having]

Inspired hope in me – KF 35 [has preserved me and] inspired hope in me

In that same hope – KF 35, [as sick fields, meadows and crops]

Like a – KF 35 like a [windblown]

Once again – KF 35 [once more]

Same – KF 35 – not present.

Become serious – KF 35 [become delicate]

Pace – KF 35 pace [has grown stronger and softer]

Coming – KF 35 [hopefully] coming

Undying – KF 35 [boundless] undying

142. <TO ANDREAS BABAMYAN>

The original is located at the MAL, KF, 2.

It was first published by K. Samuelyan (*Sovetakan Arvest*, 1971, issue 2, page 53) and later in KL 2000, page 13 and KL 2007, page 20.

In 1903, Andreas Babamyan presented a manuscript called *Manrusmunk* (dated 1315) to the Etchmiadzin manuscript library (see *Ararat*, 1904, issue 1, pages 37-39).

On 29 December 1908, Komitas gifted a photograph of the participants in the elections of the Catholicos, with the following note – "To the Highly Respected Spouses, Mrs. Arusyak and Mr. Andreas Babamyan" (MAL, memoir section, KF, unprocessed).

143. <TO VARIKO VRATSYAN>

The original is located at the MAL, KF, 1631.

The postcard is addressed to Garnik Vratsyan, Variko's brother. In the right corner of the postcard, Komitas had written "Please hand this to your sister Variko." According to the postal stamp, the letter has been sent from Bursa (Brousse) to Yerevan "Эриванск. городс. Клуб. Г-ну Гарнику Врацiян. Эривань." The reverse side of the postcard had the picture of a woman with an umbrella. The edge of the umbrella is decorated by a triple line. Komitas added two more lines and wrote the musical piece copied in the letter. The last two lines in the letter were written by Levon Yeramyan.

Levon Yeramyan (1892-1938) – Actor. The MAL Komitas Fund (number 1451) contains a poster for the concert in Kütahya on 25 July, designed by Levon Yeramyan and organized by Komitas.

I am leaving my birthplace on the 20th of this month – According to K. Samuelyan's "Annals" – "After spending around two months in his birthplace with his relatives and his childhood friends, relaxing and organizing concerts for his countrymen, Komitas left for Afyonkarahisar" (*Sovetakan Arvest*, 1971, issue 2, page 58).

144. <TO THE EDITORIAL BOARD OF THE NEWSPAPER *JAMANAK*>

The location of the original is unknown.

The letter was original published in the daily *Jamanak*, Year 2, Constantinople, 25 September/8 October, issue 599, and then later in parts in **T. Azatyan,** Komitas Vardapet, Volume One, His Life and Work, Constantinople, 1931, pages 104-106.

The 8 September 1910 issue of the daily *Jamanak* (21 September in the old calendar, issue 584) contained the interview of Komitas Vardapet by Levon Cherrahyan, printed under the title "Komitas Vardapet's views on Armenian Music. His own statements," which contains the following text in particular -

"Holy Etchmiadzin's reputed choirmaster F. Komitas Vrd. arrived in our city from Kütahya on 20 August, Friday, with the Locum Tenens of our Patriarch F. Pargev Vrd. Danielyan.

I had long wished to meet the Vardapet and had been in Constantinople when he first came, but had been disappointed to hear that he had rushed to his birthplace. I finally had the good fortune to enjoy his presence in my city, where he stayed for five days, showing his skill by singing a few segments of Armenian ecclesiastical songs, leaving a profound impression on the people of both sexes in my city.

In order to pay a visit to the honorable priests, I made my way to their residence with a group of Armenian teachers. I asked the musician Holy Priest for a separate audience there and he did not refuse; that audience occurred the following day at the Patriarchate. I offer some of the replies he gave to some of my questions I posed for the reading pleasure of the *Jamanak* daily's dear subscribers, and would like to particularly invite the attention of music lovers on certain points.

When I asked him what impression he had of Constantinople's music and musicians, his reply was the following.

'When I came to Constantinople, I had the opportunity to hear Maestro Manas' performanes in four voices. Let me just say here that the church in Galatia is completely unsuitable for singing in three or four voices, because it is not high and conducive to echoing, it is low, and the sounds is akin to being choked. For polyphonic singing, you need buildings that are broad and tall, conducive to echoing. Coming to Manas, although that man is hardworking and skilled, he has not succeeded in this piece he has prepared and he cannot succeed. All his efforts are in vain and they are pointlessly made sacrifices. Let me explain why.

Manas was educated in Italy and does not know a word of Armenian. Musical pieces should be written with inspiration, like a poem. The piece that

Manas has prepared is far from being inspired, because the melodies he has penned do not have the ability to inspire the Armenian lyrics or the Armenian spirit. They present a picture that is the complete opposite.

I met this hardworking young man personally. He is well educated but, as I said, this work has not succeeded and is not expected to succeed.

First, one should have the skill of piercing deep into the Armenian language and then to compose in a way that matches its inspiring spirit. When, for example, an Italian composer takes the Holy Mass and uses his European perception to arrange its melody, wouldn't it be completely devoid of its Armenian component and emotion? Then it would also be devoid of its value.

Our oriental melodies cannot be arranged using European perception.'

To my second question, about the opinion he has regarding Armenian musicians in Constantinople, he replied.

'The Armenian musicians of Constantinople are people who have grown and studied within the confines of Turkey, and are far from being valuable. They do not even have the drive towards self-development and, despite not being worth much, they are very confident of their abilities.'

'What is your opinion of the three-voice pieces that have been composed?'

Here, the Holy Priest broke out in laughter.

'Three-voices? All of that is nothing. They are far from being people who can compose for three voices... Even the graduates of Europe's conservatories falter at that sometimes, what else can we expect from our Turkish-Armenians, whose level of ability is not even up to the first years at those conservatories.

When Ormanyan was the Patriarch, I had received a solo composition of the Mass, which was a chaotic mass of errors from start to finish. I returned it, saying that this work was completely wrong, and it was impossible to correct it, much less convert it to polyphony.'

And he added,

'This is why I call the Turkish-Armenian musicians pretenders, because they think they are people with great skills. Let me add here that even the military bands in Constantinople are far from perfection, and very far in particular from harmony.

During the dictatorship, I read a segment in the *Manzume-i-Efkâr*, signed by someone as a 'specialist musician,' criticizing Chilingaryan's Mass in three voices and provided the hymn "Christ is revealed among us" as evidence of its wrong harmonization, with its notes, below which was a version for harmonization, supposedly free of errors. I went straight to the organ and began to sing the arrangement of that 'specialist musician' and, my God, it was such a terrible mess, even more messy than Chilingaryan – no harmonization, no meaning, and no spirit.

So you can imagine that if that specialist presents such chaos, what value can the others have?'

My fourth and final question was the following – how had he discovered the secret to Armenian music? The respected priest replied simply, 'My dear, when I say that I have discovered the secret of Armenian music, don't think these are just words; it is the truth. It has been exactly seventeen years that I have been working on this, and if I tell you about all the sacrifices I have made and the exhaustion I have suffered, you will be surprised to hear it.

There are photographs of old Armenian neumes in the Soorb Karapet monastery of Caesarea, in Bishop Trdat's possession. I wrote to the Holy Father, who was a priest then, to send me those photographs, but my requests fell on deaf ears. I wrote to the national administration after that, to the Patriarch of the time, his replacement and failed in the end to achieve my objective because the prelate of Caesarea wanted to sell the manuscripts for 300 rubles, a price which I had to reject, since I did not have the money. So I decided to go to Europe and having reached Italy, I sought the Pope and he opened the museums before me with great hospitality; I found and studied many things there. I went to other cities as well – Berlin, Paris, and then Switzerland. But they were all illegible. I needed old dictionaries to read then and that immense task greatly exhausted me. But, after a lot of searching, I finally managed to achieve my objective, and now there are now secrets left for me about Armenian music.'

And to end my questions, I asked him what we were supposed to do if people wanted to hear a three-voice composition? He replied,

'Use Yekmalyan's, where can you find a better one? Although I plan to compose a more 'purely Armenian' version of the mass in three and four voices.'

* * *

The skilled musicologist sang “Joyful Light” on 21 August, Saturday, in front of a big audience at the Soorb Astvatzatzin church. The next day, Sunday, he celebrated mass and sang the first stanza of “Come” before a large gathering. On 24 August, Father Mesrop, one of the local priests and a graduate of the Seminary where he had studied with Komitas, celebrated mass and Komitas was the choirmaster, singing “Melody,” “Holy Song,” “Amen, And Unto Your Soul,” “Amen, Holy Father” and “Lord Have Mercy” and leaving a very favorable impression on the more than three thousand attendees of both sexes, which also included foreigners.

Although the priest had planned on organizing a concert here, he could not find a suitable venue and gave up on the idea.

The people of Constantinople are lucky. They will finally get the chance to enjoy the genius of this great musicologist. The Holy Father is planning to organize big concerts with 600 people in Constantinople. He will also travel around the country for about a year, teaching European music in various cities of Turkey both to spread the love of music and waken our people.

Komitas Vardapet will leave our city on Thursday, the 2nd of the month, going to Eskişehir, then Izmit and Atabazar, followed by Petersburg via Berlin and Paris, ending his journey in Etchmiadzin.

Levon Cherrahyan
Afyonkarahisar”

Levon Chilingaryan replied to this publication with the article “Komitas Vardapet and Armenian Music,” which was published in the 17 September 1910 (30 September in the old calendar, issue 592) issue of *Jamanak*. The author of the article was unhappy with Komitas’ assessment, saying,

“In issue 584 of this important national newspaper, we read the things said in the name of Komitas Vardapet, where the respected priest had announced that the Armenian musicians of Turkey were people who have grown and studied within the confines of Turkey, and are far from being valuable. They do not even have the drive towards self-development and, despite not being worth much, they are very confident of their abilities, and so on.

It is clear that Father Komitas Vardapet, having studied in Europe, has hinted with this statement that the Armenian musicians of Constantinople are complete failures and he is the only one who isn't, he is the "ONLY MUSICOLOGIST." In this way, he has also attempted to serve a lesson in **humility** to us pretenders.

Having heard of Father Komitas Vardapet's reputation from afar, we have admired his musical skill and given his the status of "special" among us—how should I put it?—we've called him the "God of Armenian music." But we did not ask whether there was anyone who objected to this, who opposed it, and whether there was a need to declare this to the whole world? What a condescending attitude towards the Armenian musicians of Constantinople who, deprived of the wonderful patronage of someone like Mr. Mantashyan, have had the misfortune of having to study only in their own country.

We, the Armenian musicians of Constantinople, have never been pretenders. We do not grow fat on our modest abilities. On the contrary, we know our weakness well, but use whatever little opportunities we have for self-development, if not to reach the same level, then at least to follow the 'immortals' who graduate from **conservatories**.

We await the day when Father Komitas Vardapet, as a man with real skills and value, will stop condemning the modest conditions which we have today and disdaining the Armenian musicians of Constantinople by showing his own superiority over us, and will instead gather us around him and instruct us, charting a path through which we will all have to go, for the love of the church and the betterment of all the musicians. In this situation, which of us would dare to make an objection? On the contrary, we would take his advice and instructions as a clear message and fulfill them down to the last point.

On my part, I admit that we, the Armenian musicians of Constantinople, are nothing and that Father Komitas Vardapet is the only musicologist among us. So, to justify this faith that has been placed in him, he has to prove himself by displaying his work, which we will humbly follow and accept. <...>

Levon Chilingaryan
Bera, 12 September 1910"

The open letter by Komitas is a reply to this article by L. Chilingaryan.

145. <TO MARGARIT BABAYAN>

The original is located at the MAL, KF, 1350.

It was first published in K. Samuelyan's "Annals" (1971, issue 9, page 53), followed by KL 2000, pages and KL 2000, pages 38-39.

I received your letter – The letter has not been found.

In these parts – The Armenian այստեղեր has been misrepresented in KL 2000 and 2007 as այստեղ էի ("I was here").

I organized 5 concerts – He is referring to two concerts organized in 1910 in Kütahya (25 and 26 July), the concert in Eskişehir (29 August), one in Bursa in the beginning of September, and the well-known concert organized in Constantinople on 4 December at the Badişan winter theater.

From Smyrna, where I am working on the 6th one – The concert took place at the "Sporting" Hall in Smyrna on 30 January 1911.

I will go back to Constantinople and give a 7th one – The concert took place at the Union Française hall in Constantinople on 20 February 1911.

The tricks that the stupid choristers tried to pull here – He is referring to the disruption of his lecture at the Galatia Assembly building on 7 November 1910, and particularly the situation that occurred during the concert on 4 December (20 November in the old calendar) at the Badişan winter theater (for details, see **K. Samuelyan**, Annals, *Sovetakan Arvest*, 1971, issue 9, pages 54-49 and the letter to Komitas from Ghevond Vardapet Duryan, the deputy patriarch of the Constantinople Patriarchate as well as its corresponding notes).

146. <TO STEPAN AKAYAN>

The location of the original is unknown. A copy of the original was first published by Toros Azatyan (Komitas Vardapet, Constantinople, 1931, pages 114-115).

I received your letter yesterday – The letter has not been found.

I have begun immediately to write up the fundamental statute of the union and its program – In December 1910, an Armenian Music Union was created in Constantinople upon the initiative of Komitas, the purpose of which was to organize events that promote Armenian music, and later the establishment of an Armenian music school. Stepan Akayan joined the founding committee of the union. According to Toros Azatyan, in January 1911, Komitas had already prepared the following draft for the statute and program of the union –

"A. Developing Armenian Music 1. By accepting Western music as a template and example and 2. By considering oriental music as a neighbor's music. B. Promoting Armenian music 1. By organizing concerts and performances, 2. By giving lectures, 3. By printing newspapers and collections, writings and songs. C. To establish, and maintain control over 1. An Armenian music school, 2. A theater of song, dance and performance, 3. A printing house with the necessary equipment and 4. A shop selling music books, papers, and instruments. D. Maintain one permanent choir and two bands consisting of talented people with time on their hands.

Administration – A. Executive body, B. Assemblies on education, publications, printing and financial issues, C. An Organizational Assembly for 1. Song and music performances and 2. General organization. D. A supervisory body and E. General Assemblies.

Costs – A. Building rent or ownership for 1. Music school, 2. Theater hall and 3. Offices. B. Salaries – manager, officials and employees. C. Various minor expenses. D. Procurement of books, paper (musical notation), instruments and various items.

Resources – A. Main funding from citizens of the capital and the villages. B. Membership fees from the citizens of the capital and the villages, from student bursaries. C. Income from song and music performances, musical publications and invitations to perform (festivals, weddings, burials and so on) and D. Donations of money and various items. E. The founders of the union will develop the membership conditions and detailed program (*Byuzandion*, 1911, issue 4351, page 1. **Toros Azatyan**, Komitas Vardapet, Constantinople, 1931, pages 102-103).

Eat, drink and be merry – Luke 12:19.

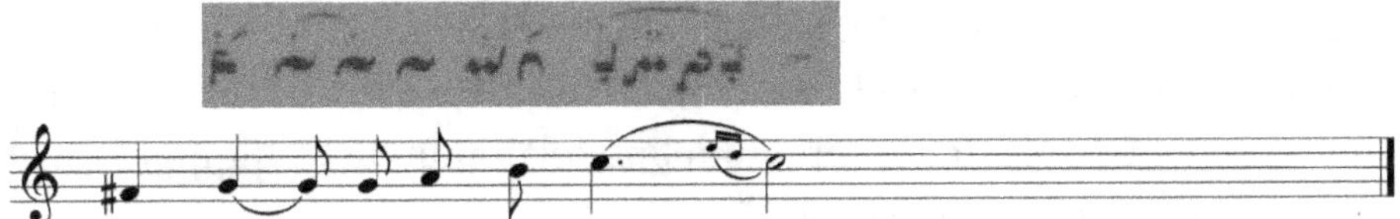

This interpretation was given by Karo Chalikyan and Areg Lusinyan.

Kertenkele – lizard (Turkish). According to the testimonials of many memoir authors, this is a word Komitas would use for his students and close friends. Aghavni Mesropyan explained Komitas' use of this word in the following way, "Komitas the Conductor, standing straight and tall, raising the white baton, would quickly divide the voices and his 'magic wand' would make a 300-person orchestra obey him. Pity those students who would come in late from distant districts and, trying to catch their breath, would seek to silently occupy their places. Such cases would not slip by Komitas. During a break, he would laugh and call them '*Kertenkele*s and Seghbos-Toros-s" (Contemporaries on Komitas, Yerevan, 1960, pages 231). Komitas has used this word on two more occasions in the letters that we currently possess (in the letter to M. Babayan dated 9 June 1913 and to his students in the letter dated 22 June 1914).

Let us be silent – Komitas had added notes for this section of the letter.

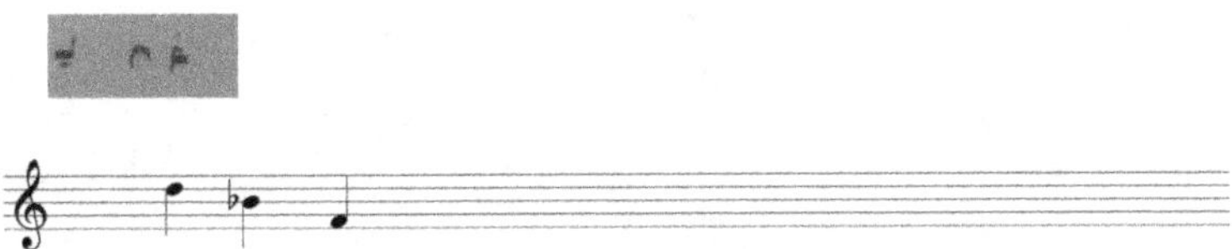

This interpretation was given by Karo Chalikyan and Areg Lusinyan.

Harents – He is referring to Astvatzatur Harents, who was a member of the founding committee of the Armenian Music Union.

Ashchyan – He is referring to Sisak Ashchyan, who was a member of the founding committee of the Armenian Music Union.

The one who endures to the end will be a spinach eater – A play on words using the New Testament passage "But the one who endures to the end will be saved" (Matthew 10:22, Mark 12:13). The Armenian "ով համբերեսցէ ի սպառ, նա կեցցէ" (read "ov hamberestse I spar, na ketstse") sounds similar to Komitas' sentence "որ համբերեսցէ ի սպանաղ կերիցէ" (read "vor hamberestse i spanagh keritse").

1911

147. <TO HOVHANNES MUTAFYANTS>

The original is located at the MAL, KF, 1570.

It was first published in *Hayreniki Dzayn*, 1968, issue 40.

See the reply my Hovhannes Mutafyants dated 16 February 1911.

I would happily take the initiative to come to Alexandria – Komitas arrived in Alexandria on 7 April 1911 (*Byuzandion*, 1911, issue 4413, page 3).

After the concert benefitting the National Hospital on 6 or 13 March – The concert took place on 27 March 1911 at the Tepe-Başi winter theater in Bera (*Byuzandion*, 1911, issue 4395, page 3, issue 4396, page 2).

The Smyrna concert is on the 30th of the month – See the letter to Margarit Babayan on 17 December 1910 and the corresponding notes.

I will leave for Constantinople on 2 February – Komitas left for Constantinople from Smyrna on 4 February (*Byuzandion*, 1911, issue 4354, page 3). The reason for the delay was a proposal to repeat the Smyrna concert which, nonetheless, did not occur.

148. <TO HAKOB>

The location of the original is unknown.

A copy of the original was published for the first time in *Kulis*, 1959, issue 302, page 8. The editor of *Kulis* printed the following note along with the copy – "Komitas Vardapet's handwriting (courtesy of photographer Mr. Yervand Aslanyan)." The letter is written on Komitas' visiting card, a copy of which is kept at the MAL A. Chopanyan Fund (no. 3386).

We are invited to Martin Hakobyan's – In the beginning of 1911, upon Komitas' initiative, a founding committee was formed in Constantinople for a music school, and one of its members was wealthy Constantinople Armenian Martin Hakobyan (see the letter written to M. Babayan on 12 July 1911 and the corresponding notes). Apparently, Komitas was referring to one of the working sessions of the founding committee, which is why we dated this letter as February-May 1911, when the Constantinople Armenian press was full of enthusiastic discussions on the opening of the music school.

Kertenkele – see the letter written to Stepan Akayan on 22 December 1910 and the corresponding notes. The use of this word suggests that the addressee, Hakob, had been one of Komitas' students.

149. <TO MARGARIT BABAYAN>

The original is located at the MAL, KF, 1351.

It was first partially published with omissions by K. Samuelyan (*Sovetakan Arvest*, 1972, issue 6, page 49), and then in KL 2000, pages 26-27 and KL 2007, pages 39-40.

Alexandrie, Eglise arm. – Alexandria, Armenian Church (French). Komitas stayed at the Armenian church during his visit to Alexandria.

My work has already reached the level of princes – According to the memoirs of Hrant Hrahan, "Everyone in Constantinople knew that the heir to the throne, Yasuf Izzidin—a lover of literature and art—was his friend, and that he was close to his younger brother, the second in line to the throne, painter Abdul Mechid, who had been awestruck by Komitas' multifaceted talent and had requested him to come to the palace frequently. Each time he enjoyed his company, he would request him to either sing or play on the piano. Abdul Mechid had also asked him to give his wife lessons in music and piano. Despite the range of other work he had, Komitas had been unable to reject the heir's proposal, taking into consideration the patriotic thought that a powerful friend in the palace could always later be useful to the Armenian people" (MAL, KF, 83, page 29).

A young lady from Constantinople, from a very good family – It is unclear to whom Komitas is referring.

150. <TO MARGARIT BABAYAN>

The original is located at the MAL, KF, 1352.

It was first partially published with omissions by K. Samuelyan (*Sovetakan Arvest*, 1972, issue 6, page 49), and then in KL 2000, pages 26-27 and KL 2007, pages 39-40.

I received your letter – The letter has not been found.

My heartfelt gratitude for the exhaustive and direct explanations you gave – See the letter to Margarit Babayan written on 12 April 1911.

The concert in Alexandria was also very successful – He is referring to the concert that took place at the Alhambra theater in Alexandria on 5 June 1911, which had had unprecedented success. According to *Byuzandion*, "Father Komitas Vardapet's concert got indescribable reactions from the public, an impeccable victory for the musicologist and an absolute success for the choir" (for details see **K. Samuelyan**, Annals *Sovetakan Arvest*, 1971, issue 9, page 54, and Tigran Kamsarakan's open letter to Komitas).

I am now in Cairo. The Armenians here wanted to transport the choir and repeat the concert – Komitas arrived in Cairo on 10 June 1911.

I hope to open a music school in Constantinople, but the plan is so far just at the level of talk – Komitas had come up with the idea of opening a music school in Constantinople in the beginning of 1911. The 2 February issue of *Byuzandion* presented the foundation program and statute of the music school in detail. A founding committee for the school had also been created, which included Arsen Arsenyan, Eduard Karageozyan, Astvatzatur Harents, Sisak Ashchyan, Martin Hakobyan, Vahram Torgomyan. - **but the plan is so far just at the level of talk** – The Armenian press in Constantinople had dedicated a number of articles with great enthusiasm to this program and the process of its implementation (see *Byuzandion*, 1911, issue 4351, page 1, issue 4371, page 3, issue 4383, page 1, issue 4386, page 1, issue 4388, page 1, *Etchmiadzin*, 1966, issue 5, page 29 (R. Zardayan's article), *Tachar*, 1911, issue 9, page 151, *Azatamart*, 1911, issue 542, page 2, *Surhandak*, 1911, issue 273, page 2, *Vostan*, 1911, issue 2, page 456).

151. <TO MR. AND MRS. LALOY>

The original is located at the MAL, MAF, unprocessed.

It was first published in KL 2000, page 68, and then in KL 2007, page 86.

According to the postal stamp, the letter was sent from Shanklin on 2 August 1911. The text is written on a postcard which has Komitas' photograph on the reverse side. The bottom right corner of the postcard has a seal that says "Alban. Alexandrie" which suggests that the postcard was printed in Alexandria. Komitas had been in Egypt in April–July 1911, from where he left for Paris and then went for two weeks with Margarit Babayan to summer resort of the Isle of Wight in England, from where he had sent this congratulatory postcard. The letter is addressed to *"Monsieur et Madame Laloy,"* i.e. to Lousi Laloy and Shushik Babayan-Laloy.

Nicolette – The daughter of the Laloys.

***Susutchki...* Margo** – This segment was written by Margarit Babayan.

152. <TO VARIKO VRATSYAN>

The original is located at the MAL, KF, 1630.

It was first published in KL 2000, page 168, and then in KL 2007, page 198.

The letter was addressed to Nikolay Karakashyan, who is probably the Nikol referred to in the letter. "Г-ну Николаю Каракашян, please hand over to Variko Vratsyan." The reverse side of the postcard depicts a scene from Shanklin.

153. <TO TIRAYR VARDAPET>

The original is located at the MM, Tirayr fund, fol. 132, doc. 43.

It was first published in *Teghekagir Hasarakakan Gitutyunneri*, 1956, issue 9, pages 109-110. According to the postal stamp, the letter reached Kishinev on 12.8.11 by the new calendar, i.e. on 25 August 1911.

The first part of the letter was written by Hambardzum Melikyan, and has been published for the first time.

St. Malo. Villa Franc-Value – H. Melikyan's summer house is located in the French city of St. Malo.

The situation of our poor Eghpaneu – It is not clear to what H. Melikyan is referring.

Hambardzum Melikyan – This is a reference to treasurer of the Armenian Union of Paris Hambardzum Melikyan (see the letters to Margarit Babayan on 7 February 1907 and Arshak Chopanyan on 12 July 1907 and 5 July 1908, as well as the corresponding notes).

Zmbltoros – *zimbali* – Having holes (Turkish).

You left Paris and ended up in the doghouses of Kishinev – Tirayr Vardapet (Tirayr Ter-Hovhannisyan, 1867-1956) had been ordained a monk with Komitas in 1894 (see *Ararat*, 1894, issue 9, pages 290-291), and left for Kishinev after graduating from the Sorbonne in 1910.

Mara Melikoff – Hambardzum Melikyan's daughter, Armine Melikyan. This note has been added to the letter most probably by Armine Melikyan herself.

154. <MARGARIT BABAYAN>

The original is located at the MAL, MAF, unprocessed.

It was first published in *Grakan Tert*, 1969, issue 22.

This is a reply to Margarit Babayan's letter sent in September 1911 from Paris, where she tells Komitas that a young man had come to her, introducing himself as a student of Komitas'. "Your student came to see me recently, he was hungry. He wants to learn *composition* here. My impress<ion> was that he has talent, but the poor thing doesn't know anything yet. What is your opinion?" M. Babayan wrote.

He had written to me from London and I had replied – The letters have not been found.

Please ask Shushik for the final copy of the dances – Komitas had sent his dance tunes to Shushik on a number of occasions (see in particular the letters to Margarit Babayan dated 23 October 1906 and 2 July 1908).

155. <TO ARCHBISHOP GEVORG SURENYANTS>

The original is located at the ANA, fn. 56, l. 1, f. 11398.

It was first published by A. Adamyan (*Teghekagir Hasarakakan Gitutyunneri*, 1956, issue 9, page 110) and then in KL 2000, page 46 and KL 2007, page 59-60.

I ask you to kindly instruct my congregational salary at Etchmiadzin to be cancelled – On 25 January 1912, Komitas' request was discussed at the Mother See and the following decision was made: "Since Komitas Vardapet has not received his congregational salary since 1 November 1911, his salary will be considered cancelled from that date onwards. F. Komitas Vardapet and the Mother See are to be informed of this decision and the case is considered closed." (ANA, f. 56, l. 1, f. 11398).

They wrote – This is misrepresented in KL 2000 and 2007 as "**I wrote**."

156. <MARGARIT BABAYAN>

The location of the original is unknown.

This section of the letter was first published by Margarit Babayan in *Komitas Vardapet Through his Letters* (see "Mshakuyt," Paris, 1935, pages 163). The original of the memoir is located in the M. Atmachyan collection at the MAL.

***Breikopt und Hartel* and will be available in one or two months, in parts** – He is referring to the collection of "Armenian Peasant Songs," the first two parts of which were published in September 1912. Considering the mention by Komitas in his letter to Margarit Babayan on 28 March 1912 that "The printing of my songs has come across a problem", this letter must have been written in December 1911.

1912

157. <TO THE EDITORS OF *HOVIT*>

The location of the original is unknown.

It was first published in *Hovit*, 1912, N 9, page 142. The letter is a reply to the information published in *Hovit* N 5 that "Renowned musician Komitas Vardapet is giving up his spiritual vocation, and he has sent a letter to this effect to the Honorable Locum Tenens" (ibid., page 79). Komitas sent the same letter to the journal *Luys* published in Nor Nakhijevan (1912, issue 10, page 13).

I have simply asked the Most Honorable Locum Tenens to cancel my salary – see the letter written to Archbishop Gevorg written on 26 December 1911.

158. <TO VAHAN MALEZYAN>

The original is located at the MAL, VMF, 315.

It was first published by Gohar Aznavuryan (*Sovetakan Arvest*, 1962, issue 10, pages 55-56). The photograph gifted to Vahan Malezyan is located at the MAL Komitas fund with the following autograph: "To dear Vahan *ef.* Malezyan. 1911. 2/7. 1911. Cairo."

I had already begun the work a month ago – He is referring to the anthem that he was to write for the Armenian General Benevolent Union (MAL, KF, 1437).

The Committee for the Armenian Music School has been organized... Sisak Ashchyan as Secretary – See the letter written to Margarit Babayan on 12 June 1911, as well as the corresponding notes.

The first performance will take place on New Sunday... the second a few weeks later – The concerts took place at the Petit Champ theater on 1 and 8 April 1912 (see **K. Samuelyan**, Annals, *Sovetakan Arvest*, 1973, issue 6, pages 54-58).

The chief of protocol for the Sultan, Ismayil Cenan *bey* came to visit me – Panos Terlemezyan has described this meeting in his memoirs about Komitas.

"Once, when I was in my studio, the cook came in, saying that there was a carriage outside decorated in gold and that they were asking for me. I came down to see the emperor's chief of protocol, Ismayil Cenan *bey*, who asked from with the carriage for permission to see my paintings.

We went up to the second and third floors of our house, and he looked at all the paintings very attentively. Going downstairs, as we walked past the door to Komitas' room, I asked whether it would please him to make the acquaintance of Komitas *effendi*. He said, 'I would like to, but I might be disturbing him.' I said, 'He won't be bothered at all' and I opened the door to Komitas' room and invited him in. They got acquainted and the chief of protocol quickly looked over my paintings that hung in that room. After drinking coffee, he turned to me, 'I don't want to be so impolite, but I would like to ask Komitas *effendi* to play or sing something.'

Komitas heard that request, softly spoken and in French, and immediately went to the piano, played a few chords, and sang a song by Schubert in German with such profound emotion that we were completely immobilized. We were quiet for a certain amount of time after he had finished too, when the Turkish diplomat could no longer hold himself back and struck the table with his hand, saying, '*Sapristi!* ('Damn it!'), we are a state with eight hundred years of history, but we have never had a temple of art and musicology like this one.'

That diplomat, in charge of the sultan's affairs, left ponderously. And after he left, I congratulated Komitas on that success and the two of us got up and danced '*Lachim nana.*'

He had learned that dance in the village of Ghrkhbulagh in Kotayk, when he was a seminary student." (*Contemporaries on Komitas*, Yerevan, 1960, page 190).

The excellent singer Shahmuradyan is now the honored guest of the Egyptian Armenians – he is referring to Armenak Shahmuradyan's tour of Egypt, which took place in February 1912. For press reviews of this tour, see **Armenak Shahmuradyan**, compiled by Khachik Safaryan, Yerevan, 1998, pages 78-80.

The Toros Azatyan fund at the MAL contains an (unprocessed) photograph of A. Shahmuradyan bearing his autograph, which was sent around that time from Cairo – "To the most talented but dear Father Komitas, with warm feelings of admiration and friendship. A. Shah-Muradyan. Cairo, 16 Feb<ruary> 1912."

I had promised to compose a song for the Union – The MAL Komitas fund (number 1437) contains the "Anthem of the Armenian General Benevolent Union," the music and lyrics of which were penned by Komitas. After this, another anthem called "Glory to the Union" was brought into use, with the lyrics by V. Malezyan and the music by H. Sinanyan (see **Theodik**, *Amenun Taretsuytsy*, 1915-16-20, pages 84-85).

159. <TO MARGARIT BABAYAN>

The original is located at the MAL, KF, 1355.

The reverse side of the third page of the letter contains Panos Terlemezyan's letter to M. Babayan. A section of the letter was first published by M. Babayan (*Mshakuyt*, 1935, page 164), followed by K. Samuelyan (*Sovetakan Arvest*, 1973, issue 6, page 56), KL 2000, pages 28-30, and KL 2007, pages 42-45.

One on New Sunday, the other the following Sunday – See the letter written to Vahan Malezyan on 24 February 1912, as well as the corresponding notes.

To start the task of the music school – See the letters written to Margarit Babayan on 12 June 1911 and to Vahan Malezyan on 24 February 1912, as well as the corresponding notes.

And drag you out here as well – The founding committee of the music school had made a decision in 1911 to establish the school in the Bera district of Constantinople and invite good quality experts from Europe, including Margarit Babayan, to teach there (see *Byuzandion*, 1911, issue 4371, page 3).

Coming to Miss Gavanozyan – Iskuhi Gavanozyan was a student of M. Babayan's in Paris.

Next to the girl I mentioned – He is referring to the young lady he mentioned earlier in the letter.

The printing of my songs has come across a problem... to Breit-kopt-Hartel - See the letter written to Margarit Babayan in December 1911, as well as the corresponding notes.

As – the Armenian պատճառաւ has been misrepresented in KL 2000 and 2007 as պատճառն.

Petersburg for a few months, as witnesses for the Dashnaktsutyun case – He is referring to the trial of the *Dashnaks* in Petersburg in 1912.

Society - the Armenian շրջանակի has been misrepresented in KL 2000 and 2007 as շրջանի.

I have also written two Turkish songs—one dedicated to the Sultan, the other to the constitution – A draft copy of Komitas' "Ittihat Anthem" (number 445) is located at the MAL Komitas fund, as well as the song with lyrics written by Turkish poet and Ittihat leader Mehmet Emin. See Mehmet Emin's letter to Komitas.

The Sultan's chief of protocol had visited me yesterday – In his letter to Vahan Malezyan dated 24 February 1912, Komitas had mentioned that on 23 February, the Sultan's chief of protocol Ismayil Cenan *bey* had visited him. Based on Komitas' reference ("The Sultan's chief of protocol had visited me yesterday"), this is the second visit by the chief of protocol, which occurred on 27 March.

Dear and respected – P. Terlemezyan's letter starts from this point.

It has been published for the first time.

Mathveev – Alexander Matveev (1878-1960) – a Russian painter and sculptor.

The Gyurjyans – He is referring to sculptor Hakob Gyurjyan (1881-1948).

160. <TO TIRAYR VARDAPET>

The original is located at the MM, Tirayr fund, fol. 132, doc. 90.

It was first published in *Teghekagir Hasarakakan Gitutyunneri*, 1956, issue 1, pages 110-111.

You remember him – The original letter says յուշում ես ("you hint at") instead of յիշում ես in Armenian.

The Holy Father – he is referring to the head of the Diocese of Bessarabia Archbishop Nerses Khudaverdyan.

161. <TO ARSHAK CHOPANYAN>

The original is located at the MAL, ACF, 3415.

It was first published by G. Aznavuryan (*Sovetakan Arvest*, 1962, issue 10, page 56) and then in KL 2000, pages 152-153 and KL 2007, pages 183-184.

Your anniversary should definitely be postponed because the situation is tense – He is referring to the 25th anniversary of A. Chopanyan's literary and social activities. Komitas' hints ("the situation is tense") refer to the situation in Turkey after the Balkan war (letters written from Turkey were subjected to censorship). Later, in the fall of 1913, Krikor Zohrab took on the brave initiative to mark A. Chopanyan's anniversary. An anniversary committee was formed consisting of Yeghishe Duryan, Krikor Zohrab, Patriarch Zaven, Ruben Zardaryan, Zabel Asatur, Tiran Kelekyan and others, but the First World War, which broke out in 1914, prevented the events from taking place.

Additionally, Krikor Zohrab had been encouraged by Armenak Shahmuradyan to take the initiative of organizing that event; the latter had written the following in a letter to Arshak Chopanyan on 16 November 1913.

"After my concert yesterday, I was sitting in the club in the evening with Mr. Martin Hakobyan and drinking tea, when Mr. Zohrab and Surenyan (dentist) came in and sat next to us. I talked nicely about your activities and spoke half-jokingly and half-accusingly of the need to organize your anniversary, as a show of gratitude and an expression of thanks for the quarter century of your artistic service. I was particularly adamant for Zohrab to take on the initiative, as a literary person and a public figure of great value. He gladly accepted this suggestion of mine, as if having made a new discovery, and promised to give it substance by forming a committee to do it, after which I told him that he should first seek your opinion.

While Zohrab writes to you about this, seated at the opposite table, I am writing you this letter with the pleasure of knowing that I have done a great thing.

Even if there had been a slight chill between us recently, I know how to appreciate the value of a person—especially a friend—irrespective of trifles. I wish with all my heart for your health and wellbeing because you are an important person in the Armenian reality, and you deserve all the appreciation of the Armenians because you are a cause of pride to them.

Please accept what I have done and what I have written to you as the sincere echo of a loving and appreciative heart. I kiss you with those sincere feelings,

A. Shah-Muradyan

P.S. If you ever feel the need to write to me regarding this, send the letter to Sertlyan. Martin Hakobyan congratulated me warmly on getting Zohrab involved." (Armenak Shahmuradyan, Yerevan, 1998, Page 49).

162. <MARGARIT BABAYAN>

The original is located at the MAL, KF, 1354.

It was first published in KL 2000, pages 30-31, and then in KL 2007, pages 45-47.

Izmit – This is misrepresented in KL 2000 and 2007 as **Izmir**.

I will go to Leipzig in two weeks. If I can afford it, I will stop by in Paris as well – Komitas left for Leipzig at the end of May to supervise the publication of the collection "Armenian Peasant Songs" ("in two weeks" i.e. on 26 May). In a letter to Father Tirayr dated 1 July 1912, Maghakia Ormanyan said, "Komitas is in Leipzig" (MM, Tirayr fund, doc. 110).

You had written about going to America – The letter has not been found.

I am sending you the photograph of me – The photograph dated 19 May 1912 that was gifted to Margarit Babayan by Komitas is located at the MAL Komitas fund. The date of the autograph suggests that, though the letter was written on 12 May, it was sent after 19 May.

Because of the war – see the letter written to A. Chopanyan on 10 May 1912, as well as the corresponding notes.

163. <TO MARINOS STAMPOLYAN>

The original is located at the MAL, KF, 711, page 16.

The letter is written in a notebook and it is unclear whether or not it was sent.

It was first published by Khachik Samuelyan (Annals, *Sovetakan Arvest*, 1974, issue 5, page 52), and then later in KL 2000, page 166 and KL 2007, page 197.

To Marinos Stampolyan – Both in the "Annals" as well as in KL 2000 and 2007, the name **Marinos** has been read and reproduced as **Marina** (with the last two letters in Armenia "-nu" resembling the letter "-ա" when written by hand), and the last name **Stampolyan** has been misrepresented in the last two publications as Stampoltsyan: KL 2007 considered it likely that Marina Stampoltsyan "is probably the cultural figure Marinos Stampolyan" (page 259). If the name had been read correctly, such an interpretation would have been unnecessary. We have written the addressee's first and last names as it was written in the original.

Lily of the valley – Song of Solomon 2:1.

Like... the choicest gold – compare this to Job 22:25 "the choicest silver for you."

164. <TO MARGARIT BABAYAN>

The original is located at the MAL, KF, 1353.

It was first published in parts by K. Samuelyan (*Sovetakan Arvest*, 1974, issue 5, pages 53, and then in KL 2000, pages 32-34 and KL 2007, pages 47-50.

N – This has been misrepresented in KL 2000 and 2007 as **Pera**.

I am truly guilty; I have not written anything to you in all this time – This letter is a reply to Margarit Babayan's letter written on 3 November

1912, where she expresses unhappiness at Komitas' long silence, "I have had no news from you for months".

You are finding success under a foreign sky – See the letter written by Margarit Babayan on 3 November 1912.

Mannik – He is referring to Retheos Berberyan's daughter Mannik Berberyan, who was being taught in Paris by M. Babayan, and by Komitas in Constantinople. On 4 May 1913, Mannik Berberyan's concert took place at the Union Française hall with Komitas' participation (see *Byuzandion*, 1913, issue 5037, page 3).

About Tigran Nalbandyan – According to G. Stepanyan, "Singer, tenor. Born in Van. Studied at the Nersisyan school in Tiflis, where he was a student of composer Makar Yekmalyan. He then studied for two years at the Tiflis music college, and continued his education from 1898 at the Petersburg conservatory as a student of Professor Gabel. He performed as a singer during those years and gained attention with his lyrical tenor. He graduation from the conservatory in 1906 and went to Italy with a scholarship from A. Mantashyan, where he developed his voice in Milan. Starting from 1909, he began giving concerts in Italy, France, Switzerland, Germany, Russia and other countries," (*Biographical Dictionary*, Vol. 3, Book 1, Yerevan, 1990, page 120).

For the moment – The Armenian դեռ եւս has been misrepresented in KL 2000 and 2007 as թերեւս ("perhaps").

Coming to Iskuhi Ghavanozyan – See the letter written to Margarit Babayan on 15 March 1912 and the corresponding notes.

My life is good. My apartment is comfortable – Komitas was staying at the apartment located at Pangalti, N 83(47), which P. Terlemezyan has described in his memoirs.

"In those days, I moved to Shidag Street in Pangalti, to live with the talented composer Komitas in one house, which had been completely given to just the two of us.

There was a pretty room on the ground floor of this house, looking out on the street, which we turned into a dining room, then a vestibule. The cook's room and kitchen were on the western side and looked out on a small flower orchard. There was a big room on the second floor on the street side, hanging out, but with a balcony that formed a part of the room itself. That room was

Komitas' workshop and reception area, where his large piano and physharmonica were located" (*Contemporaries on Komitas*, Yerevan, 1960, page 180).

A few choral songs from Wagner and Verdi – During the concert of the choir "Gusan" that took place on 12 May 1913 at the Petit Champ winter theater, under Komitas' supervision the choir performed "three pieces" composed by Wagner and Mozart that were "very well received" (see *Byuzandion*, 1913, issue 5043, page 3).

I have therefore not received my songbooks from Leipzig[26] although they are published and ready – See the letter written to M. Babayan in December 1911.

Very dear and respected - Panos Terlemezyan's letter starts from this point.

Laloy – This letter was written by Panos Terlemezyan, who jokingly added the note for "**La**" above the first syllable.

Is Mrs. Armenuhi (Carbonel) working? – That is, is she painting? (Armenuhi Carbonel-Babayan was a painter).

Bravo – Komitas wrote this section after P. Terlemezyan's letter.

Terlemezyan's letter and this section have been published for the first time.

165. <ARSHAK CHOPANYAN>

The original is located at the MAL, ACF, 3416.

It was first published in *Patma-Banasirakan Handes*, 1958, issue 1, pages 263-265, and later in KL 2000, pages 153-156 and KL 2007, pages 184-188. According to the postal stamp, the letter reached Paris on 14 January 1913.

The last page of the letter contains P. Terlemezyan's letter to A. Chopanyan.

An undying hope; we stare towards the lantern of the future... as we imagined our future lives – Here, Komitas invokes the "Lantern of the Illuminator" legend by Hovhannes Tumanyan, using the poet's imagery and

26 ["Leipzig" was written this way using Latin letters by Komitas in the original letter] – Translator's notes

words (**Hovhannes Tumanyan**, A Comprehensive Collection of his Works in Ten Volumes, Vol. 2, Yerevan, 1990, pages 127-128). Compare, for example

An undying hope; we stare towards the lantern of the future – He who looks with burning hope / Towards the future of the Armenians (Tumanyan)

Had hung... summit of Mount Aragats... an indiscernible string, so that nobody could touch it – It is hung without a rope / At the summit of Aragats... No human hand can reach it / At that terrible height (Tumanyan) and so on.

Celestial – The Armenian երկնադէտ has been misrepresented in KL 2000 and 2007 as երկնաւէտ.

Billows - The Armenian գոհակներն has been misrepresented in KL 2000 and 2007 as կոհակներն. The spelling that Komitas uses was common in informal Western Armenian at the beginning of the 20th century.

Once more - The Armenian այս անգամ այլ has been misrepresented in KL 2000 as այս անգամ, այլ and in 2007 as այս անգամ ալ. The final word in this phrase, այլ, is the old form of the Western Armenian ալ and the Eastern Armenian էլ ("again," although it varies with context), commonly use, for example, by poets like Ghevond Alishan. Komitas' usage of it is consistent with the dramatic tone of his text earlier in the letter.

In front of - The Armenian առաջեւ has been misrepresented in KL 2000 and 2007 as արջեւ. Komitas has used the classic Armenian (*Grabar*) form of the word in the original letter.

The Russian government suffered in the Far East – He is referring to the 1904-1905 Russo-Japanese war.

The union of England, France and Russia – He is referring to the Triple Entente formed from 1904 to 1907 involving Great Britain, France and Russia.

Great - The Armenian մեծ ("great") has been misrepresented in KL 2000 and 2007 as մեր ("our").

Dear, respected friend - P. Terlemezyan's letter starts from this point. It is written on the reverse side of the final page of Komitas' letter.

It has been published for the first time.

27 Dec<ember> - This note by P. Terlemezyan suggests that the letter was sent after 27 December.

1913

166. <TO MARGARIT BABAYAN>

The original is located at the MAL, KF, 1358.

It was first published by K. Samuelyan (*Sovetakan Arvest*, 1974, issue 5, page 55), and then in KL 2000, pages 34-35 and KL 2007, pages 50-51.

Flügel – a grand piano (German).

My personal work - The Armenian աշխատանքներովս has been misrepresented in KL 2000 and 2007 as աշխատանքներով.

I have not yet been able to get my songbooks from Leipzig – See the letter written to M. Babayan in December 1911 and the corresponding notes.

Shah-Murad came and left for the Caucasus – Armenak Shahmuradyan left for Tiflis from Constantinople in February 1913. On March 7, he gave a solo concert in the hall of the Artists' Society there (see *Mshak*, 1913, issue 46).

Panos – He is referring to Panos Terlemezyan.

167. <TO HOVHANNES HOVHANNISYAN>

The original is located at the MAL, HHF, 127, section 2.

The telegram has been sent from Constantinople to Baku.

On 27 April 1913, the 30th anniversary of Hovhannes Hovhannisyan's literary and pedagogical activities was celebrated at the Humanitarian Society hall in Baku. Jubilee events were also organized in Tiflis and Alexandropol. On 29 April 1913, in his letter to Karapet Ter-Mkrtchyan, Hovhannes Hovhannisyan wrote that during the event his "close friends read the telegrams, but because of a lack of time, only two or three were read out to the audience; only some of the important ones were announced" (**Hovhannes**

Hovhannisyan, A Complete Compilation of his Works, vol. 4, Yerevan, 1968, page 176).

It has been published for the first time.

168. <TO HOVHANNES HOVHANNISYAN>

The original is located at the MAL, HHF, 128, section 2.

This joint congratulatory telegram was sent from Constantinople to Etchmiadzin. On 21 May, the 30th anniversary of Hovhannes Hovhannisyan' s literary and pedagogical activities was celebrated in Alexandropol as well. In K. Samuelyan's "Annals," this telegram is mistakenly dated 20 May 1912.

It has been published for the first time.

Father Mesrop Maksudyan (1876-1918) – Mesrop Vardapet Ter-Movsisyan – philologist, translator. The graduated from the Gevorgyan Seminary. In 1902, he was ordained a priest. In 1904, he was the vice deacon of Salmast and Urmia and the diocese manager, and then the deacon of Atrpatakan (for his biography, see *Ararat*, 1918, issue 1, pages 29-31).

169. <TO SPIRIDON MELIKYAN>

The original is located at the MAL, SMF, 225a.

It was first published with multiple errors (see below) in **Spiridon Melikyan**, Articles, Memoirs, Letters, Documents, compiled by Satenik Melikyan, Alexander Tadevosyan, Yerevan, 1964, page 155-156, and then in parts in *Sovetakan Arvest*, 1974, issue 8, page 55 and KL 2000, page 114-115, KL 2007, page 139.

This Saturday, I am leaving for the Caucasus and Tiflis. I will write or wire you the date of my arrival from Batum – The day when the letter was written, 9 June 1913, was a Sunday, meaning that Komitas left from Constantinople to Batum on 15 June 1913 ("This Saturday") and arrived in Tiflis on 25 June (see *Mshak*, 1913, issue 143, page 3).

We will sit and talk to our heart's content with each other – Komitas and Spiridon Melikyan met in the summer of 1913, which Spiridon Melikyan's wife Satenik Melikyan mentions in her memoirs.

"I cannot but narrate here the meeting between Komitas and S. Melikyan in 1913; it was so warm, so personal.

Komitas' name had always been one of the most important ones to Spiridon. I could sense that on every occasion. He would speak about his worthy teacher with a special admiration. When we got married, Spiridon wrote a letter about this to his teacher. We soon received Komitas' reply, where he said that he was preparing to come to the Caucasus, so he would have the opportunity to personally congratulate us on our wedding.

It was the month of July in 1913. We had already left for our summer house in Gharakilisa (now called Kirovakan[27]) with our newborn baby Hrachik. We lived in a comfortable apartment there which belonged to Klekchonts Tatos.

Towards evening, Spiridon was sitting in his room working and I was walking in the garden, carrying the baby. I suddenly turned to look at a thin clergyman of medium height who was making his way in our direction. I guessed at once – it was Komitas. I was confused and didn't know whether to hasten to Spiridon, or not. But Komitas approached me confidently, pressed my hand lovingly and took my Hrachik into his own hands. I led him to the house. And Spiridon rushed out of the room. They embraced like father and son. Tears of joy, heartfelt words, energetic jokes. Komitas punched his student and then once again took Hrachik in his arms, throwing him up in the air and cooing at him...

I was worried, but Spiridon said,

"Satenik, don't worry. The Holy Father won't drop his grandson."

Komitas wishes me a happy motherhood, and a joyful married life, after which he turned to Spiridon and said, "But don't forget that you got married without my blessings..." (**Spiridon Melikyan**, Articles, Memoirs, Letters, Documents, compiled by Satenik Melikyan, Alexander Tadevosyan, Yerevan, 1964, page 106-107).

Even brought the heir of your royal throne into this world – Hrachya Spiridon Melikyan (1913-1942) – composer, died during World War II.

---

27 [Renamed Vanadzor in independent Armenia] – Translator's notes.

Tsteban – Spiridon Melikyan's nickname. On 20 October 1907, S. Melikyan signed the reverse side of a photograph he gifted to Komitas with the name "**Tst.**" i.e. Tsteban.

Sneeze – In Articles, 1964, the Armenian հա՛փշի՛ւն is misrepresented as հափշլուն.

Mincemeat - In Articles, 1964, the Armenian խորտուխաշիլ is misrepresented as խուրդուխաշիլ.

Hm? - In Articles, 1964, the Armenian հը՞ is misrepresented as բը՛.

I read in the news about the music union – The Armenian Music Society of Tiflis was founded in 1912 and aimed at "facilitating the dissemination of musical education, supporting the development of Armenian music and encouraging Armenian composers, musicians, instructors, and in general all Armenians with a talent for music" (ibid., page 184).

You resigned its chairmanship – S. Melikyan resigned from the chairmanship of the Armenian Music Society of Tiflis in 1913 and became the Society's deputy chairman.

Kisses - In Articles, 1964, the Armenian պաչիկս is misrepresented as պապիկս.

Face to face - In Articles, 1964, the Armenian բերանոյ is misrepresented as բերանց.

Your Satik - In Articles, 1964, this is misrepresented as "**your Satenik**."

Arazyan - In Articles, 1964, this is misrepresented as "**Araskhanyan**."

I sent the songbooks today – He is referring to the copies of "Armenian Peasant Songs" (see the letter written to M. Babayan in December 1911 as well as the corresponding notes).

170. <TO MARGARIT BABAYAN>

The original is located at the MAL, KF, 1357.

It was first published in parts in *Sovetakan Arvest*, 1974, issue 8, pages 54-55, and later in KL 2000, page 36 and KL 2007, pages 51-52.

Your open letters – The letters have not been found.

I was able to give only two concerts this year – He is referring to the concerts by the choir "Gusan" organized on 12 May and 2 June 1913 at the Petit Champ Theater.

I am going to the Caucasus this Saturday – See the letter written to Spiridon Melikyan on 9 June 1913 and the corresponding notes.

I will stay till September, when I will return to Constantinople – Komitas returned to Constantinople in the end of August 1913 (see **K. Samuelyan**, Annals, *Sovetakan Arvest*, 1974, issue 11, page 55).

Gavanoz – He is referring to Iskuhi Gavanozyan (see the letter written to M. Babayan on 15 March 1912 and the corresponding notes).

Kertenkele – See the letter written to Stepan Akayan on 22 December 1910 and the corresponding notes.

171. <TO HOVHANNES TUMANYAN>

The original is located at the MAL, TF, 757.

It was first published by G. Aznavuryan (*Sovetakan Arvest*, 1962, issue 10, page 56), and later in KL 2000, page 55 and KL 2007, pages 69-70).

I have to be in Constantinople in September – See the letter written to M. Babayan on 9 June 1913 and the corresponding notes.

Participate in the literary event organized by the Armenian Writers' Society – In a letter dated 11 July 1913 to Garegin Hovsepyan from Hovhannes Tumanyan, the latter says the following about this event – "We are planning to organize a large public literary-music event in the fall through the initiative of the writers' society, which will consist of poetry, art and music in the Armenian church. Aghbalyan will speak on poetry, but I'm going to ask others as well and I would be very grateful if you could indicate some suitable candidates.

I have asked Komitas Vardapet to organize and direct the music part, and I request you to take on the organization of the art section – to speak, to present your magical lamps, any way you wish to do it. <...> I am convinced that you would approve of a big event of this kind and that you would not doubt its success and significance" (**Hovhannes Tumanyan**, A Comprehensive Collection of his Works in Ten Volumes, Vol. 10, Yerevan, 1999, page 181). In a letter to Hovhannes Tumanyan dated 4 August 1913, Garegin Hovsepyan also refused the invitation to participate in the event (see **Tumanyan.** On Art, Yerevan, 1969, pages 200-202).

The letter to Komitas from Tumanyan has not been found.

172. <TO MARGARIT BABAYAN>

The original is located at the MAL, KF, 1356.

It was first published with slight omissions in *Sovetakan Arvest*, 1974, issue 11, pages 53-54, and the in KL 2000, pages 37-38 and KL 2007, pages 53-54.

But I have not come here to stay. There is nobody who is asking me to stay, either – Benik Vardapet (Ter-Yeghiazaryan) wrote in his memoirs about the cold reception that Komitas Vardapet got at the Mother See, after Komitas went to Aparan and visited him.

"I saw our bishops, I was given a cold reception everywhere. I heard the same questions or similar ones from everyone's lips, 'Ah, hello, hello, Komitas holy father. They say you are quite popular in Constantinople, your work is going well, they are giving you a lot of money. When are you leaving? Of course, those conditions are for you.'

I nearly lost my mind from the offense and disgust I felt. I would respond curtly in anger.

'I am here today, gone tomorrow.'

'Oh? Well, as you wish. Naturally, people should live and work where things are good for them.'

I understood that Etchmiadzin did not feel a need for me. I could no longer breathe in that atmosphere. It pained my heart, but I had to leave..." (MAL, KF, 77, pages 125-126). See also Manuk Abelyan's memoirs ("Contemporaries on Komitas," Yerevan, 1960, pages 73).

Return to Constantinople in the beginning of September – See the letter written to M. Babayan on 9 June 1913 and the corresponding notes.

I just received a letter from Chopanyan – The letter has not been found. Komitas replied to that letter on 7 August 1913.

A long time ago – The Armenian շատոնց (not commonly used in Eastern Armenian) was misrepresented as ատոնց ("to them") in KL 2000 and 2007, which made the sentence meaningless.

Awoken... monastery... you... - The ellipses have been reproduced as they were used in the original letter.

173. <TO ARSHAK CHOPANYAN>

The original is located at the MAL, ACF, 3417.

It was first published in *Patma-Banasirakan Handes*, 1958, issue 1, pages 265-266, and then in KL 2000, pages 156-157 and KL 2007, pages 188-190.

I received your letter here – The letter has not been found. See also the letter written to M. Babayan on the same day.

I have not come to stay, just to work with the manuscript library and collect peasant songs - See and compare this with the first paragraph of the letter written to M. Babayan on the same day.

I will be back in Constantinople by mid-September - See and compare this with the first paragraph of the letter written to M. Babayan on the same day.

Stay – The Armenian մնացիր has been misrepresented in KL 2000 and 2007 as մնայիր, which would cause the meaning of the sentence to change to "If only you could stay..."

Pride and joy... all prejudices to lay down their arms immediately - See and compare this with the second paragraph of the letter written to M. Babayan on the same day.

The one who works his field – See and compare with Proverbs 12:11 - "The one who works his field will have plenty of food, but whoever chases daydreams lacks wisdom" and 28:19 "The one who works his land will be satisfied with food, but whoever chases daydreams will have his fill of poverty."

You know His Holy personally – He is referring to Gevorg Surenyants V.

Toy – Komitas spells the word in Armenian խաղալիկ instead of the now common խաղալիք; the former spelling is now considered archaic.

Holy Father Karapet – He is referring to Mother See congregant Karapet Ter-Mkrtchyan.

Hussik Vardapet - He is referring to Mother See congregant Hussik Vardapet Zohrabyan.

Garegin Vardapet - He is referring to Mother See congregant Garegin Vardapet Hovsepyan.

Vardapet... - The ellipsis has been reproduced as it was used in the original letter.

Nobody even asked me once - why aren't you coming back, why aren't you staying? - See and compare this with the letter written to M. Babayan on the same day and the corresponding notes.

The singing at the monastery is worse than in a village - See and compare this with the second paragraph of the letter written to M. Babayan on the same day.

174. <TO MARGARIT BABAYAN>

The original is located at the MAL, KF, 1359.

It was first published in KL 2000, pages 38-39, and then in KL 2007, pages 54-55.

I received your letter a long time ago – The letter has not been found.

By a number of events – He is referring to the events in Constantinople dedicated to the 1500th anniversary of the creation of the Armenian alphabet and the 400th anniversary of Armenian print, in which Komitas has played an important role.

The series of articles you had written in the pages of *Azatamart* – In August-September 1913, a series of articles were published (**Levon Chilingaryan**, Armenian Peasant Songs, *Heradzayn,* 1913, issue 44) in the pages of the Armenian press in Constantinople that criticized Komitas' activities as a researcher and teacher. In particular, Komitas was accused for not publishing a separate article about Armenian music in the Music Encyclopedia published in Paris, as a result of which "It was only when writing about the music of Turkey that the notes mentioned Armenian musicians as well, but that was all" (*Azatamart*, 1913, 18 September/1 October, issue 1316). Komitas replies to these articles with the piece "Armenians Have their Unique Music" (published in the same paper), where he notes in particular that "The fact that the specialists who were editing the encyclopedia neglected our nation's music is not an issue of rights or injustice – it is simply the result of ignorance" (**Komitas Vardapet**, Studies and Articles, Book II, Yerevan 2007, pages 83). On the occasion of this debate, Margarit Babayan sent an article to *Azatamart*, where she presented Komitas' activities in detail, starting from 1906, giving him credit for the international exposure of Armenian music (*Azatamart*, 1913, issue 1329, page 2, issue 1330, page 2).

Armenak Shah-Murad was here, with me at my house. His concert went very well – He is referring to A. Shahmuradyan's 3 November 1913 concert at the Petit Champ winter theater. A. Mesropyan wrote the following about the concert in his memoirs – "On 3 November 1913, after Armenak Shahmuradyan gave a very successful concert at the Petit Champ theater, Komitas went on stage arm in arm with Shahmuradyan and, after a few emotional words, gifted a delicate symbol made of gold to him, on behalf of his choir. The hall burst into applause.

On that day, at the end of the concert, backstage, an emotional scene played itself out. Komitas embraced his former seminary student Armenak Shahmuradyan, while the members and musicians of the Gusan ensemble, who were gathered there, showered them with flowers... Komitas, the great teacher, was moved, and he kissed his former student, the hero of the day, on the forehead and said, 'My only wish is to hear you in the operas of our homeland...'" (*Contemporaries on Komitas*, Yerevan, 1960, pages 250).

He is preparing for the second one – A. Shahmuradyan's second concert took place on 15 November 1913 (see the letter written by A. Shahmuradyan to A. Chobanyan on 16 November 1913, **Armenak Shahmuradyan**, Yerevan, 1998, page 49).

I will come to Paris at the end of spring for a music conference, I have already been invited to participate with a lecture – Komitas received the invitation from the Paris office of the International Music Society on 18 August 1913 (see MAL, KF, 52, and also this publication).

I had already written that I would participate – The letter has not been found.

Please ask our Lalois – Musicologist Louis Laloy was the head of the ethnography department at the Paris office of the International Music Society at the time (ibid.)

On these two topics – For the texts of these two lectures, see **Komitas Vardapet**, Studies and Articles, Book II, Yerevan 2007, pages 131-149, 150-181, 182-193, 474-478).

Organizing a small concert—before the delegates at the conference – This proposal by Komitas was accepted, and the presidium at the Paris conference circulated a letter to all participants on 20 May 1914 informing them that, along with other performances, there would be a religious ceremony at the Armenian church led by Komitas Vardapet before the conference (see MAL, KF, 60).

Mannik, Iskuk – He is referring to Mannik Berberyan and Iskuhi Gavanozyan.

Our dear Shushik – He is referring to Shushik Babayan.

The grumbling of some people in Constantinople – See the first paragraph of this letter and the corresponding notes.

175. <TO THE CURACY OF THE ARMENIAN PATRIARCHATE IN CONSTANTINOPLE>

The original is located at the MAL, GKF, 25.

It was first published in KL 2000, page 175, and then in KL 2007, page 207.

1914

176. <TO MARGARIT BABAYAN>

The original is located at the MAL, KF, 1361.

It was first published in KL 2000, pages 39-40, and then in KL 2007, page 56.

I received your letter – The letter has not been found.

The paper to the attention of the National Assembly, where it had already been read and even published in the newspapers – M. Babayan's father, Avetik Babayan, had passed away in Paris on 25 December 1913.

177. <TO ARSHAK CHOPANYAN>

The original is located at the MAL, ACF, 3419.

It was first published in KL 2000, page 160, and then in KL 2007, pages 162-163. In KL 2007, the letter is dated "**early 1907, Paris.**" The basis for this came from the assumption of the editor that the first lecture referenced in the letter ("The first one got a wonderful reaction") was the lecture on Armenian peasant music delivered by Komitas on 13 January 1907 at the invitation of the administration of the Paris Art School. And because Komitas writes in the same letter that he is going to deliver another one, "the last lecture, on Armenian peasant music" the editor of KL 2007 wrote "We could not find any information about another lecture on the same topic" (KL 2007, page 253).

The simple reason why a search for such a lecture would never have borne fruit is that Komitas did not write this lecture in early 1907, but rather on 4 June 1914, exactly seven and a half years later. Here is why.

The letter is written on a pneumatic card and the postal stamp bearing the date and month of receipt clearly say "4.6" which confirms that the letter arrived on 4 June. The month of **June** is also clearly visible on the dispatch postal stamp – "4 *Juin*" ("4 June" in French). So the letter could not have been written in January or in the beginning of the year. The year, however, is not clearly visible on the postal stamp. Komitas mentions in the letter that he "will be reading the last lecture, on Armenian peasant music, **tomorrow, Friday, morning** around 11." This means that he will be reading the lecture on 5 June, which is a Friday. A look at past calendars reveals that June 5 was a Friday in 1897, 1908, and 1914. Komitas was in Berlin in June 1897 and in Etchmiadzin in June 1908. It was only on **5 June 1914** that he was in Paris, where he was participating in the 5th Conference of the International Music Society. Therefore, the letter refers to the first and second lectures that Komitas delivered, the first of which was on the topic of the system of intonation symbols used in Armenian ecclesiastical music, and the second on Armenian peasant music that, based on the letter, was read on a Friday, 5 June 1914.

Based on this reasoning, the letter was dated **4 June 1914**.

Pneumatique – Pneumatic post was a postal communication system (within a building or city limits) that involved a network of tubes to transport letters, within capsules or without—in which case high density paper was employed—using air pressure.

To come tomorrow to the church for rehearsal at 3 in the afternoon – He is referring to the preparations for the ceremony planned at the Armenian church located on Jean Gujon Street (see the letter written to M. Babayan on 7 November 1913 as well as the corresponding notes.

178. <TO HIS STUDENTS>

The location of the original is unknown. A photocopy is located at the MAL, VSF, unprocessed.

It was first published in KL 2007, pages 15-17. This and the next letter from Komitas are addressed to his talented students in Constantinople – Mihran Tumajan, Hayk Semerjian, Barsegh Kanachyan, Vagharshak Srvandztyan, A.

Apachyan and Vardan Sargsyan, with whom he was photographed in 1914 (see MAL, KF, 206).

The Scola Cantorum, whose manager is d'Endy – Armenak Shahmuradyan had also studied for a year at Vincent d'Endy's private school (see **Armenak Shahmuradyan**, Yerevan, 1998, pages 38-39). Komitas' library contained Vincent d'Endy's books "*Une Ecole de Musique*" and "*Cours de composition musicale*" (MAL, KF, 794, 990).

Should be able to get permission for that – The Armenian առ այդ կարծեմ թէ թոյլտուութեան has been misrepresented in KL 2007 as որ այդ, կարծեմ թէ, թոյլտուութեան.

The conference just ended today – He is referring to the conference of the International Music Society that took place in June 1914.

The introduction to the children's songbook – According to Aghavni Mesropyan, "Upon his return from the well-known conference of the International Music Society in Paris in 1914, among the many music books that Komitas had brought with him, there was a series of colorfully illustrated French and German children's music books.

Komitas dreamed of preparing colorfully illustrated books for his beloved Armenian children using those as an example, but preparing completely different content." (*Contemporaries on Komitas*, Yerevan, 1960, pages 149).

179. <TO HIS STUDENTS>

The location of the original is unknown. A photocopy is located at the MAL, VSF, unprocessed.

It was first published in KL 2007, pages 17-18.

The Armenian իմ (which translates in most contexts to "my") has been misrepresented in KL 2007 as իսկ ("while").

I have received invitations from private institutions... the Armenians of Manchester... so that I can go to England – In his letter to Margarit Babayan on 23 June 1914, Komitas mentions that he has already received the invitation to go to England and planned to leave on 24 June.

180. <TO MARGARIT BABAYAN>

The original is located at the MAL, KF, 1360.

The letter is written on a pneumatic card.

It was first published by K. Samuelyan (*Sovetakan Arvest*, 1974, issue 1, page 55-56) and later in KL 2000, page 32 and KL 2007, page 47.

K. Samuelyan (and, based on that, KL 2000 and 2007) considered the date the letter was sent to be 10/23 June 1912, which they based on the handwritten (probably by M. Babayan) text on the letter, which said "23 June 1912." K. Samuelyan added the "10" to adjust the date to the new calendar. This confused the editors of KL 2007, where the date was set as 10 June 1912. However, the dispatch postal stamp on the pneumatic card says 23.6.14 (23 *Juin* 1914), i.e. 23 June 1914. On pneumatic cards, the day and month of dispatch is usually stamped on a separate line from the year. Moreover, the letter mentions the invitation received from England, which was also mentioned in Komitas' letter to his students dated 22 June 1914. We have therefore dated this letter 23 June 1914.

At Garibyan's – He is referring to Onnik Gharibyan (see the letter to Arshak Chopanyan dated 15 April 1909 and the corresponding notes).

I will probably go to England tomorrow. I have received an invitation – See the letter written to his students on 22 June 1914 and the corresponding notes.

181. <TO ARSHAK CHOPANYAN>

The original is located at the MAL, ACF, 3420.

It was first published in KL 2000, page 160, and then in KL 2007, page 192.

The letter was written on a pneumatic card and is not dated. We have dated it based on the postal stamp - *2 Juil. 14*, i.e. 2 July 1914, Paris.

Shah – He is referring to Armenak Shahmuradyan.

182. <TO ARSHAK CHOPANYAN>

The original is located at the MAL, KF, 1447.

It was first published in KL 2000, page 158 and then in KL 2007, page 190.

I did quite a lot of work in Vienna and Philippe – According to Toros Azatyan, "Upon returning from Paris, Komitas visited Vienna. He introduced us to Armenian music during a cozy gathering there with his beautiful samples. He also stopped by Philippe, where he gave a lecture on Armenian spiritual and peasant music, at the invitation of the local Bibliophilist Society" (**Komitas Vardapet**. Constantinople, 1931, page 150).

Their school and education – This was misrepresented in KL 2000 and 2007 as "**their school education.**"

Unfortunately, Bishop Yeghishe Duryan has also played a bad role regarding my case during one of the Religious Assemblies – In June 1914, the Blumenthal brothers released a few records containing some Armenian church songs performed by Armenak Shahmuradyan, with the instrumental accompaniment of Komitas. This led to the anger and rage of the "Constantinople Armenian choristers" who considered it to be sacrilegious and brought the case to the Religious Assembly. On 5 June, the Religious Assembly came to the following decision.

"Considering that F. Komitas Vardapet has indulged in the sale of his performance of sacred songs belonging to the Holy Armenian Church and allocated to the temple of God, and that these songs are being played on gramophones everywhere, including in locations that hurt the religious sentiments of the faithful, the decision has been made to ask our Father the Holy Patriarch to request the Holy Catholicos for a censure of F. Komitas Vardapet for this course of events that are completely unbecoming of the Armenian Church."

This decision of the Religious Assembly was condemned by P. Terlemezyan, Tigran Cheokuryan, Yervand Otyan, Melkon Kyurchyan, and Arshak Chopanyan, who published an article in *Byuzandion* titled "An

Irreligious Decision" where they wrote – "The decision of the Religious Assembly is an obscenity towards beauty and is devoid of any trace of justice" (1914, issue 5384, page 1). See also **Komitas Vardapet**, Studies and Articles, Book II, pages 194-199, 478; *Byuzandion*, 1914, issue 5372, "The Persecution of Komitas Vardapet," issue 5393, "Komitas Vardapet and the Religious Assembly, issue 5397, "Against Komitas Vardapet. To Mr. A. Chopanyan").

Bishop Yeghishe Duryan (the younger brother of Petros Duryan) – philologist, poet, pedagogue, Patriarch of Constantinople (1909-1911) was the deputy chairman of the 1914 Religious Assembly. The mention that "**Unfortunately, Bishop Yeghishe Duryan has also played a bad role**" is a reply to the following section of Chopanyan's article – "The thing that causes me the most surprise is that the decision was made by a Religious Assembly, whose members are people whose names I do not know, but I do know that the chairman was Archbishop Maghakia Ormanyan and the deputy chairman was Archbishop Yeghishe Duryan. Holy Father Ormanyan was absent, he is bringing our monastery in Jerusalem to order with wonderful determination and authority. Had he been in Constantinople, he would definitely have opposed such a decision. **Holy Father Duryan was probably not at that meeting, or if he had been present, he too had definitely tried to resist this decision, but had not been heard, and the decision had been taken through a majority vote. I cannot imagine it having happened any other way** *(emphasis by the editor, G.G.)*. So how could the Religious Assembly produce a decision in a matter as delicate as this one without the presence of its two chairmen, that is something I cannot understand" (*Byuzandion*, 1914, issue 5385, page 1). Komitas hinted at the fact that Archbishop Yeghishe Duryan was both present and had voted in favor of the decision, which Chopanyan had considered "unimaginable." Later, through the intervention of the Patriarch, this decision was repealed (**Toros Azatyan**, Komitas Vardapet, page 153).

Cemel Pasha has asked about me – Cemal (Jemal) Ahemed Pasha (1872-1922) – One of the leaders of the Ittihad, governor of Constantinople and later the Navy Minister. In his letter to Yervand Hakobyan written on 13 October 1914, Komitas states that he has agreed to teach harmonization lessons at the Turkish music school.

To "I won't, I won't" - He is probably referring to S. Melikyan, who had gifted a photograph of himself to Komitas on 20 October 1907 with a friendly joke written in a local dialect of Armenian on the back – "I won't lie. I won't Lie. God is my witness... I have made this myself."

With kisses, Yours, Komitas - The Armenian Համբոյրիւ՝ Քոյդ Կոմիտաս has been misrepresented in KL 2000 and 2007 as Համբոյրիւ՝ եմ Կոմիտաս.

183. <TO YERVAND HAKOBYAN>

The original is located at the MAL, KF, 1369.

In a note attached to the original, the donor of letter had written the following note – "He wrote this letter after leaving for Constantinople via Philippe. During his last trip to Europe, he had stayed at Philippe for 4 days on his return, at the end of the summer of 1914."

It was first published in "Bulgarian Armenian Almanac" 1935, vol. 1, pages 302-303 and then in the newspaper *Azat Khosk* (1947, 17 November). The month that the letter was sent has not been mentioned in the original, but a handwritten "X", i.e. October, has been added.

Yervand Hakobyan – The Chairman of the Bibliophilist Society of Philippe (see *Byuzandion*, 1914, 1 July, issue 5390, page 1 and the letter written to A. Chopanyan on 22 July 1914 as well its corresponding notes).

184. <TO YERVAND HAKOBYAN>

The location of the original is unknown.

A copy of the letter is located at the MAL, KF, 1370.

It was first published in "Bulgarian Armenian Almanac" 1935, vol. 1, pages 302-303 and then in KL 2000, page 119 and KL 2007, page 144.

Replying to your letter – The letter has not been found.

THE LETTERS RECEIVED BY KOMITAS VARDAPET

1899

1. <FROM OSKAR FLEISCHER>

The original is located at the MAL, KF, 57.

It was first published in 1914 as a testimony to Komitas' international recognition, after articles appeared in the Armenian press of Constantinople that belittled Komitas' activities and achievements (see the letters written to M. Babayan on 7 November 1913 and to A. Chopanyan on 22 July 1914, as well as the corresponding notes on pages 222-223, 233, 474-475, 483-485).

The German original has been published for the first time.

Oskar Fleischer – He taught Komitas the history of music at the Royal Music College in Berlin. In 1898, O. Fleischer undertook the founding of the International Music Society, where Komitas had become a member and delivered lectures. This and the letter following it were written in response to those lectures. See the letter written to K. Kostanyan on 17 July 1899 and the corresponding notes.

The original letter was prepared for publication and translated from German by musicologist Artur Avanesov.

2. <FROM MAX SEIFFERT>

The original is located at the MAL, KF, 58.

The German original has been published for the first time.

According to T. Azatyan, a translation of the letter was published in "the Armenian press of Constantinople in 1914," after which it was published by Toros Azatyan in the book "Komitas Vardapet" (page 29). See the previous letter and its notes.

Max Seiffert – Secretary of the Berlin branch of the International Music Society and head teacher of the history of music at the Berlin Royal Music College.

The original letter was prepared for publication and translated from German by musicologist Artur Avanesov.

1905

3. <FROM MARIAM TUMANYAN>

The original is located at the MAL, KF, 44.

The letter was written from Tiflis on a postcard.

It has been published for the first time.

The letter was a reply to Komitas' letter dated 28 February 1905 to M. Tumanyan.

19[/]3/III <19>05 – The letter was sent on 19 February 1905 (3 March according to the old calendar).

The costs for the concert – She is referring to the concert of Armenian spiritual and folk music scheduled for 3 April 1905at the hall of the Artists' Society.

The contents of your letter – This letter written by Komitas has not been found.

She will fulfil her promise – Mrs. Ghambaryan did fulfil her promise and replied by telegram to Komitas on 25 February 1905.

Talk to you about the opera "Anush" – See the letter written by Komitas to Mariam Tumanyan on 22 January 1904, as well as the corresponding notes.

4. <FROM N. GHAMBARYAN>

The original is located at the MAL, KF, 49a.

For the context regarding why the telegram was sent, see Komitas' letter to M. Tumanyan dated 28 February 1905, M. Tumanyan's letter to Komitas dated 19 February 1905, and N. Ghambaryan's letter to Komitas dated 25 March, as well as the corresponding notes.

It has been published for the first time.

5. <FROM N. GHAMBARYAN>

The original is located at the MAL, KF, 50.

For the context regarding why the letter was written, see Komitas' letter to M. Tumanyan dated 28 February 1905, M. Tumanyan's letter to Komitas dated 19 February 1905, and N. Ghambaryan's letter to Komitas dated 25 March, as well as the corresponding notes.

It has been published for the first time.

Page 244, r. 7 - **replied to your letter by telegram** – She is referring to the telegram she sent on 25 February.

I repeat my request for you to send the program quickly – This is a response to the following section of the letter from Komitas to Mariam Tumanyan dated 28 February 1905 – "I am still not clear on whether the censor will be presented with the lyrics, or the program".

6. <FROM N. GHAMBARYAN>

The original is located at the MAL, KF, 50.

For the context regarding why the letter was written, see Komitas' letter to M. Tumanyan dated 28 February 1905, M. Tumanyan's letter to Komitas dated 19 February 1905, as well as the corresponding notes.

It has been published for the first time.

The administrator – She is referring to Karapet Kostanyan.

There is a lot of disorderliness going on in the train system – She is referring to the tense state created by the ethnic conflicts of 1905.

I still don't have your program – According to K. Samuelyan's Annals, this program was published on 24-25 March (*Sovetakan Arvest*, 1969, issue 12, page 63), although this letter and the telegram sent on the same day by N. Ghambaryan suggest that Komitas had not yet sent the program as of 25 March. The censor permitted the program for the 3 April concert to be published on 29 March, so the program was printed in the period between 29 March and 2 April (see MAL, KF, 152).

1906

7. <FROM KHACHATUR HATSAGORTSYAN>

The original is located at the MAL, KF, 49.

It has been published for the first time.

On the second page of the letter, Komitas had noted down the music and lyrics of the song that begins with the words “I have turned the field into a garden” (4 stanzas), and on the first page of the letter, at the beginning of its body, he had written, “The complete lyrics.” We present below that note by Komitas. Areg Lusinyan and Karo Chalikyan have converted the Limonjian notes into the European notation system.

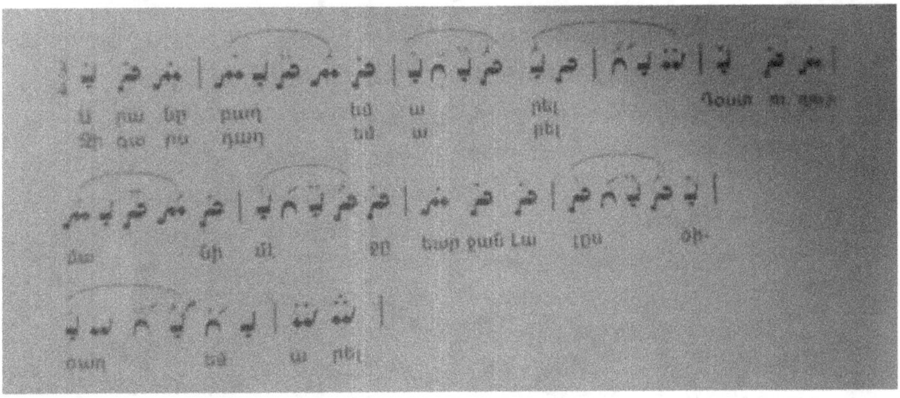

Converted

I have turned the field into a garden
I have turned my lover into a mark
Between friends and enemies, my dear
I have turned my tears into laughter.

Me and my lover are young
We have made a vow and are keeping it
May your son be cursed
He did not let us enjoy it

I went to the Bible
My lover was taken away
To the abductor, what can I say?
Half my life was taken with her.

You stand in the shadow of the mountains
In the shade of the plane tree
A silk cloth over your head
Your hair flying in the wind.

M<ister> Abeghyan – He is referring to Manuk Abeghyan.

M<ister> Altunyan – He is referring to literary figure, translator Gevorg Altunyan (1881-1947).

M<ister> Mesrop – It is unclear to whom he was referring.

8. <FROM ARSHAK CHOPANYAN>

A draft of the letter is located at the MAL, ACF, IV b, 191. It has been dated based on its contents.

It was first published in **Arshak Chopanyan**, Letters (compiled and with an introduction by Gohar Aznavuryan), Yerevan, 1980, page 87.

Armenian concert – He is referring to the concert that took place in Paris on 1 December 1906.

To allocate 1000 francs for the purpose of publishing your unpublished works – *Anahit* had published a sizeable article on this decision, which we have reproduced in full below.

"Upon the initiative of the Armenian Union of Paris, and conducted by Komitas Vardapet, the Armenian concert organized on 1 December had success that was even greater than expected. The admiring reviews of the musical critics of Paris, translations of which we present to our readers in this issue, prove that the Armenian Union of Paris has fully achieved the objective it had set for itself when organizing this concert.

Every Armenian should proudly read those expressions of wonder that the difficult-to-please Europeans lavished on our national art on this occasion. That event was organized with a very important aim – to present the Armenian tribe on the global stage as an element worthy of love and respect.

The Union spent 2321 Fr. on the organization of the event. The sale of tickets and programs, as well as donations, resulted in proceeds of 2498 Fr. The donors were Ishkhan Boris Arghutyan – 50 Fr., A. Jamharyan - 60 Fr., S. Arafelyan – 100 Fr., Mrs. Sarukhanyan – 50 Fr., Paghtasar Hakobyan – 100 Fr., Pierre Aubry – 20 Fr., Jean Psichari – 10 Fr., Bagrat Shkhyants – 66 Fr., Mirza Sarukhanyan – 66 Fr.

The Armenian Union of Paris decided to allocated a thousand Fr. for the publication of around ten songs by Komitas Vardapet. That volume, which should be printed in a few days, will be warmly welcomed, we have no doubts, by both Armenian and foreign music lovers." (1907, issue 1, page 23).

1907

9. <FROM MAURICE BASTIN AND JEAN PÉRIER>

The original is located at the MAL, KF, 1652.

Komitas mentions receiving this letter in his letter to Margarit Babayan on 27 November 1907: "Greetings to Bastin and dear J. Périer. I received their open letter and will reply". Considering the fact that it would take around a month for letters to reach Etchmiadzin from Paris, we have dated this one as November 1907.

Jean Périer wrote his text on the photograph of the postcard. The MAL Komitas Fund (number 207) includes a picture of J. Périer in the role of Pelléas, with an autograph to Komitas that said "*Au reverend et cher père Komitas. Souvenir bien bien amical. J. Périer 1909-10.*"

It has been published for the first time.

Maurice Baston – A conductor at the Paris Grand Opera.

10. <FROM KARAPET PARTIZPANYANTS>

The original is located at the MAL, KF, 55.

Pages 1-4 of the letter have been lost.

It has been published for the first time.

In your last reply – The letter has not been found.

Holy Father Ghevond – He is referring to Mother See of Holy Etchmiadzin congregant Hovakimyan (see the letter written to Mesrop Smbatyan on 6 October 1894 and the corresponding notes.

1908

11. <FROM SAMSON HARUTYUNOV>

The original is located at the MAL, KF, 48.

It has been published for the first time.

1909

12. <FROM MEHMED EMIN>

The original is located at the MAL, KF, 58.

The envelope bears the text "Istanbul Chamber of Commerce and Industry, 351, To Mr. Komitas Vardapet, Address – Yesayan School."

The original has been prepared for publication and translated by turkologist Ani Avetisyan.

It has been published for the first time.

Mehmed Emin – Turkish poet, one of the leaders of the Ittihad party.

1910

13. <FROM MARGARIT BABAYAN>

The original is located at the MAL, KF, 1651.

The letter is undated. According to the postal stamp, it arrived in Yerevan on 15 June 1910. The delivery stamp is damaged. Considering the fact that letters from London to Yerevan would arrive in 25-30 days, the letters was dated 15-20 May 1910.

It has been published for the first time.

14. <FROM GHEVOND DURYAN>

The original is located at the MAL, KF, 45.

It was first published by Toros Azatyan (Komitas Vardapet, Constantinople, 1931, page 107).

The Sacred Law and Order of the Armenian Church… on worldly stages – According to Toros Azatyan and Hakob Siruni, this letter had been delivered to Komitas on 21 November (4 December according to the old calendar) at the "Petit Champ" hall, before the concert was due to begin. "The people were upset. But Komitas Vardapet did not give in, and carried out the program without any changes, replying that he had the permission of the Catholicos. His opponents had not satisfied themselves with this much. They tried all possible machinations to ruin the concert. They had submitted a report to the municipality of Pera that the concert included conflict provoking songs. It was only through an explanation from the director of the theater that they understood the underlying cause for the report to be personal animosity," Toros Azatyan wrote (ibid.). After the concert, this episode was the cause of a major discussion in the Armenian press (see *Byuzandion*, 1910, issue 4293, page 1; *Tachar*, 1910, issue 35, page 710; *Byuzandion*, 1910, 4296, page 1; *Mshak*,

1910, issue 272, page 2; *Byuzandion*, 1910, issue 4303, page 2; *Horizon*, 1910, issue 273, page 2).

Byuzand Kechyan, referring to the decision of the Patriarchate, wrote, "Nobody is proposing that the undertaking of things which can occur only in the Armenian Church and nowhere else. A child can only be baptized in the Armenian Church. Clergymen can only be ordained in the Armenian Church, etc. etc. Who would ever think of organizing such ceremonies and observances in any of the worldly halls available? But Armenian hymns are also sung at home, during excursions, and in any hall where a choirmaster is giving lessons. There is no danger in taking a spiritual song or a prayer outside the church, because this is not a ceremony or a mystery or an observance, and it does not belong to the church building."

The first part of your program – In the first part of the concert, Komitas had included the hymns "Holy Holy," "O Wondrous," "Mother of God, You Were at the Cross," "Mary Magdalene in the Garden" and "Feet Washing."

The faithful – This word has been omitted from Toros Azatyan's publication of the letter.

1911

15. <FROM HOVHANNES MUTAFYANTS>

The original is located at the MAL, KF, 54.

The letter is a reply to Komitas' 29 January 1911 letter to Hovhannes Mutafyants.

It has been published for the first time.

16. <FROM TIGRAN KAMSARAKAN>

The location of the original is unknown.

It was first published in *Tachar*, 1911, N 22, pages 349-352, with the title "Armenian Beauties."

The evening of June 5 – He is referring to concert that took place on 5 June 1911 at the Alhambra theater in Alexandria, which had had unprecedented success.

Cicero – Marcus Tullius Cicero was a Roman political figure, orator, philosopher and writer.

One hundred and fifty children – The Komitas Fund at the MAL (number 205a) contains a photograph of the mixed choir formed by Komitas in Alexandria (190 people, photographed on 3 June 1911).

17. <FROM MARGARIT BABAYAN>

The original is located at the MAL, KF, 1651.

The postcard was sent from Paris. We have dated the letter according to the postal stamp – "18.10.11," i.e. 18 October 1911.

It has been published for the first time.

Périer was very grateful for your card – This letter to J. Périer has not been found.

18. <FROM G. RÉÏCIAN>

The original is located at the MAL, KF, 56.

The letter was a response to the concert that took place on 12 June 1911 at the Abbas theater in Cairo.

It has been published for the first time.

1912

19. <FROM AVETIS AHARONYAN, GASPAR IPEKYAN,Y. HAMAMCHYAN, HAKOB GYURJYAN>

The original is located at the MAL, KF, 1655.

The letter was sent to Siamanto's address.

It has been published for the first time.

20. <FROM MARGARIT BABAYAN>

The original is located at the MAL, KF, 1651.

The postcard was sent from Leipzig. It has been dated according to the postal stamp.

It has been published for the first time.

Your card – This letter has not been found.

Our naughty little Bay View – During the summer of 1911, Komitas went to the Isle of Wight[28] summer resort in England for two weeks. M. Babayan is referring to those days.

You will return to Constantinople so soon – Komitas had arrived in Leipzig to oversee the publication of the "Armenian Peasant Songs" collection and returned to Constantinople at the end of July 1912.

I sent you a card – The letter has not been found.

Reached you – The stamp in the corner of the postcard has been cut out, as a result of which a small portion of text is missing here.

28 [The Armenian editor and Margarit Babayan both mistakenly refer to the Isle of Wight as White Island, even when writing its name in English.] – Translator's notes.

Ipik graduated with flying colors – Gaspar Ipekyan left for Egypt after graduating from Paris University, and then went to Tiflis, from where he arrived in Etchmiadzin to work in the manuscript library (see Hovhannes Tumanyan's letter to Mesrop Ter Movsisyan dated 10 November 1912, **Hovhannes Tumanyan**, A Comprehensive Collection of his Works in Ten Volumes, Vol. 10, Yerevan, 1999, page 160).

21. <FROM MARGARIT BABAYAN>

The original is located at the MAL, KF, 1651.

The postcard has been sent to Constantinople.

It has been published for the first time.

Our White island today – See the previous letter and the corresponding notes.

Dear – this is the start of the letter from Gaspar Ipekyan.

I have graduated and am going to Egypt in 2 days - See the previous letter and the corresponding notes.

22. <FROM KARAPET KOSTANYAN>

The original is located at the MAL, KF, 1653.

It has been published for the first time.

Greta – He is referring to Margarita Babayan.

You are in Leipzig - Komitas had arrived in Leipzig to oversee the publication of the "Armenian Peasant Songs" collection. See his letters to Margarit Babayan dated 15 March 1912 and 12 May 1912 as well as the corresponding notes.

To receive your postcard – The letter has not been found.

23. <FROM MARGARIT BABAYAN>

The original is located at the MAL, KF, 1651.

The date of dispatch for the postcard has been determined through the postal stamp. The postcard arrived at Pangaldi 87(43) in Constantinople on 9 November. Komitas replied to this letter on 15 December.

It has been published for the first time.

1913

24. <FROM MARGARIT BABAYAN>

The original is located at the MAL, KF, 1651.

According to the postal stamp, the letter arrived in Constantinople in April 1913 (“4.13”). The delivery stamp has been damaged and only the day of delivery can be seen – the 10th. We have therefore dated this letter as 10 April 1913.

It has been published for the first time.

Iskuhi – Iskuhi Gavanozyan. She had come to Paris to study with M. Babayan based on Komitas’ advice (see the letter to M. Babayan dated 15 March 1912).

These monkeys – This section of the letter is written on the reverse side of the postcard, which depicts two monkeys sitting at the seaside.

25. <FROM THE PARIS DEPARTMENT OF THEINTERNATIONAL MUSIC SOCIETY>

The original is located at the MAL, KF, 53.

The letter has been dated based on the postal stamp. It was sent to Vagharshapat, and from there to Constantinople, where it arrived on 24 September 1913. See also the letter to Margarit Babayan dated 7 November 1913, as well as the corresponding notes.

It has been published for the first time.

26. <FROM ARCHBISHOP ZAVEN>

The original is located at the MAL, KF, 45a.

It has been published for the first time.

Jubilee Organization Committee – With the objective of commemorating the 1500th anniversary of the creation of the Armenian alphabet and the 400th anniversary of Armenian print, a jubilee committee was created towards the end of September 1913 in Constantinople, which included Komitas among its members.

27. <FROM THE EDUCATION COUNCILOF THE NATIONAL CENTRAL ADMINISTRATION>

The original is located at the MAL, KF, 1448.

The "old academic programs" mentioned in the letter have been preserved in two versions – draft and final copy. The draft copy is titled "Music, Elementary Course" and has a few insignificant corrections in language style and proof, compared to the final version. In these notes, we only mention the corrections made on the final copy.

The letter has been published for the first time.

Simple – Komitas has struck out the word "simple" and added "simple ecclesiastical and school."

H<oly> - This word has been added by Komitas.

Their – Komitas has changed the original Armenian իրենց to անոնց.

Eight - Komitas has changed the original Armenian ութն to ութը.

Reading the notes – Komitas has changed the word "Reading" to "Reading the notes."

Eight - Komitas has changed the original Armenian ութն to ութը.

Their – Komitas has changed the original Armenian իրենց to անոնց.

G-clef– The original contained these words in French, written using Armenian letters – Notes. *Clé de sol.* Komitas changed it to Armenian.

Double, triple and quadruple tempo – The original text was "4/4, 3/4 and 2/4" which Komitas changed.

Notes – The original text referred to neumes (*khaz*) which Komitas changed.

Previous - The original text was "intermediate" which Komitas changed.

Previous - The original text was "advanced" which Komitas changed.

F-clef– The original contained these words in French, written using Armenian letters – Notes. *Clé de fa*. Komitas changed it to Armenian.

1914

28. <FROM PANOS TERLEMEZYAN>

The original is located at the MAL, KF, 1654.

According to the postal stamp, the letter arrived in Paris on 26 March.

It has been published for the first time.

I have received your card – The letter has not been found.

Take a trip, probably towards Van – According to *Amenun Taretsuyts*, in the summer of 1914 P. Terlemezyan "left Constantinople for Armenia (the flanks of the Massis mountains, the banks of Lake Van, etc,) to conduct his field studies for the new works he was preparing" (1915-16-20, page 261).

M<ister> Portugalyan – He is referring to orator, editor, social and political figure Mkrtich Portugalyan (1848-1921).

29. <FROM THE PARIS DEPARTMENT OFTHE INTERNATIONAL MUSIC SOCIETY>

The original is located at the MAL, KF 60.

It has been published for the first time.

30. <FROM THE PARIS DEPARTMENT OFTHE INTERNATIONAL MUSIC SOCIETY>

The original is located at the MAL, KF 52.

It has been published for the first time.

31. <FROM TIRUHI KOSTANYANTS>

The original is located at the MAL, KF, 1653.

It has been published for the first time.

Page 283, r. 2-3 - **for the letter** – The letter has not been found.

Page 283, r. 3 - **Gret-Ams-Shushik** – **Gret** – Margarita Babayan, **Ams** – Armenuhi Babayan, **Shushik** – Shushik Babayan. Tiruhi Kostanyan was the paternal aunt of the Babayan sisters.

1919

32. <FROM GRIGOR VARDAPET HOVSEPYAN>

The original is located at the MAL, KF, 1375.

It has been published for the first time.

The size of a mustard seed – *Compare this to Matthew 13:31-32, Mark 4:31-32, Luke 13:18-19.*

Armenia has taken shape already – *He is referring to the First Armenian Republic.*

UNDATED LETTERS

33. <FROM HAKOB HARUTYUNYANTS>

The original is located at the MAL, KF, 46.

It has been published for the first time.
Converted by Karo Chalikyan and Areg Lusinyan.

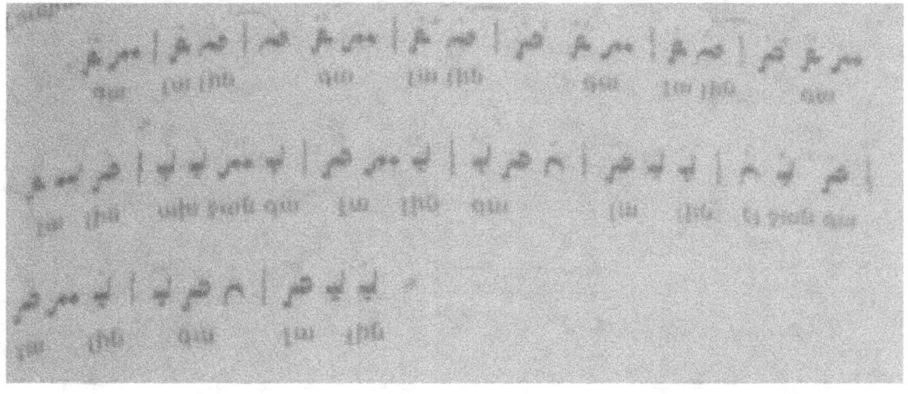

Converted by Karo Chalikyan and Areg Lusinyan.

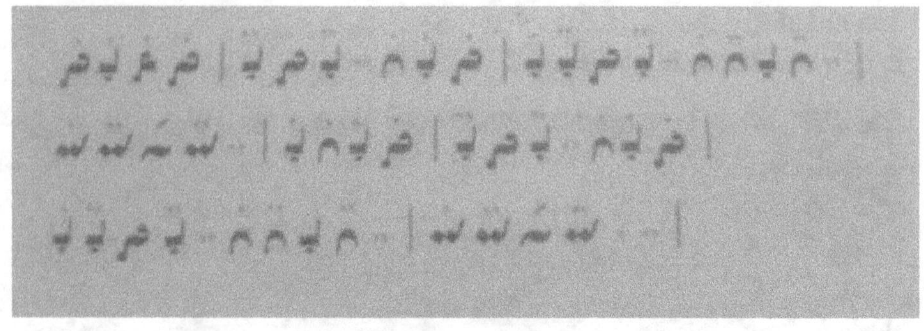

Converted by Karo Chalikyan and Areg Lusinyan.

34. <FROM HAKOB HARUTYUNYAN>

The original is located at the MAL, KF 47.

It has been published for the first time.

35. <FROM AN UNKNOWN SENDER>

The original is located at the MAL, KF, 59.

The last page of the letter has been lost.

It has been published for the first time.

Converted by Karo Chalikyan and Areg Lusinyan.

36. <FROM AN UNKNOWN SENDER>

The original is located at the MAL, KF, 245.

It has been published for the first time.

The reverse side of the postcard has "little Margarit's" photograph with the following text written on it - "Holy Father, say 'ho.' Margarit"

37. <FROM MARGARIT BABAYAN>

The original is located at the MAL, MBF, 1458.

It has been published for the first time.

There is a group photograph on the reverse side of the postcard of four young men, M. Babayan, and the "Englishwoman who heard Komitas' songs and cried." On the reverse side of another photograph of this group (MBF, 1459), M. Babayan has written "Komitas had sung our *Antuni*." Here is that photograph –

www.ingramcontent.com/pod-product-compliance
Lightning Source LLC
Chambersburg PA
CBHW070041120526
44589CB00035B/2018

* 9 7 8 1 7 7 1 6 1 3 5 8 3 *